HUMAN RIGHTS FROM THE DALIT PERSPECTIVE

HUMAN RIGHTS FROM THE DALIT PERSPECTIVE

Editor

Henry Thiagaraj

GYAN PUBLISHING HOUSE

New Delhi-110002

Human Rights From the Dalits Prospectives

ISBN: 81-212-0876-9

Reprinted in 2011 in India by
Gyan Publishing House
23, Main Ansari Road, Daryaganj,
New Delhi - 110002
Phone : 23282060, 23261060
Fax : (011) 23285914
E-mail : books@gyanbooks.com
website: gyanbooks.com

Printed at: G. Print Process, Delhi

The world owes a duty
To the untouchables,
As it does to all
oppressed people
to break their shackles
And to set them free"

Dr. B. R. Ambedkar

"Every man should have
a philosophy of life,
for everyone must have
a standard by which
to measure his conduct positively,
my social philosophy may
be said to be enshrined in three words:
Liberty, Equality and Fraternity"

Dr. B. R. Ambedkar

To my wife,
Philomena,
whose support to my work and struggles
for justice is a source of strength

HUMAN RIGHTS FROM THE DALIT PERSPECTIVE

DALIT HERITAGE IN MY BHARATAM

Source : Sunday Indian Express

"Ekalayva, denied formal tutoring because he was a Dalit, nevertheless mentally worshipped the great Dronacharya as his Guru and mastered the science of archery. Aghast that this determined pupil might surpass his chosen candidate, Arjuna, Dronacharya asked for the youth's thumb as his Guru Dakshina. Without a moments's hesitation, Ekalayva obliged." We are left to ponder: What should we do?

COURTESY: SUNDAY EXPRESS

Amidst the dominance of Dronacharyas in our country, our Dalit youth suffer continuously over 2000 years. Dalit youth leadership camps at the Delta Training Center provides an opportunity to examine our cultural traditions and realise liberation through educational programmes.

Contents

भारत सरकार
राष्ट्रीय अनुसूचित जाति आयोग
GOVERNMENT OF INDIA
NATIONAL COMMISSION FOR SCHEDULED CASTES

डा. बूटा सिंह
अध्यक्ष
Dr. BUTA SINGH
CHAIRMAN

पाँचवीं मंजिल, लोकनायक भवन,
खान मार्किट, नई दिल्ली-110003
5TH FLOOR, LOK NAYAK BHAWAN,
KHAN MARKET, NEW DELHI - 110003
Tel. (O) : 24632298, 24620435
Telefax : 24632298

Foreword

I am delighted to write this foreword for the new and third edition of the book "Human Rights from Dalit Perspective", first published in 1996 and the second in 1998. The first edition was to commemorate the historic occasion of inaugurating the National Workshop on Human Rights and Societal Changes with reference to SCs / STs jointly organized by the Dalit Liberation Education Trust, Madras and National Human Rights Commission, New Delhi on 3rd August 1996 at Chennai, for which Justice Shri. Ranganath Misra, then Chairman, National Human Rights Commission gave the encouragement and support to Dr. Henry Thiagaraj, after visiting his Human Rights Education Centre in Chennai. The second edition was published at New Delhi in December 1998 to commemorate the 50th anniversary of Universal Declaration of Human Rights by the United Nations. The demand for this book has increased after the World Conference Against Racism held in Durban in 2001. As both the editions are out of print, Dr. Henry Thiagaraj has ventured to bring the third edition with updates of the efforts in presenting the Dalit issues in the context of Human Rights.

Whenever I visited Tamil Nadu in the last 10 years I took an opportunity to visit the projects established by Dr. Thiagaraj, who is a pioneer in taking up the cause of Dalit Liberation Education as early as 1985, when he started the Dalit Liberation Education Trust (DLET). Then the word Dalit was not much known and people had misconception and were afraid to use the word Dalit because of its association with Dalit Panthers Movement in Maharashtra. Dr. Thiagaraj withstood the negative criticisms and discouragement by his commitment to the work by establishing contacts with grassroots Dalit communities and ran a model NGO with participatory and transparent objectives that for 22 years he was able to sustain the educational programmes for the liberation of Dalit people. With great deal of efforts, sacrifice and vision he empowered Dalit people through variety of activities like cultural programmes, supporting Dalit musicians who practice ancient arts of playing Drums and pipes.

Dr. Henry Thiagaraj after leaving a secured and bright Govt. career chose to serve his own Dalit people by sharing his life and education, through organizing Awareness Camps for Dalit Youth and Women brought awareness to the problems of the people and enabled them to become useful citizens by taking positive and constructive social action to be useful to the community instead of feeling frustrated defeated and neglected in life. This project is pioneering as it synthesizes human values with social action and struggles for attaining justice and equality through an educational process of group dynamics, team work, self understanding for being useful and to get integrated with the mainstream of society. The innovative educational methods of counseling and providing communication skills, opportunities of experiencing life, experience oriented exercises instead of bookish, were used to enable Dalit young men and women to realize their human dignity. It is an experience of transformation, from invalidation to empowerment, from the not-possible mindset to that of: I can achieve my goals in life.

For the first time Dr. Henry Thiagaraj made it possible for his Dalit people from the dehumanized conditions of life to experience, realize their human dignity, self worth and to develop their human potential for nation building activities. In this pioneering effort by bringing the dimension of human rights to the Dalit discrimination, which is usually called local caste issues, highlighted a dignity for the human struggle of equality and social justice.

The positive impact of the project on its immediately surrounding environment is that the participants became community organizers, facilitators, educators and formed voluntary service organizations in their villages to champion the cause of Dalits, to become leaders in their respective communities as councilors in village councils. By giving human rights education inputs it was possible to prevent violence and violation of human rights. There has been widespread appreciation from the community for the young people becoming agents for social change. Sixty women who have been trained health ambassadors in a 15-day capsule course became effective community organizers in the villages. Some degrading traditions disappeared as a silent revolution took place, when people refused to be sexually abused stopping violation of their human dignity. A simple declaration and assertion of their human rights and human dignity through educational seminars brought self-esteem to the people that their violators stopped harassing them. The project demonstrates that it is possible to effect social change through educational process in a non-violent manner.

The Delta Training Centre for Dalit youth, south of Chennai-Mahabalipuram on East Coast road is really a beautiful training campus, with international cooperation, as scholars from many countries visit this picturesque landscape with land and buildings created by the vision of Dr. Henry Thiagaraj now worth one million dollar in asset for Dalits. It is from here integrated human rights educational activities in about 100 villages were organized.

I would like to highlight some features of the pioneering and innovative Dalit Liberation Education work evolved by Dr. Henry Thiagaraj:

1. Organizing Dalit Youth Camps synthesizing justice issues with spirituality
2. His contribution in awakening the Dalit Youth in Tamil Nadu is significant as he organized Dalit Awareness Youth Camps once in three months for 16 years with the object of "Empowering Discriminated Dalits as Grassroots Agents for Social Change". The youth trained in liberation education in turn served their communities contributing to social transformation in their respective areas.
3. Dr Thiagaraj presented the Dalit issues in the context of Human Rights to the UN Human Rights Commission and in other world forums.
4. Establishing Delta Training Centre for spreading the Human Rights Culture and building a society based on human dignity and contributing to Human Rights Education Movement of India, and working in one more than one hundred villages
5. He was the first to conceive and evolve Human Rights Education Programmes to prevent violence and violation of human rights through paralegal training, mobilizing lawyers for Human Rights, etc.

I was much impressed by his philosophy of service: that he comes from the space of fullness of life that God has blessed him with good education, international experience and United Nations training, a career in Government, where he demonstrated his achievements for the state in the field of Tourism, a happy family life that he can share his blessings with others. Unlike many Dr Thiagaraj does not come from the needs and wants of projects for survival. His life and service is an inspiration to many. May this book continue to inspire scholars to take up Dalit Human rights issues till discriminatory practices end in our country and Dalit people are fully liberated.

Dr. Búta Singh
New Delhi, July 18, 2007

Commendation

I have known Dr. Henry Thiagaraj for the past more than two decades and have always found him fully engaged in the noble task of emancipation of the Dalits despite several roadblocks put on his way. In this great mission, he gives emphasis on education and awareness building, especially of the youth and has given a new sense of direction to the Dalit Human Rights movement in the country.

Consequently, I am delighted to pen a few lines to his new edition of the book "*Human Rights from the Dalit Perspective*". I am more than convinced that there is a rich background to this publication. Dr. Thiagaraj is a pioneer in Human Rights Advocacy work committed to remove discrimination against Dalits through educational efforts. In Tamil Nadu he conducted Dalit Youth Leadership Camps for a number of years to empower Dalit youth to come up and join the mainstream of life and society. His Delta Project is a living monument to his contribution to Indian society in general and to the Dalits in particular. He brought dignity to Dalit struggle for social justice by integrating the various issues into the Human Rights paradigm. He is also a forerunner in international advocacy of Dalit Human Rights since 1990.

His commitment to this great cause is total and the methodology he has adopted is innovative. An important dimension of his work is his wider experience of his work life and a deeper understanding of the Indian situation. Added to this is his unmatched tenacity and holistic approach which permeate the selection of the papers included in this enlarged publication, the authors of which are also personally known to me. How I wish to comment on these papers, but paucity of time and space prevents me from doing so! Dr. Thiagaraj's efforts to collect and publish these articles containing source materials on Human Rights for Dalits are indeed laudable. I am sure scholars in the academia and activists in the field interested or engaged in Dalit Human Rights will find it extremely informative and instructive.

Radhakant Nayak, Ph.D.
Member of Parliament (Rajya Sabha)
(Former Secretary to Government of India)

201, Brahmaputra Apartment,
11-13, Dr. B.D. Marg,
New Delhi - 110001.

Preface

India is enigmatic. India is my country. Born an Indian, educated and exposed to the world, the United Nations and western culture, enables me to see certain issues in global perspective. Despite the great progress made in the fields of science and technology, generating wealth of the nation and augmenting the riches of commercial houses and corporate giants, the problems of perpetuating poverty and socio-economic inequalities in our country, make my India a bewildering question mark on the face of the earth.

Great scholars have attempted to find answers to the poverty in India. Dr. Amartya Sen, Indian Nobel Laureate, in his works examine the question of social inequalities and the need for the governments to spend more money on social sectors like education and health. Recently, an Indian author Ramachandra Guha, on releasing his new book "India after Gandhi – The History of the World's Largest Democracy" highlighted the challenges of a multi-cultural nation. He said, "Social change is slow and incremental and during my research for this book, I've realized that there has been a change for the better overall. It's up to us to improve the quality of our democracy." He also pointed out that Palwankar Baloo, India's first great spin bowler and a dalit social reformer has been forgotten by the history books. Real history of Dalits is forgotten, suppressed till Babasaheb Ambedkar discovered the history of Dalit India.

After spending 20 years in the state government service of Tamil Nadu, I opted for voluntary retirement and embarked on a new career in the voluntary service sector. It was my privilege to work for UNICEF in India as communication consultant on the project of reducing poverty through anemia control. On researching this project, I visited several villages. I visited rural areas, urban slums and was anguished to see the spectrum of poverty prevailing in India.

India has not witnessed a social revolution which can pave way for industrial revolution. Countries like Russia and France had revolutions and change the social character of the society there which paved way for industrial advancement. Dr. Ambedkar has observed thus:

"History bears out the proposition that political revolutions have always been preceded by social and religious revolutions" *

Many of the people whom I interviewed were poor and suffering would resign to say that "it is my fate; what can I do?" Some scholars have attempted to find that poverty has its roots in its religious beliefs that after 50 years of freedom, billions of rupees spent by the government to eradicate poverty in the last 57 years have not produced any significant result in reducing poverty as it is still estimated $1/4^{th}$ of the population that is about 250 millions people still live below the poverty line of not having one square meal a day as defined by the government.

In my opinion, I find many people were living below the poverty line and accepted it as 'fate' and believe that they were born in poverty and they have to suffer and there is no easy way to escape from their plight. For some, there is hope that for the suffering they go through in this life, they may have some better chances in the next birth. So, the idea of accepting suffering is prevalent and deep rooted among people. It is in this sociological context we find that the belief in caste system is rigid, based on social occupation and people were brainwashed by religious doctrines and the laws of Manu for 2500 years. The link between suffering in poverty and the belief in caste is strong, and they go together, as caste alienates and marginalizes the Dalits, condemning them to be trapped in the bottom layers of society in India. This belief system which has reinforced in the minds of the people for 2500 years cannot easily be changed unless there is powerful tool of liberation education. Education can emancipate people from poverty, bring the social revolution of an equal opportunity for people. But education is also restricted to the few on the basis of caste that it is not easy for the millions to study and come up.

It is in this scenario some of us struggle, study, get educated and come up in life and would like to see India changes with equal opportunities and equal rights as enshrined in the Indian constitution.

---

*The full text on this subject is reproduced on page 16 of this book

After graduating from Madras Christian College, it is a rare privilege in my life that I was selected by the United Nations to be a Graduate Student Interne at the United Nations' Headquarters in New York to observe its work in 1959. An extension of the fellowship with financial support by the Quakers - American Friends Service Committee enabled me to observe the work of the Human Rights Commission and to become familiar with some members of the commission. This experience left an indelible imprint in my young mind that when I returned to India and observed the plight of the Dalits, the question often raised in my mind was: why not the UN Human Rights Commission tackle our Dalit problems of discrimination? There was no easy answer as I posed this question to several scholars. After I took my early retirement from the State Government in 1982, I was working as Consultant to NGO's, UNICEF, etc.

After exploring several paths of service, I founded two educational Trusts in 1985: Oneworld Education Trust and the Dalit Liberation education Trust. I had the opportunity to visit United Nations as a member of the World Association of Former UN Interns and Fellows and participate in the NGO consultations and Conferences, which gave me an opportunity to discuss the problems of the Dalits. While international scholars examine apartheid in South Africa, in the context of discrimination violating human rights, many of the Indian leaders consider the atrocities on Dalits as a local community problem. The Government of India's official position often stated in parliament by Ministers that caste discrimination is a local community law and order issue under the domain of State Governments. Church authorities discouraged internationalizing Dalit Discrimination till 2000, as they do not want to go against Govt. policies, till the Indian priests and nuns became target of violence.

Actually the truth is any violation of Human Rights becomes international by its very nature. Fifteen years ago I had the privilege of publishing the book: ***The International Law and the Dalits in India written by*** Dr Y.N. Kly, Professor of International Relations and Chairperson of the International Human Rights Association of American Minorities (IHRAAM). Dr. Kly's book inspired me greatly to do advocacy on Dalit discrimination issues at global level. I want to acknowledge Dr. Kly's support of solidarity to the struggles of justice for Dalits, as he is a great

African-American Champion of Human Rights both in its country and the UN Forums of Human Rights.

When I had an opportunity to celebrate the 40th anniversary of the Universal Declaration of the Human Rights in 1988 I sought the assistance of Mr. M. R. Krishna, Former Union Minister for its celebrations at Delhi. I remember that Mr. M.R. Krishna took me to the home of Mr. I. K. Gujral, who just then returned from his assignment as Indian Ambassador in the USSR and talked to us. He was very encouraging that we should celebrate the 40th anniversary of the Universal Declaration of the Human Rights of the UN with a Seminar on the Dalit issues. Justice A. Varadarajan delivered the inaugural address of the Seminar which is fully reproduced in this book. Dr. R. K. Narayanan as Union Minister for Science & Technology participated in this Seminar. It was a great satisfaction that I took a Delegation of Dalit Activists to meet him and present to him our representations when he was the President in December 1998, with the assistance of Mr. Prakash Ambedkar, grandson of Dr. B. R.Ambedkar, and Member of Parliament then.

I received an invitation to participate in the World Conference on Human Rights organized by the United Nations held in June 1993 at Vienna. Then I compiled a set of papers under the title: "The Wounded Society", documenting the violence suffered by Dalits as a background paper for human rights activists. One of the memorable experiences was that as members of the Indian NGO groups we discussed openly the problems of Dalits whom I represented. A few people came openly for our support. Dr. R. M. Pal, Editor of PUCL Bulletin is one of the persons who shared his concerns on Dalits and supported me. He introduced me to meet Justice Rajendra Sachar, then the President of PUCL who encouraged us to organize a Seminar on Dalit issues in Madras in 1993, in which several scholars participated.

The National Workshop on Human Rights and Societal changes held on 3rd and 4th August'96 at Chennai is the result of our consultations with the National Human Rights Commission which came forward to sponsor this historically significant Workshop in which several leading scholars from all over India participated. Dr. R. M. Pal assisted us as Research Consultant with useful inputs. Gyan Publishing House of New Delhi brought out a book, "HUMAN RIGHTS OF DALITS" - societal violation by Dr. R.M. Pal and Mr. G.S. Bhargava which includes the papers presented at this National Workshop.

I have collected papers presented, texts of speeches, and materials I found during the Seminars and Conferences I have organized in the last twenty years. Many friends encouraged and supported me in this effort in presenting this historical evolution taking the atrocities and violence of Dalits in India into the global paradigm of human rights. A list of their names and sources of research are listed in separate page on "Acknowledgements"

This book is based on my own personal experience and struggles in seeking justice and prevention of violence on Dalit people in India through advocacy and education for which I selected the paradigm of Human Rights. My efforts for the last twenty years in seeking social justice and providing an opportunity to empower our Dalit people at grass roots through education specially knowing the basic human rights enunciated both in our Indian constitution laws and the universal declaration of human rights in Tamil Nadu has been satisfactory though sustaining this educational work with funds has become difficult. The Agenda is not finished as I seek new methods for faster results.

I am thankful to the Gyan Books Private Limited for coming forward to publish this third edition of "Human Rights from the Dalit Perspective" updating the earlier version to meet the need of scholars.

July 11, 2007 Henry Thiagaraj

"History bears out the proposition that political revolutions have always been preceded by social and religious revolutions". The religious Reformation started by Luther was the precursor of the political emancipation of the European People. In England, Puritanism founded the new world. It was Puritanism which won the war of American Independence and Puritanism was a religious movement. The same is true of the Muslim Empire. Before the Arabs became a political power they had undergone a thorough religious revolution started by the Prophet Mohammed. Even Indian History supports the same conclusion. The Political revolution led by Chandragupta was preceded by the religious and social revolution of Buddha. The Political revolution lead by Shivaji was preceded by the religious and social reform brought about by the Saints of Maharashtra. The Political revolution of the Sikhs was preceded by the religious and social revolution led by Guru Nanak. These will suffice to show that the emancipation of the mind and the soul is a necessary preliminary for the political expansion of the people."

Babasaheb Dr. B.R. Ambedkar in
"Annihilation of Caste" p.43-44

List of Contributors

Dr. Y.N. Kly, Professor of International Law, Global Studies Deptt., Malaspina University, and Emeritus Professor, University of Regina, Canada, Consultant and Advisor to UN Human Rights Sub-Commission on Protection of Minorities. Dr. Kly founded and headed for several years the International Human Rights Association of African-American Minorities which has a Consultative Status with Economic and Social Council of the UN. He leads African-American delegations to the UN Human Rights Commission Meetings held in Geneva and organized annual Conferences on Human Rights.

Dr. Barbara R. Joshi, Emeritus Professor of Sociology, USA, Author of *Untouchable! Voices of the Dalit Liberation Movement*. London: Zed Books 1986, was associated with MINORITIES RIGHTS GROUP, UK and awakened the Western world to the plight of Dalits in India.

Justice A. Varadarajan, was the first Dalit Judge in the Madras High Court—from 1973 to 1980 and the first Dalit Judge in the Supreme Court, 1980-85, well known for his forthright judgements.

Dr. K. R. Narayanan, was the first Dalit to become the President of India, a great intellectual, diplomat who made outstanding contribution to make India a global leader in the world.

Dr. Laxmi Berwa, American Buddhist Oncologist, Veteran Dalit Activist in USA, who braved criticism and became a spokesperson of Dalits in Washington DC and author of the book: Asian Dalit Solidarity.

Justice A.S. Anand, Chairperson, National Human Rights Commission and Former Chief Justice of India, took the initiative to publish the Report on atrocities on Dalits by NHRC.

Dr. Justice K. Ramaswamy, Member, National Human Rights Commission and Former Judge of the Supreme Court of India, participated in the UN sponsored World Conference against Racism, Durban, Sept. 2001.

Mr. K.B. Saxena, IAS (Retired), assigned by National Human Rights Commission to study atrocities on Dalits and to write a Report, published recently.

Mr. Bhagwan Das, Advocate of Supreme Court, Buddhist Dalit Leader, associated with Babasaheb Ambedkar.

Dr. R. M. Pal, Educationist, Member of Faculty of Delhi University, long time Managing Editor of Radical Humanist, and Editor of PUCL Bulletin, spokesperson for Dalit Human Rights issues.

Prof. D. N. Sandanshive, Professor of Law, Mumbai, an articulate speaker and writer, scholar on Ambedkar's writings served as Member, Law Commission of India.

Mr. Udit Raj is the National President of Justice Party and Chairman, All India Confederation of SC/ST Organisations and led mass conversion movements to Buddhism.

Dr. Mrs. P. Nagabooshanam, Formerly Vice Chancellor of Govt. B. R. Ambedkar Law University of Tamil Nadu, Chennai and Champion of Women's Rights.

Prof. Arvind Nirmal, a Dalit Theologian, highlighted the Dalit people's struggles for justice in theological schools and churches in India.

Dr. K. Wilson, Emeritus Professor of Philosophy, Osmania University, Hyderabad, and Author of Twice Alienated Dalit Christians of India.

Mr. Ibrahim Fall, Secretary General of the World Conference on Human Rights—June 1993, and high ranking UN Official, gave impetus to Human Rights Movements and NGO participation in the UN Forums.

Fr. A.X.J. Bosco, S.J. was provincial of Andhra Pradesh Jesuit Province, Secretary, SC, ST, BC Commission, Andhra Pradesh Bishop's Conference, Dalit Christian Activist, participated in World Conference against Racism, Durban, Sept. 2001.

Dr. Geetha B. Nambisan, Professor in Zahir Hussain Centre of Education Studies, Jawaharlal Nehru University.

Dr. Henry Thiagaraj, is the recipient of the UN Alumni Award by the WAFUNIF, given "In recognition of his work in advancing the goals and principles in the charter of the United Nations through the promotion of education for peace, development, and all human rights for all especially for the poor and disadvantaged at the grass-roots level..." September 25, 1998. He was in Tamil Nadu Government Service for 20 years, excelling in different positions, in

Education, Public Relations, and Tourism. He served the University of Madras for a term as the Head of the University's Student Advisory Bureau and was Consultant to UNICEF. At present he is the convener of the Human Rights Education Movement of India and Director of Dalit Youth Training Centre, which he founded near Chennai. A Dalit Activist, Founder of the Dalit Liberation Education Trust, is engaged in Human Rights Advocacy globally.

Ms. Julie Thomas, Visiting Scholar from USA, was a student of Semester at Sea and stayed in a Dalit Village to study the living condition of Dalits.

Ms. Patricia Nickels, International Field Program Coordinator for the Institute for Shipboard Education, University of Pittsburgh, USA, organized several visits to rural India and Dalit villages.

Prof. Hans Küng, Author of "Global Responsibility", an eminent Swiss theologian, and a prolific author. Since 1995 he has been President of the Foundation for a Global Ethic (*Stiftung Weltethos*). At the University of Tübingen as a professor of Ecumenical Theology, serving as Emeritus Professor since 1996.

Dr. R. K. Nayak, M.P. (Rajya Sabha) formerly Secretary to Govt. of India and Retired IAS officer, encouraged NGO's to involve in poverty eradication programmes, housing for rural poor, etc. for writing the Commendation of the book and for his continued support to my work.

Sardar Dr. Buta Singh, Chairman, National Commission for Scheduled Castes, Govt. of India, and former Union Cabinet Minister for Home, a veteran Congressman, and Statesman, for writing the *Foreword* and for his encouragement to fight for justice.

Dr. John C. B. Webster, Emeritus Professor of History, Baring Union Christian College, Batala, Punjab, Author of Several books on Dalit Liberation, and Editor, Dalit International Newsletter, USA, for permission to reproduce articles from Dalit International Newsletter.

Prof. Claude E. Welch, Jr., SUNY Distinguished Service Professor (Political Science), Director, Program in International and Comparative Law.

Director, Human Rights Center, Department of Political Science, STATE UNIVERSITY OF NEW YORK, Buffalo NY 14260 USA and Virginia A. Leary, Editors of "Asian Perspectives on Human Rights" for Dr. Barabara Joshi's article.

National Human Rights Commission, Govt. of India, New Delhi

for permitting to publish extracts from their Reports.

Mr. Y. S. R. Murthy, Director of Research, NHRC for his encouragement to my Human Rights Advocacy work, for obtaining permission of NHRC.

Prof. Anita Manuel Thomas for going through the manuscript and suggestions to improve the third edition.

Messrs V. Ramachandran and Sundar, for their patient work in putting this book in proper shape through computer skills.

For all those who supported me in my struggles against oppression of many kinds and assisted in production of this book.

1

International Law and the Dalits in India

Dr. Y.N. Kly

Foreword to Dr. Y.N. Kly's book International Law and the Dalits in India by Justice A. Varadarajan

I had the privilege of reading Dr. Y.N. Kly's International Law and the Dalits in India. "Dalit" is a new name by which the scheduled castes, who are considered to be untouchables, are referred to now. The author has mentioned with authority some of the many atrocities and indignities to which the scheduled castes are subjected. He has noticed that regardless of the fact that the Indian constitution has officially abolished untouchability the custom and tradition against the scheduled castes continue and the gross violation of the human rights of the Dalits persists as daily witnessed by the innumerable acts committed against these communities. He has rightly observed that it is not difficult to understand that the group in power believes in the maintenance of the economic, social and political privileges, which would vanish if the racism on caste ideology was dismantled.

Dr. Kly is right in saying that the Indian Government and the state Governments know that the laws enacted by parliament and state legislatives to end the cruel and illegal humiliation and exploitation of the Dalits are not enforced properly but do nothing to put an end to such attitude on the part of their officials, a vast majority of whom are caste Hindus. He has correctly noticed that the Indian Government has not seen it fit to recognize the Dalits as a distinct national minority. The Dalits should seriously endeavour to make the Government of India do that right thing.

It should be noted that Article 46 of the constitution of India to which reference has been made by Dr. Kly contains the directive principles of state policy and that the whole of their part of the constitution of India is unenforceable.

The question posed by the author concerning the effectiveness of the national laws in reaching implementable decisions and interpretations which may run counter to the custom on religious belief of the rulilng elite in India, and to what degree international law can be expected to assist, is a very legitimate and appropriate one with the conditions prevalent in India.

Dr. Kly has rightly noticed that the Dalits and other minorities have no other peaceful choice than either to submit to the will of the Aryan descended castes or appeal to international human rights law. He has made a welcome implied suggestion that the Dalits should officially request or demand recognition as a minority for the purpose of international protection without which such protection is unavailable.

As rightly observed by the author, the existence of the Dalit communities (for purposes of record) inside Hinduism is exploited and their existence (openly) outside Hinduism is ignored, denied or punished, depending upon the circumstances and interests of the ruling Hindu elites. It should be noticed that the Dalits do not belong to any of the four *Varnas*, namely *Brahmins*, *Kshatriyas*, *Vaisyas* and *Shudras* who alone are Hindus according to Hinduism and there is no possibility at all for the Dalits to get integrated with any of these four sections of Hindus, and no attempts are made for assimilation or integration of the Dalits who are considered as outcastes.

In the conclusion portion the author has stated that the oppression of the Dalits and the deep rooted social practises against them continue: "although India is reported to have implemented the International Declaration of Human Rights and Covenant on the social and Economic Rights and that all parts of the international covenants which may have significant impact on the situation of the Dalits and other minorities have been interpreted to suit the will of the ruling group". It may be stated that the international covenants on economic, social and cultural rights are only treaties who state parties have formally agreed to abide by their provisions to respect, ensure and take steps for the full implementation of a wide range of rights. By October 1987, 91 states including India had become parties to the Economic, social and cultural covenant and 87 states including India had ratified the civil and political rights covenant. The optional protocol, an adjunct instrument to the covenants came into force in 1976. Simultaneously with the covenants after they had been adopted by the general assembly in December 1966. The states according to the optional protocol empower the human rights committee established under the covenant to receive complaints from individuals who allege violation of their rights set out in the covenant. Though 39 states had become parties to the optional protocol, India has refrained from becoming a party thereto. The result is that no individual can complain to the human rights committee against any violation in India of any right protected by the treaty of the United Nations. India's official excuse is that ratification of the optional protocol would mean foreign countries interfering with its sovereignty. India has noticed its concern vehemently in world bodies and elsewhere against apartheid which is sanctioned by law in South Africa. This could be only on the assumption on basis that apartheid is an international problem and not an internal problem of South Africa alone. If apartheid is assured or treated by India to be international problem one fails to understand how the age long oppression and discrimination of the Dalits and scheduled tribes in India and not an international problem. The fact that apartheid is sanctioned by law in South Africa and that the problem of the Dalit is in spite of the laws in India can hardly distinguish the two.

Advocates for conversion of the Dalits to Buddhism or other religions may note that the Dalits would lose their historical identity by conversion, as also the special rights provided for them in the constitution, though honestly implemented, and that the international law view of minority rights does not accept assimilation law view of minority into the culture of the larger race on ethinic groups; unless it is the will of those people accurately secured through internationally supervised democratic means.

I appreciate the reference made by the author to Mr. V.T. Rajashekar who has been forcefully championing the cause of the scheduled castes, though unlike me, he does not belong to them.

I congratulate Dr. Kly on his venture.

15th sept. 1989.
Madras, S. India

A. Varadarajan
Former Judge,
Supreme Court of India.

Introduction to the book : International Law and Dalits in India

Dr. Y.N. Kly

The constitution of ancient societies was not favourable to the development of international law. International law can only exist where a number of communities acknowledge a mutual equality before the law and its authority. This condition did not prevail amongst the nations of antiquity such as those inhabiting the territory we now call India. For the most part a state of hostility characterized the relationship between a nation and other races; might was regarded as right. Neither persons nor property were considered sacred. In the ancient world, all relations among nations were guided by self-interest. The stranger was regarded by them as a spy and the normal condition of things was war, during which all was permissible. [1]

The ancient Hindus (Aryans) of the north who conquered and enslaved the Dravidian (Dalit) civilization preferred to base the rules of interest group relationship on dharma (rules of duty as codified in their religious scripture). Today it continues to have a significant influence on the actual rules governing the Hindu relationship with peoples conquered during antiquity, such as the Dalit.

Most scholars of ancient India agree that the Aryan all-embracing definition of religion as given in the Rajadharma-Prakaraw, the Santiparva of the Mahabharata formed the bases of all conception of righteousness in India.

The ancient Hindus recognized the truth of the well-known maxim that "custom is the king of all things" [2] for India over the centuries, religious customary laws was more pertinent to the conduct of daily life than were secular laws. The realization of this fact raises the question the question of which should be emphasized, Indian religious law or Indian constitutional law, to most honestly and effectively highlight the nature of the Dalit dilemma in India and to show why the actual rules governing their treatment may violate international law.

We shall attempt an answer to this question in the conclusion of this effort. However, to begin this relatively modest monograph, we have decided to supplement the work of the many scholars who have written in this area by reflecting wherever appropriate the politico-historical roots of this Indian dilemma. The listing of atrocities against the Dalit in India is an unending task. Regardless of the fact that the Indian constitution has officially abolished untouchability, the custom and traditions continue to rule.[3] The recent effort of the Indian government to implement the human rights covenants seem to have failed, since the gross violations of the human rights of the Dalit continues, as daily witnessed by the innumerable acts committed against this community.[4] In the testimony of Dr. Laxmi Berwa to t h U.N. Sub-Commission on human rights, Geneva, August 31, 1982, it is noted:

For 2000 years the untouchables, who make up one seventh of India's population (approximately 105 million by the governments estimates) have been assigned to the dirtiest, lowest paid jobs and are landless slave labourers, shunned socially by higher castes (*Brahmins*, Kshatriya, Vaisya) and neglected in social services and education.

In this monograph, we shall attempt to provide an understanding of how such a situation as that of the Dalit has been carried down through the ages in order to suggest that the uniqueness of the Indian oppression of Dalits is only in the fact that the conditions of Indian development permitted its primitive customs and beliefs (which at some time in history were probably shared by all civilizations) to be transmitted into the present. An understanding of this factor will permit us to human rights, as it relates to the Dalit oppression, to provide direct international intervention in the implementation of human rights for Dalits.

Indeed, we will view the problem of the Dalit not as just a problem in India, but as a problem of ancient history that has not yet been resolved in India, a problem of the implementation of international human rights law – as our problem, not just theirs.

INTERNATIONAL LAW AND THE DALITS IN INDIA

RACISM AS CASTE IDEOLOGY – A TOOL TO MAINTAIN THE STATUS QUO

Often in human history, the past conquest of one people by another and the desire to maintain the advantages and privileges gained during that earlier period of outright conquest or enslavement serves as the emotional and material fuel that fires and maintains beliefs in caste and racism. In such situations, the belief in caste or racism that began in antiquity as simply the irrational "peur des autres", became a deliberate effort to provide the ideological basis for the creation or maintenance of a politico-socio-economic situation of exploitation, inequality or segregation. While South Africa today may be perhaps the most obvious example of this type of racism (they continue to use racist ideology to justify the maintenance of the system of apartheid while they show few qualms about participating with Blacks in events outside South Africa), a closer look at the Dalit situation in India, or even the Afro-American situation in the U.S., may reveal a similar use of racism or caste as an ideological basis for the maintenance of the status quo, however in all such cases, what is not difficult to understand is that the group in power believes in the maintenance of the economic, social and political privileges that would vanish if the racism or caste ideology was dismantled. As Dr. N.D. Kamble writes concerning India:

After the introduction of the concept of ownership, exploitation of man by man started. The property relationship as such that one who owned it dominated one who did not, and in the process the latter was made a slave by the first. The present bonded labour system is the same slave system which existed for centuries together in India. It is not only the culmination of the debtor-creditor relation into a slave and master relation. It is also an outcome of the unequal social-economic system prevailing in India. The system provided a built-in-mechanism for continuation of exploitation of the under-privileged sections by the privileged sections of the society. The caste system (racism or caste) functioned as a transmission belt to pass on such slavery from one generation to another.[5]

The Indian caste system is probably the longest surviving hierarchical system in existence in the world today where a section of society is regarded by others to be so inherently inferior that it is polluting to other humans: untouchable.

The segmentation among the various castes is so rigid that no one can change from one caste to another caste, and it is something in which one is born and remains until death. Moreover, in addition to segmentation, it defined the work to be allotted to each particular caste. The Dalits or so-called Untouchables have been at the bottom of this totem pole for centuries in all spheres of their lives: educationally, society, economically and politically. As a conquered people once maintained by their conquerors in a condition of slavery and apartheid, formally forbidden Hindu practise or entry to Hindu temples, they have at one and the same time been politically integrated but not assimilated "within" Hinduism as outcastes, defined by it as "untouchables"; rejected by it yet controlled by it.[6] They are known for official purposes various names—schedules castes and tribes, depressed classes, and Harijans (coined by Mahatma Gandhi). Unwilling to see the Dalit as a separate nation, the Government of India does not recognize the Dalit by the name they have chosen for themselves.

Although the Dalit number only one seventh of the Indian population, its actual size is staggering; between 105-110 million, possible more (because this figure does not include converts to Buddhism, Sikhism, Islam and Christianity) at the time of the 1984 census. This is almost as much as the combined population of the United Kingdom and France. Indeed, one may say that one out of every forty people in the world today spends a lifetime battling with the stigma of being born untouchable.[7]

It is appropriate to analyse the 1971. Indian census of approximately 750 million to give an idea of the stratification in Indian society, which plays such an important role in determining attitudes and the potential of the Dalit minority to achieve equal status by formal state lawa:

1.	The Hindus	82.75%
2.	The Muslims	11.20%
3.	The Christians	2.60%
4.	The Sikhs	1.89%
5.	The Buddhists	0.71%
6.	The Jains	0.42%
7.	Other (Parsi, Jews, etc.)	0.40%[8]

Note that in the Indian census, the Dalit are included in the Hindu population.

The Hindu group is divided as follows:

		1971	**1984[9]**
A. Varnas	The *Brahmins*	0.5%	0.50%
	The *Kshatriyas*	0.50%	0.50%
	The Vaishayas	0.50%	0.50%
	The *Shudras*	50.00%	50.00%
B. Non-varnas	Untouchables	12.50%	15.00%
	Tribes	6.50%	7.00%

The Commissioner for Scheduled Castes and scheduled Tribes for the years 1979-1981 wrote a 30-page statement in his 27th report published in 1983 in which it says, "Caste prejudice with the accompanying evil of the practise of untouchability against the scheduled castes continues to prevail in the various parts of the country". This is despite the Untouchability (Offenses) Act of 1955 and recently promulgated Protection of Civil Rights Act of 1976. The act provides penalties for preventing a person on the ground of untouchability from entering a place of public worship and offering prayers or taking water from a sacred tank, well or spring. Penalties are also provided for enforcing any kind of disabilities such as denying access to any shop, restaurant, public hospitals or educational institution, hotels or any place of public entertainment, or denying the use of any road, river, well, tank, water tap, public bathing and washing area, cremation ground or sanitary convenience, etc.

A study of the situation of the Dalit may reveal that a less obvious, and thus more difficult and dangerous, form of racism is maintained in India through the use of its ancient social system and religious penal code. The possibility that such an insidious yet devastating form of racism could have existed for so long in a country often cited for its democratic processes and adherence to the philosophies of humane non-violent development, etc., leaves us with the starling realization that India's successful implementation of such exploitation over more than several centuries may encourage the adoption of such principles into the systems of other multi-national states as an easy and profitable answer to their minority question. If so, this would pose a problem for the international system, and in particular for the implementation of international law as it concerns minorities.

This book International Law and the Dalits in India is important because it attempts to provide information in such a way as to allow western and other civilizations to better see the historically primitive and economic motivations for this form of racism. In short, it attempts to remove the nature of Dalit oppression from behind the particularistic veils of Hindu religion, demystifying it, and thus perhaps rendering it less acceptable to the population concerned than their concept of racism itself. By exposing the principle historical and economic foundation of this form of racism, we open the vision of our reader to discern, hidden in the dark recesses of socio-culturally supported so-called racism, an even more disquieting and illegal resultant; "domestic colonialism". The manner in which the application of the principles and rules of international law as it concerns minorities are applied must lead India away from its dark and primitive past.

The question of the Dalits of India is the question of economic exploitation under the ideological veil of racism (as imbued in Hinduism) and the question of the caste system as a final solution to its total and insidious implementation, a socio-cultural implementation that may even resist Indian constitutional and nation law.

In India, untouchability is abolished, and if (practised) is punishable (by law), but who can punish the upper caste rulers who practise untouchability? They are the (law) so who can punish the lawbreakers (who make the law).[10]

When we look more closely at the historical development of racism in relation to the Dalits, we see that it appeared at such a primitive period and under such primitive circumstances as to permit the conquest of a people and their subsequent subjection in the conqueror's society to be solidified into part of the conqueror's religious belief, their culture, their customs, etc. This is the same religious, cultural and social milieu in which the conquered were, at a later date, forced to assimilate. Perhaps this is why Dr. Donald McGavran writes:

What happened in India had happened in almost all countries – the strong have oppressed the weak. However, in India, the Aryans 4000 years ago devised a religion that made them a superior race...... This religious sanction of racism is one of the greatest enemies of humankind...... No matter how much (the Dalits) organize, they will make no real gains until they renounce the Hindu religion which is sanctified racism.[11]

However, no matter how unacceptable we view "sanctified racism" to be, it should not b e difficult to understand how such a situation, used so deviously politically today, occurred so naturally during early human development, not just in India. All tribal people saw conquest as proof of their superiority over the conquered. None accepted the conquered tribe into the community under conditions of equity, and who did not hold and encourage superstitious beliefs in regard to others?[12]

Politico-Historical Origin of the Dalit Problem

Dr. A.A. Carvallo in this book, Dalit People: A socio-political Study of the Caste-Oppressed, takes the traditional view held by most scholars that the Dalit were part of an ancient highly developed non-Aryan civilization living in what is now southern India.[13] These people, referred to as Dasyas, Dasas or Dravidians by most historians, are also recorded to have had distinct African features and cultural characteristics.[14] V.T. Rajshekar, one of the Dalits' most prominent present day spokesmen tells us:

The Dalit were the original inhabitants of India and resemble the African in physical features. It is said that India and Africa were one land mass until separated by the ocean. So, both the Africans and the Indian untouchables and tribals have common ancestors. Some portion of these came to India and founded the Indus Valley civilization. These original inhabilitants of India put up a strong fight against the Aryan invaders. However, the latter, working through deceitful means, defeated the innocent but hard-working original inhabitants who had built the world's most ancient civilization in the Indus valley.[15]

A comparison of Mr. Rajshekar's description of the origins of his people, the Dalit, with that of various other scholars, presents no significant contradiction to traditional explanations; however it provides a more concise or useful understanding. As demonstrated in the last section of this monograph, this understanding of the Dalits' origin will be important for determining their minority status in international law because it suggests that the Dalits are a national minority in India and not the lowest section or caste of the Hindu nation.[16]

What is not so easy for people of our present age to understand is how the Aryans, around 1800 B.C., could have so successfully established a political economic and social system which materially, socially and psychologically gradually relegated the Dalits to the position of so-called Untouchables. To understand this point, we must remember the degree to which (that which we today call) magic held authority in all ancient societies, and imagine how the primitive and savage beliefs of these early Aryans may have been transformed into the ritual (indeed magic) of that society, to become the foundation for their religion, social stratifications, economic production, etc. To emphasize this understanding, and keeping the case of India in mind, let us digress a moment to comment on the role of magic or ritual in all ancient civilizations.

McLennan observed in 1870 that all primitive groups developed a cult around some beliefs; such beliefs became their totem. On this conception, confirmed by observation of primitives in Australia more "primitive" than any then known, new theory was erected. It was founded on the conception of primitive mentality. If Vico had been able to imagine the "fathers" deliberating their common interests and consciously creating the "People", if Rousseau had represented an assemblage deliberating, weighing the advantages of freedom and its dangers, of isolation, of a social contract, it is because their era was profoundly ignorant of the nature of primitive man.

The primitive group, which lived a narrowly collective existence, maintained itself only by a constant vigilance against all which threatened it in nature-death, sickness, the upcropping of accidents-or the imagined malignity of an outcaste people that pollute. All evil resulted from an intention to destroy. The small discomfiting event is only a warning of this intention which soon enough will deploy all its strength. It is necessary thus to hasten to neutralize it by whatever rites may be capable of so doing, even if such rites lead to the permanent subjection and enslavement of other human beings, or for that matter, human sacrifice of individuals from one's own society.

Nothing, neither the unaccustomed prolongation of winter which exhausts the provisions of the group, nor the torrid dryness which exterminates beasts and men, nor famines, nor epidemics nor even the child who breaks a leg-nothing is by chance. All evil thus may be prevented by appropriate conduct and ceremonies among one's group as well as towards one's enemies and servants. Only by proper conduct can one assure a place for oneself in the life after death.

In some societies, perhaps such as the early Aryans, there may have developed the idea of an intercessor government. A man capable of ruling no longer men but invisible forces, gods, etc. and of rendering them favorable, would of course have been recognized as leader, and would find scapegoats in both men, animals and things to explain those occasions when he fails to ward off injury or evil. His function would have been to disarm bad intentions and to maintain the natural vegetative cycles. Thus, as an ancient song from Easter Isle attributed to royal virtue the growth and multiplication of potatoes and the like, many of the taboos of Hindu society attribute ill occurrences to "pollution" from the Dalits, once the enemies of their ancient rules.

What appears more and more certain, to the extent that we advance in ethnological studies, is that most primitive societies do not fit in our modern classification of governments. Individual behavior and collective action was not prescribed by the will of one alone, of many or of all, but rather was necessitated by the powers which dominated society and which certain were skilled at interpreting (certain religious leaders). Thus, present day society may never be able to completely understand the source of many primitive customs or fully appreciate the consequences of primitive fears on conquered people.

Often historians depict primitive peoples holding assemblies, creating primitive democracies, but in reality we should be more modest. It is a gross error to believe that in all societies such as that of the early Aryans, civilized assembles took place, and that this gathering was destined to expose arguments for or against whatever decision, after which the tribe would range itself on the side of the most probing, in many societies, such assemblies were hardly deliberating; it is better to see them rather in the manner of black masses whose object is to arouse the god in order to make his will understood.

India notwithstanding, even in the history of the least religious people of all, those of Rome, we read that before opening a debate, they proceeded with sacrifices and consulted augurs. Our modern consciousness only sees a ceremonial preface to the session. But certainly, in the beginning, the examination of entrails and their interpretation constituted the session itself.[17]

Natural interpreters of god, the ancient Aryans lent to him their own attachment to ancient customs; humanity marched across an unknown earth, seeded with traps, and knew security only in a narrow space which shows itself only to the old ones whom the next generation followed, putting their steps in those of the preceding generation. Thus, in some societies like that of India, divinity and custom became Indivisible.

Summer Maine cites an example which gives a feeling of how much primitive peoples living in modern times still withdraw from modern government by deliberating decisions. While a civil servant in the Indies, he saw the administration create irrigation canals and put the water at the disposition of the communities of villages, which then had to apportion it out. The delicate work of apportionment, once finished, and the arrangement hardly in place, the villagers willingly forgot that the partition came from a human authority. They persuaded themselves that the lots of this totally new water had been assigned by a very ancient custom.

Ancient Customs vs Constitutional Law

The problem the Dalit in India pose for international human rights law is how to protect a minority whose human rights have been historically violated over thousands of years under the cover of ancient custom, culture, and the right to religion. Like the right of conquest, this conception of the right to religion as practised by the Aryan Hindus against the human rights of the Dalits ceased to be acceptable in international law yet remained entrenched in Indian culture to such an extent that one may question the degree to which it can be remove by the formal erection of constitutional guarantees. The Indian government has attempted to respond to the Dalit problem by creating legal and constitutional devices to end the cruel and internationally illegal humiliation and exploitation of the Dalits and other classes of Indian citizens. However, it has not seen fit to recognize the Dalit as a distinct national minority for the purposes of international protection.

Most scholars indicate that the Indian government has sincerely attempted to bring about improvement in the status of the Dalits. Article 46 of the Indian constitution reads: "the state shall promote with special care the equational and economic interest of the weaker sections of the people and, in particular, of the scheduled castes and scheduled tribes and shall protect them from social injustice and all forms of exploitation." It is interesting to note that the Indian government defines the Dalit as the weaker sector of the population (similar to the manner in which the U.S. laws refer to the powerless when dealing with African-American problems). While the legal meaning of this definition is not clear, it is clear that by legal definition the Dalits or scheduled castes etc. are legally considered the weaker subgroup of Hindu people. An important implication of this official position is that the solution to the Dalit problem must be limited to conceptualization in national law and is not a problem for international involvement.

However, due to the ancient inculcation of the Dalits' status and the manner in which we suggest that this exploited status is interweaved in the custom, culture and very identify of India, itself, the Dalit problem is one in which the efficacy of using only the resources of national law becomes doubtful. In the case of most national minorities, the resources of national law are usually not enough. Why would it be different in the case of the Dalits, who under Indian law do not qualify for the status of national minority?

The specific problem of the use of national law alone to deal with national minorities' problems is always the difficulties involved in obtaining consistent implementation, just interpretation and timely formulation. In the case of the Dalit, these are reported to fall critically short of requirements. It may be said that the present Indian law, if implemented rigorously and interpreted equitably, would suffice to remedy the problem of the Dalit minority within the context of their assimilation into the Hindu population, yet most scholars surveyed agree that even this may not be possible within the foreseeable future. Nothing is said about the rights of the Dalits to seek equal-status outside of the assimilationist frame work. Also on this point, even the Indian constitution is silent.

Thus, the Dalit problems, more than most such problems, bring us face to face with questions concerning the effectiveness of national law in reaching implementable decisions and interpretations that may run contrary to the custom or religious belief of the ruling elite, and to what degree international law can be expected to assist. We propose that while international law may be extremely limited in what it can do, if used both politically and legally, it always acts to help ruling elites and their minority populations come face to face with the nature of their real problems, if only by calling attention to deviations in interpretations and implementations of national law that result simply from the difficulty of ruling elites to apply disadvantageous rules to themselves. This latter difficulty is so important to understanding the need for the intervention of international human rights law in the national minority question and particularly that of the Dalit that we will devote the next chapter to commentary on why such difficulties exist in all states when dealing with minority demands, and consequently why minorities are traditionally seen as requiring international legal protection.

Why do Minorities need International Law?

Present day rulers and ruling elites no longer find in their own society the concrete powers of exposing of containing their power. This is true although they may limit themselves theoretically before the abstract power of law. The supremacy of law is a central idea of all political science, but it is necessary to understand that in situations significantly to the interest of the ruling ethny or elite, it presupposes and necessitates a law that is senior to and above the state. Because if the law is something that the ethnic group in power elaborates, how would it ever become an obstacle, judge or guide to that ethnic group?

Popular wisdom, unconsciously repeating the medieval theologians, demands that those who direct society be just. But what is justice? It is, as the institutes of Justinian tell us, "the unshakable and permanent will to attribute to each his rights". Nothing more clear. We each have rights, which we call subjective rights, which are situated in an objective law, the elaboration of a moral rule imposing itself on all.

We may say willingly with Duguit: "the end of public power is to realize the law." No matter which group holds that power, it legitimates itself with subject group when it is exercised in conformity with the law. But what, finally, is this national law? Let's ask the jurists. The majority answer that "the law is the whole or corpus of rules of conduct handed down by a competent authority." In a way, that which conforms to the law is good, while that which strays from it is bad, thus, the art of distinguishing the just from the unjust gets mixed up with the art of understanding and applying the law.

What a vicious circle. The political authority must be just, that is to say to act in conformity with the law. But the law, we are told, is only the whole of rules handed down by that ethny or authority. The law-making ethny or authority is thus just, by definition.

What a sophism! But even Kant reached this undefined justification of national power. We read in the metaphysics of morals:

Against the supreme legislature of the state, there is no legitimate resistance on the part of the people; because a juridical state is only possible thanks to the submission by all to the legislature will. We cannot thus admit in any manner the right of sedition, still less that of rebellion...

The duty the people have to endure the abuse of supreme power, while it may even seem unbearable, based on the idea that resistance to the sovereignty of legislature power is never other than illegal, and even as overturning the whole legal constitution. Because, for the people to be authorized to resist, it would necessitate, beforehand, a public law which would permit it, that is to say, it would necessitate that the sovereign legislation contain a disposition by which it would no longer be sovereign. [22]

The reasoning is marvelous. Only the law makes the Law. Thus, all that is law is Law, and there are no rights against the law. From this standpoint, it is an illusion to seek in national law a rampart against national power. National law is, as the jurists say, "positive".

The essence of the rule of law, specifies a contemporary master, is to be sanctioned by immediate means of coercion, in other words, by human means. The law necessarily thus presupposes a public authority capable of constraining individuals to observe the rules that it itself has emitted. By the same logic, it is manifest that he could not conceive, concerning law, any but positive law. [23]

Is it necessary then, ceding to such authorities, to renounce as illusion the idea of national law as capable of constraining national power, and to recognize in it simply the creature of the state, powerless against its creator?

Doesn't history show us a more dignified law, based on Divine Law, treaties among nations, international customs, the scholarly search for justice and equity, and the aspirations and morals of mankind? Doesn't sentiment bear witness still today that all which is national law (such as apartheid in South Africa) is not really Law? Let's reflect a moment, therefore, on how the aberration for which we have just cited so many witnesses, was introduced, how this servitude of national law was produced.

Historic Basis for Our Belief in the Supremacy of National Law:

We are here at the point of convergence of errors of very different sources. The error of Hobbes, the illusions of Rousseau and of Kant, large faults especially of the utilitarian and materialist school, of the very influential minds of Helvetius, the Benthams, the Destutt of Tracy.

Hobbes, we know, saw in Power the only author and maintainer of order among men. Before it or without it, there is nothing but the brutal collection of appetites. Also, "when a Republic is instituted, there are laws, and nothing beforehand." And "Civil law is for each subject the whole body of rules that the State, verbally, by writing or by any other sufficient indication of its will, makes its will known to the end that it is used to discern the Good and the Evil, that is to say, that which is against the rule."

How much this definition resembles that of certain modern jurists who favor the absolutism of nation state legal sovereignty, not only in India but in numerous other states! (Note the legal argument against the Rev. Martin Luther King during his campaign of civil disobedience in the U.S..*) What results from these principles?

The ruler of a republic, whether it is a (majority) assembly or a man (or an ethnic group), is no longer subject to civil laws. Because having the power to make and unmake laws, he can, when he pleases, set himself apart from this subjection by abrogating those laws which inconvenience him and by making new laws.

*In his campaign of civil disobedience, Dr. King claimed the right sanctioned by Divine Law to disobey unjust national laws; his opposition insisted that all law must be obeyed until it is changed or annulled.

Hobbes at least had seen and wished for the consequences of the principle he advocated. He was pleased to imagine a total power; he traced the frightful portrait with the fanaticism of a logician; master of all properties, censor of all opinions, unable to be reproached no matter what it does, as the sole judge of social good, and of moral good as derived from social good.

For minorities like the Dalits, the Catholics in Northern Ireland, the African-Americans, etc., the philosophical influences for the model of absolute sovereignty of national law under which they struggles have an additional heritage; the influence or heritage of Rousseau and Kant. They constrain themselves from conveying this unlimited legislative power on a monarch or an assembly. No, they wish only to divide it among the whole people, and this condition seems to them without danger. For, as Kant reasons:

When someone decides something with regard to another, it is always possible that he does some injustice; but all injustice is impossible in that which one decides for oneself.[25]

This reasoning is rigorously supported if all the minorities or subjects of the law without exception effectively give their deliberated consent to each law. However, in most cases, the necessary justice of the legislative power leads to numerous fictions. Fiction first that the majority supposedly pronouncing themselves deliberately could not take an injust decision against a certain minority among them. Fiction, finally, and of paramount importance, that the people, including the minority, are consulted on each law. This doesn't happen except in Switzerland, whose harmonious relation between national minorities is almost universally recognized.

Thus, this unlimited legislative power with which Rousseau and Kant endowed the whole of a state, including its minorities, must inevitably pass to that of the majority, from the majority into the hands of several men, a race, class, or often into a single hand. Also this solution to freedom that the rulers of India and many modern states). Saw in the whole social body no other reality than man, and his search for equalitarian justice.

The materialist and utilitarian error is more grave. It is the extreme fruit of the rationalist crisis.

"There is nor good in itself but," says Helvetius, "the diverse peoples throughout the centuries and in all countries have only accorded the name of virtuous to those actions which were, or at least were believed in be, useful to the public."

But they were mistaken in their ideas that all rulers would pass law to obtain what is most useful to the public rather than what is most useful to their race, social class, class, caste or personal self-interest. However, the influence of this orientation on the thinking of modern opinion-leaders in modern democracies suggests that it is necessary first to entirely banish the moralist prejudice of a morality "given" and necessary in itself. Thus, the atrocities committed against the Dalits can be accepted in India while an anathema elsewhere.

It is an ancient and absurd error, says Destutt de Tracy, to believe that moral principles are infused in our heads and that they are same in all and from this dream, to presuppose for them who knows what celestial origin...... Let's recognize that morality is a science which we make up like all the others..... each man has his moral system which is appropriate to him, or rather a confused mass of ideas without consequences, which hardly merit the name of system, but which, in him, take its place.[26]

The reader perhaps would shrug his shoulders, thinking Tracy is not a thinker of the first order nor has exercised great direct influence. Without doubt, but he describes marvelously the array of beliefs and sentiments pertinent to the rationalist upheaval in modern liberalism. The Good and the Bad, the Just and the Unjust, have become a matter of opinion. Such thinking is used by oppressors in various countries such as India to explain why the oppression of certain minorities in their society is perfectly natural and understandable, and how its uncompromising elimination would not serve the interest of the good. But by what crude means does such high-sounding philosophy render the oppressed docile?

The most powerful of all the moral means and besides which all others are almost nil, are the repressive laws and their perfect and complete execution.

In Search of Effective Law

The modern Dalit problem is posed for us here. There is no national law in India supported by common belief throughout the whole society; the law, or its interpretation is indefinitely modifiable at the will of the Aryan-descended Hindu upper castes. The Dalit and other minorities have no other peaceful choice than either to continue to submit to the will of the Aryan-descended caste or to appeal to international human rights law.

Let us take note: the continuing flow of ancient Aryan caste-orientated custom should not create the law that governs the human rights of the Dalit minority. These are the translations of the thrust of interests, of the fantasy of opinions, of the violence of passions, laughable in their disorder and omissions and odious in their inimical order because they emanate from Power gathered in a brutal caste-orientated land. They only merit and obtain the respect that constraint procures them. They are anti-social because they are all based on a false and immoral conception of humanity.

The necessary cohesion of a potentially beautiful and ancient society such as India can't be procured by the power of the rulers alone. There must exist a profound equitable community of sentiments rooted in a common and just faith, translating themselves in an uncontestable morality, supporting inviolable human rights. The fundamental human rights of minorities must extend outside the reach of state power. When law is delivered to arbitrary caste predisposed interpretations, implementation and legislation, then without a doubt caste interest not only can but must extend itself. It is up to international law to re-establish by acceptable but constant intervention a compromise cohesion.

Amid a concert of protest, Duguit enunciated the true doctrine of the role effective law plays:

..........it is necessary to affirm energetically and tirelessly that the activity of the state in all its manifestations is limited by a law superior to it, that there are things that it must not do, that there are things it must do, that this limitation doesn't imposes itself only to such and such an organ, but rather that it impose itself on the State itself.......The main thing is to understand and affirm, with an indefatigable energy, that there is a rule of law superior to public power, which comes to limit it and impose duties upon it.[28]

While Duguit probably assumed an effective law as emanating solely from the state, in the case of minorities, it led to the following question:

When one speaks of instituting the reign of law among nations, what can that mean if an unlimited right to determine its actions exists within each state?

However desirable the idea of the rule of divine or international law imposing itself on state power may be, to put it in action in our time poses great difficulties. For if one admits the principle that law must be in conformity with law, what will prevent the state power representing law from pretending that it is the expression, manifestation and realization of Law. And when international law would judge it inimical, one need only say that the international legal conception in relation to minorities is not law.

The modern spirit instinctively finds itself moving beyond state law, yet it is completely vain to expect the defense of an uncertain international law from a hesitant public sentiment. The ideal of sovereign state law is still very much alive. Only the most naked violence revolts public sentiment sufficiently to call for support. Let us hope that the level of violence presently being visited upon the approximately 110 million Dalits will be sufficient to activate the appropriate use of the necessary human rights machinery.

The Need for International Law

There is in international law an unalterable portion that is derived from the cumulative highpoints of human thought and realization, and that remains outside the reach of any one state power. Humanity is not capable of constant flux, of a mixing of ceaselessly new truths. Ideas are, to the contrary, rare points of water in the desert of human thought which, once discovered, are forever precious, regardless of the stupidity and ignorance they may engender.

Too often in Indian as in all human history, state law has been the toy and instrument of the majority race or ruling elites and their passions. If a wave carries a despot or a tyrannical party, class or caste to power, they can deform in the most fantastic fashion that which already no longer has any certain form. The conclusion being that the philosophic factors that go into the creating and maintenance of state law are too open to elite manipulation.

Given this understanding of the problems faced by state law, we need no longer question the obligation imposed on international human rights law and institutions to make every effort to intervene in every way legally acceptable to encourage the Indian government to bring an end to this several thousand year old Dalit nightmare.

INTERNATINAL LAW AND THE PROBLEM OF MINORITIES

The problem of minorities is of particular importance to scholars of international human rights law because a major reason for the existence of this discipline is to establish principles whereby rules for the harmonious and peaceful relationship among groups may evolve and be discerned. The sacredness of the minority idea, of the right of a people to remain themselves in all significant ways in which still enjoying equal status relationship with all other peoples who live in the same multi-national state, ahs found recognition in the principles of 20th century human rights law. It is elaborated in the legal and constitutional instruments for minority protection in most of the progressive modern states, and in the human rights machinery of international organizations, including the United Nations.

Although the principle of minority equal status protection may be said to have only recently (with the work of the U.N. Human Rights Commission and its sub-committee) begin to be recognized in modern international law, its most well-known modern origins can be said to go back to the dismantling of the European empire with the occurrence of European nationalism and the introduction to the world of the concept of nation-states as well as the concept of the right to self-determination. From this moment on, the concepts of the rights of minorities to equal status and self-determination entered the lifeblood of the developing modern world and eventually found its place in domestic and international legal instrumentation.

The self-consciousness of nations is a product of the nineteenth century............Nations were already there, but it is not the things which are simply 'there' which matter in human life....apprehended (legally and politically conceptualized) ideas as well as a fact before it can become a dynamic force.[29]

True! This European nationalism, this concept of the nation-state, but seldom did it actually lead to the creation of its ideal, the nation-state. Instead, it generally led to the creation of the multinational state, states in which not one but often several ethnically defined nations co-existed. Yet the ideal of the nation-state remained to serve as a force toward which all states and nations were drawn, and as an ideal concept to which they attempted to conform. Regardless of the fact that they were multi-national, their ruling ethnics or elites presented themselves as working towards or having accomplished the goal of nation-statehood.

Why did development take this turn? The answer perhaps can be attained from the observation of the historical fact that not only (as Ernest Baker noted) the idea of the nation-state must be comprehended before it matters, but also the people or ethny that conceives of itself as a nation must have the circumstance and consequently power to win their freedom from those who claim them. The people of every European state-to-be fought difficult struggles for their liberation. However many peoples, for whatever reasons, did not achieve statehood, although remaining attached to and aware of their nationhood. Having not achieved statehood, they remained a part of the states of the more powerful or successful peoples or nations. The goals of these more powerful nations among whom they live was usually to absorb their less strong countrymen (e.g. Britain and France) at the more positive end of the scale, or to use or exploit them (e.g. South Africa, U.S., India) at the lower end of the scale. However, both of these earlier processes have in general historically failed, and in the process of failing have constantly posed threats not only to the peace, progress and well-being of states and regions concerned, but also to the world. An important goal of the League of Nations was to cap the minority problems that were threatening international peace and order.

The attention of international organizations to these threats to world progress as well s their regular involvements in minority conflicts played an important part in encouraging the recognition and development of international human rights law, particularly as it relates to minorities. In essence, the involvement of international law with the question of minorities can be said to have occurred as a natural response to the failure of the methods in place by multi-national states to absorb or provide acceptable status to their minorities, as well as their tendency to present legal or informal circumstance that prevented the members of minorities from experiencing civil rights on an equal footing with other citizens. Following World War II, international law, through the instrumentality of international organizations entered this most volatile area of minority rights by first encouraging states to afford to minorities the same equal protection and civil rights as enjoyed by other citizens; then through the tumultuous years of decolonization, it found the authority under such conditions to promote the right to self-determination in cases where minorities (usually redefined as colonial subjects) were obviously being exploited, and where minorities were being absorbed into the majority ethny against their declared will. (This did not include states like the U.S. where minorities were seen as having chosen to assimilate or having been already assimilated.) When the French citizens of Algerian descent sought separation of the area in which they were a majority from the remainder of France, the U.N. saw fit to grant this minority colonial status and to accept the right of the territory in which they were the majority (Algeria) to independence. Obviously this was a way to resolve the problem of a minority such as the Algerian (whose armed revolt was considered a threat to regional peace) without raising the general urgent but volatile question of the rights of all minorities in multi-national states. But regardless of how successful the conversion of the minority question into a colonial status question, it still did not prevent the question of minorities rights and self-determination from being raised by minorities in situations far removed from the well-accepted decolonization process. The continuing struggle of the Kurds in Iraq. Iran and Turkey, the French Canadians in Canada, the Irish in Northern Ireland, the African-Americans in the U.S., the Dalits and Muslims in India, all serve as witness that the question of the needs and rights of the ethnic nation or minority is far from fading into the sunset.

When we consider the minority rights that are already acceptable principles of international law: equal protection, the right to be different, the right to special measures, etc. in conjunction with the international support given to minorities seeking colonial status, we see that when states can be shown to be refusing to grant minorities rights, international law implicitly upheld the right of minorities to engage in armed struggle.

In short, international law attempts to establish the moral environment that will encourage the evolution of circumstances that will permit nations or minorities within multi-national states the possibility of achieving self-determination, equal status or civil rights with minimum or no armed conflict and particularly without the necessity for conflict with the international system itself. Thus, the necessity to raise the question of whether international organizations should intervene in the domestic affairs of a country to define and encourage minority rights in case of gross violation of their rights, such as India in relation to the Dalits, in South Africa in relation to the blacks, in Israel in relation to the Palestinians, etc., is essentially a procedural response to Article I (non-intervention in domestic affairs) of the U.N. Charter and other human rights instrumentality, and as such is almost always provoked and conditioned by power politics. To raise this question apart from power politics is totally academic.

Power Politics and Minority Rights

The possibility for the successful use of inter-national human rights law in relation to a given minority (the Dalit, for example) depends not only on the prevailing interpretation of minority rights in international law, but also on existing power relations within the international system: the relative power position of India within that context, and within the context of the redress being requested.

Recent history has seen the world essentially divided between the proponents of the western system and the proponents of the system of the socialists. This means that major powers tend to have a disproportionately high influence on what other states accept as rules and principles are interpreted, and on what is emphasized. In this manner, major powers may disproportionately influence the law-creating and law-determining sources and thus human rights law itself. In order to interpret the effect of power politics on the law-influencing declarations, resolutions, etc. of the U.N. as it concerns minorities, we have examined the human rights emphasis of both socialist and western liberal countries as it concerns minority rights. We have found that minority rights are chiefly promoted by the socialist bloc in accordance with their domestic and international ideologies, and that minority rights are chiefly de-emphasized by the western states. We have also found that the capacity of each major power bloc to exert influence in the U.N. was related to their relative power position in the international system, that is, that their period of maximal influence in U.N. output coincides with their period of maximum strength in the international system. It is only in recent years, as the socialist bloc gained in power relative to the western democracies, that minority rights have taken on special importance in the U.N. When considering the question of the Dalit in India, similar consideration must be given to power politics to avoid the adoption of a legal strategy that is unable to fit into the demands of the international political configuration.

Just as the League of Nations reflected the predominant concerns and policy orientations of the European nations who dominated the world scene at its creation, so too did the new United Nations, created after World War II, reflect the new international order. The minority rights question, which had received pre-eminent attention in the League, was de-emphasized in the U.N., largely due to the western bloc concept of human rights. The western bloc embarked upon a policy of de-emphasizing minority human rights in the U.N. in favor of an emphasis on individual civil and political human rights and assimilation of minorities. It was the U.S. concept of human rights that has been adopted by India since independence, and applied to the problem of the Dalits. The Indian Constitution was greatly influenced by that of the U.S.

However, as the Eastern bloc's power and influence represented a counter to western power in the new international order, so too has it served to counter American de-emphasis of minority human rights in the U.N. Having perceived that by lessening tensions and avoiding conflict in Europe, Eastern bloc powers could heighten the western

European Powers' awareness of their geo-political interest, thus leading towards greater European unity and reducing the threat of war. The Eastern bloc focused its foreign policy initiatives on avoiding confrontations in Europe while encouraging self-determination for minorities in European empires (colonized 'peoples' of the Third World). This strategy, which opened the way to the process of certain minorities achieving colonial status and hence to decolonization, was reflected in the U.N. by a new emphasis on minority rights, and in particular, on the political right of self-determination.

Yet the chances for more meaningful international responses to the needs of minorities are increasing. One reason for the multilateral inaction has been (the ideology of assimilation propounded in the United Nations (by the U.S)

Most unfortunately for the capacity of international law to fulfill the role it has been called upon to play in relation to the question of minority rights in various social systems, is the still very important influence of the assimilationist concepts in determining what international organizations do. A sincere analysis of the situation of minorities such as the Dalits, African-Americans, Irish Catholics, Kurds, etc. in present day multi-national states should have convinced assimilationist advocated that even if such a policy had worked among Europeans in the U.S., it is not necessarily transportable to most other countries, and that the continued effort to encourage the international adoption of such a minority rights concept only further exacerbates regional, national and world political contradictions, and further isolate this U.S. policy as reactionary. It would no doubt be better to combine the traditional minority rights concept with that of the assimilationist concept in such a manner as would best preserve their collective and individual rights features. Such an unlikely combination may produce a genuine alternative to self-determination in multinational states. The minority rights models of such countries as Switzerland, Belgium, Yugoslavia, U.S.S.R., Sweden, Nigeria and Canada should be studies, analyzed, and legal and political principles made available to countries such as India in her good faith search for a solution to the Dalit question.

Minority Rights and the U.N.

The Principles upon which the concept of minority rights in international law are based can be found in treaties among states, in the recognized legal and political internal practises of states, as well as in the U.N. resolutions and declarations and, most importantly, the U.N. Covenant on Civil and Political Rights.

Although the United Nations initiated many conferences to discuss and to encourage respect for minority rights, it is only the general principle (in Article 27 as a part of the Covenant on Civil and Political Rights), that has received universal formal acceptance as a legal principle by the member states of the United Nations. The final text of this article reads:

In those States in which ethnic, religious or linguistic minorities exist, persons belonging to such minorities shall not be denied the right, in community with the other members of their group, to enjoy their own culture, to profess and practise their own religion, or to use their own language.

Article 27 of the Covenant on Civil and Political Rights has been said to contain two important requirements. According to the Human Rights Sub-Commission on the Elimination of All Forms of Racial Discrimination, it calls upon states to take the following two steps:

(1) Officially recognize the existence of the minorities living within their borders. This means recognize their right to peoplehood with equal rights but as a different people from the majority, that is, a different people with the same statehood or citizenship.

(2) Provide for special measures where required in order for the minority to maintain its ethnic identity and achieve political, economic and social equality with the majority. (We should note that ratification of the major human rights treaties is encouraged by the United Nations in order that minorities may benefit through domestic law from internationally protected minority rights. So, far, India had not yet had occasion to grant the Dalit this first and most fundamental right. Thus, the Dalit are not recognized by India as a minority for the purpose of international protection, and thus, they do not benefit from the secondary rights. Furthermore, there is no evidence that Dalits have ever officially requested such recognition.

One of the most important secondary rights that are often discussed in connection with minorities, once they have been so recognized in accordance with the general principle, is the right of self-determination as well as right to armed struggle if equal status is refused.

1. Recognition

From a study of the practises of states, we observed that in accordance with, but not necessarily because of, the general principle, most nations having minority provide clauses in their constitutions or body of laws to the effect that the state is composed of certain minorities or national groups. This provides the minority with a legal and political identity. We assumed that it is exactly this manner of recognition that is called for by international human rights law. Such concepts have been historically practised by states. Article 19 of the Austrian Constitutional Law of December 21, 1867 states.

All the ethnic minorities of the State shall enjoy the same rights and, in particular, have an absolute right to maintain and develop their nationality and their language. All the languages used in the provinces are recognized by the State as having equal rights with regards to education, administration and public life.

2. *Special Measures*

Although the component principle of special measures involves more than does that of recognition, it too can be abstracted from the practises of civilized nations. In essence this principle simply means that, when required in order to achieve the purposes of the general principle, special actions (U.N. intervention, studies, inquiries, fact-finding commissions, etc.,), or special laws (affirmative action, financial and/or particular political institutions) should be established to assure the equal status of a minority. However, even with this explanation, the principle of special measures still remains somewhat vague. This is so because its precise definition depends on the specific requirements of the state and minority concerned. The general understanding is that it can be whatever produces equal status.

The three traditional types of special measures to which Professor Joseph B. Kelly calls attention in his article, "National Minorities in International Law," (op. cit.) are frontier revision, population transfer, and the development of a new autonomous state. However, it would appear that Dr. Kelly's concept of special measures only became required by the general principle, if the state is unable to offer or apply less extreme measures such as pluralistic integration or voluntary assimilation.

The international law view of minority rights does not accept assimilation of the minority into the culture of the larger race or ethnic group unless it is the "will of the minority," and the will of the minority can only be accurately secured through internationally supervised democratic means.

Safeguarding Minority Rights

1. To entrench safeguards for minority rights usually requires constitutional amendments or legislative decisions by more

than a simple majority before protected rights can be changed or abolished; a "weighted" majority, for instance, more than two-thirds or more than three-quarters of the votes, in place of a simple majority. An example of an entrenched safeguard is the concept of a blocking mechanism which enables a particular minority to prevent, or at least to delay, and national legislation which it considers to be against its vital interests. For example, under the present Belgian Constitution, three-quarters of either the Dutch or the French national minority groups in Parliament can refer back to the Council of ministers any proposed legislation which they consider harmful to relations between the communities. The two national minorities have equal representation in the governing council, although Dutch speakers are a majority in the country. Also most minority safeguards include some arrangement that permits the minority to receive, for its collective use, some significant portion of taxes paid by its members to the state.

2. There can be special representation of minority groups in the legislature. There are several forms. In Belgium, Switzerland and other countries a second chamber is designed to give particular weight to distinctive groups. In Belgium, for example, there are separate cultural councils, each comprising all the members of the appropriate group in both Houses of Parliament. Such councils could represent the interests of their particular communities and have a final say on such minority community matters as education, social services, family planning, or religious or linguistic questions, etc.

The possible examples of special measures are endless, because in essence this principle calls for governments to provide their minorities with the same rights as the majority in addition to investigating the minority's situation and instituting any feasible measures which are necessary to promote the survival and equality of that minority with the majority. All component principles of the general principle aim at the acceptance of the minority's right to be different and the survival of the minority in an equal-status relationship with the majority. The key words are "right to be different," "equal-status" and "survival". If the arrangement does not lead to both survival and equal-status, it does not pass the requirements of international law, and thus more effective special measures involving such concepts as U.N. fact-finding, inquiries, commissions, supervision, trusteeship or self-determination becomes necessary.

Minority Rights and the Dalits

In considering the possibility of the Dalit question being raised as a question of minority protection in international law, the chief approach determining how international human rights law can be most effective will be conditioned by the response to the following:

1. Are the Dalits a minority for the purpose of international protection and
2. Is Dalit oppression governed more by the ancient customs and religious rules by which it evolved during the past 1,000 years than by the written or formal laws of India, and if so, what contribution can international human rights law make to the resolution of this problem?

In the following section, we shall do our best to highlight the appropriate perspective and provide data that we feel is appropriate for providing our reader with a sound basis upon which to respond to the aforementioned questions.

Dalits and Other Minorities

One of the chief difficulties in attempting to ascertain legal rule concerning the Dalit and other similar minorities from the legal principles of international human rights law is the tendency of states such as India to classify their minorities as social minorities and to prevent them from understanding that they are a national minority for the purpose of international minority protection. In looking at the practises of civilized nations, we may quickly see that the international needs or rights of all types of minorities (sub-groups, social and political minorities, etc.) that are domestically recognized have no international personality, and thus no enforceable claim to legal rights as minorities in customary or institutional human rights law.

In general, customary international law, as far as minorities are concerned, deals almost exclusively with only two types of minorities for the purpose of international legal protection; national minorities and immigrant minorities, which can be further divided into linguistic, ethnic and religious groups. While no differences in the type of rights accorded to each distinction is mentioned in U.N. law, they can be ascertained from customary international law. However, for the purpose of international protection, the Human Rights Sub-Commission drew the following distinctions:

"historical", "classical", or "involuntary" minorities, resulting from the events of a historical or geographical character (for example, changes in the borders, transfers of population and slavery) and "minorities by election," "voluntary minorities" or "new minorities" composed of persons who had recently and voluntarily left their country of origin and moved to other countries (such as immigrants).

In relation to the origin of groups and their situation in relation to the State, the following types of minorities were mentioned by the Sub-Commission:

(a) Groups which existed in the country before the establishment of the State..........

......(c) Groups formed by persons having a common origin, religion and language who have become national of the State (Example: Italian, Polish and other immigrants. Their internationally protected rights (found in customary law) are limited to civil rights and the right to assimilate (or integrate while maintaining) their culture and language, or (to) return to their homeland.)

While the Indian government appears to have taken action that recognizes the Dalits as an Indian or Hindu sub-group minority for the purposes of affirmative action, it has not recognized them as a minority for the purpose of special measures and international protection. The law speaks of the Dalits as the lower sector of the Hindu population and attempts to grant them civil rights for the purpose of assimilation or integration.

However, in his book, Dalit: The Black Untouchables of India, the Dalit leader V.T. Rajshekar, affirms the conclusion of other scholars that the Dalits are the descendants of the Indus Valley civilization that was conquered by the Aryans (who later were called Hindus). The Dalits were first classified within Hinduism as Scheduled Castes during the British rule of India despite their centuries-old denunciation by Hindu sacred writings as being outside Hinduism, or outcastes, pariahs or untouchables. The maintenance of this classification of Dalits as Scheduled Castes within Hinduism subsequent to Indian independence was, according to Mr. Rajshekar, for the purpose of consolidating Indian unity on the basis of Hindu dominance. Prior to this, the condition of Dalits in relation to Hindus was that of a conquered people, an enslaved people, a people living in a condition of culturally, socially and religiously enforced apartheid. Most scholars studying the various Dalit populations have provided data that indicate that they are not just the poor and oppressed of the Hindu nation, but that they are also a distinct ethnic group.

Judging from this data, U.N. classification of minorities, and numerous other authorities, we believe that the evidence presented by most scholars demonstrates that the Dalits are not just a sub-group or social minority, but a national, historical and involuntary minority, but a national, historical and involuntary minority, thus possessing the right to international protection in the meaning of international law. National minorities (such as we feel the Dalits to be) have the right to international legal protection. Social or sub-group minorities do not. Even immigrant minorities are not seen as having the same type of international legal protection as national minorities:

Many delegates representing countries of immigration stressed......that persons of similar origin who entered their territories voluntarily, through a gradual process of immigration, could not be regarded as minorities, as this would endanger the national integrity of the receiving States; while the newcomers were free to use their own language and follow their own religion, they were expected to become part of the national fabric.

Another Sub-Commission Commentary States

In historical surveys of the origin and establishment of ethnic, religious and linguistic minorities in the country, it should be indicated in particular whether the presence of these minorities is due to the existence of an autochthonous population, immigration, or an alteration of the country's borders.

Most governments which accepted the need in general for national and immigrant minority protection felt it should not be extended to types of immigrant minorities that were not permanent (migratory immigrant minorities).migrant workers represents a new and special category of minority, possibly a "social minority". It was also noted that special problems arose in developing countries, and that the case of tribes should not be confused with that of minorities in industrialized countries.

Governments, such as that of the U.S.A. and India, indicated that the objective of their policy is 'cohesion and unity if their people and the creation of an atmosphere in which the various ethnic, religious and linguistic groups may find the opportunity to transcend the differences between them.' On the basis of that assumption, the tendency of such governments has been to not recognize the minority's right to be different, and often even to deny their existence altogether.

The response of the Sub-Commission to such arguments can be seen in the conclusions it reached, which were adopted by the Human Rights Commission:

............While equality and non-discrimination imply a formal guarantee of uniform treatment for all individuals, protection of minorities implies special measures in favor of members of a minority group; the purpose of these measures none the less is to institute a factual equality between the members of such groups and other individuals. The prevention of discrimination on the one hand and the implementation of special measures to protect minorities, on the other, are merely two aspects of the same problem. The guiding principle is that no individual should be placed at a disadvantage merely because he is a member of a particular minority.

The Sub-Commission further Stated

From available information, harmonious relations between various ethnic, religious and linguistic groups within a country depended to a large extend on the attitude of the dominant political forces of the society of that country and on their willingness to allow members of each group to pursue their economic, social and cultural development according to their own tradition in an atmosphere free of discrimination.

The Sub-Commission further concluded that the principles of international law require states to officially recognize the existence of their minorities with the understanding that "the objective presence of sufficient evidence to indicate that the minority exists is sufficient to make applicable the pertinent international rules, foremost of which is Article 27 of the Covenant on Civil and Political Rights." As for the question of implicit recognition, "general constitutional provisions forbidding discrimination based on race, national or ethnic origin, religion or language cannot be interpreted as constituting a recognition of ethnic, cultural, religious or linguistic minorities"; that most of the objections to the application of Article 27 to all U.N.-defined minorities can be classified under the following headings:

(1) risk of interference in the internal affairs of States, (2) the diversity of situation, and (3) the threat to the stability of the State. These objections are basically the same as those raised for many years in respect to international protection of human rights in general......Furthermore, governments would prefer to have a free hand in the treatment of their minorities. While some states on their own initiative have devised effective protection systems and models, the idea that every State must conform to international standards and a degree of international control encounters great opposition.

In order to fulfill its mandate to come up with a suitable definition of the term minority, the Sub-Commission approved and submitted the following definition:

.........the term 'minority' may be taken to refer to: a group numerically inferior to the rest of the population of a State, in a nondominant position, whose members, being nationals of the State, possess ethnic, racial, religious or linguistic characteristics differing from those of the rest of the population and show, if only implicitly, a sense of solidarity, directed towards preserving their culture, traditions, religion or language.....Extent of the subjective factor involved is the extent to which the desire, whether expressed or not, of the ethnic, religious or linguistic group to preserve its own characteristics, constitutes a factor relevant to the definition of the term 'minority'. Whether the number of persons belonging to the ethnic, religious or linguistic group is relevant depends on whether it is sufficiently numerous for it to be practical for the country concerned to maintain minority institutions......

Certainly the focus of international law on the Dalit problem will afford scholars in international organization an excellent opportunity to investigate the elusiveness of state law in dealing with certain very serious and gross violations of minority rights that go beyond civil rights violations, and to test the usefulness of various international human rights instruments in dealing with a problem governed by entrenched ancient custom and religious rules:

.........While equality and non-discrimination imply a formal guarantee of uniform treatment for all individuals, protection of minorities implies special measures in favor of a member of a minority group; the purpose of these measures nonetheless is to institute a factual equality between the members of such groups and other individuals....

..........From available information harmonious relation between various ethnic, religious and linguistic groups within a country depends to a large extent on the attitude of the dominant political forces of the society of that country and on her willingness to allow members of each group to pursue their economic, social and cultural development according to their own tradition in an atmosphere free of discrimination......

The above quotations call attention to the social system and attitude of the dominant political forces. The social system and consequently social attitudes that evolved out of the 2,000 year old Aryan conquest in regard to the Dalit still reflects the savage commands of antiquity.

The Present State of Affairs

Not only has the Indian government not provided the Dalit minority with its right to international protection, but neither has it been able to implement their civil rights (see Table 1).

Number of violations registered under the Protection of Civil Rights Act of 1955

Name of State/Union Territory	*1970*	*1979*
Andhra Pradesh	151	144
Karnataka	426	550
Maharashtra	1283	1604
Orissa	106	151
Tamil Nadu	547	603
Madhya Pradesh	398	307
Rajasthan	168	126

A police officer in Tamil Nadu is reported to have remarked. "If we (the police) take this law seriously (PCR 1976), half of the population of Tamil Nadu will have to be arrested. In any case, the police have better things to do than go poking their noses into the private affairs of the people."

What is more disturbing are reported that the police themselves are sometimes the aggressors. One of the most conspicuous reported was documented in the city of

Agra where police, outraged by the persistent Untouchable protest, went on a rampage in the Dalit residential area, killing 9 and seriously injuring more than 100, burning huts and leaving the walls of an Untouchable Buddhist shrine riddled with bullet holes.

In the past ten years there have been documented reported of an increase in brutal killings, rapes, violent crimes against the Dalit. This corresponds to the increased efforts of the Dalits to internationalize their struggle without the protection of international organizations, resulting from their increasing awareness of their internationally protected human rights. This increase in incidents has been widely reported in many sources in India and abroad. The commissioner for scheduled castes and scheduled tribes in his 27th report (1979-81) published in 1983, charged, "In spite of the firm resolve of the government to check the incidents of atrocities on the persons belonging to scheduled castes and scheduled tribes, such incidents continue to be reported in considerable number from all parts of the country. It is all the more disconcerting that at times atrocities on weaker sections are allegedly committed by persons who themselves happened to be in charge of protecting their life and honor. On occasions when influential persons are involved directly or indirectly in the incidents of atrocities on scheduled castes and scheduled tribes, it is alleged that attempts are made to weaken the cases. It seems that so far the Indian state administrative machinery has not been properly geared to check exploitation of scheduled castes and scheduled tribes."

According to the figures released by the Home Minister for 1982, "on an average, two women belonging to the scheduled caste are raped, two men are murdered and three members of the community suffer grievous injury every day in the country."

Out of the total cases in which offences were reported only a few cases were tried and punished. Such statistics strongly indicate a trend that, if correct, probably means that the ancient attitudes and social customs developed throughout the past 2,000 years act to prevent the formal implementation of equality laws from being realized in reality, and underscore the unacceptability of the Dalit nation to the Hindu nation for the purposes of assimilation.

Of course, the Hindu social system and civil rights itself mitigate against the ability of the government to create the will and scope of fair play necessary to give real assurance to those in the position of authority that equal-status law should be enforced. It should be noted that:

(a) There is no major mixing of high caste and low caste in terms of intercaste or intercultural marriage. Where it does occur, it is an exception to the rule, and generally it occurs if this favors the Hindu high caste financially.

(b) Members of the Dalit nation are still considered "Pollution". The late Babu Jagjiwan Ram, a Dalit leader, inaugurated a statue, which was then "purified" by a Hindu high caste priest with holy water from the Ganges River. Several months ago another Dalit leader. Mr. Ram Dhan, was asked to inaugurate a statue, and after he left, again the statue was purified by the Hindu high caste.

(c) In 1978-79, as reported in a personal interview to Dr. Berwa, Harijan Sevak Sangh conducted a sample survey of untouchability in 1.155 villages from districts throughout India. In 613 villages, Dalits were not permitted access to the public well. In 821 villages, Dalits were denied access to the public temples. In 496 and 473 villages respectively, Dalits were turned away from local cafes and barber shops. In 603 villages, Dalits were denied the services of local washermen. At the same time, the nation's courts handed down only 198 convictions for untouchability offenses under the Protection of Civil Rights Act.

(d) According to the rules (affirmative action), scheduled castes and scheduled tribes should have 15% and 7% reservations respective in the public sectors. But indeed, quotas in high level jobs are not met, according to the government's own data (1982) and the representation in menial jobs which Hindus do not want to do due to social stigma is almost completely Dalit.

(e) In the Indian constitution, declaring India a sovereign, secular and democratic republic there was no reference to the religion of the people listed under scheduled castes in the year 1950. But in the same year, presidential orders came into force which declared that "No person who professes a religion other than Hinduism shall be deemed to belong to the Scheduled Castes." In 1956 this order was amended to include those scheduled castes who professed Sikhism. These kinds of laws deny the political rights of professing Dalit Buddhists, Christians, and Muslims to contest seats to the Parliament and State Legislatures reserved for the so-called Hindu scheduled castes and scheduled tribes (Hindu Dalits). Indeed, the requirements of international law suggest just the opposite, which is that such reservations be made for all national minorities, not just for a lower segment presumed to be of the majority ethny.

It appears that reservation laws in India are designed not to assure equal-status to its minorities but to penalize national minorities that do not accept political assimilation at the bottom of the Hindu nation. Christians, Muslims, non-Hindu Dalits, etc. were not entitled to the affirmative action quota in the professional courses like law, medicine and engineering, or to affirmative action programs for government jobs. While the existence of the Dalit community inside Hinduism is exploited and humiliated, its existence outside Hinduism is either ignored, denied or punished, depending on the circumstance and interest of the ruling Hindu elites system.

In India, much is written about the continuation of the discrimination against the Dalit regardless of the actions of the Indian government. However, very little is written by non-Dalits on whether the Dalits are a part of the Hindu nation, or a conquered minority forced to suffer a one-sided assimilation in order to provide the Hindu with an adequate menial labour force free from the possibility of international intervention. It is their history, their heritage, social customs, and consequently their culture and collective identity that serves to identify them for the purpose of Hindu exploitation.

Conclusion

The International Covenants: Non-Acceptance of the Accepted

In this monograph, we have taken pains to suggest that the application of international law was necessary in seeking solutions to minority problems because (1) the elaboration, implementation and interpretation of domestic law usually follows the interest and will of the ethny or group in power; and (2) the caste-orientated religious customs of India can be depended on to maintain the oppression of the Dalits although the formal written law appears to abolish this oppression. This implies the need for application of a law that can not only be elaborated outside of India, but also interpreted outside of India. Thus, when we speak of the necessity of international law to help end the gross violation of the human rights of Dalits, we must logically foresee the necessity for international intervention in both the interpretation and implementation process.

We have seen in India the official abolition of the heinous crime of untouchability, a form of socio-political, economic, religious and cultural oppression which had been successfully applied to the Dalit people over centuries. We also know, however, that the Dalit populations continue to suffer from this oppression due to the cultural enrootedness of the social practises acting against them and lack of effective implementation of legal protection by the Hindu rulers. This continues although India is reported to have also implemented the international Declaration of Human Rights (The Covenant of Civil and Political Rights and the Covenant on Social and Economic Rights). However, when we examine the actual implementation process we find that all parts of the international covenants which may have significant impact on the situation of the Dalits and other minorities were reinterpreted to suit the law (India's Constitution) or the will of the ruling group.

When we compare the Indian Constitution to the U.N. covenants on human rights, we find that it seems to give the Indian people many of the same fundamental rights. A completed table of the similarities showed that the "right to liberty of movement," "freedom to choose his residence", "right to hold opinions," "right of peaceful assembly," and "right to freedom of association with others" are provided in the Covenants is laid down under Article 23 of the Constitution. "Right to life and security of person" and the right of a person to remain "equal before the Courts and Tribunals" are guaranteed respectively under Articles 21 and 14 of the constitution. That any one who is arrested shall have a right to be informed at the time of arrest is provided under Article 22. Equality before the law and prohibition of discrimination on the ground of religion, race, caste and sex and equality of opportunity in matters of public employment have been guaranteed under the Constitution respectively under Article 14, 15 and 16(1). Freedom from being prosecuted and punished for the same offence more than once is recognized under Article 29, Para (2). No person accused of any offence shall be compelled to be a witness against himself is guaranteed under Article 20 para (3) etc.

However, when we come to the rights in the Covenants that would make the above rights truly accessible to the oppressed minorities who need fundamental human rights in order to guarantee the implementation of the above civil rights in relation to themselves, the Indian government distorts the rights in the covenants to conform with the will of its ruling elite expressed in its constitution by the use of the concept of acceptance with reservation.

1. *Right of Self-Determination*

Para 9(1) of Article 1 of the Covenant lays down that all peoples have the right to self-determination. Para, (1 of the Indian Declarations makes it clear as to their stand. It says that Article 1 shall

Only apply to the peoples under foreign domination and that these words do not apply to sovereign independent States or to a section of a people or nation- which is the essence of national integrity.

It means that the right of self-determination cannot be invoked by any section of the people of any part of the country on the basis of the stipulation supposedly accepted in the Covenant.

2. *Protection against Arbitrary Arrest and Detention*

The Covenant under Article 9 provides various safeguards against the arbitrary arrest and detention of a person. Under Article 22 of the Indian Constitution, however, these provisions are different. For instance, the right is not available to any enemy alien or to a person arrested or detained under a preventive of the Advisory Board, and, although the detaining authority is required to furnish to the detained the grounds for detention, disclosure of facts which are considered by the authority to be against public interest may not be furnished to the detained. India has made this position clear by making reservation under Para(2) of the Declarations which says that Article 9 shall be so applied as to be in consonance with the provisions of clauses (3) to (7) of Article 22 of the Constitution of India. As far as the Covenant's enforceable right to compensation to the victims of unlawful arrest or detention, the Declaration expressly provides in Para II that under the Indian Legal System, there is no enforceable right to compensation for persons claiming to be victims of unlawful arrest or detention against the State.

Thus, the provisions relating to preventive detention stipulated in the Covenant including that of compensation would not be applicable to India. Because of the aforesaid reservations, the provisions of the National Security Act, enacted in 1980 are not considered contrary to the provisions of Article 9 of the Covenant.

3. Rights of Aliens

Article 13 of the Covenant lays down that an alien lawfully in the territory of a State Party may be expelled therefrom only in pursuance of a decision reached in accordance with law and shall, except where compelling reasons of national security otherwise require, be allowed to submit the reasons against his expulsion and to have his case reviewed. This has not been recognized by India. Para III of the Declarations provides that with respect of Article 13 of the International Covenant on Civil and Political Rights, the Government of the Republic of India reserves its rights to apply its law relating to foreigners.

4. Right to Freedom

Article 19(1) of the Indian Constitution provides various rights to a person which includes freedom of speech and expression, right to peaceful assembly, right to form associations or unions, and the right to move freely throughout the territory of India. These rights are recognized in the Covenant under Article 12, 19, 21 and 22, but along with India's restrictions which are different from those provided in the Covenant.

The Government of the Republic of India declares that the provisions of the said Articles shall be so applied as to be in conformity with the provisions of Article 19 of the Constitution of India.

5. Emergency Provisions in India and the Covenant

By the Thirty-Eighth Amendment Act, 1975, Article 352 was amended to provide the President with Power to issue different proclamations on different grounds even if a proclamation already issued on one ground is in operation.

During the 1975 emergency individuals were completely denied their rights guaranteed under the Covenants and Constitution. It was done by making Constitutional amendments and legislative changes. During this period, the whole ideology of human rights and fundamental freedoms was annulled.

However, the Covenant expressly lays down the provisions for an emergency. Para 1 of Article 4 of the Covenant lays down that in time of public emergency which threatens the life of the nation and the existence of which is officially proclaimed, the States Parties may take measures derogating from their obligations under the present Covenant. But the provision does not mean that the State shall have complete freedom to abuse other provisions of the Covenant.

Firstly, there cannot be any derogation in respect of certain rights. Even in time of emergency, they are not suspendable. Such rights are as follows:

(a) Prohibition against arbitrary deprivation of the inherent right to life (Article 6)

(b) Prohibition against torture, cruel, inhuman or degrading treatment or punishment or subjecting a person without his free consent to medical or scientific experimentation (Article 7)

(c) Prohibition against slavery, slave-trade and servitude (Article 8, Paras 1 and 2)

(d) Prohibition against imprisonment merely on the ground of inability to fulfill a contractual obligation (Article II)

(e) Prohibition against retroactive penal offences and punishments thereunder (Article 15)

(f) Right of recognition of everyone, everywhere as a person before the law (Article 16) and

(g) Right to freedom of thought, conscience and religion (Article 18).

In the Indian Constitution, no express provision has been made for any of the above safeguards mentioned in the Covenant. On the contrary, in time of emergency there was a provision for the absolute suspension of fundamental rights provided under Article 19 and also the enforcement of other rights conferred by Part III of the Constitution by a simple declaratory order to that effect by the President (see Article 358, 359).

Rights stipulated in the Covenant on Economic, Social and Cultural Rights find place in Part IV of the Indian Constitution, which lays down the "Directive Principles of State Policy."

The significant difference between the "fundamental rights" in the covenant and the "directive principles" in the Indian constitution is that while the former is enforceable before the Courts of Law, the latter is not justifiable. Instead, the courts are required to interpret the laws in light of the social and economic values set out by the directive principles.

Also in this Covenant, Article 1,(which)lays down the right of self-determination shall apply only to the people under foreign domination and not to sovereign independent States or to a section of a people or nation. Further, Articles 4 and 8 of the Covenant shall be so applied as to be in conformity with the provisions of Article 19 of the Constitution.

and Article 7(c) of the Covenant shall be so applied as to be in conformity with the provisions of Article 16(4) of the Constitution.

The effect of the reservations that India made to both international covenants, in supposedly implementing them, is that the Indian government is not required to take any step beyond that which is guaranteed in its own constitution. Now we can see how even international law, if left to the interpretation of national power, becomes the creation of that power. It is necessary that both the interpretation and the implementation of international law be left in the hands of international organizations or tribunals.

Recommendation

Apart from the civil rights and affirmative action steps already undertaken, *international law requires that the Dalits be first recognized as a national or historical ethnic minority, as a separate nation from the Hindus for the purposes of international protection.* International human rights law envisages that the maintenance of ethnic identity and of equal-status and development by minorities be achieved, first, by the minority's official (constitutional/legal) recognition by the state in which it lives. A *value of such recognition is that the minority so recognized is thus made eligible for international intervention (for the application of the provisions of international treaties or covenants concerning minorities which are presently in existence or which will be in the future.)'* Such recognition also makes permanent rather than compensatory or provisional [61] the concept of special measures and gives the minority a significant voice in deciding what special measures should be implemented, and how. *Minorities that are not the same, to be equal, must have the right not to be the same as well as to be equal.*

Secondly, international human rights law envisages that state governments undertake to provide economic measures in order to assure their economic as well as cultural development. These economic measures are measures other than those applied to the general population, measures which are applied to minorities by virtue of their being national minorities which are economically, politically or socially unequal. All special measures have, in short, two main functions:

(a) to protect, preserve and distinctive aspects of minority culture, and
(b) to promote the minority's social-political equal-status with the majority.

Also we must note that official recognition and special measures themselves act as prevent the continued applicability to the Dalits of a policy of forced or coerced assimilation which in their past has been only a tool for domestic colonialism and exploitation.

International Law and Assimilation

While international human right recognized the possibility that assimilation might be a desirable objective in certain multi-national countries, it does so always with the proviso that the minorities involved wished to assimilate and that assimilation leads to equal status or equality. 62 This has not been the case for the Dalits in India.

The objective of a policy of assimilation would be the establishment of a homogenous society in which persons belonging to minority groups would have to abandon, even if gradually but not forcibly [emphasis added] their traditions, the culture and the use of their language in favor of the traditions, the culture and the language of the dominant group63

Any assimilation which might take place must be clearly voluntary, and not resulting from the humiliating enforcement of a sense of inferiority. For a policy of assimilation to be voluntary, the minority concerned must both be advised that this goal is intended, and be queried for its consent. Such action should be supervised by a mutually agreed upon international organization.

It is a widespread belief that if member of different groups came into contact with one another, friendlier attitudes will develop as a consequence. This is not always true. No amount of contact between (members of different groups) is likely to improve relations (in) cases (where) judgements of superiority or inferiority may merely be reinforced. What is needed is equalstatus contact, in which the members of the ethnic groups which meet, represent comparable levels of position and prestige. Research has further indicated that contact has the best results when the two groups work together to achieve a common goal, particularly when success depends on co-operation. [64]

In India, it is obvious that the situation of thc Dalit, after hundreds of years of humiliating oppression under the policy of assimilation, calls now either for a policy of some form of pluralism or self-detennination. The continuation of forced assimilation of the Dalits into a humiliated exploited caste is not only blatantly illegal but also morally bankrupt.

The important question is: what type of special measures can be taken to speed up the process of ending the gross violations of human rights of the Dalits and other minority populations in India?

In similar situations, the U.N. organs have often employed such special techniques as fact-finding, enquiry, commissions, conferences, and out and out supervision. However, given the present political climate and the similarity of the Dalit problem to the problem of other minorities trapped in situations of forced assimilation (exploitation) in politically powerful multinational states, we would feel that a first step demands an urgent effort to convene a United Nations conference on the subject of Dalit oppression and the problem of forced assimilation of minorities trapped in multinational states.

Footnotes

1. International Law and Custom in Ancient India.See also Barbara N.Joshi, "The Enemy Within," "The Untouchable! Voices of the Dalit Lib Zed Books, London, 1986.
2. Attributed to Pindar by Herodotus Book III, 38 (Vowu Ravtwy Bagidea), Arthasatras VII, 18, Satra IV, VII 89: "One should follow moral rules so long as one is powerful. People remain friends until then: Just as the wind is the friend of the burning fire."
3. See Barbara N. Joshi, op. cit.
4. Nandu Ram, "Law and Atrocities on Weaker Sections in India," Indian Bar Review, Vol. X. No.3, 1983.
5. Dr. N.K. Kamble, "Bonded Labour in India, in Untouchable! Voices of the Dalit Literation Movement, op. cit., p.60
6. V.T. Rajshekar, DALIT: The Black India, Clarity Press, 1987.
7. Dilip Hiro, The Untouchables of India, Report No. 26 of the Minority Rights Group, Dalit Sahitya Akademy, 1984.
8. Laxini M.Berwa, unpublished
9. Ibid.
10. Dalit Voice, Vol.6, No. 18, August 1-15, 1987, p.14.
11. Dalit Voice, Vol. 6, No. 10, April. 1-15, 1987, p.18.
12. Eugene Cavaigne. Histoire Universelle (De. Boccard, ed.); Fichte, L'etat commercial ferme, Gibelin, Paris, 1802; William Christie McLeod, The Origin of the State reconsidered in the light of the data of aboriginal North America.
13. A.A Carvallo, Dalit, People: A socio-political Study of the Caste-Oppressed.
14. Ivan Sertimus and Larry Williams, ads., Great African Thinkers: Vol. 1: Cheikh Anta Diop, Transaction Books, Rutgers, 1986.
15. V.T. Rajshekar, op. cit.
16. This question is complicated by the fact that Indian constitutional law suggests that the Dalits are a sub-group of Hindus, not a separate ethnic group like the Muslims or Sikhs.
17. G.L. Gọmme, Primitive Folk Moots, London, 1880.
18. See Articles 338 (3),340 (1), 341, 342 of the Indian Constitution. Also see bibliography. All the authors mentioned note

improvement, but feel that the problem still remains. They also cast doubt on the ability of the problem to be handled uniquely by the Indian legal system.

19. India does not accept the Dalits as a national minority, although they do so qualify in international law.
20. Barbara R. Joshi, op. cit.
21. See Barbara N.Joshi, "Legislatures, Courts, Public Policy," Untouchables, op. cit, pp. 118-140.
22. Retaphysique des moeurs, trad. fr. Barni, Paris, 1853, h' partie, XLVI.
23. Carre de Malbert' Contribution a la theorie generale de L'Etat, Paris. 1920, p.57, note 6.
24. T. Hobbes, Leviathan, 2nd part, chap. XXVI of the first edition of 1651.
25. Op. cit.
26. Destutt de Tracy, Elements d'ideology, t. iv., p.456-459.
27. Ibid, p.454.
28. Duguit, Taite de Droit constitutional, t.III, p.547,
29. Ernest Baker, National Character and the Factors in its Formation, Methuen & C p. 247.
30. Such scholars as Professor J. Claydon ("The Transnational Protection of Ethnic Minorities: A Treatise Framework for Enquiry," The Canadian Yearbook of International Law, Vol.XIII, 1975, pp. 25-60) and Professor J.B. Kelly ("National Minorities in International Law," Denver Journal of international Law and Policy, Vol. 3, No. 2. fall 1973, pp. 153-73) show how the assimilationist influences work against emphasizing minority rights in the U.N. The Soviet system has often been attacked by the U.S. on charges of violation of individual rights. Such charges are historically well known. However, the problem encountered by Jewish and other individuals seeking the right to leave the U.S.S.R or to publicly express certain individual non-communist opinions often resulted from the past narrowness of the U.S.S.R's effort to establish socialism and a classless society, and are nowhere close to the gross violations of the human rights of the Dalits in India. Seldom, however, does the U.S. ever see fit to raise this a testimony to the political natural for human rights.
31. George Schwarzenberger and George W. Keeton, the Inductive Approach to International Law, Stevens and Sons, London, 1965. Also see Wolfgang Friedmann, Oliver J. Lissitzyn and Richard C. Pugh, International Law: Cases and Materials, West Publishing Co., St. Paul, Minnesota, 1969, pp. 11-33.
32. J.13. Kelly, op. cit.

33. Not only is this one of the terms of U.N. Doc. E/CN.4/Sub.2/384, but it can also be abstracted from the practises of civilized nations.
34. Equal status and equal access to the resources of the society and land concerned, etc., as implied in Article 27 of the Covenant on Civil and Political Rights.
35. U.N. Doc. E/CN.4/Sub.2/384/Add 1.
36. Ibid., p.29.
37. U.N. Doc. E/CN.4/Sub.2/384/Add 2, p. 80.
38. Op. cit.
39. U.N. Doc. E/CN.4/Sub.2/384/Add 2, p. 66. 40 Ibid.
41. Ibid, p. 10. National minorities by definition would compose autochthonous populations.
42. In our view, such a social minority would be included under the sub-group minority denotation.
43. Ibid. The problem of tribe or extended families seems to arise out of the unique political needs facing underdeveloped countries. Under-developed countries need special considerations, but the principle of minority rights is perhaps more important in such areas.
44. E/CN.4/Sub.2/384/Add. 3, p. 16.
45. E/CN.4/Sub.2/384/Add. 3, p. 17.
46. E/CN.4/Sub.2/384/Add. 1, p. 31
47. Ibid
48. E/CN.4/Sub.2/384/Add. 1, p. 5
49. E/CN.4/Sub.2/384/Add. 5, p. 97
50. Add. 3, Op. cit., p. 17.
51. Ibid.
52. Civil rights simply refers to those laws which were recently made a part of the Indian constitution; legal status, designed to formally end untouchability as a legal institution in India and to provide the Dalits with the same rights as other Indian citizens. These include the affirmative action law designed to make up for past discrimination (reservations). The most important of these law are mentioned in the concluding section of this paper under Implementing the Universal Declaration of Human Rights in India.
53. Laxni M. Berwa, unpublished paper.
54. Ibid.
55. Report No.26, minority Human Rights Group, op. cit.
56. Laxmi M. Berwa, op. cit.
57. Nandu Ram, "Law and Atrocities on weaker Sections in India," Indian Bar Review, Vol X, No.3, 1983.
58. Laxmi M. Berwa, op. cit.
59. Personal interview with Laxni M. Berwa.

60. It is the various secondary minority applicable by the general principle that actually tend to define and fix the rights of minorities for the purposes of international protection.
61. This permanent recognition prevents minority rights from being recinded by states upon any conflict of same with the interest of the majority.
62. While we have suggested that in several state practises immigrant minorities are generally expected to assimilate, the international law view of minority collective rights as represented in Article 27 of the Covenant on Civil and Political Rights does not yet distinguish between national and immigrant minorities for the purpose of international protection.
63. E/CN. 4.Sub.2/384/Add. 1, p. 69.
64. Ibid.

2

Human Rights as Dynamic Process: The Case of India's Untouchables

Dr. Barbara Joshi

If a Shudra (low caste person) listens to a recitation of the Vedas (Hindu religious texts) his ears shall be filled with molten tin or lac. If he recited Vedic texts his tongue shall be cut out. He who teaches law to a Shudra and he who teaches him religious observances, be indeed together with that Shudra sinks into the darkness of the hell called Asamvritta.

—Dharam Sutra (Traditional Hindu Religious Text)

"Untouchability" is abolished and its practise in any form is forbidden. The enforcement of any disability arising out of "Untouchability" shall be an offence punishable in accordance with law.

—Constitution of India, Part III, Article 17

Do the oppressed castes have a right to live? Is it a crime for the poor to be economically independent, to be educated and grow in self respect? Is the price of such development death by bullets in one's own home?

—Memorandum presented to the Chief Minister of Gujarat

By survivors of a massacre of Untouchables in the Village of Golana in January 1985

Introduction

There is a precarious volatile quality to the human rights status of India's large Untouchable population. Modern constitutional law guarantees a full range of social, economic, and political rights. Tradition insists that those born into Untouchable castes are inherently inferior beings. Daily reality is a constant struggle between past and possible future. Any evaluation of Untouchable status thus becomes a study of human rights as dynamic process.

The untouchables' unfolding story is a particularly complex one. It is not a simple case of "State" vs. "Citizen," nor is it a study of contrast between relative freedom in a simpler past and eroding rights in a complex modern state structure. Instead, the Untouchables' struggle today is shaped by the continuation of a very old pattern of exploitation and oppression that was legitimized and enforced through a variety of institutions-religious, social, and economic, as well as political. The realization of full and equal human rights for Untouchables thus requires changes in the relationships among different groups of citizens within each of these arenas.

The Untouchable population is vast: more than 100 million people, approximately one out of every seven Indian citizens, is born into one of the many different hereditary castes that traditionally have been regarded as belonging at the bottom of the steeply hierarchic social order. Classical Hindu philosophy used the theories of ***karma*** and reincarnation to justify systematic suppression of the Untouchable castes, those who had sinned especially grievously in some past existence were reborn into Untouchable castes and were thus inherently inferior to all others in society.

"In" is a critically important word here, for although untouchability imposed a variety of humiliating forms of physical segregation, the Untouchables were very definitely not shut out from the realm of the dominant society. Untouchability rationalized one way of limiting potential competition from a large hereditary category, while at the same time keeping this human category available as a readily exploitable labor force. Given the tremendous advantages this system offered to all others in society, it is hardly surprising that untouchability as a systematic denial of group rights has expanded beyond the ideological border of orthodox Hinduism. For generations both the Sikh and Christian communities have preserved untouchability in spite of theologies that deny the legitimacy of caste hierarchy. On a secular plane, a number of modern Indian opponents of radical status change for Untouchables have borrowed freely from the West's ever-evolving arsenal of rationalization for its own racial variation on a theme of inequality.

For most people, the details of rationalization are not especially important. "They" are not like "Us" and have no business laying claim to a share of "Our" dominance of land, the professions, political authority. The only important question is how to keep "Them" in their rightfully subservient position. It is the sheer vicious ferocity of some of these efforts that attracts attention, but violence is only a small part of the total picture. Most efforts to block Untouchable claims to human equality are far less conspicuous but in the aggregate they are far more destructive. The endless maneuvers of denial by higher caste bureaucrats, businessmen, landowners, judges, and teachers function as form silent violence and violation.'

All of this stands in stark contrast to the legal provisions that abolish untouchability. It also stands in open conflict with increasing resist; from the Untouchables themselves. What was once a far more uniformly enforced pattern of inequality is now the focus of intense social tension and open, large scale conflict. The current status of Untouchable human rights is thus the net result of sharply contradictory pressures in Indian society. No simple summation is possible because the balance among contending pressures is in such a state of flux and differs also from one region to another within India. The following analysis employs series of case studies to illustrate the dynamics of the Untouchable rights picture, while exploring variations in the key factors affecting change: the nature of the existing political system; long-term structural change in the Indian economy; and changing attitudes and values, especially within the Untouchable population itself. We begin in the western state of Gujarat, first with a recent incident then the larger state context in which it occurred. This is followed by two shorter comparison studies illustrating the Untouchable struggle in differing regional settings.

Gujarat: This Time, Golana

Golana is a relatively minor incident as conflicts over Untouchable rights go.[3] Five Untouchables were killed in January of 1985 when local Darbar Rajput landlords set out to reestablish dominance over Untouchable villagers. A number of factors had led to changes in the Untouchables' status and attitudes, but the immediate focus of conflict was their effective use of government programs established to promote the rights of Untouchables and other low status citizens. The states role was ambiguous, however. Three days before the attack the local state legislator-who is the son of the most influential Rajput landlord in the region, and also a member of the Congress (I) party that initiated many of the policies in contention-visited the village to urge the Untouchables to "compromise" by retreating from exercise of legal rights. The attack itself took place in daylight, began at the village bus stop, and involved an armed mob of more than 50 men, but an armed police contingent that had been posted in the village as the result of an earlier disturbance failed to intervene.

The village is an afternoon's bus ride south of the state's capital and key industrial city, Ahmedabad. The Darbar Rajputs who dominate the village were originally revenue collectors for the Moghul kings, then filled the same role for the British, then used their economic base to gain access to modern education and the new bureaucracy. Darbars now share dominance of the region's administration with the Patidars, another landed caste. In spite of recent land reforms, the Darbars, who are 20 percent of the village population, still control between 60 and 70 percent of the arable land, which is cultivated for them by tribal and low caste wage laborers and sharecroppers. In spite of slow changes in local labor relations, Darbars were still accustomed to a cheap and docile labor force and had only recently experienced serious threats to their dominance.[4]

The largest Untouchable caste in the village, the Vankars, had traditionally been weavers. Gradually the people whose skills had attracted Western traders to Gujarat had been displaced by industry first by mill cloth from imperial Britain, then by cloth from the mills of the indigenous Indian industrialists whose profits fueled the nationalist movement. Vankars throughout Gujarat became increasingly dependent on agricultural labor for local landed elites, though a few did find employment in semi-segregated departments of the new textile mills of Ahmedabad and Bombay, or worked as unskilled urban labor. The urban labor market expanded slowly, however, and urban working conditions were generally as exploitative and precarious as those in agriculture.[5]

The efforts of higher caste Indian nationalists to gain domestic and international support during the independence movement of the 1930s and 1940s did lead to a series of human rights policies focused on the Untouchables, but these have borne fruit slowly and grudgingly in Golana-or elsewhere. Ahmedabad was home to Mahatma Gandhi's first Indian *ashram* and the early campaigns that led to the Constitutional abolition of untouchability, the subsequent Untouchability (Offenses) Act, and the newer Protection of Civil Rights Act. Recent Gujarat survey data reveal that the imposition of untouchability is still more pervasive in Gujarat than in many other regions, but both law and the Gandhian tradition have undermined the legitimacy of these once universally accepted social controls.[6]

Policies to expand Untouchable rights in the Indian economy have also taken effect slowly, but they too have affected once secure high caste dominance. A three-cornered maneuver among the British, Gandhi's Indian National Congress, and the key Untouchable leader of the era,

Dr. Ambedkar, produced an extensive set of incentives and affirmative action programs for education and public sector employment of Untouchables and tribals that have been expanded slowly by subsequent developments in Indian politics.' These programs have been so hampered by the existing poverty of the target groups and the determined sabotage of higher caste elites that we easily overlook their long-term impact. By the 1970s, there were several well educated Untouchable youths from Golana families. Some were employed as teachers, others were in government civil service jobs.

Gradually, these developments have eroded the Darbars' dominance. Now the pace of change is accelerating, for the new jobs give Untouchables independent access to information about the operation of other redistributive policies. Over the past few years, Golana Untouchable families have been awarded small quantities of land under the Tenancy Act, the Land Ceilings Act, and programs for distribution of house sites to previously landless villagers.

Cooperatives have been another source of informal Untouchable education and mobility in Golana, though the Darbars initially welcomed the innovation. The first major cooperative in the village was established by AMUL, the government-sponsored chain of dairy cooperatives that has served as a conduit for international dairy development aid." At first the Darbars controlled the local cooperative, though a large number of members were Bharwads, a cattle herding tribal community. The Bharwads eventually insisted upon giving a strategic technical position to an educated Christian Vankar youth, then slowly wrested administrative control from the Darbars. The Darbars succeeded in having the AMUL unit closed down, but the Vankars had already learned about the resources available through government programs for cooperatives.

With the encouragement and advice of higher caste social activists and an Indian Christian agency in Ahmedabad, the Vankars set up their own cooperative. This unit linked Vankars from several surrounding villages, and united Hindu Vankars with the small number of Vankar Christian converts. The cooperative improved incomes by pooling lands received by individuals in grants from the government, and using part of this land to develop a sideline in charcoal production to provide paid employment during the agricultural slack season. This reduced Vankar dependence on Darbar loans during the slack season and thus increased Vankar ability to negotiate for good wages during peak farming seasons. Cooperative members also became increasingly willing to assert legal rights. They persisted in building homes on house sites assigned by the state, in spite of intense Darbar opposition, and three months before the fatal attack the cooperative commenced cultivating 40 acres that the Darbars had forcibly withheld ever since it was granted to Vankar families by the government in the mid 1970s.

The Darbar attack on January 25th was well organized. The Darbars first attempted to use one of the many caste distinctions within the Untouchable population; a few members of the local sweeper caste were egged into a quarrel in which they injured a Vankar youth. The Vankars merely prepared to take the boy to a hospital and to seek official intervention from the district headquarters town. As they boarded a passing truck the Darbars themselves attacked, then spread out through the village in a hunt for officials of the cooperative. The five Vankars killed were all leading figures in the cooperative movement; two were shot at point blank range, the others were beaten to death.

A few days later, Untouchable activists in Ahmedabad mobilized massive demonstrations. The mass media had paid scant attention to the massacre, but Untouchable organizations had collected and circulated their own information independently. The rallies carried a clear public message: although policies promoting Untouchable rights might generate political headaches for the governments that had formalized those policies, political retreat would also have a price.

The Untouchables had good reason to feel the message was necessary. Since 1981 Gujarat has been racked by waves of anti-Untouchable violence, much of it organized on a state-wide basis by high caste urban university students and professionals trying to turn back the programs that encourage higher education and public sector employment for Untouchables and other severely disadvantaged groups in Gujarat's profoundly unequal society. A number of observers have argued that something much larger than specific affirmative action policies is at stake, that the agitations represent diffuse high caste fear of any low caste mobility and all that such mobility would represent for the potential collapse of a system of hierarchy and caste privilege. The analysts have gone on to point out that although Untouchables are a relatively small proportion of the state's affirmative action program, "Untouchable" bulks large in the popular imagination as the symbolic floor of the entire social hierarchy, and Untouchables thus become the special focus of resistance to more generalized change.[9]

The nature of this potential change is clearer if we examine the state's current socio-economic arithmetic.[10] The so-called "Forward Castes" that have so thoroughly dominated business, the professions, bureaucracy, and land holding-the Brahmans, Rajputs, Banias, and the landed Patel/Patidar complex-are actually an elite minority, 25 percent of the population. Pushed to the bottom of society have been the Untouchables and the tribals, 7 percent and 13 percent respectively. Between these two clearly defined poles are a wide array of Hindu castes and religious minority communities, some relatively independent and prosperous, but many so hobbled by linked high caste discrimination and economic exploitation that their condition often approximates the Untouchable and tribal experience. Slowly, haltingly, the pressures of democratic politics have built upon the Independence era policies of affirmative action for Untouchables and tribals, expanding the range of settings covered by the programs and also extending limited coverage to the communities now referred to as "Socially and Economically Backward Classes" (SEBC).

The resulting programs actually preserve the Forward Castes' prominence in society's prestige positions, but the threat to familiar, unquestioned monopoly has triggered panicky resistance. For example, the programs under attack in 1981 had set up university admission and government hiring targets of 25 to 30 percent for a variety of the most seriously disadvantaged groups, the exact proportion varying for different programs. The Forward Castes continued to be free to compete for the remaining 70 to 75 percent of the positions, plus all positions from the affirmative action pool unfilled "for lack of suitable candidates." In the five years prior to the 1981 riots, riots initiated by high caste medical school students, only 4 percent of the seats in the state's medical schools had gone to students from the affirmative action pool. Although the agitators wrapped their actions in the rhetoric of "defend the merit system," they did not challenge the common practise of reserving a significant number of slots for the children of "donor" families able to make substantial financial contributions to schools. Untouchables were the primary targets of violence-thousands were left homeless and seven were murdered-but Untouchables were the smallest of the beneficiary categories that included tribals (13 percent) and SEBC (10 percent) as well as Untouchables (7 percent). Numerically, neither this nor subsequent waves of anti-Untouchable violence associated with the affirmative action programs made much sense. Symbolically, their meaning has been clear to everyone, including the politicians who are simultaneously actors and audience.

There has been no consistent pattern to political party support-or opposition-to the efforts to open avenues of mobility for the state's long-suppressed majority. Both a series of Congress governments and the one opposition party coalition that governed in the late 1970s have supported various extensions of the policies. At the same time, each outbreak of violent resistance has seen involvement by a variety of politicians from both opposition and ruling parties, though the politicians appear to play secondary roles. Throughout, the initiative has come from high caste students and professionals. The most serious outbreaks, in 1981 and 1985, came hard on the heels of overwhelming electoral victories for the governments subsequently challenged by the violence. Agitation and violence have become the weapons of recalcitrant elements of a small high caste elite that has been losing its ability to control electoral politics.

This strategy of agitation has brought occasional victories for the higher castes, but the political arena continues to be relatively open in Gujarat. For example, shortly after the Golana massacre, Untouchables and the small group of high caste social workers supporting them demanded the appointment of a Special Prosecutor, a move that would greatly increase the likelihood of effective prosecution and simultaneously signal state support *for the* still frightened Untouchable villagers. Prominent Vankar politicians, including the Congress Whip of the state legislature and a central government Cabinet member, were pressed into service. Golana's Rajputs responded by mobilizing the aid of caste fellows in the Congress party and the bureaucracy in an effort to block prosecution, only to discover that the new Chief Minister was far more deeply beholden to Untouchables in his party than to the Rajputs. A Special Prosecutor was appointed, a Rajput police official who had blocked collection of evidence was transferred, and the case was finally sent to trial under the draconic provisions of the Terrorism Act. It is common for even the most blatant attack on Untouchable rights to go unpunished, but in this case supporters hoped for convictions and stiff penal sentences.

Both the reservation wars and events like the Golana massacre illustrate some of the intense conflicting pressures that operate throughout Indian politics. These political factors deserve further exploration, for they directly affect the way state power is used to sustain-or deny the human rights of Untouchables. Details vary widely with time and region, but there are some common themes inherent in India's blend of social hierarchy and fragmentation with electoral politics. For example, the Congress (I) party that has governed Gujarat during both the antireservation agitation and the Golana massacre is based on a relatively new variation of the precarious socio-political coalitions that have appeared in various forms in Gujarat since independence. The current coalition is referred to locally as KHAM-Kshatriya (including Rajputs), Harijan (Untouchable), Adivasi (tribal), Muslim. The Rajputs, including the Darbars of Golana, played a prominent role in developing this coalition, even though their influence within it is now beginning to wane. Shortly after independence, some of Gujarat's Rajputs set out to increase their influence vis-a-vis other landed elites by mobilizing a diverse group of castes claiming "Kshatriya" or "warrior" status; some were themselves powerful landed elites, others were impoverished lower status castes seeking to gain prestige and economic support from the alliance. When Mrs. Gandhi's populist policies of the 1970s split the old Congress party the Rajput "*Kshatriyas*" saw an opportunity to take control of the newly formed Congress (I) party, but to do this they had to forge an even wider alliance with long-term Congress supporters from the Untouchable, tribal, and Muslim communities, all severely disadvantaged groups for whom the redistributive policies of the Congress (I) were vitally important.

These traditionally dispossessed groups made strange bedfellows for the likes of Golana's Darbar Rajputs, but together the Untouchables, Tribals, and Muslims were nearly 30 percent of the state's voters, and there were special institutional reasons for any political coalition builder: to take the Untouchables and tribals into account. The pre-Independence struggle between the British Raj and predominantly high caste nationalists gave the late Untouchable leader, Dr. Ambedkar, enough ; leverage to insist upon guaranteed proportional legislative representation for Untouchables (Scheduled Castes) and tribals (Scheduled Tribes) in an effort to protect their long-term policy interests. The national formula sets up "reserved" constituencies in which only Scheduled Caste (or, elsewhere, Scheduled Tribe) individuals may stand for office, but in which these legislators are elected by all local residents. Since" Untouchables-and in many regions, tribals-are a dispersed minority, social geography adds to the effects of economic dominance in giving higher caste voters considerable influence over these representatives. However, high caste divisions do leave occasional room for maneuver, and whenever there is cooperation with other disadvantaged groups, as there has been intermittently in Gujarat, the margin of influence for Scheduled Caste and Scheduled Tribe legislators increases accordingly."

Predictably, the internal tensions within such socially diverse governing erning parties (or opposition coalitions) are routinely intense-as witness the small world of Golana, where conflicts are being played out among segments of the ruling KHAM coalition. Gujarat's political parties are not alone in facing such conflicting pressures. Indeed, the programs in dispute in Gujarat are based on national policies key elements in the affirmative action programs were written into the national Constitution as a result of pre-Independence negotiations; the land reform programs are a spill-over from nationalist efforts to mobilize support from middle as well as lower caste tenantry; and village house site distribution was a feature of the 20-Point Programme with which Mrs. Gandhi sought to broaden her own base of electoral support.

The most common political solution to juggling the demands of a small elite and a massive underclass has been to combine such redistributive policies with administrative inaction that is either tolerated or explicitly encouraged. So, pervasive is this practise that it has led one of India's leading legal scholars, Upendra Baxi, to describe it as a routinized system of "governmental lawlessness" in which government

Official regularly violate the government's own law[12].This "Solution" is under increasing pressure, however long -term changes in society and economy, combined with even marginal effects from a generation of redistributive policies, have raised the level of pressure from the dispossessed themselves.

One important factor in this rising level of pressure from below has been the increasing Untouchable capacity for independent mobilizing. We have already seen glimpses of this development, on a local scale in Golana, and in the efforts of Untouchables in Ahmedabad to bring state pressure to bear on behalf of Golana villagers whom most of the Ahmedabad activists had never met. In most areas of the country, including Gujarat, the ability to launch efforts like these is still so new that sometimes it seems to startle the Untouchables as much as the higher caste elite. However the change has been part of the slow and uneven build-up of new attitudes and resources within the Untouchable population.

There is no one style, strategy, or philosophy that conveniently summarizes the new mobilizing efforts within the Untouchable community, but one of the organizations behind the initial Ahmedabad rallies protesting the Golana massacre, the Dalit Panthers, serves to illustrate several of the more common characteristics of the larger scale efforts.

The local Panther organization is part of a larger movement that began in the early 1970s among young Untouchables in working class districts of Bombay. The movement drew its inspiration from both the late Untouchable leader, Dr. Ambedkar, and news of America's Black revolution and Black Panthers. The original Dalit Panther organization soon broke into a number of different, and often competing, fragments, but at the same time the movement spread rapidly along the rail and highway lines that already carried increasing numbers of migrating Untouchable workers and students. Several features of Panther ideology have remained influential constants during this process of diffusion.[13] The Panther emphasis on assertive self-respect includes specific rejection of the inequalities of both class and caste, an outlook that sustains critically important links between the resources of the small new strata of educated Untouchables and the much larger block of Untouchable laborers. The concept of "Dalit" itself-"the oppressed"-is consciously inclusive of all forms of both cultural and economic oppression, and greatly expands the potential arena of both personal identity and group alliances. One recurrent Panther theme has been efforts to break down traditional social barriers between Untouchable castes, and between Untouchables and other oppressed groups.

Panther group active in Gujarat do not regard themselves as a match for high caste organizations with far greater resources, but during the 1980 anti-reservation riots they succeeded in mobilizing the first strike since independence in Ahmedabad's massive textile industry. Untouchables are a minority of the mill workers, but the patterns of discrimination that clustered them together in semi-segregated departments produced unexpected leverage. When Untouchable mill workers heeded the Panther call for a strike to protest the riots, production quickly ground to a halt. Private industrialists who had backed high caste students leading the agitation quickly saw the need for moderation, and the agitations that had run a bloody course for months rapidly subsided. Obviously this particular success was temporary, but local Panther units continue to be one channel through which support for a-new vision of rights and identity change is mobilized within the Untouchable community.

Several hundred miles to the northeast, in Delhi, another branch of the same movement has become a factor in one more struggle to implement Untouchable rights.

Delhi: Bonded Labour, Brick Kilns and Dalit Panthers

There is a building boom in Delhi-five-star hotels, more space for government bureaucracy, the elegant offices of multinational industry and banking, convention centers in which local authorities and international consultants discuss the future of computers in a proposed chain of special government Model Schools. The laborers who produce the building boom are part of another world, a world of child labor, make-shift shanties, little or no education, and poor wages. Intermittently there have been reports of debt-bondage labor.[14]

Typical cases have involved urban employers who acquire laborers from distant villages by giving them an advance that will allow the laborers to pay off existing village debts, then transporting them to the work site where they are kept confined while working off the new debt. The employer provides subsistence rations and materials for shanties, but most of the substandard wages are withheld until the monsoon season terminates construction work. At this point the employer deducts what he chooses-transportation costs, astronomical interest rates, the employer's own estimate of time lost and rations provided. If he needs a few laborers for between-seasons maintenance work, some will be found still in debt to the employer and kept at the work site. Most will be paid enough to return to their home villages, where they will scramble to find new employers for the ensuing agricultural season.

The practise clearly violates a number of Indian laws and international conventions. Its appearance in areas like Delhi has also shaken belief that debt bondage is just a relic of rural feudalism, for obviously it has made the transition to urban capitalism. Prominent voluntary agencies have become involved in the attack on debt bondage, and some of the resulting legal cases, including the discovery that government financed contractors were using bonded laborers to construct civic improvements in Delhi prior to the 1982 Asiad Games, have become Supreme Court landmarks. However one of the earliest and most effectively sustained local struggles against debt bondage and the conditions that create it has received less attention than it deserves. It involves Untouchable activists of the Dalit Panther movement and the predominantly Untouchable labor force of brick kiln workers on the rural periphery of Delhi.

Their collaboration began in 1973 when one of the laborers took the unusual step of seeking help in a suburban village and was taken to Bapurao Pakhiddey, a Dalit lawyer and Panther leader. The immediate legal problem was relatively simple even in the years before the highly publicized 1975 Ordinance against bonded labor. Pakhiddey filed a case of wrongful confinement, and a Delhi court ordered the release of 29 men, women, and children. However it quickly became apparent that this was not an isolated case, and that the law was the least of the laborers' problems. The liberation of the kiln workers became a central feature of the local Panther program.

The project was daunting. There are several hundred kilns scattered around the perimeter of Delhi's 1,500 square kilometer territory. Even workers who were theoretically free were isolated in shanties constructed on separate and privately owned kiln sites, and kiln owners routinely used violence, private property laws, and ties to the local police to drive off meddling intruders. The Dalit Panthers were-and are-a small organization in Delhi. They now have one jeep that improves access to the kilns, but even this was missing in the early years. Still, Panther goals demanded that they try to do something about the kiln workers and bonded labor.

There is ample evidence that debt bondage does indeed symbolize the conditions that the Dalit Panthers are committed to changing: social oppression linked to economic exploitation and the psychology of dependency. Survey research shows a strong correlation between caste status and debt bondage. For example, a national survey conducted in 1977 by the Gandhi Peace Foundation found that the Scheduled Castes, who constitute 15 percent of the total population, were 61 percent of the bonded laborers.[15] These figures reflect long-standing patterns of unequal rights in the agrarian economy, a situation that has *deteriorated* throughout the country in recent decades. Between the 1961 and 1971 national censuses, the proportion of Scheduled Caste workers recorded as landless agricultural from 34 percent to 52 percent of the total Scheduled Caste workforce. (Corresponding figures for the total Indian population rose from 17 to 26 percent.) Scheduled Caste data collected in the 1981 census is only now being released, but new data distinguishing "marginal workers" (those unable to find work for more than six months in a year) are deeply disturbing. Further, the massive oversupply of farm labor has generally held wages down, while the price of food has risen. By 1975 the national Rural Labour Enquiry showed that the incidence of indebtedness among all agricultural laborers had risen from 61 percent in 1965 to 66 percent in 1975; for Scheduled Caste laborers it had risen from 66 to 71 percent.i[6] Debt bondage labor in Delhi's building industry is not an anomaly. Internationally supported agricultural policies that have relied on privatized top-down development have unquestionably increased food production and prosperity for some, but for others the price has been increasing desperation.

The Panthers are quick to add that there is an important cultural element reinforcing debt bondage, a combination of traditional social codes and the psychology of dependency. Many of the workers expected to trade total submission to economic exploitation and social humiliation for the promise of subsistence. This has been the law of village survival for centuries, and it is not an easy set of attitudes to break. Pakhiddey speaks with grim sympathy about workers who are accustomed to begging the "malik," the master, for a box of matches, not demanding higher wages with which to buy the matches. These attitudes are endlessly reinforced by practical realities. Where are the alternatives to starvation? How does one deal with the malik's private goon squads, or his ties to police and public officials? Better to keep one's head down and beg for the matches.

However, by the early 1970s several factors produced a slight tilt in favor of Untouchables' rights in the Delhi area, and gave a small group like the Panthers increased leverage. The maliks themselves were making some changes in worker attitudes inevitable: both rural malik and urban malik were now part of large-scale cash economies that make it impractical to sustain laborers year round in seasonal production units, whether in wheat or in bricks. A pattern that bounces workers from one short-term master to another eventually leads some laborers to question the value of old patterns of personalized dependency.

The combination of some Untouchable mobility and the Panther ideology also made it possible for the Panthers themselves to symbolize their message of change in ways open to few others. The Panther activists are from Untouchable castes and most are from impoverished working class backgrounds. They are openly proud of their roots, but at the same time all are educated, and several are successful professionals, walking proof that caste is not destiny, that poverty is not the unavoidable stigma of hereditary caste shame.

Finally, national politics and conditions in the capital city itself made it easier for the Panthers to build upon their message of rights and self respect. During the 1971 national election Mrs. Gandhi had popularized the slogan *Garibi* Hatao-"eliminate poverty." Her landslide victory was widely attributed to support from the massive Indian underclass, and the slogan came to shape political competition in the public arena. Opposition parties turned increasingly to "more committed than thou art" mobilizing of workers and socially oppressed, in spite of the fact that most of the national opposition parties, like the Congress (I) itself, draw most of their leadership and financial support from the small social and economic elite. A period of prolonged and escalating social upheaval ensued.

In this setting even a small group of independent activists could exercise some influence. After Pakhiddey's first court case in 1973, local Panther activists spent more than a year meeting laborers at kiln sites in rural Delhi trying to help workers lose their fear and awe of the owners. They argued that the maliks had no right to the labor conditions they were imposing; the workers not only had a right to freedom, they had a right to better wages.

In March of 1975 a few hundred kiln workers in South Delhi rallied in support of wage increases, and then decided to march to neighboring kiln sites. The movement grew rapidly and all work at local kilns came to a halt, but the outraged kiln owners dug in their heels. The Panthers had no resources with which to sustain a prolonged strike, but they knew how to use local politics. On April 12th, 5000 ragged kiln workers, including 3,000 women and children, demonstrated in front of the official residence of the Prime Minister,. many spending the night on the pavement in front of her home. On April 13th, Mrs. Gandhi's Personal Assistant instructed the Delhi Union Territory officials to arbitrate. The administration was hardly aggressive in its dealings with the kiln owners, but the workers were encouraged. The strike quickly spread to kilns in North Delhi. Workers at rural kiln sites who had been isolated from each other as well as the larger society were now part of a common strike and national politics. By April 19th the kiln owners agreed to wage increases that put kiln wages in advance of the Delhi minimum wage.

At this point the political setting itself changed abruptly. In June of 1975 Mrs. Gandhi declared a State of Emergency that sharply curtailed the possibility of using agitational politics for any purpose. There were no kiln strikes-and no wage increases-until after the Emergency was lifted in 1977, though the Panthers did continue to work with the kiln laborers and formed a stronger organizational base at the kilns. There were several legal initiatives during the Emergency, including the Bonded Labour System (Abolition) Ordinance of 1975, which became an Act of Parliament in 1976. The legislation was not in fact a major departure from existing Indian law, and it certainly did not dramatically alter existing social and economic realities, but it did add to the environment of the 1970s in which political legitimacy required at least verbal support for radically egalitarian change.

When the national election of 1977 brought the new Janata coalition to power, the Panthers returned to public mobilizing to-increase' the kiln workers' leverage. By the end of 1982 there was a registered kiln workers labor union. Wages have continued to exceed the Delhi minimum wage, and the Panthers have turned their attention to improving a wider range of kiln worker conditions.

The new agenda is a stark reminder of the limitations of this effort at mobilization from below. The kiln workers are still more than miles from the internationalized glamour of downtown Delhi. Their housing sites are a nightmare landscape at the end of rutted lanes a mile or more from paved roads. Medical facilities are non-existent, and tuberculosis is rampant. Access to food supplies is a running battle. Education remains a severe problem. There are approximately 100 children at each kiln site, government schools are normally miles away, families migrate from their native villages in the middle of the school year, and parents are desperate for help molding bricks or tending smaller children. The Panthers have established one informal school, and have clearly shown that both parents and children can be motivated, but public funding is needed to extend the demonstration project to other kiln sites. Adult education in the literacy and basic arithmetic needed to hold employers to honest accounting is desperately needed, but this too is missing.

And yet it is progress for at least one branch of the Delhi construction industry, progress that has been achieved by organizers who started with little and workers who started with less. kiln workers themselves are now spreading the movement. Brick workers often move to new kiln sites in other states, and by now workers with experience in Delhi have triggered similar projects in the state Gujarat, Madhya Pradesh, and Rajasthan, sometimes recruiting local Panther allies. Nor are the workers' home villages immune. Panthers who traced one set of kiln workers during the agricultural season found them organizing fellow village farm workers around the English the Panthers had used in Delhi- "strike."

The really serious problem is that in most conditions independent assertion of rights, whether in labor strikes or otherwise, is still extremely dangerous, legal protections notwithstanding. This is conspicuous in events like the 1986 Arwal massacre in the state of Bihar, where at least 21 sharecroppers and laborers from a variety of low castes were gunned down in an enclosed courtyard by police, the logical extension of increasingly conspicuous Bihar government cooperation with landed elites determined to quash the state's own land reforms.[18] The mind boggles at Arwal, and promptly turns to denial mechanisms: this has to be gross deviation from the norm, and after all "Bihar is like that." Unfortunately Arwal is not really so far from the norm, and although Bihar is indeed "like that," Bihar is not alone. Massacres are common, and so is state involvement before the event or conspicuous state inaction after the event.

The provocations can fall short of organized demands for agrarian change. When assertion of rights comes from Untouchables, the provocation can be very minor indeed.

Karamchedu: The Bleak Side of Democracy and Development

Karamchedu is the center of a prosperous agricultural region on the eastern coast of the state of Andhra Pradesh.[19] It is also an influential center of support for the state's Chief Minister, N. T. RamaRao, and the landed Kamma caste that has been the backbone of his Telegu Desham party. The village is the home of Venkateshwara Rao, NTR's son-in-law and himself the independently powerful head of the youth wing of Telegu Desham. Venkateswara's father still lives in the village and is a prominent figure in the local Kamma community.

On July 17, 1985, a mob of several hundred Karamchedu Kammas attacked the Untouchable Madiga community. Five Untouchables died where they fell, another died the following day, and a pregnant woman who had been raped later aborted. Scores of severely wounded were hospitalized; reports of the number of these who subsequently died range from two to four. On the preceding day, two young Madigas, a crippled youth and a young woman, had dared to protest when a Kamma dirtied the pond the Untouchables depend on for drinking water. The Kamma attack was launched in broad daylight by a mob that made no attempt to conceal its identity, and local Kammas later bragged to reporters that their political influence would prevent "interference." To a considerable extent they have been proven correct. It must be understood that there is no clear evidence directly linking the state Chief Minister or his son-in-law to the organized assault, and that equally blatant and barbaric incidents during the preceding decades of Congress party rule in the state were also swept under the political rug. Karamchedu is just an unusually clear example of the persistent importance of the status distinctions summarized in "Untouchable," and the way in which political and economic factors can tilt against Untouchable rights.

Although Karamchedu is usually referred to as a village, the term understates local prosperity and the role of the Kammas in it. Changes over the past thirty years have increased local affluence in ways that strengthen the correlation between caste and control of economic resources, and reinforce the value of untouchability as one way of rationalizing continued subordination of a large part of the local workforce. Earlier in the twentieth century, the Kammas themselves were deeply divided: a few families prospered as moneylenders, and absorbed increasing proportions of the lands of other Kammas; most were hard pressed as small farmers and, increasingly, tenants. Poorer local Kammas were important in the Communist Party, recruiting lower caste villagers, including Untouchables. However in the late 1950s, Kamma tenants expanded into tobacco production just as changes in international markets produced a surge in tobacco prices. State investment in irrigation and drainage projects generated more options in commercial agriculture. Kamma tenants did have to borrow heavily from wealthy Kammas to take advantage of these new opportunities, but caste ties ensured relatively easy access to credit and economic changes led to profits that more than paid the debts. Earnings from commercial agriculture were reinvested in the film industry, transportation, and milling.

The ensuing economic expansion greatly reduced class differences among local Kammas and increased the sense of caste-defined social and economic dominance. This solidarity found political expression in Telegu Desham, a new regional party led by the charismatic movie actor, N. T. RamaRao, that became a vehicle for statewide Kamma efforts to wrest political power from another landed caste, the Reddies. By 1985 Karamchedu was awash in television sets, trucks, and political power brokers.

Some of the economic change did improve the living standards of Untouchable villagers who were able to move into slightly better economic niches vacated or created by the Kammas. As once impoverished Kammas have gone on to better things, some local Untouchables have moved from wage labor to openings in sharecropping or tenancy. To this extent they are better off than most Andhra Untouchables, 71 percent of whom are now agricultural laborers. Those who are still wage laborers in Karamchedu are able to supplement agricultural work with work in the tobacco sheds, albeit at low wages. Nevertheless, the local Untouchables are still dependents, and the Kammas clearly perceive the Untouchables' function to be that of filling whatever economic duties the Kammas find it convenient to assign them.

For the most part, the local Untouchables have not openly challenged the Kammas, but most of them have failed to follow Kamma support for the Telegu Desham party. In Andhra, as elsewhere, the massive Untouchable population is politically diverse: it is possible to find supporters of everything from various "Naxalite" insurgency groups to conservative organizations like the BJP (Bhartiya Janta Party). A large proportion, apparently including most of the Karamchedu Untouchables, has continued to support the Congress (I). There are several villages elsewhere in Andhra where local Kammas attacked Untouchable hamlets suspected of supporting the Congress; four Untouchables were killed and 80 homes burned in Pakirikuppam in the aftermath of the 1983 election that brought Telegu Desham to power, and far more widespread violence occurred during the 1984 parliamentary election. There had been no attacks in Karamchedu, but local Kammas were already concerned about Untouchables "forgetting their place."

Certainly the immediate cause of the July massacre makes sense only in terms of the symbolism of inter-group dominance and subordination. A crippled Madiga youth protested when a Kamma chose to wash a water buffalo on the steps of the pond the Untouchables use for drinking water. The Kamma responded by striking the boy with a cattle whip. A young Untouchable woman intervened, striking the Kamma with her water pitcher. A group of Kammas later descended on the Madiga settlement, beat up the young woman, and demanded that her father-in-law appear before a Kamma caste court that has no legal standing but regularly dispenses its own brand of justice in the village. The old man failed to appear. Kammas spent the night rounding up caste-fellows from surrounding villages, and launched a massive attack the next morning. Mala Untouchables, who had been slapped into place three years before, were ignored; this time it was the Madigas who would be taught a lesson.

The sequel to the attack further underlines the nature and significance of Untouchable identity in the incident. A number of reports describe the victims as "Scheduled Caste," but this in not strictly accurate. They were all Untouchable Madigas, but many were Christians. As we noted earlier, Christian Untouchables are excluded from the official Scheduled Caste category and its attendant aid programs on the legal fiction that only Hinduism ever permitted untouchability. In social practise, however, an Untouchable is an Untouchable. The Kammas, like the Rajputs of Gujarat, made no religious distinctions in their attack. The Madigas who fled took shelter in a Christian church in nearby Chirala, but aid mobilized first by local Untouchables, then by Untouchable organizations all over Andhra, was shaped by Untouchable identity. Progressive organizations, whether predominantly Christian or predominantly Hindu, expressed horror at one more attack on Untouchables, but in a country where inter-religious conflict commonly unifies the victimized group, most high-caste Christians betrayed a fine sense of social distinctions and said not one word.

As news of the massacre spread, a variety of Andhra Untouchable organizations mobilized to demand prosecution of the guilty and suspension of a Deputy Superintendent of Police accused of active collusion with the attackers. *Rasta rokos* and *rail rokos* (human blockades of highways and rail lines) were organized in several districts, and Untouchables in the state capital who held public service jobs under the national affirmative action program took mass casual leave to join a demonstration in the state legislature.

Unfortunately, the social configuration within the Andhra political arena still offers fewer of the options that have begun to emerge in Gujarat or Delhi, and the balance still tilts heavily against the rights of Untouchables and other long-dispossessed groups. Shortly after a daylight attack by several hundred Kammas, 11 minor figures were arrested. Several months later, a state police force that has displayed great tenacity as well as brutality in its pursuit of "Naxalite extremists" – in practise, any citizens who have raised any type of protest against existing inequalities-was still unable to locate the many Kammas named as key figures in the attack by Untouchable survivors.[21]

Untouchable activists in the state continued to press the case but privately they express doubt that there will ever be serious prosecution Their disgust is shared by a journalist who concluded his own observations by wondering "what would have happened if it had been the other way around and the labourers had attacked the landlords and killed half this number? One shudders to think what would have happened then." [22] Indeed.

Conclusion

Gujarat, Delhi, Andhra. Three different reflections of the complex dynamics of the struggle to implement human rights. Obviously there are circumstances in which recent changes have altered both attitudes and the balance of power significantly, but the impact of these changes on development of Untouchable rights has been mixed. Value change within the Untouchable community has generally outpaced value change in the rest of society, with recurrently explosive results. Long-term economic changes have added to the ability of Untouchables to mobilize independently on behalf of a new vision of their own humanity and equality, but economic changes have also increased the repressive capacity of higher status groups. A similar pattern has emerged as a result of structural changes in the political arena.

As these three case studies indicate, "Untouchable" is a status category that has persisted through profound changes in polity and economy. It has done so in ways that underline important parallels with a variety of other forms of pervasive discrimination and exploitation. There is, for example, nothing fanciful in the Dalit Panthers' adaptation of symbols and strategies from continuing Black struggles against Western racism. Understanding the present and possible future of the Untouchables will be easier if we put aside the tendency to view their experience as a problem that is uniquely Indian and inherently medieval.

"Untouchable" symbolizes one of several status systems that require some humans to subsist as dependent, subservient, and ultimately expendable populations serving the needs of others. As technologies and economic structures have changed, the nature of subordinate roles that serve the convenience of dominant groups have changed. Ideological rationalizations also have shifted: recently, reliance on overtly hereditary definitions of "inferiority" are being displaced by the theoretically achievement oriented concept of meritocracy, combined with continuing dominant group manipulation of definitions of "merit" and mechanisms by which one may achieve it. A variety of controls once exercised locally and informally are increasingly being transferred to institutions of the modern state-professional bureaucracy, police, courts. Democracy, even as a utopian system of majority rule, does not necessarily serve the interests of minorities in a population, and where traditionally dispossessed groups are concerned, political reality is often shaped by economic inequality and dominant group exercise of sheer brute force.

At the same time several factors have tended to loosen dominant group controls in a number of hierarchic societies. The very concept of equality has become an increasingly disruptive force. Indian elites who adopted and popularized the concept of equality in their own struggle against Western colonialism now find they have become one more in a long line of dominant groups grappling with the impact of this subversive notion on varying forms of internal colonialism. On balance, both democracy and meritocracy have added to elite problems. Though both frequently serve the interests of established elites, a few of the dispossessed do slip through, and of these a few act in ways that add to pressures for further change. Over time, such slippage also increases the resource base for further struggle. In India, these pressures have been accelerated and sustained by the special Independence-era programs that have increased Untouchable access to a widening range of positions in the economy, bureaucracy, and politics.

Such changes are threatening, however, especially when they come from human categories that traditionally provided the conceptual base line for an entire social order. Conflict is hardly surprising, and for several reasons that conflict is likely to continue to be increasingly visible in India: the locus of social controls continues to shift from the local and personal to the large-scale and institutional; changes in the values and resources of the suppressed group make resistance to continued oppression increasingly likely; and value change now divides the dominant society itself, creating small cracks of support or, more often, simple ambivalence, where once there was a far more solid wall of conviction.

"More of the same" hardly seems an optimistic prognosis, and yet it represents a bitter progress. The real question is whether even this limited progress will be sustained by future shifts in the current precarious balance of social forces.

Notes

1. A note on terminology is in order here. Legally there are no more Untouchables. The government is required by the Constitution to define a list or "schedule" of castes deemed to be still handicapped by persisting problems of untouchability, and these castes are guaranteed certain compensatory programs. These "Scheduled Castes," 15 percent of the national population, include Untouchable converts to Sikhism but exclude converts to Christianity and Buddhism. The excluded groups, who in fact continue to be treated as Untouchables, may constitute another two percent of the population. "Harijan," the term used by Mahatma Gandhi in his reform campaign, is regarded by many Untouchables as demeaning and its use is declining. "Dalit," a term meaning "the oppressed," is an assertive term of self-identity increasingly used by Untouchables for themselves but also for a wide variety of other oppressed groups. I use the term "Untouchable" here as being more precise and more likely to convey the significance of persisting problems to a broad audience.
2. I have discussed these patterns in "Whose Law, Whose Order: Untouchables, Social Violence, and the State in India," *Asian Survey, vol.* 22, no.7 (July 1982), pp. 676-87. The views of a number of

Untouchable intellectuals appear in Barbara R. Joshi (ed.), *Untouchable: Voices From The Dalit Liberation Movement* (London: Zed Books, 1986). Another summary is Minority Rights Group, Report #26, *The Untouchables of India* (London: MRG, 1982), a revised edition of the report by Dilip Hiro.

3. This study of events in Golana is based on conversations with social activists in Gujarat as well as the following published sources: *Lokayan Bulletin* (Delhi), vol. 4, nos. 3 and 4, pp. 74-79; Sudarshan Iyengar and Sujata Patel, "Golana: Symptoms of Crisis," *Economic and Political Weekly* (Bombay), vol. 21, no. 7 (February 15, 1986), p. 287; and *Social Action* (Delhi), "The Golana Tragedy," vol. 36, no. 2 (AprilJune 1986), pp. 201-08. 1 am also indebted to Fa. J. M. Heredero for a chance to read the manuscript of his study of the Golana cooperative movement.
4. Some interesting parallels in relations between Brahman landlords and tribal laborers are discussed by Jan Bremen in his studies of southern Gujarat: Patronage and Exploitation: Changing Agrarian Relations in South Gujarat (Berkeley: University of California Press, 1974); and *Of Peasants, Migrants,* and Paupers: Rural Labor Circulation and Capitalist Production in West India (Delhi: Oxford University Press, 1985).
5. This is clear in two accounts of the current labor scene in Ahmedabad that include extensive data on labor roles heavily populated by Untouchables: Sujata Patel, "Contract Labour in Ahmedabad Textile Industry," *Economic and Political Weekly, vol. 21,* no. 4 (October 11, 1986), pp. 1813-20; and Jennifer Sebstad, *Struggle and Development Among Self-Employed Women* (Washington: Agency for International Development, 1982).
6. Key research on the actual practise of untouchability in Gujarat owes much to the late Dr. I. P. Desai. A recent review of the national scene is included in P. Mathew and Simon Stephen, "Untouchability and the Law," *Social Action, vol.* 36, no. 2 (April-June, 1986), p. 183-94.
7. The most extensive study to date of Indian affirmative action law is Marc Galanter, *Competing Equalities: Law and the Backward Classes in India* (Berkeley: University of California Press, 1984). Regarding the continuing interaction between changing Untouchable status and Untouchable pressures for further changes in public policy, see Barbara R. Joshi, *Democracy in Search of Equality* (Delhi: Hindustan Publishing, 1982).
8. Golana provides an interesting footnote to debate about AMUL. See for example the critical analyses in Claude Alvares (ed.), *Another Revolution Fails* (Delhi: Ajanta Press, 1985); and the more positive analyses of K. T. Achaya and V. K. Huria, "Rural Poverty and Operation Flood," *Economic and Political Weekly, vol. 21,* no. 37 (September 13, 1986), pp. 1651-56.

9. Some of the most thorough descriptions and analyses of these riots are Pradip Kumar Bose, "Social Mobility and Caste Violence," *Economic and Political Weekly* (April 18, 1981), pp. 713-16; 1. P. Desai, 'Anti- Reservation Agitation and Structure of Gujarat Society," *Economic and Political Weekly* (May 30, 1981), pp. 819-23; Achyut Yagnik and Anil Bhatt, "The Anti-Dalit Agitation in Gujarat," *South Asia Bulletin, vol.* 4, no. 1 (1984), pp. 45-60; and Anon., "Caste War in Gujarat: A Report from the Field," in Joshi (ed.) *Untouchable . . . , pp.* 72-76.
10. For statistical data on relative proportions of Gujarat caste populations, see Ghanshyam Shah, *Caste Association and Political Process in Gujarat: A Study of the Gujarat Kshatriya Sabba* (Bombay: Popular Prakashan, 1975). All contemporary calculations are based on projections from the last Indian census to tabulate the population of all castes, the census of 1931. Since birth rates have tended to decline more rapidly for the better educated higher castes, it is widely assumed that these projections overstate the current relative proportion of the higher castes.
11. My own earlier background commentary appears in Barbara R. Joshi "ExUntouchable: Problems, Progress, and Policies in Indian Social Charge,": *Pacific Affairs, vol. 53,* no. *2, pp. 193-222;* and *Democracy in Search of Equality*
12. Upendra Baxi, *The Crisis of the Indian Legal System* (Delhi: Vikas, *1982).* A number of commentaries express similar critiques in analyzing failure to implement policies specific to low status castes, as for example V. R. Krishna Iyer's brief pamphlet for the Indian Social Institute, *Justice in Words and Injustice in Deeds* (Delhi: *ISI, 1984);* or K. S. Subramaniam, "Violence against Scheduled Castes in India," a study presented for discussion at Oxford University.
13. One of the original versions of the "Dalit Panther Manifesto" appears in Joshi (ed.), *Untouchable, pp. 141-46,* and provides a broad overview of the ideology that, with variations, shapes the movement.
14. The following segment owes much to a wide variety of social activists in Delhi who kindly shared views, pamphlets, and time. Some of the key events described below have also received some coverage in the New Delhi press.
15. Sarma Marla (For the Gandhi Peace Foundation), *Bonded Labour in India* (Delhi: Biblia Impex, *1981), p. 155.* See also the informative study of Karnataka by the Dalit scholar N. D. Kamble, *Bonded Labour in India* (Delhi Uppal Publishers, *1982).*
16. *Government* of India, Ministry of Labour, *Rural Labour Enquiry, 1974-, 75: Final Report on Indebtedness among Rural Labour Households* (Delhi; Labour Bureau, *1978).* See also the companion volume on rural wages. The government has yet to publish more current comparable data.

17. Panther organizers have worked with the better known, and much better funded, Mobile Creche program that attempts to provide some services for children of construction workers at sites within the city itself. They have drawn from the Creche program but modified it in ways they hope will decrease dependency and increase self-motivation among kiln workers.
18. Several prominent human rights organizations have monitored the Bihar situation for several years, including the Delhi-based Peoples' Union for Democratic Rights. A recent PUDR report is summarized in "Bihar: Peasants, Landlords, and Dacoits," *Economic and Political Weekly, vol. 21,* no. *35 (August 30, 1986), pp. 1531-35.* Other useful background sources are Smitu Kothari, "Bihar's Jalianwala and After," *Lokayan Bulletin, vol. 4,* nos. 3 and *4, pp.; 79-95;* and Anon., "Agrarian Movement in Jehanabad," *Economic and Political Weekly, vol.* 21, no. *19* (May *10, 1986), pp. 813-15.* The perspective of one of the more radical activist groups is recorded in Vinod Mishra, *From the Flaming Fields of Bihar* (Calcutta: Prabodh Bhattacharjee, *1986).*
19. *Two* published analyses of Karamchedu are of relatively easy access: K.B., "The Karemchedu Killings," *Economic and Political Weekly, vol. 20, no.31* (August *3, 1985), pp. 1298-1300;* and D. Narasimha Reddy, "Karamchedu: Dialect without Development," *Economic and Political Weekly, vol. 20,* no. 37 (September *14, 1985), pp. 1546-49. 1* have also relied on interviews and two publications by Andhra Untouchable activists, *Prajabandhu,* edited by E. V. Chinnaiah of Nellore; and the *1985* report of the Confederation of Depressed Classes Organizations.
20. One excellent source of information on problems of Untouchable Christians and Christian progressives is the Indian Social Institute of New Delhi, which publishes both monographs and the periodical *Social Action.* A useful summary is the pamphlet by Dr. Jose Kananaikil, *Christians of Scheduled Caste Origin* (Delhi: ISI, 1983). For comments of some of the more outspoken Untouchable Christian activists, see Rev. M. Azariah, *The Unchristian Side of the Indian Church* (Bangalore: Dalit Sahitya Akademy, 1985); and Dr. K. Wilson, *The Twice Alienated* (Hyderabad: Booklinks Corporation, 1982).
21. Amnesty International has commented repeatedly on the activities of the Andhra police. Extensive background material is available in A. R. Desai (ed.), *Violation of Democratic Rights in India* (Bombay: Popular Prakashan, 1986), pp. 326-407 and 456-609. A useful source of continuing coverage is the series of articles contributed to *Economic and Political Weekly* by Dr. K. Balagopal of the Andhra Pradesh Civil Liberties Union, himself under attack by the state police.
22. "The Karamchedu Killings," *Economic and Political Weekly, p.* 1300.

Source: " Asian Perspectives on Human Rights" edited by Claude E. Welch, Jr., And Virginia A. Leary.

Bibliography

Ambedkar, B.R., Annihilation of Caste, Bheem Patrika Publications, Jalandhar, India, 1982.

– The Buddha and His Dhar ma, Siddharth Publication, Bombay, 1957.

– Castes in India, Bheem Patrika Publications, Jullundur.

– The Untouchables, Jetavana Mahavihara, Shravasti, Balrampur, 1977.

– Why Go For Conversion? Dalit Sahitya Akademy, Bangalore, 1981.

Baker, Ernest, National Character and the Factors in its Formation, London: Methuen & Co., 1948.

L.R. Balley, An Open Letter to the People of the World: Violation of Human Rights in India, Bheem Patrika Publications, Jullundur.

Bandyopadhyay, Pramathmioth, International Law and Custom in Ancient India, New Delhi, Ramanand Vidya Bhawan, 1982; originally published University of Calcutta, Calcutta, 1920.

Bhatia, H.S., ed., International Law and Practice in Ancient India, Deep & Deep Publications, New Delhi, 1977.

Berwa, Laxini N., "The Untouchables of India and their Human Rights Violations," Unpublished paper presented at the New York Conference on Asian Studies, State University of New York, Brockport, N.Y., 1987.

Carvallo, A.A., Dalit People: A socio-political Study of the Caste-Oppressed.

Claydon, J., "The Transnational Protection of Ethnic Minorities: A Treatise Framework for Enquiry," The Canadian Yearbook of International Law, Vol. XIII, 1975. The constitution (india) Darwin, H.G., FactFinding and Commissions of Inqurry, Report of a Study Group of the Davies Memorial Institute of International Studies, 1976.

Das, Bhagwan, ed., Thus, Spoke Ambedkar, Vol. 1, Bheem Patrika Publications, Jullunder, 1977.

– Thus, Spoke Ambedkar, Vol. 2, Buddhist Publishing House, Jalandhar.

– Thus, Spoke Ambedkar, Vol. 3, Ambedkar Sahithya Prakashana, Bangalore.

– Thus, Spoke Ambedkar. Vol. 4, Ambedkar Sahithya Prakashana, Bangalore.

Dubey, Sumari Nurain, Administration of Policy and Programs for Backward Classes in India, Ratna Murdia, Bombay Somaiya, 1976.

Friedmann, Wolfgang, Oliver J. Lissitzyn and Richard C. Pugh, International Law: Cases and Materials, St. Paul: West Publishing Co., 1969.

Galanter, Marc, Competing Equalities: The Indian Experience with Compensatory Discrimination, Berkeley: University of California Press, 1984.

International Declaration of Human Rights.

– "Untouchability and the Law" in A.W. Murphy,et al (eds.), Law and Poverty, Bombay: N.M. Tripathy, 1973.

Hingorani, R.C., Human Rights in India, Oxford IBH, New Delhi, 1985.

Hiro, Dilip, The Untouchables of India: Report No.26 of the Minority Rights Group, London, Dalit Sahitya Akademy, Bangalore, 1984.

Joshi, Barbara R., Untouchable! Voices of the Dalit Liberation Movement, Zed books, London, 1986.

Kelly, J.B., "National Minorities in International Law," Denver Journal of International Law and Policy, Vol. 3, No. 2, Fall 1973.

Kly,Y.N., International Law and the Black Minority in the U.S., Clarity Press, Atlanta, 1985.

Meron, Theodor, Human Rights Law-Making in the United Nations, Clarendon Press, Oxford, 1986.

Moreley, William Hook, The Administration of Justice in British India: Its Past History and Present State, Metropolian Book Co., 1976.

Rajshekar, V.T., Ambedkar and his Conversation, Dalit Sahitya Akademy, India, 1983.

DALIT: The Black Untouchables of India, Clarity Press, Atlanta, 1987.

Ram. Nandu, "Law and Atrocities on Weaker Sections in India," Indian Bar Review, Vol. X, No.3, 1983.

Ramcharan, B.G., International Law and Fact-Finding in the Field of Human Rights, Martin Nfj"hoff Publishers, The Hague, 1982.

Rural Development and Human Rights in South Asia: Report of a Seminar held in Lucknow, India, 4-9 December 1982, International commission of Jurists, Switzerland, and the Human Rights Institute, Lucknow, India, 1984.

Sandanshiv, D.N., ed. Law and Social Justice. Bombay: Siddharth Publications, 1978.

Schwarzenberger, Georg and George W. Keeton, The Inductive Approach to International Law. London: Stevens and Sons, 1965.

Sertima, Ivan Van and Larry Willialms, eds., Great African Thinkers, VoL 1. Rutgers: Transaction Books, 1,985.

Shakir, Moin, Politics of Minorities: Some Perspectives, Manta Publications, 1980.

Shulka, P.D., Administration of Education in India, Vikas, New Delhi, 1983.

States of Emergency: Impact of Human Rights, International Commission of Jurists, Switzerland.

Van Dijk, P., Judicial Review of Governmental Action and the Requirements of an Interest to Sue, Smithoft & Noordhoff, Netherlands, 1980.

Wadhwa, Kamlosh Kumar, Minority safeguards in India: Constitutional Provisions and Their Impli.mentation, Thomson Press, India, 1975.

3

Human Rights Violations and the Dalits

Justice A. Varadarajan

There are human rights violations in respect of the poorer sections of various people in this country. Human rights violations are more pronounced so far as the untouchables and the Scheduled Tribes are concerned. So, I will deal with this problem in general in respect of the poorer sections of the people of the country and in particular of the untouchables and Scheduled Tribes of India.

There are three characteristic features of the Hindu Organisation:

1. Castes; 2. Hierarchical system among the castes; 3. Sub-class system, cutting into the caste system.

The Rule laid down by the Hindu Law giver Manu is that there are only four *varnas* of Hindus and that there is not to be a fifth *varna*. The four *varnas* are: 1. *Brahmins*, 2. Kshatrias, 3. Vysias and 4. Sudras. The *Brahmins* are said to have been born out of the shoulder, the Vysias out of the abdomin or thigh and the Sudras out of the feet.

According to sage Brighu, Brahma created only *Brahmins* and other sections of the Hindus, namely, *Kshatriyas*, Vysias and Sudras came into existence on the basis of the extent to which the Original *Brahmins* deviated from the principles to be observed by them. Gandhi and others in their campaign against untouchability contended that the untouchables and the schedule tribes fall under the fourth category, namely *sudras* on the basis of manu's statement that there shall be only four *varnas* and there is not to be a fifth one. Dr. Ambedkar has pointed out that this theory is not acceptable because Manu speaks of untouchables as varna Bahayas, which means those out-side the varna system. The four classes of Hindus are called Savarnas, while those outside the four classes like the untouchables are called *Avarnas*. Manu has stated in his smriti that the dwelling of the *Chandalas*–Shapakas shall be outside the village, that they must be made apapatras and their wealth shall be dogs and donkeys, their dress shall be garments of the dead, they shall eat their food in broken dishes, and black iron shall be their ornaments. They must wander from place to place, and they shall not sleep in villages and towns at nights. It is well known that in villages the untouchables live in separate localities variously called as *cheris* or colonies, etc. while the other caste Hindus live in the main village. It cannot be denied that the untouchables are not part of the Hindu Society and they must remain separate and segregated.

The first general census in India was taken in 1881. Thereafter, there were census operations once in 10 years. In 1911 the Census Commissioner laid down 10 tests for ascertaining the total population of the untouchables Scheduled Castes, and Scheduled Tribes. They were those who:

- denied the supremacy of *Brahmins;*
- did not receive the mantras from any Brahmin or other recognized Hindu Guru;
- denied the authority of the *vedas;*
- do no worship Hindu gods;
- were not served by good *Brahmins;*
- have no *Brahmins* priests;
- have no access to the interior of ordinary Hindu temples;
- cause pollution;
- bury their dead, and
- eat beef and do not revere the cow.

Efforts were made in the subsequent census operations also to ascertain the population of the untouchables in British India. The Simon Commission, which came to India in 1930 stated that the population of untouchables was 44.5 millions. When the Lothian Committee came in 1932, the Hindus refused to accept the figures given by the Simon Commission and they even denied the very existence of untouchables in some provinces realizing the danger of admitting their existence and giving up representation enjoyed by the Hindus, in fact, due to the untouchables. In 1931, the Census Commissioner stated that the population of the untouchables was 53 millions, and it was contended that it must be between 55 and 60 millions.

Though, there was slavery in ancient Rome and America. The laws of slavery permitted emancipation. Once a slave always a slave was not the fate of the slave there. But in untouchability, there is no escape. Once an untouchable always an untouchable has been the position. To tell the untouchable, "you are free, you are a citizen; you have all the rights of citizen" and to tighten the rope in such a manner as to leave him no opportunity to realise the ideal is cruel deception. Of the two orders, untouchability and slavery, untouchability is beyond doubt the worst.

The master of Roman slave or the American Negro took much trouble to train the slave and initiate him to higher forms of labour and culture. It was undoubtedly with motive of gain, for a skilled slave as an item was more valuable than an unskilled one and if sold he would fetch a better price and if hired he would bring in more wages than an unskilled one. That has not been the case of untouchables, who are kept in a low level without any initiation into the finer things. In the competition with the scales always weighing against him by reason of his social stigma the untouchable is the last to be employed, and the first to be fired or removed from employment.

By now the problems faced and the indignities suffered by the untouchables have been repeated from several platforms and are more or less well known. So, it is not necessary to make any detailed reference to them here except to cite a few instances. There have been several agitations and *Satyagrahas* against the practise of untouchability. The right to wear any kind of dress and ornaments are some of the rights which the British Indian Law gave to untouchables along with the rest, along with the right to use public utilities, such as, wells, schools, trams, railways, public offices, etc. The untouchables agitated by petitions and protests prior to 1920 and by direct action from about 1920. *Satyagraha* was organized in 1923 against denial of the right to take water from Chavdar tank situate in Mahad Town of Holaba District in the Old Bombay Presidency and Valkkam struggle in the Travancore state in 1924 which was for vindicating the right of use public roads which skirted the temple at vaikkam. The mahad satyagraha ended in favour of the untouchable by a court verdict in the Bombay High Court, which confirmed the decision of the sub judge, mahad on 20.12.1927 as part of the chowdar tank agitation.

Gandhiji condemned the Mahad Satyagraha by the untouchables against caste Hindus, while he preached that civil disobedience was a weapon. Which could legitimately be used by Hindus against the British for securing their freedom. Curiously, Gandhiji argued that untouchability and that Satyagraha for the removal of untouchables because they were not the sinners but far from being sinners they were the sinned against. The untouchables replied that if that was so British must be asked to offer satyagraha and not the Hindus as the British imperialism was a sin of the British and not of the Hindus. Curiously Gandhiji was in favour of the Vaikkom Satyagrah carried on under the auspices of the political party to which he belonged and he blessed and encouraged and the Scheduled Tribes continue unabated.

India became independent in 1947. Before the grant of independence, the British Government wanted to settle the problems of the untouchable Scheduled Castes. This section of the Indian population wanted separate electorates in the future parliament and legislative bodies. This demand for separate electrorate was opposed by the caste Hindus. There were Round Table Conferences in London in connection with this problem, but as there was no agreement between those sections of the population and the caste Hindus, the British Prime Minister offered to give his own award on the question, provided that all the parties concerned agreed in writing to be wholly bound by the award. It is a matter of history that the parties including Gandhiji accepted that offer and undertook in writing to abide by the award. Unfortunately Gandhiji went back on that undertaking after the award for granting of separate electorate and separate representation to the scheduled caste was given by the British Prime Minister and he resorted to a fast unto death demanding the withdrawal of the award so far as the scheduled castes are concerned, though he had no objection to the grant of separate electorate to the muslims and certain other bodies. Dr. Ambedkar, who along with Dewan Bahadur Retta Malai Srinivasan represented the scheduled castes and scheduled tribes as their nominee in the Round Table Conference was made to given up this demand of separate electorates to the Scheduled Castes and Scheduled Tribes and to be satisfied with the Joint Electorates as Gandhiji's life was otherwise in danger. Thus, came the Poona Pact in 1932.

Dr. Ambedkar knew very well and the scheduled castes could see from the way their representatives chosen by the Joint Electorate function in Parliament and in legislative Assemblies in the country that they do not really represent their interest in those forums, Rao Bahadur M.C. Rajah, who was originally a party to the demand for separate electorate to the scheduled castes and scheduled tribes, later came under the influence of Dr. Moonjie of the Hindu Maha Sabha and began to contend that the grant of separate electorate to the scheduled castes and scheduled tribes would be harmful to them and he campaigned for the grant of the joint electorate. It would suffice to give one instance of how joint electorate works. Rao Bahadur Rajah has stated in his letter dated 25.8.1983 to Gandhiji, thus:

> "The Congress party men in Madras representing the caste Hindus deviated from the Legislative Assembly have to follow the caste Hindus blindly in every measure the Ministry may bring and vote with them even in matters which deeply affect the interest of the community. The recent debate on the Temple Entry Bill in the Madras Legislative Assembly has exposed the ugly fact that all the Depressed Class Members driven by the discipline of the Congress Party in the Assembly voted solidly against the Motion for referring the Bill to a Select Committee. Could anything more unnatural and more humiliating proving, as it did, the subjugation of my community by the Caste Hindus represented by

> Mr.Rajagopalachariar, ... who stood up and opposed the Bill and requested me to withdraw it, saying he will introduce another Bill only from Malabar and not for the other Districts. The effects of Mr.Rajagopalachariar's speech was to defeat my Motion with my own community men registering their votes against a measure introduced to secure their social and religious elevation."

Rajah has stated in his subsequent letter dated 21.9.1938 to Gandhiji:

> "So, the question of our being in the joint electorate with caste Hindus and the attitude of the Congress Ministry towards the raising of the Social and religious status of our community are mutually and vitally connected. If we are not free to enter into Hindu Temples, we are no Hindus, and if we are not Hindus, why should we have a joint electorate with them? Is it for swelling their numbers as against Muslims and other communities?"

Gandhiji has stated in reply dated 5.10.1938 to Rajah:

> "The temple entry question is a mighty religious problem. I would like you to apply your religious mind to it . If you will, you will give your whole hearted support to Rajaji and make his move a thorough success."

Now a very large percentage of the Schedule Castes and Scheduled Tribes feel that nothing could be lost by the deletion of Articles 330 and 332 in the Constitution of India, which grant separate representation by joint electorate. Gandhi said before the Poona Pact was signed in 1932 that the superior class of Caste Hindus have to do penance for having neglected the untouchables for ages and that it can be done by active social reforms by making the lot of the untouchables more bearable by acts of services. In the Second Round Table Conference, he did not participate in the First Round Table Conference–he contended that the Hindus had seriously taken up the cause of the untouchables and therefore there is no need to give them political safeguards. Now more than 60 years have passed after the Poona Pact was signed and the miracle which Gandhiji thought would happen has not happened and the degradation and very poor economic and social condition of the Scheduled Castes and Scheduled Tribes remains mostly unchanged.

The Constitution of India provides for reservation of the Scheduled caste and Scheduled Tribes in Government Employment in Articles 16(4) and 335. Everybody knows about the extent to which these communities have benefited by these constitutional provisions. It is negligible. There is no reservation in matters relating to science and technology, with the result that these people are not represented at all in those field. There are 512 posts of High Court Judges in the Country, but there are only 13

Scheduled Caste Judge and no Scheduled Tribes Judge at all in the other High Courts. These people are not represented at all in the other High Courts. The representations of these people in Class I and Class II posts inclusive of the Secretariats of the President and Prime Minister is far below the percentage of these People compared to the total population of the country. The position in the services in the States is not in any way the better. This State of affairs exists mainly due to the antipathy entrusted with the implementation if the Constitutional provisions and safeguards.

It may not be out of place here to mention that when the agitation of some misguided people was going on against the implementation of the Mandal Commission's recommendations for the grant of 27% reservation in the Central Services to the Backward Classes, the Class I Officers in the capital of the country went to the extent of passing a resolution urging the removal of the reservation provided to the Scheduled Casts and Scheduled Tribes, thus proclaiming to the world their antipathy to these classes of people. The representation of these people in business and industry is very negligible.

The Constitution provides for compulsory primary education. But in 1985, it was stated by the Government in the Rajya Sabha that illiteracy was 78.62 percent in the case of Scheduled Casts and 81.65 percent in the case of Scheduled Tribes in the Country. In Tamil Nadu, it was 71.33 percent amongst the Scheduled Castes and 79.55 percent amongst the Scheduled Tribes. This admission of the Government of India shows to what extent Articles 45 and 46 providing for compulsory Primary Education have been implemented over the past 40 years.

Article 17 of the Constitution says that untouchability is abolished. The protection of Civil Rights Act has been passed by the Parliament in 1955. But untouchability is practised even now in the villages and towns and even in the National Capital City, Delhi. Whenever clashes occur between caste Hindus and the Scheduled Castes in regard to taking water from taps and well-provided by the Government instead of taking proper action against the erring caste Hindus. The officials provide separate taps and wells to the oppressed untouchables leading to their further segregation. Separate Schools and hostels are provided to the children belonging to the Scheduled Castes and Scheduled Tribes by the Governments. This results in segregation of these children from the children belonging to the other communities. The Scheduled Castes and Tribes people have been forced in the past to live in segregated colonies far away from the caste Hindu localities. The position continues to be the same even now. The small houses provided by the Government to the scheduled caste and scheduled tribes people are located in segregated areas far away from the residential areas of caste Hindus resulting in segregation being practised even at the instance of the Governments.

There are even separate burial grounds for these people. The position is that the untouchables remain segregated from birth to death.

The universal Declaration of Human Rights was proclaimed in 1948. the first two Article of the Declaration emphasize that all human beings without distinction are born free and equal in dignity and rights. Those two Article set out the basic principle of the Equity and non-discrimination in the enjoyment of the Human Rights and Fundamental Freedoms. The next 19 articles relate to the civil and political rights to which all Human beings are entitled. The international Covenants of Human Rights are treaties whose states parties have formally agreed to abide by the provisions and to undertake to respect, ensure and take steps for the full achievement of a wide rage of rights. There are two such International Covenant. They are: the International Covenant of civil and political rights and the International Covenant on the Economic, social and cultural rights. The two Covenant were adopted by the General Assembly in December, 1966. They came into force in 1976. The Optional protocol, which is an adjunct instrument to states acceding to the Optional Protocol empower the Human Rights Committee to receive complaints from individuals, who allege violation of their Human Rights. By October 1987, India and 86 other countries became parties to the Covenants and 39 nations became parties to the Optional Protocol, but not India. India refused to become a party to the Optional Protocol contending that acceptance thereof would result in foreign intervention with its sovereignty.

Accordingly to Sumantha Banarji, Human Rights violations take two forms in India. They are (1) Direct Violation by the State as cited in the Amnesty International Reports and (2) State's indifference to such violations. The problems of the untouchables in India are not India's internal problems, but are undoubtedly international problems. Apartheid was practised by the South African Government under Law. The General Assembly of the United Nations and the Security Council had declared Apartheid as being incombatable with the United Nations Charter and termed the policy of the South African Government as a crime against humanity and called upon all other nations to take appropriate action to end it. India also raised the South African Apartheid issue in the World Forums and observed 1978-79 as Anti-Apartheid Year. Fortunately, Apartheid has ended in South Africa and the South African Blacks are getting equal political and other rights with the White South Africans. It cannot be contended that untouchability in India cannot be equated with Apartheid in South Africa merely because Article 17 of the Constitution of India says that untouchability is abolished and the Civil Rights Protection Act has been passed in 1955. The position is the same though Apartheid was practised under law in South Africa and untouchability continues to be practised in India inspite of the Laws against it.

These provisions are not seriously enforced. The untouchables in India have by now come to know their rights and are no longer prepared to bear their sufferings and indignities any more. The youth of these class of people have awakened and are trying to and bent upon asserting their rights. This has no doubt resulted in increased violence against these people. The Scheduled Castes cannot continue in the present state of suppression and degradation, which may undoubtedly lead to great turmoil sooner or later. The Central and State Governments should therefore, rise and take real, active and abiding interest in the uplift, of these classes and stop cruelty and oppression which are caused day in and day out in one or other part of the Country.

Though the United Nations Organisation cannot force Government to change their policies and practises, and pursuation is the only tool available for bringing about improvement in the observation of Human Rights, the General Assembly, the Trusteeship Council. The International Court of Justice and the Economic and Social Council deal with Human Rights questions in one way or another.

Now a Human Rights Commission has been constituted in India under an ordinance and a revised Bill was introduced in Parliament. It is hoped that the machinery to be constituted will be more effective than what has been achieved till now under Article 17 of the Constitution and the protection of Civil Rights Act 1955 and other relevant provisions. Unfortunately, the body which has since been constituted does not contain any representation of these sections of the population in this Country, namely – the Scheduled Castes and the Scheduled Tribes who form a vast majority of those who are subjected to Human Rights Violations in the Country. These people will watch keenly how the Committee is going to deal with their Human Rights violations.

On the day following the 45th Anniversary of the Proclamation of the Universal Declaration of Human Rights by the General Assembly of the United Nations Organisation (UNO), on behalf of untouchables Scheduled Castes and Scheduled Tribes people of India, I express my gratitude for the yeoman services being rendered by the Organisation for putting an end to Human Rights violations all the World over and wish the Organisation every success in its endeavour. I urge the Scheduled Castes and Scheduled Tribes people and other weaker sections in the Country to be vigilant and protest strongly against any Human Rights violation to which they may be subjected, and agitate for their rights in a united and concerted manner.

4

Untouchability in Contemporary India Worse than Apartheid

Justice A. Varadarajan

There are discriminated people all over the world, such as the African-Americans of the United States of America, the Blacks of South Africa, the Jews of Israel and the people of the Scheduled Castes and Scheduled Tribes, who are the original inhabitants of India as it was before the Partition of the country in 1947. Those original inhabitants who were subjugated by the Aryans came to be dubbed as Untouchables who now belong to the Scheduled Castes, while those who fled to the forests are now the Scheduled Tribes. The Indian society, barring the Christians, Muslims, Parsis and Sikhs, is a caste-based one consisting of Hindus. According to Hinduism, there are four sections of Hindus, namely *Brahmins* at the top, *Kshatriyas* below them, Vaisyas coming third and the *Shudras* coming last.

A.K. Roy wrote in July, 1985, "The Indian caste system, without any parallel in the world, is not merely a feudal superstition. It effectively determines the division of labour in Society and defines mental attitudes towards physical labour. In the tenth book of the *Rig Veda* it is written that from the head of the Creator came the *Brahmins*, from the arms the *Kshatriyas*, from the waist the *Vysyas* and from the feet the *Shudras*."

Article 338 of the Constitution of India provides that the President shall appoint a Special Officer for the Scheduled Castes and the Tribes. Article 340 likewise provides that he may appoint a Commission to investigate the conditions of the Backward Classes and suggest measures for their development. The first Backward Classes Commission, of which Kaka Kalelkar was the Chairman, submitted its report in 1955 identifying 2399 castes as backward including all women, and 837 castes as the most backward and suggesting reservation in services for them. That report, though placed before Parliament, was never discussed and has been forgotten. The Second Backward Classes Commission constituted in 1978 with B.P. Mandal as Chairman, submitted its report in 1980. This Commission has not hesitated to suggest Castes as the basis of reservation.

The Scheduled Castes, who at one time were sought to be labeled as *Panchamas*, do not fall under any of those four sections. According to Hinduism and Hindu Law, Hindus are born and not made. There are Scheduled Castes even amongst the Sikhs. So, there is no possibility at all for the Scheduled Castes and Tribes getting integrated with any of the four sections, not even with the *Shudras* who themselves belong to many different castes. Every election is fought on caste basis and even *Brahmins* (*Indian Express*, dated 25.11.1988) asked the political parties to field at least 15 Brahmin candidates in the on coming Tamil Nadu elections, stating in a press release made on behalf of the Tamil Nadu Association and the *Brahmins* Youth Association that *Brahmins* decide the winning candidates in at least 25 constituencies and are in a majority in 15 other constituencies.

The problem of these minority Scheduled Castes and Tribes persists for thousands of years. The Scheduled Castes, both men and women, have been suppressed and made to engage themselves in the meanest of jobs such as scavenging and removing dead animals, and denied the human rights such as freely walking in the streets where caste Hindus live, wearing any dress apart form those allowed by the caste Hindus, drawing water from drinking water sources, receiving education, going to religious places and the like. They are segregated and made to live away from the residential areas of the caste Hindus in what are known in Tamil Nadu as "Cheris". Even the residential hutments called houses, built by Government of India, are in separate areas away from the residential areas of the caste Hindus. The officials responsible for construction of these hutments are either unwilling or unable to find places to enable the scheduled castes to live side by side with the Caste Hindus. They are forced to have even separate burial grounds for disposing of their dead. In small towns and cities even educated officials amongst the Scheduled Castes cannot obtain rental accommodation in caste Hindu areas, unless they hide their caste.

The *Times of India* (March 31, 1983) stated thus: "and backward areas of the country, notwithstanding the enactment six years ago of the Civil Rights Act providing for enhanced and stringent punishment for offenses arising out of this social evil....

"The prevalence of untouchability in large parts of the country was revealed by an All India Survey conducted by the All India Harijan Sevak Sangh in the 12 states of the country sometime ago. The findings have been confirmed by the Commissioner for Scheduled Castes and

Tribes in its latest report presented in the Rajasthan Vidhaan Sabha here last week."

India's ruling class does not want to abolish untouchability which provides a lot of socio-economic benefits to the other people and also serves to provide vote banks which pay for mere promises and which are soon forgotten and repeated next time.

Whenever the Scheduled Castes revolted against the ill-treatment to which they are subjected, they are attacked with deadly weapons and killed, their houses are burnt, their women are raped, molested or dishonoured and their belongings are destroyed. This ill-treatment and hardship of the Scheduled Caste continues unabated even now, mostly in the villages where the majority of the population of this country lives.

Untouchability is practiced even in New Delhi where our Union Government functions. The following is the report (*Indian Express*, Delhi dated 10.12.1988) about a cruel and inhuman act of untouchability which was committed in that city recently.

According to the report, "Nathu Lal Dhinvar's birth caught up with him on Saturday. For 20 years, as he ran his stall in Sri Venkateshwara Mandir in R.K. Puram, he thought he had left it behind. But, on Saturday, the aggarbatti and coconut that he sold to devotees were hurled aside and he and his wife were thrashed by goondas. Nathu Lal was reminded that he had been born a "Harijan".

"For 20 years his wares were offered at the temple and the poojari considered them pure. Suddenly, people have remembered his caste, I don't understand," said a senior member on the temple committee. Nathu Lal doesn't understand either. He was given a stall at the temple by N.Rajagopal Iyengar, a Supreme Court Judge, and every morning, along with his wife Anokhi, he would make a small offering to God, which God accepted. Then, he would provide devotees with their offerings, until a few months back when the poojari and some people on the temple management decided that offerings bought from a Harijan were not good enough for God.

In June, Nathu Lal could see his birth catching up with him. The poojari told him to pack off. A temple committee member said that Nathu Lal refused and prayed to God instead. Apparently, God did not need him. His stall was ransacked.

Nathu Lal persisted. He laid out his wares and went to court. Then the management devised a new method. The poojari began rejecting the offering that devotees bought from Nathu Lal on the ground that they were 'impure'.

The crunch came on Saturday. As Nathu Lal and Anokhi were laying out the agarbatti and coconut, some goondas came and hurled them aside. The couple were thrashed. Offerings to God lay scattered on the ground.

Nathu Lal can only pray. Pray that his offerings are good enough for God. May be, God will need him then.

Independence was obtained in 1947 after Partition, and India became an independent sovereign republic by the adoption of the Constitution on January 26, 1958. The conditions of the Scheduled Castes and Tribes remains much the same even so many years after independence and the adoption of the Constitution. The improvement made is negligible. The Constitution has abolished untouchability, but untouchability laws are not enforced seriously, for a caste majority of the law enforcing authorities are Caste Hindus who are not bothered about the practice of untouchability by their fellow caste men, and the Scheduled Caste officers who are sometimes posted to enforce these laws are not effective enough due to fear of their Caste Hindu Superior officers. The prosecution of the offenders under these laws is very negligible and not even heard of.

Education

The Constitution of India provides for compulsory primary education. But in an answer to a question in the Rajya Sabha it was stated on December 12, 1985, that illiteracy was 78.62 per cent among the Scheduled Castes and 81.65 per cent amongst the Scheduled Tribes in the whole country. It was 80.35 per cent in Andhra Pradesh, 85.04 per cent in Uttar Pradesh and 89.60 per cent in Bihar, In Tamil Nadu, it was 71.33 per cent amongst the Scheduled Tribes.

The Constitution of India provides for reservation in education and Government employment to the Scheduled Castes and Scheduled Tribes. Though a comparatively small number of these people have come up in life through education and Government Employment, the progress of these minority people in these fields is tardy and negligible. This is due to the antipathy or lack of interest, nay animosity of the caste Hindus manning the machinery, through which these beneficial measures are administered. The quotas fixed for these people are not filled under the pretext of "efficiency" and even the statistics relating to the number of persons benefited by these measures are not forthcoming and are not effectively insisted upon by the higher authorities. The Government of India instructed the Chief Justices and the Chief Ministers of the States in August, 1980 to locate Scheduled Caste and Scheduled Tribes persons who could be appointed as Judges to give them proper representation, and those instructions were reiterated in May, 1984. But when a question was asked in Parliament, after due notice, it is stated in February, 1986 by the Minister of State of Law and Justice that he was unable to get the information from the State Governments. The Government of India was unable to get this information inspite of all facilities of communication like telephones, telex and wireless network due to the apathy and indifference of its Caste Hindu bureaucracy. If the matter rests there, would not this show the following two factors?

Half-Heartedness of the Government of India

About the apathy of the Chief Ministers of the States regarding appointment of Scheduled Castes as Judges, A.K. Roy wrote :

In July, 1985: "Despite reservation this is true even today with the high positions, whether in politics, the services or education, dominated by the upper castes (even among Nazalites).

In the trading and cultivating communities the backwards are to be found and amongst class IV employees, the sweepers and tillers, Harijans and Adivasis. The statistics collected by the Mandal Commission were revealing. In the Class I and Class II services of the Central Government, the percentage of SC and ST are only 5.68 and 18.18 and that of the backwards 4.69 and 10.63 though together they constitute 70 percent of the population. Individually, in the President's Secretariat, out of 35 officers only two are SC/ST. There are no Backwards. Similarly out of 162 Class-II Officers in the President's Secretariat the SC/ST number 26 and in the Prime Minister's Secretariat the figures are 13 and 4 out of 107 officers. The Home Ministry has totally 409 Class I and 1301 Class II Officers in which SC/ST number 15 and 140 and the Backwards 13 and 27 respectively. . . The question of reservation of Backwards has always left the Central Government uneasy. Unlike the SC and ST, the Backwards are physically and numerically strong (above 50%) and they matter in terms of voting power and so cannot be ignored. Moreover, if by chance wisdom dawns and they unite with the SC and ST then the 1000 years' rule of the forward Castes would end in no time to the horror both the Left and Right."

The reservations, which have provided opportunity for only a small minority of the Untouchables and Scheduled Tribes, and should continue, have not solved the problem of equal rights and human dignity of their masses, not even of elite amongst them, for even their elite still suffer from discrimination and antagonism as untouchables. But some amongst the Hindus belonging to advanced communities envy these reservations of the untouchables and they do not hestitate to eat into the reservation quota by obtaining false community certificates and impersonation-crimes which are sought to be justified even by cinematograph films. The discrimination, antagonism, suffering and ill-treatment of the Scheduled castes and Tribes are so grave and intolerable that large masses of these communities are forced to embrace Buddhism, Christianity and Islam, inspite of the fact that they are aware that by conversion they would lose the benefits of reservation. As antonym Doss Gupta says :

"The untouchables know perfectly well that they will lose privileges, concessions, grants and subsidies on their conversion to Islam. Yet they are willing to embrace Islam. What is the motive ? (a) Social inequality is the primary reason for the untouchables losing faith in Hinduism. (b) Nobodv ever heard of a Muslim women being raped or molested or dishonoured. Black untouchable women want exactly this. They hope to get this protection only by embracing Islam, rather than Christianity which in India is nothing but modified Hinduism, as it still observes the caste system."

The Universal Declaration of Human Rights, the basic international pronouncement of the inalienable and inviolable rights of all members of the human family was proclaimed in a resolution of the General Assembly of the United Nations Organisation on December 10,1948. The first two Articles of the Universal Declaration emphasises that all human beings, without distinction, are born free and equal in dignity and rights, and they set out the basic principles of equality and non-discrimination in the enjoyment of human rights and fundamental freedoms. The next Article 19 deal with the civil and political rights to which all human beings are entitled. The International Convenants on Human Rights are treaties whose States Parties, which are nations which have formally agreed to abide by their provisions, undertake to respect, ensure and take steps for the full achievement of a wide range or rights. There are two such Convenants : (a) The International Convenant on Civil and Political Rights, and (2) the International Convenant were adopted by the General Assembly in December 1966, and they came into force in 1976. The optional protocol, and adjunct instrument to the Convenants, also come into force simultaneously in 1976. The States acceding to the optional Protocol empower the Human Rights Committee established under the Convenant, to receive complaints from individuals who allege violation of their rights set out in the Covenant. By October 1987, 91 States including India became Parties to the Economic, Social and Cultural Convenant, 87 States including India had ratified the Civil and Political Rights. Covenant and 39 States become parties to the Optional Protocol. India has refrained from becoming a party to the Optional protocol. The result is that no individual can complain to the Human Rights Committee against any violation of the right protected by Treaty of the United Nations, This is what Article 1 of the Optional Protocol to the Inter-National Covenant on Civil Political Rights says: Right without remedy is a mere shadow.

Sumanta Banerjee, a noted caste Hindu columnist, has written thus:

"On almost all counts India has been violating the Covenant. The conservative figures cited by Amnesty International in its annual report are quite revealing"

The United Nations Organisation cannot take action concerning India's violation of the Convenants because India has refused to sign and ratify the Optional Protocol. India's official excuse is that ratification of the Optional Protocol would mean foreign countries interfering with its sovereignty. Sumanta Banerjee says that Human Rights violation takes two forms in India–firstly direct violation by the State as cited in the Amnesty International Reports, and secondly State's indifference to such violations, and he concludes that such indifference-

> "amounts to violation of other international covenants such as the Covenant on Economic and Social Rights to which India is a Party–a Country ratifying this convenant (like India) has its responsibility to protect all of its people from economic and social exploitation".

The Problem of the Untouchables in India is not India's internal problem, but an international problem. Apartheid is a systematic form of institutionalized racial discrimination and segregation practised by the Government of South Africa as its official policy since 1948. Under apartheid the Black South Africans are not allowed to participate in the political life of the country and are subjected to hundreds of repressive laws and regulations. The General Assembly of the United Nations and the Security Council have declared apartheid as being incompatible with the United Nations Charter and have termed that policy as a crime against humanity and have called on all states to take and promote action to end it. Did not India raise South Africans Apartheid issue before the World Bodies and discuss it even in its own Parliament ignoring the South African Government's protest that Apartheid is an internal issue and outsiders have no right to interfere with it? India observed the International Anti-apartheid year in 1978-79.

Even last month (*Indian Express* dated 14.11.1988) our Prime Minister assailed the Developed World saying that Apartheid would have collapsed a long time ago, if the Developed World had not maintained economic and defence relationship with the racist Pretoria regime.

This is what Dr. Ambedkar, the most revolutionary figure in modern India, has stated about the untouchables:

"The Romans had their slaves, the Spartans their helots, the British their Jews. So, the Hindus have their untouchables. But none of these can be said to have been called upon to face the fate which is worse than the fate of the untouchables. Slavery, serfdom, villeinage have all vanished. But untouchability still exists and bids fair to last as long as Hinduism. The untouchable is worse off than a Jew. The sufferings of the Jew are his own creation. Not so are the sufferings of the Black Untouchables. They are the result of a cold, calculating Hinduism which is not less sure in its effect of producing misery than brute force is. The Jew is despised but is not denied all opportunities to rise. Yet nobody seems to take any notice of the Untouchables muchless espouse their cause"

In his anguish he has also stated :

"Indians have not written about Untouchables for they lack courage and honesty and the foreigners have avoided the subject for fear for offending the orthodox Indian masses".

In some quarters a distinction is sought to be made between apartheid in South Africa and untouchability and the consequent denial of human rights to and the oppression and cruel treatment of the untouchables in India on the ground that whereas in South Africa Apartheid is practiced and permitted by law, in India Untouchability has been abolished by the Constitution and the Civil Rights Act and Anti-Untouchability laws have been passed against the practice of untouchability and acts of denial of human rights law and Untouchability and acts of denial of human rights and of aggression are practised and committed against the Scheduled Castes and Tribes in India are graver than those of the Blacks in South Africa. The responsibility of the Government and the people in India vis-a-vis the sufferings of the Scheduled Castes and Tribes does not cease by the mere fact that certain laws have been passed in this country. Therefore, the fact that the constitution has abolished untouchability on paper and the not seriously enforced Civil Rights Act and Anti-untouchability laws have been passed in this Country would hardly render the problem of the Scheduled Castes and Tribes in India is an internal problem and not an international one.

If Apartheid is not the internal problem of the South African Government, the problem of untouchables in India, which is far worse, cannot be the internal problem of India. If India could condemn Apartheid in the World Bodies and call upon the Developed World not to maintain economic and defence relationship with the racist Pretoria regime, there can be no reason why the problem of the Untouchables in India could be said to be an internal problem of India and that it cannot be raised and discussed in the World Bodies. Therefore, the reason for India refusing to accede to the Optional Protocol of the United Nations Organisation is either that India considers that there is no violation of the Human Rights of the Untouchables in India or that it considers the problem to be so bad as to be not in its interest to be discussed in World Bodies. It is necessary to recall what Dr. B.R. Ambedkar has stated :

"On January 26, 1950, we will have equality in politics and inequality in social and economic life. We must remove this contradiction at the earliest moment or else those who suffer from the inequality will blow up the structure of political democracy"

He has further stated :

"The Hindus practice injustice and tyranny against Untouchables only because they are weak. Firstly untouchables cannot face social and religious persecution so long as they remain weak and divided. Secondly, they do not possess enough strength to face the tyranny. With those two conclusions, the third one automatically follows. That is the strength required to face the tyranny needs to be procured from outside".

The Untouchables in India, have, by now, come to know their rights and are no longer prepared to bear their sufferings any more. The youth of these Classes are awakened and are trying to assert their rights. The Scheduled Castes and Tribes cannot continue in the present state of suppression and degradation. I appeal to the Government of India and the State Governments to raise and take a real, active and abiding interest in the upliftment of these classes and the World bodies for action to remove their Human Rights violations by raising the issue before the United Nations Organisation as done by Mrs. Jeanne Kirkpatrik, United States Ambassador to the United Nations Organisation, for which we thank her.

Though the United Nations Organisation cannot force Governments to change their practices or policies and persuasion is the only tool available to it for bringing about improvements in respect of human rights, the General Assembly, the Trusteeship Council, the International Court of Justice and the Economic and Social Council deal with Human Rights in one way or another. The Organisation's opposition to racial discrimination dates back to the United Nations Charter and the Universal Declaration of Human Rights. This has been repeated in successive resolutions of the General Assmebly, which in 1963 adopted the Declaration on the Elimination of All Forms of Racial Discrimination. In 1965, it adopted the International Convention on the Elimination of All Forms of Racial Discrimination. The Committee on the Elimination of Racial Discrimination was set up in 1969 under the convention to consider reports by State Parties on the measures adopted by them for implementation. The General Assembly has created four voluntary Funds–the United Nations Trust Fund for South Africa, the United Nations Educational and Training Programme for Southern Africa, the Trust Fund for Publicity against Apartheid and the Fund for the Victims of Apartheid which is administered by the Council for Namibia. In 1973 the General Assembly adopted the International Convention on the suppression and punishment of the crime of Apartheid and opened it for signature by Member States. The United Nations has sponsored or co-sponsored World Conference and Seminars on how to eliminate apartheid. In 1981, the International Conference on sanctions against South Africa called for further International action to isolate South Africa.

In 1985 the Security Council urged Member States to adopt a number of economic measures against the Racist Regime. Africa was held, and the Declaration adopted by the Conference called for a World Wide Comprehensive System of mandatory sanctions for bringing an end to apartheid in South Africa and against the Country illegally occupying Namibia and attacking neighbouring states. These are but a few of the many steps taken by the World Body. The Organisation has been rendering commendable service for the emancipation of the discriminated people of the World. I salute the world Body in appreciation and appeal to it to intensify its sanctions against discrimination in the World, especially India.

I also appeal to the Scheduled Castes and Tribes, especially the youth, to rise and revolt against the evils to which they are subjected in the name of caste and untouchability. Educate and organize themselves, and agitate unitedly for their birth right in this our country. We should not remain content with reservation in Government services alone, but should strive to engage in business and industry.

5

The Caste System and Human Rights Violation

Dr. R.M. Pal

There is now a general acceptance of the 1948 statement Universal Declaration of Human Rights, adopted by the UN General Assembly as a common standard of achievement for all peoples and all nations. That human rights include civil and political rights, as also economic, social and cultural rights is clear from the subsequently adopted two international Covenants (legally binding on those countries who have become a party to these Covenants)—*The International Covenant on Economic, Social and Cultural Rights, and The International Covenant on Civil and Political Rights.*

The very first two Articles of the 1948 Declaration make it clear that freedom, equality and fraternity are the very basis of human rights. According to Article I, "All human beings are born free and equal in dignity and rights. They are endowed with reason and conscience and should act towards one another in a spirit of brotherhood." According to Article 2, "Everyone is entitled to all the rights and freedoms set forth in this Declaration, without distinction of any kind, such as race, colour, sex, language, religion, political or other opinion, national or social origin, property, birth or other status..." It is therefore clear that any system–social, political, religious–which is in contradiction with the values set forth in the Declaration, violates human rights.

It is in this context that we may examine the caste system which has sanctioned indignities to be heaped on a section–a very large section indeed–of our population, with a view to pointing out how the system is in contradiction with what the Declaration and other Covenants state. It is not possible to go into a detailed examination of the system because of constraint of space. In any case it is hardly necessary to enumerate this in details. I, however mentioned the main characteristics of the system, as divinely sanctioned in the Gita and also in Manusmriti. Lord Krishna tells Arjunal (I quote), "The works of *Brahmins*, Kshatriyas, Vaishyas and *Shudras* are different... The work of find joy in their work... Greater in thine own work, even if this be humble, then the work of another, even if this be great. When a man does the work of another, even if this be humble, then the work of another, even if this be great. When a man does the work God gives him, no sin can touch this man. And a man should not abandon his work... Because thou art in the bondage of Karma, of the forces of thine own past life; and that which thou, in thy delusion, with a good will does not want to do, unwillingly thou shall have to do."

Our society is thus based on this hierarchical order in which social hierarchy is determined by birth–under divine sanction. (I should, however, add at once that social hierarchies and occupation based on heredity exist in other societies also, but this divinely sanctioned one is exclusively ours).

We all know about the intellectual and moral support that has been given to the caste system by the doctrine of *varna-vyavastha*. There have been any number of sophisticated commentaries by scholars and social analysts who have asserted that the system has served very useful purpose in India. In fact, you cannot be a scholar if you take the ground realities into account! In any case I haven't inclination to reply to all these arguments which rationalise the irrational. However, go a little deep, and you won't fail to observe that most of our scholars, both ancient and modern, have almost always practised the art–successfully–of rationalising the irrational–in fact the modern have practised this art with the vengeance.

Let us now have a quick glance at what our recognised law-giver Manu has prescribed for us: Brahma created the Brahmin, the Kshatriya, the Vaishya and the Shudra from his mouth, his arms, his thighs, and his feet respectively; and this Brahma did "for the sake of the prosperity of the world". He assigned separate duties and occupations to them, and that, too, Brahma did to "protect" this universe. The first three were created for teaching, protecting, citizens, trading lending money on interest, etc. and the *Shudras* were created by Brahma for serving the first three *varnas* without being critical of them. *Shudras* (and also women belonging to all *varnas*) are not allowed to study. *The Dalits* are described as *varna-sankara* born out of the intermixture of the "pure" *varnas*). They are outside the system–they are the outcasts.

I have already referred to Article 1 of the Universal Declaration (i.e. all human beings are born free and equal in dignity and rights), and plainly and simply our caste system is inconsistent with the provisions of the Article, for our system gives different status to different persons on the basis of birth; some of the unprivileged ones are treated as the untouchables. Denial of education to some people including women violates Article 26(1), according to which, "everyone has the right to education...".

Our system requires a person to join the occupation of the caste to which he is born, and this violates Articles 23(1) which states, Everyone has the right to work, to free choice of employment, to just and favourable conditions of work and protection against unemployment. Compulsion of marriage within the caste alone is violative of Article 16(1), which says, "Men and women of full age, without any limitation due to race, nationality or religion, have the right to marry and to found a family. They are entitled to equal rights as to marriage, during the marriage and at its dissolution". Our system does not permit certain sections of the people including women to enter temples, to learn Sanskrit, to read religious books, to be priests, and this goes against Article 18 which prescribes, "Everyone has the right to freedom of thought, conscience and religion; this right to freedom of thought, conscience and religion; this right to freedom to change his religion or belief, and freedom, either alone or in community with others and public or private, to manifest his religion or belief in teaching, practice, worhsip and observance". Some people *(Dalits)* are forced to live in the outkirts of villages and this violates Article 13 (1) which states that "Everyone has the rights to freedom of movement and residence within the borders of each state". There are a number of other prescriptions which one could quote, and which are violative of human rights as enunciated in the Universal Declaration: denial of right to vote violates Article 4. (A begdar, i.e. laborer, generally of lower caste, according to Manusmriti, is obliged to work without payment; if a Brahmin forces a twice-born to work for him, he is to be punished, but if a Brahmin forces a Shudra to work for him, on payment or without payment, he is not to be punished; penance for a Brahmin for killing an animal or a shudra is the same; in fact the killing of a cow is more heinous than killing a shudra).

Apart from the above blatant violations, there are also other violations which are indirectly related to cast system, such as torture, rape and death in custody. Civil liberties and Human Rights (HR) groups have published any number of reports about such cruelties. Those of you who read the PUCL Bulletin would know that different units of PUCL have investigated into a large number of incidents of violence against Dalits and adivasis and have given detailed accounts of how they have been frequently tortured and raped, and killed in custody, by police and others in collusion with police. Many of you perhaps know that even today there are many places in the country where a Dalit girl is obliged to sleep with the village landlord on the first night of her wedding.

Now, we are told that the malpractice does not exist anymore or has started disappearing. Well, I don't know; in any case, I'm not sure that caste identities have disappeared even from metropolitan cities, not to speak of the rest of the country. There is no limit in our country to holding up a fiction to obscure facts. Let us refresh our memory–our memory is very short, and that too conveniently–about what happened in north India during the anti-reservation stir? In Delhi University, where the anti-reservation stir started, it was impossible to remind people that a coin has two sides. Even the Vice-Chancellor who always likes to be known as a human rights activist spoke in a language of "either or neither nor" and desired the faculties to give their opinion on the subject, even though he was not called upon by anyone to do so. Anyone who was for Mandal was not allowed to speak in any meeting; even invited speakers were turned out from a meeting in Delhi School of Economics which is known as the citadel of Marxism. The Delhi University Teachers' Association took up Mandal on trade union level and waged a regular warfare. During my long association with the University I'm unable to recollect any other occasion when the teachers' body ever took up similar issues. In a meeting of the Academic Council of the University, to discuss an item on reservation for SC/ST candidates, some faculty members received thunderous applause when they declared that "Mother goddess Saraswati's clothes will be desecrated" if SC/ST candidates became teachers. Many of the banners put up in colleges in Delhi, mostly by women students in women's colleges, expressed their fear that if Mandal were introduced they'd be compelled to marry SC/ST boys. Even some radical humanist colleagues of the well-known activist Mr.Tarkunde, and communists and Marxists–quite a few of them my colleagues–maddening upset, if not wild, and became the best examples of how thoughtful people could think so thoughtlessly. Many life-long friends have now stopped being on even speaking terms! does anybody really believe that the stir was against reservation? Everyone knows that the stir was engineered by the upper castes to maintain the status quo; they would fight back any movement and struggle for human rights and social justice by the depressed. They made it known that it is insult to their person if they saw any SC/ST walk with their heads erect on their shoulders. The north Indian middle class (Rajni Kothari calls this class "lumpenished") felt threatened, not because they would be deprived of jobs, but because their caste identities were at stake. The "lumpenised" class made it clear that those who do not belong to the twice-born castes must respectfully submit to the norms that have been prescribed by our ancient law-makers and holy scriptures. And yet, look at the hypocrisy–no political party was opposed to reservation, and yet they lent their support to it; in fact, some of the parties funded the stir ! You should have been in Delhi to see what happened on the day when V.P.Singh resigned–Diwali was celebrated that night–throughout the night; it is nobody's concern that none could sleep that night. Nineteen per cent of the population had waged a war and won the battle; social justice and human rights paled into insignificance.

The real issue relates to the institution of caste which has been a stumbling block for social justice and human rights; and a clear acknowledgement of the fact that every human being given favourable conditions is capable of developing unlimited powers of intellect and will, and that those conditions have not yet been created for those who deserve them the most.

We have any number of do-gooders amongst us. They would have us believe that since the Constitution has abolished untouchability and has made special provisions for the uplift of SC/STs, and now for OBCs, there is nothing more that needs to be done. Rapid increase of crimes committed against Dalits, however, tell a different story which unfortunately not many of our countrymen, not even human rights groups, are willing to take note of. Some do-gooders when confronted with this fact suggest that if there are more judges from amongst SC/STs things would be allright. Yet others like Swami Agnivesh have prescribed that SC/STs must be given arms to teach a lesson to the upper castes and the evils of the system, but not the system, will disappear! And the system must not be disturbed. I don't know of many do-gooders who are prepared to look beyond the constitutional provisions (which has not yet made any dent) and look at the system with a view to dismantling it. There are some liberals Gandhians with many of whom I hope to work, and quite a few of them are my friends who follow the Christian dictum, namely that, a gentleman is one who does not inflict pain on others. Yes, they don't inflict pain on SC/STs, indeed they are ashamed of the fact that this kind of discrimination exists in our society. These well-intentioned people who cherish two values of democracy suggest that there should be a vigorous reformist movement, along with the implementation of constitutional provisions, to do away with the malpractice. But the sad story is that until now, all attempts to reform the Brahmanical religion, including religious and social reformist movements, have failed.

Buddha tried and appeared to succeed but only to be "expelled" from the country. Nanak, Kabir and Chaitanya also made brave attempts—the results are for all to see. During the British regime, a number of reformists fought relentlessly. And yet, no less a man than Ishwar Chandra Vidyasagar at one stage, while fighting the cause of widow-remarriage, got so exasperated by the cunning arguments put forward by Sanskrit scholars and Pandits against widow-remarriage, that Vidyasagar felt constrained to exclaim in utter disgust: "In a country where men have no sensitivity, let not unfortunate woman be born there. Oh, women, what sin have you committed that you should have been born in India!" It is also painful to add that Mahatma Gandhi's valiant efforts and life-long struggle came to nothing – and it is sad, indeed. All these liberals wanted to see an end to this cruel discrimination that exist in our society, but without touching the basic structure of the system.

How can one think of remedying the situation without questioning the very authority that has sanctioned this impregnable wall? The absence of sensitivity and concern for human rights and social justice are contradictions in terms to which I have referred in relation to some of the Articles of the Universal Declaration. Let us not pretend that the system has vanished from our society. We must accept the ground reality, namely that, even though the Indian constitution is not based on the Manusmriti and the Gita, and has aboilished untouchability and has made provisions for equality before law, the impregnable walls built by the system remain. The constitution has merely prescribed, but has not given any description of the ground reality. We can make a dent only if we reorganise the fact that the caste system is a major source, indeed an obnoxious one, of human rights violations. I for one feel sad that even this recognition is not there, not even amongst many liberals and human rights activists. I feel our activists must pay adequate attention to this aspect of our society, so that the objectives of the Universal Declaration, to celebrate which we have assembled here, become, realizable goal. Constitutional provisions are of course important, but without a philosophical revolution which will ensure uprooting of the system, a change for the better does not appear to be attainable.

Finally, I suppose we could do with a little less arrogance and also a little less hypocrisy-arrogance manifested by the "divine" twice-born; and hypocrisy in all two parties' hailing Dr.Ambedkar and 'owning' him (for reasons which I need hardly elaborate) and yet not, saying a word about eradicating the 'divine system' with a view to bringing about a society where social justice will be realised, when all persons, at last when they are born, will be equal.

6

Human Rights Status of the Dalits

Prof. D.N. Sandanshive

On Dec. 10, 1948 the General Assembly of the United Nations Organisation proclaimed the Universal Declaration of Human Rights. In order to commemorate the day as a landmark in the history of mankind, reassertion of the greatest idea of human rights a gift to the entire humanity, mainly the depressed and suppressed.

Here I analyse the human rights status of the Dalits and to conceive and design a possible futuristic agenda for the Dalit actions and agitations in order to ensure further meaningful development and expansion of the categories of human rights keeping in view the present scenario and emergence of the 21st century within the six years. In the given constraint of time, I would do my best to render justice to the theme on the various aspects.

The oldest human rights organisation – the Anti-Slavery Society was founded in 1839. Slavery was abolished in the British Empire in 1833 and in the United States in 1862. Agrarian slavery in India was abolished in 1843 and untouchability was abolished in 1948. The agrarian slaves were sold and bought with the lands and they were treated as things and not as humanbeings and therefore they had no rights under the system. Abe Dubais in his book: *Hindu Manners, Customs and Ceremonies* has observed that the pariahs were reduced to agrarian slaves and made to suffer severely, as if they were not humans. Untouchability, according to the thesis of Dr. Babasaheb Ambedkar, originated around A.D. 400 out of struggle for supremacy between Buddhism and Brahmanism "which so completely moulded the history of India and the study of which is so woefully neglected by students of

Indian history. The Untouchables in some parts of India were reduced to servitude as agrarian slaves. The origin of agrarian slavery was in their untouchability. Even though agrarian slavery and untouchability are abolished, even now bonded labour still prevails and untouchability is still practised in most parts of India.

Historically and sociologically, the Dalits are the progenies of the Buddhists because our forefathers much before they were reduced to the status of untouchables practised and professed Buddhism. After the decline of Buddhism, the *Brahmins* persecuted and tortured the Buddhists for centuries. The persecution and torture forced the Buddhists to become Muslims. The partition of India in 1947 was the ultimate result of Buddhism in India. Those who did not become Muslims were reduced to the status of Untouchables in the graded Hindu Society. The Hindus denied to the untouchables even elementary civil rights in order to take revenge against them for being Buddhists in the past. The untouchables were foreced to merely exist without rights. The rights are absolutely necessary for the development of any individual. Even then the entire community of Untouchables constituting almost one-sixth of the population of the country were forced to live a rightless life. This is the origin, mechanism and development of untocuhability.

The untouchables were denied the use of public roads, public lakes, wells, admission in schools and entry into the temples. Barbers and washermen refused to render them service. They were treated as sub-humans, less than men, worse than beasts by the Hindus. They were deliberately kept illiterate and ignorant and all public services including police and military were closed to them. They were forced to follow hereditary occupations such as street-sweepers, scavengers and shoemakers. Thus, being deprived of social, religious, economic, educational and civil rights, they had no chance of bettering their conditions. They were born as untouchables, they lived as untouchables and they died as untouchables. The stigma of untouchability persisted from their birth till their death.

Untouchability of the rightless untouchables was sanctified by the Hindu religious scriptures and ruthlessly perpetrated, practised and enforced by the *Brahmins* for their material and political gains. The kind of duties the untouchables were performing had developed an object obedience to the exploiters who were benefited by the untouchables, but who never gave any benefit to the Untouchables. Untouchability implied not only mere denial of rights, but the organised and systemised denial of rights, exlusively on the basis of birth, sanctified by religion and was regarded as divine, natural and eternal as a result of the sins of the past Karma and rebirth as untouchables. Their minds were conditioned to do such work and perform such duties which benefited and supported the hierarchical social order evolved for the selfish ends of the *Brahmins*.

Nowhere in the world any country had in the course of social development devised a system of Untouchability which was an off shoot of the poisonous branch of the caste system, rooted in Vedicdharma, of Chaturvarna as it was done by the *Brahmins* in India. Peculiar to this country, untouchability epitomised an immoral, unethical, unjust and reprehensible woes of Indin culture and civilisation.

Phule, Ambedkar and Periyar E. V. Ramaswami had inherited such a social system, in the strangle-hold in which lived the rightless human Untouchables. Phule established the first school in 1848 for the untouchables in Poona. Ambedkar asserted the right to drinking water at the Mahad Chavdar Lake in 1927. Thanthai Periar burnt the Manu Smirti in 1924. Ambedkar repeated the feat in 1927. These daring acts of those great leaders were the first signs of the assertion of human rights of the Untouchables. Ambedkar succeeded in the Round Table conferences in placing the plight of untouchables and their claims for social, economic, civil and political rights on the world agenda. The Hindu leaders had to be defensive. The Communal Award declared by the British Prime Minister recognised the separate electorate to the untouchables. Gandhiji protested and went on a fast unto death. The political deadlock was resolved by the Poona Pact of 1932. But one fact emerged through this battle between Ambedkar and Gandhi. That fact was the recognition of untouchables as a group which was denied human rights and who needed constitutional and legal recognition of their human rights. This happened hardly sixty two years ago. Ambedkar succeeded in restoring humanity to the untouchables. He had performed a man-making mission. He came out triumhantly in making the Constitution of India on the basis of individuals and granting fundamental rights to all citizens. Thus, he transformed the untouchables into citizens of a republic by the constitution of India in 1950. He was the Chief Architect of the Constitution.

The rightless unotuchables have now become citizens entitled to the human rights. The story of human rights status of the Dalits thus began 44 years ago. Most of us born as Untouchables became citizens with the entitlement of rights since 1950. Before the constitution came into force, the British Government had granted certain concessions, and provided with some safegards to the untouchables. They were mainly with regard to access to education and public services. Some progressive princely states like Mysore and Baroda had also done good work in facilitating the progress of the untouchables.

Untouchability is abolished by Article 17 of the Constitution and the untouchabes are defined as the scheduled castes under Artilce 366 (24) read with Article 341 for the purposes of the Constitution. Besides the fundamental rights as their entitlements as citizen, the Constitution guarantees them protective discrimination and provides affirmative actions programmes in the matters of three types of reservations. One, reservations of seats in educational institutions; two, reservations in services under the State and three, reservations of seats in Parliament and the State Legislatures. Educational and service reservations have no time limit. But political reservations was originally intended only for ten years. However, it was extended from time to time at the end of every ten years from 1960. It is to lapse by 2000 A.D. However indications are, it will be again extended by ten years. Besides the fundamental rights, the Directive Principals of State Policy clearly impose the duty on the State to secure social justice to the Scheduled Castes. The fundamental rights are justiciable and the Directive Principles though non-justiciable are still enforceable as they impose the duty on the State to apply them, while laws are made in order to secure social and economic justice. Primacy of the Directive Principles over the fundamenal rights is broadly recognised by the Judiciary. For the Dalits, the Directive Principles are more fundamental than the Fundamental Rights, because the state is required by the Constitution to create environment conducive by implementing the principles for the purpose of the enjoyment of the rights.

The Scheduled Castes are given a new label since early seventies as the Dalits. The label has changed, but the stigma of untouchability still persists in various forms. Untouchability is abolished only in law, but not in practise.

Rights of men are not only against the Government, but against the people collectively. Humanity is one enormous extended family with all the obligations of family membership. Both the government and the people are responsible for the Dalit mobility, advancement, emancipation, and empowerment.

The Constitution has given a definition to the people who were Untouchables. Therefore, the Dalits are a definable group. The Constitution has also provided a safety net to the Dalits and Income Tax provides a ladder for their upper mobility and higher integration into the mainstream of society. The activist state is to enforce protections, safeguards and promote the rights of the Dalits. Social Darwinism is shunned by the Constitution.

The test of human rights is not whether the prosperous, with access to the law courts, are well-protected, or whether living standars for the majority are improving, but whether the weak are helped by the strong. Paul Sieghart once remarked, "The ultimate measure of whether a society can properly be called civilized is how it treats those who are near the bottom of its human heap." Measured by this test Indian civilzation can hardly be called civilization as despite more than four dcades of operation of a Republic Constitution the Dalits are even now at the bottom of the social pyramid. Their poverty is still staggering, illiteracy is more wide spread, unemployment is massive, housing conditions are undesirable and their exploitation goes on as usual as before.

Dr. Babasaheb Ambedkar had administered the words of admonition in 1949 while speaking in the Constituent Assembly:

> "We must make our political democracy a social democracy as well. Political democracy cannot last unless there lies at the base social democracy. What does social democracy mean? It means a way of life which recognizes liberty, equality and fraternity as the principles of life."

He further Said:

> "On the 26th January, 1950, we are going to enter into a life of contradictions. In politics we will have equality and in social and economic life we will have inequality.... We must remove this contradiction at the earliest possible moment or else, those who suffer from inequaltiy will blow up the structure of political democracy which this Assembly has so laboriously built up."

It is now common knowledge that social justice is an objective of the Constitution and social justice demands preferential treatment to the Dalits in order to correct the historical imbalance existing in our society. Human rights are a means for securing justice. Enforcement of Directive Principles by the state is meant to create conducive environment of use and exercise of human rights. If such suitable conditions are not created by the State for the Dalits, human rights will remain merely as paper rights to them.

Human rights operate in a social milieu and cannot exist in a cultural and economic vacuum. They are understood and respected to the extent of the educational and economic level of society. It is a noble maxim that it is better for a man to go wrong in freedom, rather than go right in chains, but it sounds like empty rhetoric to the Dalits who still live in economic and social chains.

Every society is divided into a dominant class and a dominated class. But in all societies, excepting Indian society, the division is based on the economic conditions and it is not fixed, rigid and sanctified by religion and enforced ruthlessly after deprivation of humanhood of humans. But the contrary happened in India. Therefore, the claim of India to be one of the oldest civilizations and cultures suffers from the inhuman, cruel and evil social practises. Untouchability was one such cruel practise. Some call it an aberration and others as unfortunate development and only the congenitally incorrigible defend untouchability. And no sane person can justify and defend untouchability though the Sankaracharya of Dwarka once publicly said that it was eternal and natural. The Dalits had then condemned him. But no *Shastris* and *Pandits* condemned the objectionable and criminal statement of the Shankaracharya.

In spite of an egalitarian facade and legislative State and affirmative action programmes, the deprivation of the Dalits of use and enjoyment of rights still continues. Now the Dalits have rights, but they cannot enjoy and exercise these rights; social justice, economic equality and educational development are still a distant dream to the Dalits. The Dalits are still at the bottom of social pyramid and the official view is paternalistic in its attitude towards Dalits. Dr. Ambedkar was conscious of this fact. Like the Constitution, his concerns were radically different. For him the priority was not how to integrate the social reform sub-agenda into the freedom struggle the overwhelming goal to which all other objectives must be subordinated. It was how to give centrality to social justice and social welfare agenda as part of building a new, equal, free, open, non-hierarchical modern India. He had no interest whatever in making Hinduism and Hindu society shine forth. He had already changed the course and adopted and taken a route of conversion of the Dalits to Buddhism. For, he wanted the hierarchical social structure to be destroyed and he had planned to rebuild a casteless and classless society on the principles of liberty equality and fraternity as envisaged in the Constitution and contained in the social doctrine of Budhism. He wanted the Dalits to be elevated and integated on a higher social plane, economic development and political empowerment. For he know that democracy in India was merely a top dressing on the undemocratic social order.

Let it be mentioned that untouchability in the sense of touch me 'notism' has been vanishing under the pressure of modern development in all walks of life. But untouchability still persists in varied forms. The caste Hindus invent and change forms of observance of untouchability. Its practise is overt or covert, visible or invisible, crude or sophisticated, but practised, it is, with ingenuity, is a fact of life. And the practise of untouchabiltiy makes the human rights status of the Dalits doubtful and meaningless. They need the State support strongly to enjoy human rights. But the State is found faltering in supporting the Dalits in respect of exercise of their rights. The State support can make the human rights status of Dalits meaningful.

Violence and atrocities against the Dalits are increasing and not decreasing. Discriminations are practised in countless number. Researches have shown a close correlation between levels and targets of violence and discrimination and relative degree of upward mobility among Dalits. Subtle and invisible humiliation and discrimination practised by the Hindu intellectuals, bureaucracy, judiciary, police, political executives and politicians against the Dalits in the cities and towns are far more dangerous and destructive mentally and psychologically. Artocities in the rural India are becoming more pronounced in the form of revenge against the self-respect and self-elevation shown by the Dalits. In my opinion mere legislative measures cannot and would not protect the Dalits because of improper and biased enforcement of laws by the Hindu officers. Therefore, the Dalits must have their own organisations. The Dalit Liberation Movement and the Dalit Lawyers Associations in Madras are representing the need of the hour.

To a great extent the Dalit intelligentsia have played a decisive role in integrating the Dalit masses through Dalit literature and folk culture in a dynamic community. Through their literary works and organisational activities, they have spread far and wide across the country the democratic ideology, rational outlook and human rights consciousness to the level of the Dalit masses. However, the Dalits are still taken for granted and they are being manipulated by the government and the politicans. The Dalit Organisations and voluntary agencies have to zealously guard against unjust policies, improper enforcement of programmes and unscrupulous politicians and they have to ensure the effective and prompt implementation of affirmative action programmes.

Dr. Ambedkar was awfully aware of these problems and therefore, he preached the grand universal law that liberty is never recognised as a gift. It has to be fought for. Self-elevation is not achieved by the blessings of others, but only by one's own struggle and deed. The Dalits lacked courage and needed a vision and a mission. Dr. Ambedkar gave them courage, a vision and a mission. He was driving them to action by acting himself. He was inspiring them to fight battle for their human rights. He argued. "If all these communities are to be brought to the level of equality, then the only remedy is to adopt the prin ciple of inequality and to give favoured treatment to those who are below the level."

He held that equality meant raising the level of the lower classes to the level of the higher classes. He warned the Dalits that education alone would not solve their problems. They should join political agitations and get political power in their own hands in order to secure their human rights and redress their economic and social grievances by law and political policy. Nothing could be achieved, he said, if the Dalits did not adopt an aggressive attitude and prove by their thoughts, words and deeds that they would not tolerate insults and disabilities any more. Further, they must create fear in the minds of those who ill-treat them. That alone would dishearten and demoralise their tormentors. He told the Dalits:

"What you have lost others have gained. Your humilia tions are a matter of pride with others. You are made to suffer wants, privations and humiliations not be cause it was preordained by the sins committed in your previous birth, but because of overpowering tyranny and treachery of those who are above you. You have no lands because others have usurped them. You have no posts because others have monopolised them. Do not believe in fate. Believe in your strength."

I would like to emphatically point out and clearly impress upon you that the significance of the human rights cannot be understood by you unless you realise and accept that you are human beings like the *Brahmins*. You have dignity, self-respect and brains like the *Brahmins*. You can achieve excellence in any field of knowledge as the *Brahmins* claim they have achieved excellence in various fields of knowledge. I know that you need opportunities. Opportunities were denied to you because rights were denied to you. You have no good environment? I say create with your own efforts a good environment. You have no tradition of learning? I say you create your own tradition of learning. You can be the masters of your own development, change and empowerment. You can fortify your human rights status and impart meaning and life to the rights granted to you under the Constitution. If the State fails to support you, make the State do so because it is under constitutional obligation.

You demand the enforcement of your collective rights provided under the Directive Principles of State policy. Tell the Government that the days of charity are over. It is now the era of your rights and the Government is duty bound to act for the Dalits under the Constitution.

Rights will not be given to you by others. Opportunities will not be given to you on a silver platter. You have to grab the rights and the opportunities. You have to create such conditions as will make others start admiring you ultimately. I want you not to believe in the Hindu Karma doctrine and the sins of previous birth theory. Believe in your self-efforts and raise yourself on the social plane. Nothing is impossible collectively. You have to unite, educate and agitate until the goal of social justice is attained. That is the real message of this day. Remember that mere declaration of human rights is useless unless those who have rights are vigilant to use and exercise the rights. It is true to say that the eternal vigilance is the price of liberty. Human rights may be summed up in one word liberty. Isaiah Berlin noted that there are more than 200 definitions of liberty. A Dalit definition of liberty is emancipation, empowerment and integration of the Dalits on the higher levels in Indian Society. You have to use liberty for this definite goal. Liberty is merely a means to achieve your goal.

I would now like to proceed to itemise the futuristic agenda for the Dalit empowerment and higher integration:

(1) The fact is that until the humanitarian efforts for educating the Untouchables were made, education was monopolised by the *Brahmins* for their selfish ends. Now the State decides the education policy under the Constitution. Under the present law, education is free, but not compulsory and there is no policy of retention of students with the education system. Adequate scholarships are not given to the Dalit students. Moreover, the education policy is unequal and iniquitious. As a result illiteracy of people is very high, the rate of drop-outs of students is mind-boggling and the Dalits get low quality of education. A demand, therefore, should be made to revise and modernize the education policy. Unless the Dalits get quality education with adequate financial support, they will continue to remain poor, but illiterate Dalits will remain always poor. For poverty removal, quality education is necessary. It is proved now that education is the most effective contraceptive against population explosion. Therefore, a demand to give equal and quality education to the Dalits is justified and can not be opposed on any ground.

(2) Historically, the Dalits were isolated and forced to live in the miserable conditions of insufficient accommodation and insanitary surroundings. An exclusive Hostel System for the Dalit students was, therefore, conceived and developed. The system has revealed many deficiencies and flaws. It needs to be abolished. The mixed hostel system must be developed in order to provide a wider exposure to the Dalit students for increasing competitiveness and social integration on the higher place. In a new system, the bills for food, clothes, books and stationery should be paid directly to the suppliers by the Government treasury and a minimum attendance of 75% of the classes held be made compulsory and the Dalit Students should be held accountable for the performance in their examinations. The successful students must be rewarded and the failures punished suitably.

(3) The policy of reservations in services has provided jobs to suitable Dalits, but it has failed in many respects. Firstly, it has alienated some, made others docile and those who serve with self-respect are harassed and discriminated against. Secondly, reservation quotas are not faithfully filled in and a bogie of merit and efficiency is raised without empirical studies. Thirdly, the Mandal judgement has deprived the Dalits of initial recruitments for some posts and promotions for all posts without hearing them. Fourthly, with the new economic policy and privatisation of industry, job opportunities under the State are shrinking and the policy of reservation of seats is not applicable to the private sector. Fifthly, the market economy is a curse to the Dalits unless they become consumers by securing jobs in the employment market. All these grounds call for a review of the policy of reservation in services under the State. A suitable constitutional amendmend and an enactment on reservation in services in public and private sectors and under the State placed in the Nineth Schedule of the Constitution alone will solve the accumulated problems and enable the Dalits to secure adequate representation in the services.

(4) The studies have shown that the Dalit politicians have failed the Dalits. Once elected they and their party men do not represent Dalit interests and claims, but work under the party discipline in order to get ministerial berths and tickets for the

next elections. Therefore, the Dalits should have the right to call-back the Dalit legislators in order to make them accountable. This demand would need a constitutional amendment.

(5) The new economic policy has serious repercussions to the Dalits in many respects. The policy has failed to resolve the accumulated problems of poverty, illiteracy, unemployment and low standards of living of the Dalits. No specific conditions for use and exercise of human rights by the Dalits have been so far created and the active role of the state in creating necessary conditions and also in determining the priorities of economic development and of economic equality is willfully ignored and neglected. It is obvious that the new economic policy has deviated from the constitutional goals of socio-economic justice. The Dalits are the most obvious sufferers of such unscrupulous attitude of the government. A demand for implementation of the Directive Principles of State policy must, therefore, be voiced. Such a demand is justified because the fundamental rights are to the individuals what the Directive Principles are to the deprived communities like the Dalits. And it is the duty of the State to implement them for securing socio-economic justice.

The above are some items of the future agenda for the Dalits. I expect a debate and actions, if need be, agitations on these and other relevant items which would determine the Dalit future. I would like to impress upon you that silence nourishes oppression. The Dalits have suffered more than enough. They have to rediscover their humanity by reassertion of human rights. They can even, if situation demands, approach the National Human Rights Commission for the purpose of enforcement of the constitutional guarantees of human rights. We have also to activise the National Commission for the Scheduled Castes and the Scheduled Tribes. Let it be brought in the centrality of the Dalit activities for securing social justice. You must be convinced that if the Dalits were to accomplish their mission of empowerment it would not be as a result of any liberation of attitudes among the Hindus but rather in spite of their opposition.

Dr. Ambedkar gave the Dalits human rights status. Now it is for the Dalits to assert the rights bestowed on them. I hope they will do so by their own right in order to elevate their social status, so that they become the competitive participants in the various processes of decision-making and development and change in our society.

The strength of a chain lies in the weakest of its links. As long as the Dalits remain weak, democracy in India would remain weak and the nation unstable. The economic development without human face and social justice would be tantamount to violation of the Constitution. If the Government fails to give justice to the Dalits, then the National Human Rights Commission must intervene and the SC/ST Commission must act on behalf of the Dalits. If these Commisssions also fail, then the Dalits shall not tolerate injustice any longer.

There is one universal law. That law is justice. Justice social, economic and political-forms the cornerstone of our Constitution. Therefore, the duty-bound government should implement the constitutional directive of social justice in order to achieve the goal of empowerment of the Dalits so that their human rights status is invested with actual benefits and gains as their entitlements.

7

President of India— Speaks to the Nation

Dr. K.R. Narayanan

Fellow-citizens, on the eve of the golden jubilee of our republic I have the privilege to extend to all Indians living in India or abroad, my heartiest greetings and felicitation. I also send my greetings to the brave personnel of our armed forces who stand guard to defend the unity and territorial integrity of the nation. And I pay my homage to the memory of those who laid down their lives in the defence of the republic from external aggression and intermittent terrorist attacks across the border.

On this solemn occasion our thoughts go back to the father of the nation who lived and died for the freedom and unity of our nation, and to the countless men and women who followed him into the arena and faced immense hardships and sufferings in the heroic struggle for independence. Our thoughts also go back to the founding fathers of our constitution whose far-sighted vision and arduous labours gave us a constitution which enshrined the traditional concepts of liberty, equality and fraternity adding to them the concept of justice-social, economic and political and declaring our nation a sovereign democratic republic.

President Dr. K. R. Narayanan delivered the Republic Day speech on 26.01.2000 which was radically different from the usual ceremonial and traditional speechs. Dr. Narayanan came out strongly on the problems faced by the Dalits, Tribals and Women in our society. His comments on the privileged sections which are opposed to reservations and the need for continuing with affirmative action deserves wide publicity.

The word 'republic' is no ordinary word. It is a commitment to the effect that, in our state, supreme power is exercised not by some remote monarch but by the people. It is an affirmation that the wielder of power in India the *adhinayaka* is the great aggregation of our people as a whole, whom Rabindranth Tagore has immortalized as the *jana-gana*. Let us, on this anniversary, hail that proclamation and commitment. Let us celebrate the exceptional status we enjoy, the status of being the world's largest democracy. Given the chequered career of democracies elsewhere, we can be grateful to be citizens of this republic: where an individual, be he ever so high, the constitution and the laws made by the people remain higher than him; and where the executive remains accountable to parliament.

Thanks to our early and visionary support to science and technology we have made advances in that field as would excite human imagination anywhere; thanks to our kisans and mazdoors and entrepreneurs, the wheels of our agriculture, commerce and industry turn steadily with the world; and thanks, above all, to the striving of our agricultural communities, our granaries remain full.

From the 1970s when our GDP grew at only around 3.5 per annum, the economic growth rate has accelerated to around 6.5 per cent. It is not generally realized that in the 1990s, India has become one of the 10 fastest growing economies in the world. We can be justly proud of the abundance of our entrepreneurial ability, the high levels of domestic private savings, and also of the high level of managerial and technical skills. All these have enabled our economic reforms to have a solid and a stable base for further and more rapid growth. This is a day when we take pride in our achievements, but it must surely also be a day of honest self analysis and self-questioning about where we, as a people and a society, are headed.

Fifty years into our life in the republic we find that justice-social, economic and political-remains an unrealized dream for millions of our fellow-citizens. The benefits of our economic growth are yet to reach them. We have one of the world's largest reservoirs of technical personnel, but also the largest number of people below the poverty line, and the largest number of children suffering from malnutrition. Our giant factories rise from out of squalor; our satellites shoot up from the midst of the hovels of the poor. Not surprisingly, there is sullen resentment among the masses against their condition, erupting often in violent forms in several parts of the country.

Tragically, the growth in our economy has not been uniform. It has been accompanied by great regional and social inequalities. Many a social upheaval can be traced to the neglect of the lowest tier of society, whose discontent moves towards the path of violence. Dalits and tribals are the worst affected by this. In parts of rural India forms of sadism seem to be earmarked for dalit women. From the time of Draupadi our womenfolk had been subjected to public disrobing and humiliation as a means of vendetta–individual, social or political. For dalit women it has become a common experience in rural areas; but what is astounding is that it has been extended as one of the methods of ragging in our elite colleges and universities.

To open a newspaper or to hear the news over television now requires nerves of steel. Violence in society has bared a hundred fangs as advertisement driven consumerism is unleashing frustrations and tensions in our society. The unabashed, vulgar indulgence in conspicuous consumption by the *nouveau riche* has left the under class seething in frustration.

One half of our society guzzles aerated beverages while the other has to make do with palmfuls of muddied water. Our three-way fast lane of liberalization, privatization and globalization must provide safe pedestrian crossings for the unempowered India also, so that it too can move towards equality of status and opportunity. "Beware of the fury of the patient man, "says the old adage. One could say, "beware of the fury of the patient and long-suffering people." We cannot and ought not halt the movement in the trajectories of our modern progress. Factories will and must rise, satellites must and will soar to the heavens, and dams over rivers will rise to prevent floods, generate electricity and irrigate dry lands for cultivation. But that should not cause ecological and environmental devastation, and the uprooting of human settlements, especially of tribals and the poor. Ways and methods can be found for countering the harmful impact of modern technology on the lives of the common people.

I believe that the answer to the ill-effects of science and technology is not to turn our back on technology, but to have more science and technology that is directed to human needs and for the betterment of the human condition. While the Government must be held responsible for the environmental and human consequences of mega projects, the responsibility for environmental protection cannot however lie with the Government alone. It must also be borne by civil society. There is a need to improve the tone of our social and economic life through an improved work ethic and environmental behaviour. Far too many of us lack the professional pride to see a task well performed, a responsibility well borne.

Accountability in the delivery of public services is shockingly low. One reason why our infrastructure remains weak is that the quality of civil work executed is poor compromised by sub-standard materials, corrupt practices and sloppy supervision. We ignore the social dimensions of our actions and practices. The late Dr. Malcolm Adiseshiah, one of our prominent economists and academicians, wrote about his mother that she was a high-born lady who kept her house spotlessly clean. Every morning she used to sweep and clean the household herself and then dump the rubbish in the neighbour's garden.

Self-regarding purity and righteousness ignoring others has been the bane of our culture. It has created a gulf in our society between people even with regard to the basic needs and fundamental rights. For example, water is a basic need and a fundamental right of the people are struggling to get adequate clean drinking water. Less than 150 years ago, there was hardly any Government sponsored water supply scheme in India. But India had a long standing strong tradition of water management, which was built on the technology of rainwater harvesting. Not only does that tradition still survive in the northeast and a Himalayan region like Ladakh, but remnants of that tradition can be found in Tamil Nadu, Andhra Pradesh, Karnataka, Rajasthan and other states. There is no reason why we cannot revive this tradition of our forefathers. Water is required for not only drinking, but for agriculture and animal husbandry. Good water management can help increase water supply and regenerate rural ecology and rural economy. Government's efforts to increase water supply can be supplemented by a people's movement to capture and conserve rainwater. We have to organize people's movement for stopping the pollution of our rivers and groundwater reserves. This would be a great contribution to our economy as well as to public health.

I have referred earlier to the question of illiteracy in our country. It is today an accepted fact that literacy and education are at the root of human as well as economic development. Why is it that as a nation we do not feel the desperate urgency of making our people literate? I hope that vested interests have not been fearful of awakening the masses through education. On the contrary, we should have faith in the people. We should organize a mass movement for literacy. Can we not involve the millions of our students, teachers and civil servants to spread literacy among the masses, at least on a part-time basis? Through such a movement not only literacy but national and social causes like population control and environment consciousness could be spread among the people, not to speak of awareness of and opposition to many ills that are plaguing our society. Fortunately, civic actions in India have multiplied during the recent years.

Civil society should be further encouraged to grow and address social, cultural and environmental challenges confronting the nation. We need a comprehensive policy to promote the growth of civil society interacting with various branches and levels of government. Even in a developed and affluent society like the USA, there are around 6 million such organizations disposing of 8 per cent of the country's GDP in their activities. Not only the Government but the private sector also has an important role to play in a comprehensive civic action plan. We have a model for us in the constructive programme chalked out and implemented during the independence movement by Mahatma Gandhi.

I said a little earlier that this is an occasion for honest self-analysis. I think it would not be wrong to say that as a society we are becoming increasingly insensitive and callous. Gandhiji had tried to popularize the Gujarati song which describes the 'true vaishnava' as one who knows the other person's pain. He may not find too many of that description in India today. Be it the way cars and buses are driven in our city roads, the way garbage-and, particularly, middle-class plastic garbage-is strewn around, the way public servants treat the public, or the public handles public utilities, the manner in which we squander or pollute precious reserves like water, the way owners of vehicles allow toxic gases to be spewed into the air that we breathe, the way we allow children to be exploited, the disabled to be passed by, speaks of a stony-hearted society, not a compassionate one that produced the Buddha, Mahavira, Nanak, Kabir and Gandhi. And then there is our greatest national drawback-the status of our women; and our greatest national shame-the condition of the dalits, the erstwhile untouchables.

Fifty years after our constitution, the plain truth is that the female half of the Indian population continues to be regarded as it was in the 18th and 19th centuries. It is more than 170 years since Raja Rammohan Roy caused Sati to be abolished. But the infamous pratice still manages to raise its head and what is worse, even gets explained away as 'suicide' or as 'saintly sacrifice'. What one finds disconcerting is even the absence of political rhetorich on these social ills. Commenting on the male-female disparity in India, Gandhiji wrote in 1931, "You cannot have one set of weights and measure for the one and a different one for the other. Yet we have never heard of a husband mounting the funeral pyre of his deceased wife". Unless the status of women in Indian society changes, the 'equality' spoken of in our preamble will remain hollow. It is against this attitude of society and the habit of discrimination prevalent in society that the demand for constitutional reservation for women in the legislatures and parliament has become a compelling necessity.

We have to ponder over the condition of not only women in our society, but of the dalits, the tribals and other weaker sections. Untouchability has been abolished by law but shades of it remain in the ingrained attitudes nurtured by the caste system. Though the provisions of reservation in educational institutions and public services flow from our constitution, these provision remain unfulfilled through bureaucratic and administrative deformation or by narrow interpretations of these special provisions.

It seems, in the social realm, some kind of a counter revolution is taking place in India. It is forgotten that these benefits have been provided not in the way of charity, but as Human Rights and as social justice to a section of society who constitute a big chunk of our population, and who actually contribute to our agriculture, industry and services as landless labourers, factory and municipal workers. There are signs that our privileged classes are getting tired of the affirmative action provided by constitutional provisions. On this golden jubilee I would like to say that let us not get tired of what we have provided for our weaker sections; for otherwise, as Dr. Ambedkar pointed out, the edifice of our democracy would be like a palace built on a dung heap. If on an occasion like this golden jubilee of our republic we ponder some of these issues, it would be the better for us. While there is a need to be honest with ourselves, I must emphasize, we must act, not despair. In moments of crisis we rise gloriously to the occasion as few societies do. The late war in Kargil showed it; the cyclone in Orissa did so too. And, even more recently, the stoic fortitude with which the nearly 170 passengers and crew aboard the hijacked plane showed how we are capable of the highest endurance, calm, fortitude and human care. But we do not have to reserve our best qualities for national or natural calamities; they should manifest themselves in our daily life. The Biblical exhortation, 'do not do unto others what thouwouldst not others do unto thyself', was anticipated by Vyasa in his words, *Aatmanaha pratikulaani pareshaam na samaacharet.*

The world watches us with a combination of admiration and concern: admiration at what we have achieved despite great odds, and concern over the fact that, even with great investments of money and energy we remain far from our goal. Indians do well, they say, India does not. We must examine the import of that observation and try to rectify the situation. Of course the rest of the world, too, is faced by crises. The end of the cold War has not ended all conflicts, it has only changed its character. Even as we want equality amongst ourselves, so do we want equality among the nations of the world. This does not and cannot mean that all countries have the same of everything. But it does mean that no nation or continent can seek over lordship over others claiming political, economic, technological or strategic superiority. We are privileged, as Indians, to have played a leading role in the decolonizing of the mighty continents of Asia and Africa. We are the initiators of the concept of non-alignment in the world when it was bitterly divided by the Cold War; and whether the great powers now recognize or not the role of non-alignment in ending the Cold War, the fact of its contribution remains for all to see. And we are also co-authors with the People's Republic of China of the five principles of peaceful coexistence which provide the world a code of conduct in international relations. The principles, like the respect for the territorial integrity and independence of nations, non-interference in their internal matters and mutual benefit and equality are precious concepts which cannot become redundant in a world of globalization.

We are privileged also to be playing a role to see that in the new millennium all the nations of the world, enjoy the same political status and have a level playing field, economically and technologically. This will be our endeavour in all world bodies of which we are proud to be members or associated with the United Nations, the Commonwealth, the non-aligned movement and the new formations such as the WTO and important regional grouping like ASEAN, SAARC..... We are proud to belong to South Asia and to the Asian continent, we celebrate this year the 50th anniversary of the establishment of diplomatic relations with China. We wish that country and its people every happiness. We want to live in peace with Pakistan. We want the relations to conform to the best traditions of good neighbourliness, eschewing terrorist interventions and the propaganda of hatred, in the spirit in which Jawaharlal Nehru declared in the constituent assembly, to the sister-continent of Africa, the Commonwealth of nations, the European Union, the United States of

America and Latin America, to Japan, and to the Arab nations and the countries of the pacific and central Asia with whom we have traditional ties of friendship. To Russia, with which our political economic, cultural and strategic relations remain strong, we reiterate our fraternal goodwill.

I once again extend my greetings to all fellow-citizens. May all of us cross the golden milestone and march along the vision of the founding fathers of our republic.

Jai hind.

8

Economic Equality Ensures Equality for Dalits in Indian Society

Dr. Laxmi Berwa

I admire the vision and dynamism of Senator Pandithan and his associates, who made for the first time, their efforts to focus on "the new vision towards a casteless society". In this perspective I would like to throw some light on the economic problems of Dalits and how a better economic position can help achieve equality. As any student of India's culture and caste system knows, social, economic, and religious issues are intertwined as causes of our problems as Dalits. Here, I shall concentrate upon the economic issues of Dalits. For past many centuries, Dalits have been totally deprived of social, economic, educational, and religious interaction as equals with the rest of Indian society. In a nutshell, about 15 to 17% of India's population has been totally emasculated and reduced to physical and mental slavery to this very day.

Knowing the impact of social sanctions against Dalits, the British Government through legislation started affirmative action programs to improve the condition of Dalits in educational and other matters through the Government institutions. After India gained independence, the founding fathers—Mahatma Gandhi, Pandit Jawaharlal Nehru, Dr. Rajendra Prasad, and Dr. B.R. Ambedkar, Chairman of the Constitution Drafting Committee-had a vision of India becoming a democratic, secular and socialistic society in which Dalits would be equal partners. In that spirit, Constituent Assembly abolished the practise of untouchability through Article 17 of the Constitution and the successive Governments have enacted various Acts for their civil rights protection.

In addition, Parliament enacted in favour of Dalits the constitutional provisions for reservations in governmental, civil service and educational institutions. Article 338 of the Indian Constitution provided for a special commissioner for Scheduled Castes and Tribes to be appointed. It continues to be in action to this day.

Unfortunately, successive Indian Governments regardless of political affiliations, although most have been Congress governments, have treated the office of the Commissioner for Scheduled Tribes and Castes with indifference. Its report sometimes comes out 7 or 8 years later and nothing is said about it and the problems of Scheduled Castes and Tribes.

Now let me take up the economic status of Dalits in India today. The total population of India today is about one billion. Dalits are about 16% or 160 million of that total. Dalit in India, therefore, are about six times more than the total population of Malaysia. India is a country of villages in which 84% of all Dalits live. Seventy percent of Dalits live below the poverty level and more than 70% of them depend upon the agricultural sector. Eighty-five percent of rural Dalits are landless or near landless. Only a very small section of Dalits have crossed the boundary of poverty line. This is mainly due to the reservation policy of the Government of India and the state Government as well as of educational institutions. According to Dr. Anand Teltumbde, who presented a paper at the University of Oxford on 8th November, 1996, "Out of the total Dalit population of 138 million, the number of Dalits in the domain of reservations does not exceed 1.1 million; a mere 0.8%."

Before I dwelt upon some of the issues of the Government programs, it is clear that the private sector has contributed a big zero to the economic empowerment of Dalits. In the private sector, Dalits are the last to be hired and the first to be fired. This is because of the deep caste prejudice harboured by private sector employers against Dalits.

First let me address the issue of reservation policies in the Government of India. According to the Central Government's reservation policy as of January 1, 1995, the proportion of jobs is fixed for Dalits at 15% of the total population of India. The actual employment figures for Dalits in the four categories of Government jobs are as follows: in the first class category only 10.15% of jobs, in the second class category 12.6% of jobs. Obviously, the high caste *Brahmins* and Banias do not like to do the fourth class jobs of cleaning latrines or streets. After fifty years of independence, Dalits have a sufficient pool of highly educated and competent persons who are capable of fulfilling the job requirements, but because of deep caste prejudice by the high caste, these jobs cannot be fulfilled. When it comes to the sincerity of the bureaucracy, there continues to be many attempts to derail and undermine the reservation policies, either because of "no suitable candidate", or because the job was filled by a high caste person.

The second issue concerns the Government of India's program on comprehensive and human resources development. This came into being during the Fifth Five Year Plan. Before 1978-79, the funding was only under the welfare of backward classes sector of the annual plans of the state which allocated only a minuscule amount compared to the dimensions of the problems. Thus, the Government of India realized that a more concerted effort had to be taken in order to improve the economic well-being. Thus, during the Sixth Five Year Plan, there was a special plan called "Special Component Plan" on family and beneficiary-oriented development schemes. This special component plan was to be financed from four sources viz., (1) flow from the state's plan, (2) flow from the central sector and centrally sponsored schemes, (3) special central assistance, (4) institutional finance. The special component plan envisaged identification of schemes in the general sector of development which would be of benefit to the Scheduled Castes, quantification of funds from all programs under each sector, and determination of specific targets in terms of the number of families who were to be benefited from those programs under each sector to enable them to cross over the poverty line.

Special Component Plans were formulated by the majority of the states and Union territories, according to the Commissioner for Scheduled Castes and Tribes. The working group on the development of Scheduled Castes during the Seventh Plan pointed out that some of the major departments of the states were avoiding the strenuous exercise of ear-marking funds some specifically for the development of the Scheduled Castes and it was mainly due to their inertia. The working group termed this as an "attitudinal problem and lack of proper orientation".

The main argument advanced by the state Governments for not earmarking funds under the special component plan in proportion to the percentage of the Scheduled Caste population was that a large portion of the total state plan outlay was indivisible in sectors like power, irrigation, communication, roads, transport, etc., which of them accounted for about 60% of the total plan outlay. The report of the Commission for Scheduled Castes and Tribes (28th report in 86-87), states that the working group pertinently pointed out that the benefits from these sectors, especially the economic benefits, did not automatically or significantly go to the Scheduled Castes in view of their poor ownership of assets and, therefore, incapacity to utilize this infrastructure either for stepping up their production or to produce marketable surpluses to be transported to market.

The report of the working group on development and welfare of the Scheduled Castes and Tribes during the Eighth Five Year Plan 1990-1995, Ministry of Welfare, was reviewing the Scheduled Caste development strategies during the Sixth Plan, 1980-85, and the first four years of the Seventh Plan, 1985-90, noted the following major deficiencies:

1. Physical and financial targets under various sectors were not disaggregated and communicated to the Districts and Blocks by the Departments concerned,
2. Equity and viability of the schemes were not carefully ensured,
3. The implementing agencies were structurally weak for absorption of large amounts of funds under different programs,
4. Due to the lack of coordination and proper type of linkages, special central assistance funds made available to the states could not be properly and fully utilized,
5. In some states, the district magistrates and collectors were not directly involved with the special component plan schemes either at the stage of formulation or at the stage of implementation with the result that focus on proper implementation of the schemes' programs had blurred,
6. There was no commitment to the welfare of the Scheduled Castes on the part of most of the officers entrusted with schemes,
7. There was no accountability,
8. There was no effective supervision, and
9. There was no proper follow up.

The Eighth Five Year Plan's working group suggested the following:

1. The strategy of the special component plan, Scheduled Castes development corporation, etc. should be continued and further intensified during the Eight Five Year Plan by pursuing the indicated objectives and ensuring adequate thrust on economic and educational development of the Scheduled Castes.
2. The special component plans of the Union Government as well as of the states should provide for fully meeting the minimum needs/basic amenities of all Scheduled Caste habitations with a view to improve their quality of life generally.
3. The special component plan should also provide for a judicious mix of beneficiary-oriented programs and human resources.
4. The schemes taken up should be viable and, as far as necessary, diversify Scheduled Castes into newer areas of economic activity.
5. There should be provision for meeting the backward and forward infrastructure needs by projecting the approach as far as necessary.
6. The schemes taken up should be open ended for the development of the Scheduled Castes.

7. The delivery system has to be effective.
8. The organization and association of the beneficiary group should be given due preference.

These are all great ideas, but unless there is an effective machinery to implement them, the Dalits will not benefit from the schemes. Mr. N.G. Uke, Coordinator of the Ambedkar Samaj, remarked on the social and economic development of Dalits, saying "The trickle down theory, that when the country as a whole is developed economically and socially even the lowest section of society will get proportionate benefits of development, proven wrong and government had to create special component plans for the Scheduled Castes and Scheduled Tribes. In spite of these special plans for SC and ST and a number of projects undertaken for the development, the outcome has been dismal. From the funds provided for the development, only 15% could reach the target people, the remaining 85% having been eaten away by the administrative and other expenses."

The next important issue is that of land reform. It was beautifully summarized by the Eight Five Year Plan working group when it stated:

"In the rural society, land not only provides subsistence base but also a social status to its holder. It also acts as a measure of securing other benefits of various development programs. Scheduled Caste comprise as the most vulnerable of the rural landless group. The largest percent of the Scheduled Castes are agricultural labourers. Most of them have been deprived of their tenancy rights. The ideal solution to providing security to the tiller of the soil would be to nationalize land. But, this needs reforming of the major political decision. The Government has been pursuing the land reform. And, if governments are to achieve success in their efforts to provide security to the tenants/share-croppers, and also to secure some land for allotment to the landless poor, they have to undertake certain special measures."

The report states that "loopholes in the agricultural land sealing legislation should be removed."

This means a fresh look at the entire land reform issue is needed because it is the landlessness which is the cause of the problems of poverty and social oppression which results in the rise of horrible atrocities. Those two problems and their result are directly linked to land. Without land reform, Dalits continue to be the lease-holders, rather than the owners, of India. Thus, the Indian government must undertake radical measures, if it wishes to help the Dalits.

The final issue is that of the impact of the new economic reform policies on the Dalits. For the past several years, since the Government of India started a new economic liberalization under the finance Minister, Mr. Manmohan Singh, there have been major negative repercussions on

Dalits. Professor S .K. Thorat, in a leading article in *Dalit International Newsletter*, Volume I, Number 2, 2 June 1996 wrote:

> *"The negative impact of the new measures are already visible. After the new reforms were implemented in 1990, both unemployment and poverty levels have increased. The number of Dalits employed in government services has declined from 628, 000 in 1991 to 604, 000 in 1992, while those in public sectors dropped from 432, 000 in 1990 to 369, 000 in 1992."*

In his concluding remarks, Prof. Thorat warns,

> *"With no protection against the caste based discrimination in the private sector, the Dalits are going to find the future upward mobility more difficult. Thus, unless some steps are taken to protect Dalits from job discrimination in the private sector, the positive trends that Dalits have experienced through the government plan effort since independence may be reversed."*

In other words, the clock may be turning back. This was the very thing which Dr. Ambedkar dreaded the most when he remarked:

> *"With great difficulty, I have brought this caravan where it is seen today. Let the caravan march on despite the hurdles that may come its way. If my lieutenants are not able to take the caravan ahead, they should leave it there, but under no circumstances should they allow the caravan to go back. This is the message to my people".*

Similar sentiments were expressed in a seminar, "Economic Reforms and Dalits in India" held by Oxford University in England on November 8 1996, where one of the speakers, Dr. Anand Teltumbde, concluded, "The Dalits in India being the poorest of the poor, have been hit the hardest. There are social disabilities, largely reinforced by, and sustained on, economic deprivation, and are bound to become sharpened with these policies." He suggested that:

"(As) pre-requisites to reform, there could be radical land reform infrastructural projects, universalization of primary education, a primary health care system and reinforcement of positive discrimination in favour of Dalits. The policy of positive discrimination in favour of Dalits will have to be reinforced much more vigorously in all sectors of economy than even RYS before."

Alarmed by the negative impact of the Indian Government's new economic reform policy on the Dalits, the National Commission for Scheduled Castes and Scheduled Tribes Chairman, Mr. H. Hanumanthappa, urged the Government to extend job reservation to joint and private sector companies as well as to whosoever deals with the Government in the matter of licensure, loans, special permits, tax relief or for that matter any other dealings with the Government.

The issue of structural reforms is vast and complex. The question usually comes down to who decides and monitors the politics and procedures of Government, and whether the Government is doing what it is supposed to do and doing it effectively. From all research I have done, the Government is not to be trusted, because high caste bureaucrats are hell-bent on torpedoing the well-intentioned policies of the Government of India, because of deep-seated caste prejudice. Thus, the onus is now left with the Dalit intellectuals and legislators. Until and unless we fight vigorously for our own rights, no one is going to give it to us. As Dr. Ambedkar in his editorial in *Bahiskrit Barat* on 27th November 1927 wrote: "Lost rights are never regained by begging and by appeals to the conscience of the usurpers, but by relentless struggle... Goats are used for sacrificial offerings and not lions."

I have a few suggestions to improve our economic well-being:

(1) As for Land Reform, since land reform laws are like a sieve having too many holes, the best way to address this issue will be to nationalize the land like nationalizing the banks during the late Mrs. Indira Gandhi's time. This will ensure that the Dalits will have land as a source of livelihood. In addition, the Dalits must be given physical possession of the land and those who are perpetrators or are not cooperating must be punished. Extreme action must be taken against them.

(2) A separate ministry of rehabilitation for the Dalits and Tribes must be urgently constituted to devote its energy exclusively to economic empowerment through land reform, to full implementation of reservation policy in the central and state Governmental agencies as well as the private sector; small scale industrial development for Dalits, the banks to give low interest rate loans and many other human resource program, especially in the field of education and high technology. That will relieve some of the burden from the ministry of social welfare. This ministry should also take legal action against those who are violating the laws concerning land reform, reservations, banking, etc. This ministry should also coordinate work with other ministries.

(3) The Scheduled Caste and Tribal Parliamentary Forum must take more aggressive approach to Dalit issues in parliamentary debates, especially those on the reports of Commissioner of Scheduled Castes and Scheduled Tribes and the National Commission on Scheduled Castes and Scheduled Tribes. The Forum should make sure that the above two reports are brought up annually and in a timely fashion. It's recommendations must be carried out, followed through, and monitored. The ministries are responsible only to the members of Parliament. Outside people have little recourse other than going to the court of law, for which Dalits do not

have financial resources. Thus, our Dalit members of Parliament have to be more hawkish. They must also work in coordination with the Dalit intellectuals and consult them on the issues of a technical nature or on issues needing a second opinion. Actually one of the members of the Forum must be a direct liaison with the minister concerned in each ministry, so that the minister will give a direct liaison with the minister concerned in each ministry, so that the minister will give a direct response to the parliamentary Forum and subsequently necessary action can be taken. The Forum must also monitor the activities of the bureaucracy, the police, and the judiciary for violations of the law. Stern action must be taken against, and punishment given to, those involved in criminal activity, whether it be a departmental secretary or a low-level peon. But, those who are implementing the government's policy must also be rewarded.

(4) Dalit intellectuals cannot remain on the sidelines. They are the eyes and ears of ordinary Dalits. They must continue to be vigilant in championing Dalit issues rather than be selfish.

(5) Urgent reservations in the private sector must be implemented.

(6) Fifteen percent of the central and state budget monies must be appropriated to Dalit upliftment, through land, small business, educational institutions, etc.

Let me remind all of you of the famous words of Dr. B.R. Ambedkar, Chairman of the Constitution Drafting Committee. He said:

"On the 26th January 1950, you are going to enter into a life of contradictions. In politics we will have equality and in social and economic life we will have inequality. In politics we will be reorganized by the principle of one man, one vote and one vote of value. In our social and economic life, we shall, by reason of our social and economic structure, continue to be denied the principle of one man, one value. How long shall we continue to lead this life of contradiction? How long shall we continue to be denied equality in our social and economic life? If we continue it for long, we will do so only by putting our political democracy in peril. We must remove this contradiction at the earliest possible moment or else those who suffer inequality will blow up the structure of political democracy which this assembly has so laboriously built up."

9

Dalit Discrimination and the Indian Constitutional Provisions

Dr. Justice K. Ramaswamy

Any discussion about racism, racial discrimination, xenophobia related intolerance holds, in reality, a mirror to the soul of each of us. Our comments, therefore, require a degree of introspection and honesty not always associated with the expression of views. Mrs. Robinson has been right in observing:

"There has never been a United Nations Conference where there has been such a strong quest for the recognition of historical injustices".

and in asserting further:

"In different parts of the world, people are hurting because of problems of inequality or injustice and are pressing their case at this Conference."

Indeed, no part of the world is exempt from such pain and India is no exception.

The National Human Rights Commission of India, has therefore considered it its duty to listen attentively to those in our country who have been the victims of historical injustices, and who are hurting because of discrimination and inequality. I refer in particular to those who, under our Constitution, comprise the Scheduled Castes and Scheduled Tribes–the Dalits and Adivasis of India–with the protection of whose Human Rights Commission is itself deeply involved. It was to hear their voices, and to benefit from an exchange of views with them, and with eminent jurists, academics and Human Rights activists, that our Commission

---

* Member, National Human Rights Commission (NHRC) presented a position paper of NHRC at Durban - United Nation World Conference against racism Sept.2001.

organized two major consultations in August 2001, in Bangalore and Delhi respectively, as steps preparatory to the formulation of the views of our Commission for this Conference.

With these introductory words, may I now outline the views of Human Rights Commission, as succinctly as possible, on certain issues that are particularly germane to my country.

1. There can be no doubt that in India–as everywhere else in the world–history and society have been scarred by discrimination and inequality.
2. It was in recognition of this–and to end such injustice–that Part III of the Constitution of our Republic dealing with Fundamental Rights, contained powerful provisions to combat all forms of discrimination, including notably those forms which were based on race, caste or descent. These provisions of the Constitution, which are justiciable, include, inter-alia:
   - **Article 14**, which stipulates that the State shall not deny to any person equality before the law or the equal protection of laws within the territory of India. This also applies to non-citizens.
   - **Article 15**, which expressly declares that the State shall not discriminate against any citizen on grounds only of religion, race, caste, sex, place of birth or any of them. It specifically adds that no citizen shall be subjected to any disability, liability, restriction, or condition with regard to access to shops, public restaurants, hotels, and places of public resort maintained wholly or partly out of State Funds or dedicated to the use of the general public. In addition, Article 15(4) permits the State to make special provision for the advancement of any socially and educationally backward class of citizens as well as Scheduled Castes and Scheduled Tribes. It is under this provision that the States of the Union are permitted to make reservations in educational institutions for these groups of citizens.
   - **Article 16,** which provides for equality of opportunity in matter of public employment. It also stipulates that no citizen shall on grounds only of religion, race, caste, sex, descent, place of birth, residence or any of them, be ineligible for, or discriminated against in respect of employment or office under the State. This Article further provides for affirmative action, through the reservation of appointments or posts, in favour of any backward class

of citizens which, in the opinion of the State, is not adequately represented in the services of the State. It also covers promotions and provides further for the carry-forward of unfilled vacancies of the quota for succeeding years.

- **Article 17,** which abolishes "Untouchability", and forbids its practise in any form.
- **Article 21,** which protects life and personal liberty.
- **Article 23,** which prohibits trafficking in human beings and forced labour.
- **Article 29(2),** which prohibits denial of admission to any educational institution on grounds only of religion, race, caste, language or any of them.
- **Further, Article 38 (2),** of the Constitution, in Part IV, setting out the Directive Principles of State Policy, requires the State, in particular, to strive to minimize the inequalities in status, facilities and opportunities, not only amongst individuals, but also amongst groups of people residing in different areas or engaged in different vocations.
- **Article 45,** calls upon the State to provide for free and compulsory education for all children until they complete the age of fourteen years.
- **Article 46,** enjoins the State to promote with special care the educational and economic interests of the weaker sections of the people, and in particular of the Scheduled Castes and the Scheduled Tribes, and to protect them from social injustice and all forms of exploitation.
- **Article 51(c)** enjoins the State to foster respect for international law and treaty obligations.
- **Article 325,** prohibits disenfranchisement on grounds of caste.
- **Articles 330 & 333,** provide for the reservation of seats for members of the Scheduled Castes and Scheduled Tribes in Union and State Legislatures.
- **Article 335,** states that the claims of the members of the Scheduled Castes and Scheduled Tribes shall be taken into consideration, consistently with the maintenance of efficiency of administration, in the making of appointments to services and posts in the affairs of the Union or of a State. In order to strengthen this provision, the Eighty Second Amendment Act of 2000 provided that nothing in this article shall prevent in making of any

provision in favour of the members of the Scheduled Castes and the Scheduled Tribes for relaxation in qualifying marks in any examination or lowering the standards of evaluation, for reservation in matters of promotion to any class or classes of services or posts.

- **Article 341,** makes possible the specification of the castes, races or tribes which shall be deemed to be Scheduled Castes.
- **Article 366(24),** defines Scheduled Castes to mean such castes, races or tribes or parts of or groups within such castes, races or tribes as are deemed under Article 341 to be Scheduled Castes for the purpose of the Constitution.

3. To give clear expression to the constitutional provisions, an impressive range of legislative measures have been enacted to end discrimination against Scheduled Castes and Scheduled Tribes. These, inter-alia, include :
    - The Protection of Civil Rights (Anti-Untouchability) Act, 1955.
    - The Bonded Labour (Abolition) Act, 1976.
    - The Scheduled Castes and Scheduled Tribes (Prevention of Atrocities) Act, 1989.
    - The Employment of Manual Scavengers and Construction of Dry Latrines (Prohibition) Act, 1993.
    - And various land reform acts.
4. In pursuance of the Constitutional provisions and legislative measures just enumerated, it can with good reason be said that India has embarked on a programme of affirmative action which is, perhaps, without parallel in scale and dimension in human history. It is all the more remarkable for being undertaken in a country that has demonstrated, in the 54 years since its Independence, an unshakable faith in the capacity of its people to effect fundamental social, economic and political change through the processes of democracy.
5. Despite this, however, and the powerful role of the judiciary in ensuring respect for the Constitution, the laws and affirmative action programmes of the country, it is widely recognized that much remains to be done to bring to an end the discrimination and inequality that have been practised for centuries and that this requires both sustained effort and time. There are manifest inadequacies in implementation which are deeply frustrating and painful to the Scheduled Castes and Scheduled Tribes and, indeed, to all Indians who strive to end injustice that persists in several forms and the atrocities that occur.

6. Because of its history and convictions, it was India that proposed that the word "descent" be introduced in Article 1(1) of the Convention on the Elimination of All Forms of Racial Discrimination (CERD) when it was being drafted and adopted in 1965. And it was also India that proposed that the concept of affirmative action be included in Article 1 (4) of that Convention so as to make the latter consistent with the Constitution of India and the aspirations of its people.
7. The National Human Rights Commission of India believes it is essential that all Member States, including India, respect the international human rights regime established under the auspices of the United Nations, and observe the discipline of the treaties to which they are States Party. It, therefore, attaches the highest importance to the views of the Treaty Bodies established, inter alia, under the Covenants on Civil and Political Rights, and on Economic, Social and Cultural Rights, as also under the Conventions dealing with the Elimination of ll Forms of Racial Discrimination (CERD), the Elimination of All Forms of Discrimination against Women (CEDAW) and the Rights of the child (ROC), all of which have commented on the country reports of India and on the efforts being made, and the difficulties being faced, in promoting and protecting the human rights of Scheduled Castes and Scheduled Tribes. It is worth mentioning, in this connection, that Section 2 (d) of the Protection of Human Rights Act 1993, which establishes the National Human Rights commission, defines "human rights" to man the rights relating to life, liberty, equality and dignity of the individual guaranteed by the Constitution or embodied in the International Covenants.
8. Respect for the UN Treaty system, the Commission believes, is also consistent with the landmark judgement of the Supreme Court of India which has dealt with the applicability of international conventions to the country; the Apex Court held: "...Any international convention not inconsistent with the fundamental rights and in harmony with their spirit must be read into these provisions to enlarge the meaning and content thereof, to promote the object of the constitutional guarantee.... regard must be had to international conventions and norms for construing domestic law when there is no inconsistency between them and there is a void in the domestic laws" (*Visakha vs State of Rajasthan* [1997(6) SCC 241].
9. In the light of this, the Commission is of the opinion that the exchange of views on Human Rights matters, whether at the

national, regional or international level, can all contribute constructively to the promotion and protection of such rights there are opportunities to the international community to deal openly and courageously with the vexed issues of discrimination and inequality as they exist all over the world, in all of their variety, including the forms of discrimination that persist in India and all other countries. In such a context, it is not so much the nomenclature of the form of discrimination that must engage our attention, but the fact of its persistence that must cause concern. Given this perception, the Commission is of the view that the debate on whether race and caste are co-terminous, or similar forms of discrimination, is not the essence of the matter. The Constitution of India in Article 15 expressly prohibits discrimination on either ground, and that Constitutional guarantee must be rigorously implemented. In this connexion, the commission believes deeply in the value of engaging Governments, non-governmental organizations, national institutions, and all concerned elements of civil society in the process of fighting discrimination, and urges that this process be conducted at all levels in a spirit that in genuinely interested in the furtherance of Human Rights, and not vitiated by self-righteousness or by political and other extraneous considerations.

10. As far as its own role is concerned, the Commission has been deeply engaged, ever since its establishment in October 1993, in the promotion and protection of the Human Rights of all of the people of India, acting in a manner that is complementary to that of the higher Courts of the country. The Commission has been especially concerned with the rights of the weakest sections of society, notably the Scheduled Castes and Scheduled Tribes. Under the provisions of its Statute, contained in the Protection of Human Rights Act 1993, the Commission is expressly required to review the safeguards provided by or under the Constitution or any law in force for the protection of Human Rights and recommend measures for their effective implementation; it is expected to review the factors including acts of terrorism that inhibit the enjoyment of Human Rights; and to study treaties and international instruments and make recommendations for their effective implementation. In the light of its Statute, therefore, the Commission has a clear responsibility to ensure the proper observance of international conventions, including CERD.

11. In furtherance of its statutory responsibilities, the Commission has thus accorded the highest priority to ending discrimination against Scheduled Castes and Scheduled Tribes and in seekig to eradicate, in particular, two pernicious practises which largely affect members of these communities: these relate to manual scavenging and bonded labour. In respect of both of these matters, the Commission is coordinating its activities closely with all Governmental and Non-Governmental Organizations concerned in an effort to end these practises and to rehabilitate those who have been affected by them. In both cases, too, the Commission has sought to involve the political leadership of the country, at the highest level, in the tasks that remain to be accomplished. Thus, as recently as 14 August 2001, on the eve of the 55th anniversary of India's Independence, the Chairperson of the Commission wrote to the Prime Minister of India and the Chief Ministers of all States, urging measures that should be taken to end the scourge of manual scavenging by October 2 2002, the birth anniversary of Mahatma Gandhi. He described this practises as a "national shame."
12. The Commission has also taken up the issue of the right of persons displaced by mega projects, specifically those affected by the construction of large dams, many of whom are tribals. The efforts of the Commission in this respect are greatly facilitated by the presence of the Chairperson of the National Commission for Scheduled Castes and Scheduled Tribes, who is also an ex-officio Member of the National Human Rights Commission.
13. In the final analysis, the Commission believes that the promotion and protection of the human rights of the weakest sections of society are clearly related to their full and proper empowerment. That is why the Commission has urged the adoption and implementation of policies and the Central and State levels that will open the doors of opportunity to them: free and compulsory primary education upto the age of 14 years, as the Constitution requires; access to proper primary health care; freedom from malnutrition and maternal anaemia, and the re-allocation of resources to back such programmes in a manner that has true meaning. In addition, the Commission has continued to receive and redress numerous individual complaints that it has received daily from persons who are included among the Scheduled Castes and Scheduled Tribes; these have alleged acts of discrimination,

"untouchability", violence against the human person, atrocities of various kinds, and high-handedness by public servants and others.

14. Economic upliftment and empowerment of Dalits is the most effective tool to combat casteism. More avenues must be opened for the economic betterment of the disadvantaged. Experience shows that economic upliftment and improvement in the status of Dalits eliminates inequalities. It is the poor who remain vulnerable. The fight to eradicate poverty must be intensified. National policies must be so formulated, and that is the mandate in the Directive Principles in Part IV of the Constitution of India. The National Human Rights Commission takes these factors into account in the discharge of its functions and in making recommendations to Government for improving the quality of goveınance. The Commission's involvement in the areas of illiteracy, malnutrition and lack of adequate healthcare, which afflicts the majority of Dalits, is to achieve this end.

Conclusion : The Commission is acutely aware that the journey to end discrimination, injustice and inequality will be long and often frustrating. But it is convinced that, in this mission, the Constitution of the Republic has shown the way. Legislative and affirmative action programmes are firmly in place, but unquestionably need to be far better the grounds contained in he Constitution of India, and these include race, caste and descent, constitute and unacceptable assault on the dignity and worth of the human person and an egregious violation of human rights. Such discrimination must, therefore, be eradicated, as must other forms of discrimination covered by United Nations treaties. The Commission holds the view that the instruments of governance in our country, and the energetic and committed non-governmental sector that exists, can unitedly triumph over the historical injustices that have hurt the weakest sections of our country, particularly Dalits and Scheduled Tribes. This is above all a national responsibility and a moral imperative that can and must be honoured.

10

National Human Rights Commission's Deep Concern on Atrocities Against Scheduled Castes

Justice A.S. Anand

Deeply concerned about the historical injustices faced by certain sections of the society, the founding fathers of our Constitution enshrined the ideals of Justice-social, economic and political-in the Preamble of the Constitution, and included far-reaching protective provisions under the Chapter on Fundamental Rights. The Universal Declaration of Human Rights, 1948 and the subsequent international covenants of Human Rights sought to make on-discrimination a cornerstone of international Human Rights system.

At the World Conference against Racism, Racial Discrimination, Xenophobia and Related Intolerance held in Durban in 2001, the National Human Rights Commission opined that it was not the "nomenclature" of the form of discrimination that must engage our attention, but the fact of its persistence. The Commission observed that the Constitution of India, in Article 15, expressly prohibits discrimination on grounds both of "race" and "caste" and that constitutional guarantees had to be vigorously implemented. The Commission held the view that the instruments of governance in the country, and the energetic and committed non-governmental sector of society that existed, could unitedly triumph over historical injustices that had hurt the weakest sections of our country, particularly the Dalits and the Adivasis. The Commission

Foreword of Justice A.S. Anand, Former Chief Justice of India & Present Chairperson NHRC, New Delhi - to the report on the Prevention and Atrocities against Scheduled Castes - published by NHRC with their permission.

concluded that this was, above all, a national responsibility and a moral imperative that can and must be honoured.

Despite elaborate provisions in the Constitution and other laws, it is an unfortunate reality that social injustice and exploitation of Scheduled Castes and Scheduled Tribes and other weaker sections persist. There are reports in the press about atrocities against persons belonging to these groups and the frequency with which they occur is a cause for disquiet. The humiliation which persons belonging to the Scheduled Castes in general and the Dalits in particular suffer even today, more than half a century after India proclaimed itself to be a Republic, is a matter of shame.

For the National Human Rights Commission, the protection of Human Rights is essential for defence of democracy itself-a democracy that is inclusive in character and caring in respect of its most vulnerable citizens. The Commission holds the view that Human Rights must be made the focal point for good governance. The Commission has been quite vocal and outspoken in defence of Human Rights particularly of the vulnerable sections of the society.

The National Human Rights Commission, being deeply concerned about the atrocities against persons belonging to Scheduled Castes, requested Shri K.B. Saxena, IAS (Retd.) to carry out a study in this regard and suggest appropriate recommendations. Shri K.B. Saxena, accordingly, undertook the study and has submitted his comprehensive and detailed report. With a view to monitor the implementation of the recommendation contained in that report, a Dalit Cell has been set up in the Commission and placed under the charge of a Member. The Commission proposes to have this Report printed in different languages, with a view to disseminate it widely and thereby sensitize the Civil Servants, NGOs and other key stakeholders regarding the protection of the rights of Scheduled Castes.

11

Violence: the Social Edifice

Shri. K.B. Saxena, I.A.S. (Retd.), NHRC

Organised violence directed against members of identified groups/communities has been a distinct feature of the Indian society for quite sometime. Though violence does take place in the process of change in many societies, and particularly so when radical alterations take place in the existing social and power relations, it usually does not choose its victims on the basis of birth in a given social entity. In India, however, this is precisely what has defined the character of violence in relation to certain groups. The country has witnessed an increase in both caste and communal violence since Independence which the processes of modernization have not abated. Rather, in some respects, it has been intensified by them.

While communal violence is a relatively recent phenomenon rooted in the events leading to partition, caste violence has a much longer history and a firmer anchorage. It also has the distinctiveness of being embedded in the social structure of the dominant community itself which lays down the norms of conduct between its more privileged groups and the subdued and subordinated segment. It is this age-old caste relationship in Hindu society which is getting disturbed by pressure of forces both from above and below. The frequency and intensity of violence is an offshoot of desperate attempts by the upper caste groups to protect their entrenched status against the process of disengagement and upward mobility among lower castes resulting from affirmative action of State Policy. The violence takes brutal forms and turns into acts of atrocities against a whole group of people, such as massacre, rape, burning of

---

From the Report on the Prevention and Atrocities against Scheduled Castes - published by NHRC, New Delhi with their kind permission.

houses and through more subtle methods like social boycott, which are intended to block their access to basic necessities and services. This phenomenon has to be positioned in the larger perspective of State-Society dynamics in order to understand why it happens and how it can be checked.

The target of caste violence is largely the people belonging to the lowest rung in the hierarchy of Hindu social order, who are known as the *'untouchables'*, or *Scheduled Castes* bound to the rest of the caste society in immutable relationship of rights and obligations. The practise of *"untouchability"* characterizes this relationship. The emergency of untouchability in the caste based social order has a complex history with little consensus or clarity on its origin. While some have attributed it to the growth of agricultural civilization in the country and the emergence of agricultural castes, who needed assured access to manual labour for agricultural operations, others have traced its genesis to expansionist phase of Indian civilization which led to the conquest of indigenous inhabitants and their consequent enslavement by the Aryans. The *'shudras'* in the social hierarchy towards the end of the Rig Vedic period represent these enslaved persons who were assigned inferior status, which was related to their birth in that community[3].

Whatever be the explanation of its origin, the institutional structures which governed social conduct in the society are subsumed under the nomenclature of 'Caste System', which broadly represents a vertical arrangement of social division of the Hindu population into four major groups, known as *'Varnas'*. At the top of this arrangement are the Brahmans (priestly class), followed by 'Kshatriya' (the warrior class), and 'Vaishya' (trading and artisan class). 'Shudra' (labouring and service class) stood at the bottom of hierarchy. The 'untouchables' were not a part of this scheme. However, over a period of time, the exigencies of situation led to the addition of a Fifth group to this classification which was not given any 'caste status' as such, but nonetheless integrally linked to the social order and is referred to as 'untouchables' or 'outcastes'. The membership of this group was determined by birth and could not be changed by individual effort or social acceptance. These four *'varnas'* subsequently transformed/got divided into hundreds of sub-castes, known as 'jati', each 'jati' having its own norms of social conduct. The caste structures is characterized by six important features.

1. Segmented division of Society,
2. Hierarchy,
3. Restrictions on commensal relations and social intercourse,
4. Lack of unrestricted choice of occupation,
5. Civil and religious disabilities and privileges of different sections, and
6. Restrictions on marriage.

The segmentation of society into four groups represents a tightly divided arrangement, of both status and occupation which is linked to each other in a hierarchical relationship. Brahmins occupy the top slot in the hierarchical ladder and 'untouchables' the bottom. As the caste hierarchy operates around the concepts of 'purity' and 'pollution', while the 'untouchables' are considered as the most degraded, because they perform polluting tasks. The restrictions on commensal relations and social intercourse incorporates code of conduct for each caste on what one can see and cannot see, what one can and cannot touch and what can or cannot be accepted by a person of one caste from a person of another caste. Restrictions on occupation are intended to prevent any destabilization of hierarchy. Civil and religious disabilities mandate 'untouchables' to live at a distance from the main village, not to draw water from village well, enter the village temple, wear the sacred thread, acquire education or recite the religious texts.

Untouchables are required to undertake the most polluting and degrading occupations, such as cleaning filth, including human excreta, flaying dead animals, digging graves, etc. The absolute restriction on marriages outside the caste and, in fact, even sub-castes ensures that there is not mobility from one group to another. Thus, the untouchables face total segregation in all matters, subjected to their status. The transition from caste disabilities to commission of atrocities has been traced from the very 3rd and 4th century A. D. when varna system faced crisis of deviations from the prescribed social conduct and the need was felt for coercive measures to enforce caste discipline and boundaries. The kind emerged as the upholder of the system. Those who violated the system were subjected to severe punishment as well as performance of various rituals. This is how physical violence by higher castes on the lower castes was sanctified. This situation continued for centuries. The persons of suppressed communities acquiesced in this arrangement, as there was no option for them to escape from it. Perhaps, they may have been made to believe that life in the next birth may be better if discipline imposed by existing status is adhered to.

During the medieval period, some saints like Kabir, Nanak, Ravidas were critical of existing social order and preached a religion of love, compassion and consideration and a more tolerant social arrangement. But there was no protest against the caste system and its social ramifications as such. The prevailing laws continued to support the caste system and the rulers upheld them. During the Muslim Rule in India, some people from the suppressed communities might have converted to Islam as a way out of their degraded status, but there is no evidence that the Muslim rulers ever tried to interfere with the Hindu caste system or reform it. Their strategy of governance may have prevented them from doing so.

However, the British established the rule of law which was based on a concept of equality. The law applied to all persons irrespective of their social or economic position. This was a major departure from the pre-British judicial system where caste distinctions were not only recognized, but also enforced and differential punishment was awarded, for the same offence, depending on the caste status of the offender. In any case, the suppressed castes neither had the courage, nor resources to seek any relief under the new system. But even during the British period caste distinctions remained relevant in matters relating to the Hindu Law. The general features of the legal system did not change the status of lower castes, as the overall British policy remained one of non-interference. In matters such as entry to temples, ritual pollution and rights to exclusiveness, the Courts supported the customary laws of Hindus and their view was upheld even at the level of Privy Council. There was, however, some difference in the attitude of Courts towards secular public facilities such as streets and roads where such disabilities were not enforced. However, the courts did not provide any support for removing caste disability in matters which came up before their consideration.

On a social plane, the period witnessed many reform movements in Hindu Society, such as Brahmo Samaj, Prarthana Samaj, Arya Samaj, Ramakrishna Mission, Theosophical Society, the Social Conference which attacked the caste system and some other features of Hindu social order. These movements, while supporting the four *varnas*, condemned the inhuman practise of untouchability. Later, during the freedom movement, Gandhiji contributed a great deal towards abolition of untouchability and later founded the All India Harijan Sangh for this purpose. In south, self-respect movement was launched against Brahminical tyranny. It was Dr. Ambedkar, who took up the fight against caste oppression more vigorously through the All India Depressed Classes Federation. Around 1909, the issue of untouchability acquired political significance when proposals were made for special legislative representation for the untouchables. In 1917, the Congress passed anti-disabilities resolution. In the 1930s anti-disablities were introduced in Central Legislative Assembly, Madras and Bombay Legislatures. In 1938, Madras Legislature passed the first comprehensive law to remove social disabilities making it an offence to discriminate against the untouchables. In fact, in the publicly supported facilities, such as roads, wells, public transport vehicles, etc. as also in other secular institutions, such as restaurants, hotels, shops, the law prohibited judicial enforcement of any customary right or disability. This was followed by similar legislations in other provinces. Later, initiative was also taken by Madras to facilitate temple entry for Scheduled Castes by making it a criminal offence for any person to prevent any Hindu from entering or worshipping at any temple. Similar Acts were passed in other provinces subsequently.

However, the British Government never took positive action to improve the condition of *shudras* and untouchables and to remove their disabilities. Apparently, the larger consideration of consolidating their rule prevented them from interfering with the customary practise associated with indigenous religions. Thus, at the time of independence, the traditional status of untouchables and caste disabilities, which prevented them from leading a life of dignity and self-respect continued to prevail. It was, therefore, left to the Constitution of India after independence to make the first comprehensive break with the past and to pronounce the policy of abolition of untouchability and declare total equality for the *shudras* and untouchables in Indian society. The Constitution also laid down means to achieve these objectives.

12

Judiciary – Least Honest and Least Accountable

Udit Raj

Every human being is product of social structure in which he is born and brought up and so is the case with Indian Judges. Do they perform marriage, rituals and other essential expressions of life outside caste and customs, barring a few? How can we expect that they will behave completely differently from ordinary citizens? A person who had not suffered poverty and hunger, how can he be expected to feel the pain of the have-nots? Nearly a hundred years ago, the US president Roosevelt said in the decisions of the courts on economic and social philosophy." A judge's mind is not a mechanical legal slot machine. His judgment is influenced, at least unconsciously, by his likes and dislikes, prejudices and predilections, his entire philosophy of life in the atmosphere of the ongoing social struggles in the country, the resultant bitterness can not leave the judge without being influenced in their judgment as to the right or wrong of the struggle – being members of the struggling community.

The then British policy of divide and rule; the emphasis on industrialization at the expense of villages; frustration among "meritorious" people because of reservations." The so called learned judge is a by product of our caste ridden social system. Can a dalit expect any justice from judges in respect of reservation, who are so

---

Mr. Udit Raj is the National President of Justice Party and Chairman - All India Confederation of SC/ST Organisations, Off. : 5, Pusa Road, IIIrd Floor, Karol Bagh, New Delhi-110005 This paper was presented on 2nd August,03 in the convention held on Judicial corruption and accountability at Agha Khan Hall , Bhagwan Das Road, N.Delhi.

biased? A learned judge biased goes completely out of context. In 1996, the Supreme Court held that there are three parties in any litigation and two of them are litigants and third one is judge himself. If it appears that the litigants are hand in glove and are not assisting the court to reach at conclusion, then it becomes the duty of the judge to extract the truth from witnesses. The Best Bakery case is often cited as an example how things go wrong.

The constitution is the mother and the judiciary , Executive, Legislature are its children but the judiciary has now defiled its mother by misinterpreting and diluting it in many ways,. In 1981 in the 1st Judge case - S.P. Gupta V/s Union of India (1991) the Supreme Court held that the opinion of the Chief Justice of India does not hold primacy in appointment and transfer matters of judges and constitutional functionaries like the President, P.M., Governor, Ministry of Law as per article 217 of the Indian Constitution must be consulted. In 2nd Judge case S.C. Advocates on Record Association V/s Union of India, 1993, Supreme Court held that the Chief Justice of India holds primacy in transfer and posting of judges and the process of selection of judges of Supreme Court must be initiated by the CJI. This is complete departure from constitutional provisions. In the case of reference case (1998) it again confirmed the primacy of CJI. Unfortunately , there is no law to govern judiciary.

A dalit judge in Allahabad had to suffer from the behavior of his colleague upper caste incumbent Judge , Ashok Srivastav, who washed his chamber and furniture with Gange's water on 3rd June,1997 and when the matter was reported, the humiliated judge, Mr. B. Brashad, was reprimanded and was compulsorily retired. The distt. judge who shielded the erring judge was promoted to the High Court . A judge of Jaipur revealed his caste feeling in case of Bhanwari Devi ,he said how can upper caste rape her? A High Court judge of Delhi compounded the sentence under civil procedure code when a matter went before him after sentence was conferred under Food and Adulteration Act by lower court. Number of culprits went scot free by just paying a few thousands of rupees whereas they would have languished in jail for months and years. Can there be such lawlessness elsewhere and erring persons allowed to go scot free ! Impossible .

A committee on the welfare of Scheduled Castes and Scheduled Tribes (1999-2000), comprising of 30 Members of Parliament headed by one Mr. Karya Munda ,M.P., presented a detailed second report to Lok Sabha on 15-3-2000 and the same was laid in Rajya Sabha on 15-3-2000. This report was with special reference to appointment of SCs/STs judges in higher judiciary. The committee recommended that the relevant articles 124 and 127 of the constitution may be amended suitably to include especially judiciary wing of the state within the ambit of reservation, and simultaneously a Judiciary Act may be enacted to spell out the governing principles of the proper functioning of the judiciary, the Supreme Court and High Court.

The Committee further noted that at present, majority of the High Courts have made provisions for reservation in services for SCs and STs under them by framing suitable rules of recruitment. However, no such rules have so far been made by the Supreme Court. The whole attitude of the Supreme Court is very surprising. Its Registry has intimated that the requisite information regarding representation of SCs and STs is not available with that office.

It is further noted there has been not only no reservation for SCs and STs in the appointment of officers and staff of the Supreme Court but framing of codified rules regarding their recruitment has also not been finalised during the last half century. How can the weaker sections of the society have any faith left in such a court. The committee was, therefore of the view that when the Supreme Court is receiving the salaries from the Consolidated Fund of India for its staff, it is a condition that the Chief Justice and companion judges of the Supreme Court as well as high Courts should also implement reservation in recruitment and promotion of the officers and servants at various levels at the prescribed percentage and the backlog of vacancies in the categories of Scheduled Castes and Scheduled Tribes must be filled up by conducting special recruitment drive.

When the Committee wanted to have clarification on the uneven policy followed by the various High Courts in regard to reservation in employment for SCs and STs in their establishment and whether this question was ever discussed at the Chief justices' Conference held periodically, the Ministry of Law, Justice and Company Affairs in their post-evidence reply have stated that the agenda of the Conference is finalized by the Supreme Court and the Department of Justice has no role to play. They have further stated that as per information available with them, the question of reservation in employment of SCs/ STs in the establishments of High Court has not been discussed in the Chief Justices' Conference held during the last eight years. However, the information in this regard was not supplied by the Supreme Court of India.

On enquiring about figures of actual representation and percentage of SCs & STs in the total number of officers and staff separately for Subordinate Judicial Services, Higher Judicial Services and Ministerial Service for each state, the Ministry of Law, Justice and Company Affairs in their post-evidence reply have stated that primarily the Subordinate Judicial Services and Higher Judicial Services are the concern of the respective state Government and its High Court. The control of the Ministerial service in the establishment of the High Court is the exclusive domain of each High court. The information in respect of actual representation of SCs and STs in various High Courts' establishments is as under:-

State	*Total No. of Employees*	*No. of SC Employees*	*Per (%)*	*No.of ST Employees*	*Per (%)*
Allahabad	2583	Information not received			
Andhra	1304	106	8.12	9	0.69
	(OBC 231)				
Bombay	2171	238	10.96	23	1.06
Calcutta	563	38	6.75 8	1.42	
Delhi		Information not received			
Gauhati	462	41	8.87	37	8.00
Gujarat	685	60	8.76	43	6.28
H.P.	351	55	15.67	2	0.57
J & K.	354	22	6.22	11	3.11
Karnataka	1253	103	8.22	20	1.60
Kerala*	400	30	7.50	—	—
M.Pradesh	1224	48	3.92	21	1.72
	(OBC 271)				
Madras	1277	146	11.43	2	0.15
Orissa	595	68	11.43	5	0.84
Patna	1151	115	10.00	49	4.25
Punjab & Haryana	684	70 (SC +ST)	10.23 SC+ST)		
Rajasthan	933	42	4.50	5	0.54
Sikkim	107	9	8.41	37	31.58

*Ministerial Services

From the information furnished, the Committee found that the said information relates to only total number of employees and the number of SCs and STs among them and not according to categories as asked for. However, two of the High Courts, namely Allahabad and Delhi, have not furnished any information at all in this regard which cannot be expected from these esteemed organizations. The Committee also observes that the representation of SCs and STs employees in the establishment of various High Courts is deplorable. The Committee desired that full information relating to officers and grade wise service wise details in respect of employees of all the High Courts with the break-up of SCs and STs therein should be made available to the Committee at an early date.

The Committee noted that a proposal for setting up of National Judicial commission was made by the Commissioner for Scheduled Castes and Scheduled Tribes more than a decade ago, which had also been reiterated by the Law Commission of India in its 121st Report. The Committee regretted to note that the matter was still under examination by the Government. The Committee, therefore, strongly recommended that a National Judicial Commission including one member from Scheduled Caste and one member from Scheduled Tribe be set up early in dealing with the appointment, transfer and placement of the judges of the High courts and Supreme Court. This should be supplemented by constituting an All India Judicial Service.

The committee was surprised to see that out of 481 High Court judges only 15SCs and 5STs were in position as on 1-5-1998 . It held a view in the reports that the judges take oath that they uphold the constitution and the laws. But the Supreme Court and a few High Courts claiming power above the constitution, practice untouchablity and are disobeying the constitution with regard to Ats. 16(4) and 16(4A).

Recent incidents regarding behaviour of judges have left no doubt to leave the system like this would spoil the whatever democratic values are left. Poor Sumit Mukherjee was jailed because he was not enjoying immunity and such characters are not a few but must be in plenty. They hear those lawyers who have face value , tacit understanding and ,of course, their relatives. Judges should not be posted in the places where their relatives are practicing law but examples of Delhi High Court will put to rest all doubts where 12 judge's relatives are practicing and in Allahabad, such judges are 27 in number .Thus present set up judiciary is neither honest nor accountable. On behalf of All India Confederation of SC/ST Organizations and Justice Party, I assure the august gathering that our movement is with this pious mission.

13

Legal Education for People

Dr. Mrs. P. Nagabooshanam

In this year of empowerment of women, Human Rights Education Movement of India is inaugurating the Human Right Lawyers Forum, Madras Chapter today. I wish to congratulate them and hope and pray they succeed in all their endeavours to do their best to educate on Human Rights, preserve and protect Human Rights in this region.

I thank the organization of this solemn function for inviting me to represent the field of legal education.

Education is the foundation for almost all the activities of our lives. The foundation is not visible for the outside world. As long as it is strong and sturdy nobody bothers about it. If it is not so the cracks develop fast in the walls, the construction gets affected and one fine day even without any terrorist hit, it collapses.

Education is quite natural for women because mother is the first teacher of a child and in many occasions even for grown ups. If that first teacher is neglected, ill-treated, her rights are violated, responsibilities are many told beyond endurance, What will happen? The world has been witnessing the result for a pretty long period, several centuries have passed in silent sufferings of the women for no good reasons.

In recent times I often think the prehistoric period was less problematic and more secured generally and more particularly for women.

Text of welcome speech delivered by Mrs. Nagabooshanam, Formerly Vice Chancellor, Dr. Ambedkar Law University Tamil Nadu.

When the enormous strength of women particularly their mental strength was realized by men, they pushed them to the peak and almost endeavoured them under the pretex of protecting them.

When this anomaly has been realized by righteous men and women of the world nations, the Human Rights declaration, conventions and other treaty agreements have emerged to set their rights in order to protect Human Rights. The aim and goal of Human Rights is to reaffirm faith in fundamental Human Rights, in the dignity and worth of the human person and of nations large and small, universal declaration of Human Rights 1943 Act 2, 16, 25 (2) are particularly for women, the rest are for other men & women. Later it was realized Human Rights is women's right. Convention on the elimination of all forms of discrimination against women emerged from the 1st World Conference on women in Mexico City in 1975.

In 1979, UN General Assembly adopted the women's convention that addressed comprehensively women rights within political, cultural, economic, social and family life.

The convention defines discrimination against women mandates state parties to ensure a legal framework including all laws, policies and practices that provide protection against discrimination and embody the principle of equality. Declares the need to modify social & cultural patterns, family education to recognize the social function of motherhood and the common responsibilities for raising children.

The convention obligates state parties to suppress traffic in women and the exploitation of women. Particularly of women in political life at national and international level on equal basis with men. Equality in education, employment, accesses to health facilities, financial and social security to ensure for women.

Rural women have these problems with inadequate means to solve them. Equality in legal and civil matters, equality in family law are all to be ensured.

A Committee to evaluate progress made in implementation of the convention rules, procedures, members tenure of office, how to settle the dispute all have been provided for in this convention.

Almost all the Human Rights convention provisions and the convention on the elimination of all forms of discrimination against women are having parallel or similar provisions in the fundamental rights part of the Indian constitution law.

To mention a law Act 12 to 32; special provisions like 330 (reservation SC/ST) to 342 are also there.

We have 1). The protection of Human Rights Act, 1993 2). The SC/ ST prevention of atrocities Act (1989) 3). Protection of civil rights Act 1988 4). The National Commission for Minorities Act (1992) 5). The National Commission for Women Act (1990) 6). The SC & ST (prevention of atrocities rules 1995, etc. to take enough care of almost all the provision in under national conventions of Human Rights, women rights, etc.

That apart, in our civil and criminal law systems, protection to women is provided to some extent, e.g. IPC, CPC Police Act, Property Right, etc.

One area where women could not enter until recently is also open to their choice now namely, the defence services.

Dowry Prohibition Act, Eve Teasing Prevention Act, Equal Pay For Equal Work, some of the labour legislations protecting the rights of women employees we have almost everything except that the system is inadequately insulated.

1. For proper understanding and implementation of these provisions we must have authorities without any fear or favour. Do we have this insulation adequately? I leave it to your guess.
2. Proper understanding and realization of one's own faith without affecting others interest is something which is again exposed very dangerously by the fanatics and fundamentalists who ruthlessly impose their views on others and claim that it is their religious duty and Jihad and what not.
3. Our habits of slave preventability to the rituals, sentiments and traditions due to identity crisis fear psychosis.
4. The social set up which has a very poor rate of tolerance, more of inclusive and interfering tendency, inhuman instinct of a few who suffer from egoistic problem who are capable of triggering off violence, terrorism, etc, leading to chaotic conditions.
5. Ignorance on the part of tradition bound women who are not aware of their rights / no means to attain it, accept humiliation, etc, as fate and silently suffer and pass on this ignorance and insecurity to their succeeding generations.
6. The invisible link between law and reality has to be identified and the better has to be removed restoring self-respect.
7. The vested interest group who promote, propagate and perpetuate the violations of Human Rights in general / women's right in particular must be identified and made them

realize the havoc due to their behavior and correctional measures to be adopted to prevent them from committing further damage to the harmonious coexistence.

8. Women must be made to realize the discrimination against them which have neither legal nor moral / religious sanction. Therefore they need not have any fear whatsoever to fight for their rights and undertake responsibilities successfully.

Finally what is essential in today's world is proper understanding of the "Life", the gifts is abundance in nature, enjoying the gifts without eliminating them, mutual tolerance, love and affection towards fellow being. In short have the simple motto "Live and Let Live". Thank You

14

Societal Scenario in Contemporary India

Prof. Arvind Nirmal

When challenges are posed to the secular ideal of our democracy, when our secularism is also threatened by the revivalist, fundamentalist forces. Violence in Punjab, Kashmir and Assam is threatening the federal structure of the nation. It is time, indeed, that we took a serious note of "Societal Scenario in contemporary India", It is true we do some fresh thinking and search for new directions and new solutions for our vexing socio-economic and political problems. My own task is to look at the "Dalit Scenario".

The Significance of Dalit Perspective

It is beyond the scope of this chapter to give an exhaustive account of the Dalit Scenario in Contemporary India. All that I can hope to do here is to raise some issues related to the Dalit Scenario which need our attention. This does not mean that the question of the Dalit Perspective is not important. On the contrary, it could be argued that no adequate account of "Societal Scenario in Contemporary India" could be given, unless one takes a serious note of Dalit issue. Indeed, some scholars feel that the question of Dalits is central for contemporary India. Alexandra George writes : The future of the Scheduled Castes is indeed the touchstone on which India's future in the modern world and perhaps its whole political system will be tested. For the question of the Scheduled Castes is but one segment of the dilemma facing Hindu Society in the attempt to restructure for India its ancient eroded foundations. Traditional

---

Speech delivered at the Centre for New International Economic Order, Chennai,

attitudes towards the Scheduled Castes are merely an extreme example of attitudes towards other minority or linguistic groups. The whole, question of the plurality of Indian Society and the achievement of a new harmony no longer dependent on hierarchy will depend considerably on the capacity of upper caste-leadership to restore confidence among the Scheduled Caste.' (Social Ferment in India, PP 202F)

Prof. M.N. Srinivas, too, recognizes the importance of dalit issues and writes : "A depressing Scenario for the future concerns the conflict between dominant, and owning Castes and Scheduled Castes. This is likely to become increasingly violent and bitter, and will be a primary arena for the struggle of equality in India. There is a positive aspect to the conflict between the dominant and high Castes and the Scheduled Castes, which death, and rape have to be seen as integral parts of the process of translating into reality the rights which the to say this is not to condone the savage attacks, but to economic and political change".

(*On Living in a Revolution*, India 2000; The Next Fifteen Years. PP 16-18)

The dalits thus become the test case for deciding whether or not we want to translate the ideas of "liberty, equality and fraternity" enshrined in the Constitution of India into reality. This is why I want to maintain that the question of dalits should become the important one for a nation wide debate. The Mandal controversy have demonstrated once again how sensitive this area is and how deep-seated the hatred against the dalits is. I would like to present the dalit perspective keeping in mind the following aspects; (1) Dalit History and Culture (2) Dalit Religion, (3) Dalit Sociology, (4) Dalit Economics, (5) Dalit Politics, (6) Dalit Movements and (7) Dalit Literature.

(1) **Dalit History and Culture:** The question of the history and culture of dalits is important for the dalit identity. There are several theories about the historical origins of the caste-system. What must be noted, however, is that the dalits are outside the four-fold caste system in India.

They are the *Avarnas*. The question of dalit identity is the question of these people's roots and their historical consciousness. History is important for them, but the current dominant historiographer is not on their side. The academic historian demands historical sources, particularly written sources or archeological findings. When we consider the question of the history of the dalit, they face several problems. More often than not the dalit people have no written folk traditions. Their histories are oral based on oral traditions. Added to this difficulty is the fact that by general consensus dalits were the conquered people. Their history, therefore, has to be constructed from hostile sources. What is needed is the historical scholarship that is 'interested' in dalit issues and which will look at their oral traditions more sympathetically and consider them as the 'alternative' historical sources.

Having studied carefully the question of the historical orgins of the dalit people and having based this study on the *Rigveda* and about the other religious text, Prabhati Mukherjee concludes thus : It is true that history of that period is based more on conjectures than on facts. Nevertheless, valid conjectures made by piecing together the various strands of indirect evidence would result in a working hypothesis. Further researches may then prove or disprove the validity of arguments and supply materials for the lacunae of the present study belonging to one of the shadowy periods of Indian history. The next part of the study, if possible, will be based on oral history from the untouchables.

That is to say, an empirical investigation is planned to find out what they themselves think about their origin, future, betterment of their lot, etc., Thus, we shall have views on untouchables from the "top" and the "bottom", and also from 'Outside and Inside'. (Beyond the Four *Varnas* : The Untouchables in India P.16)

Standing within the current tradition of the academic historiography. Mukherjee uses such words as 'Conjectures', and 'indirect evidence' but she does recognize the importance of 'Oral' history, views from the 'bottom' and also from 'inside'. Another important piece of historical research is Malati Shendge's *The Civilised Demons of the Rig Veda*, (Abhinav Publications, New Delhi, 1977).

Among dalit historians, there seems to be emerging a consensus that the dalits and tribals were the original inhabitants (Mul Bharatis, Adivasis) of India and, therefore, their history and culture are not only Pre-Aryan' but also Pre-Dravidian. If so, this claim of being the indigenous people of India needs to be examined. Apart from the Dalit oral histories, it is also necessary that the rituals, rites, festivals and other ceremonies of dalits are studied with a view to understanding their distinctive history and culture.

Professor Siddhalingaya, a member of the legislative Council, Karnataka, made an interesting and illuminating presentation on dalit culture. It was based on his painstaking research which analysed the myths and folksongs of dalits. He made the following points :

(a) That the Dalit Deity was a servant of the people. (b) That the Dalit Deity refused to dwell in temples and identified himself/herself with the homeless. (c) the Dalit Deity is a God of the poor. (d) Dalit culture maintains both the need as well as the worth of daily works. (e) Most of the dalit deities are female. (Arvind Nirmal (Ed.) From "No People" to God's People" PP. 2gf.)

Dalit Religion : From the above section, we note that both religion and culture of the dalits were different and distinctive from that of Brahmanic religion and culture. Prabhati Mukherjee writes :

"Overt reasons given for the Rigvedic people's enmity toward these groups were religious, cultural and ethnic. The Asuras did not worship Agni, the god par excellence of the Suras and others were culturally inferior and ethrically different. It was candidly admitted that, since they did not worship the same god or offer sacrifices like the Rigvedic people, they ought to be subjected."

What exactly the features of the religion of dalits were is difficult to say. A study of some of their prevailing religious practices indicate that they worshipped their ancestors and as mentioned above they also worshipped female deities. The social system was based on matriarchy. Historically, the Aryans seem to have inflicted double injury on the dalits. Through the subjugation of the dalits, the Aryans without making the dalits full members of the Hindu society, brought them into the Hindu fold only to assign them a subservient role, so that they could be exploited as the cheapest possible labour anywhere in the world. As far as the religion was concerned, the dalits were not given any access to the temples, denied worshipping rights, but the exploitative doctrine of Karma Samsara was used to make them believe that their status as dalits was determined by their Karma during their past lives. This was nothing less than double deprivation. The question of dalit religion, therefore, is important for understanding the modern dalit movement. In fact, the modern Dalit movement starts with the phenomenon of mass conversion movements.

Unfortunately, these mass conversion movements of the dalits have not received a proper attention from Indian historians. The modern dalit movement is inseparably bound with this mass conversion movements. Dr. John Webster writes :

The defining characteristic of the first stage in the modern Depressed Classes movement was mass conversion, especially to Christianity, as this was the most dramatic and alarming step the Depressed Classes took in the nineteenth Century to improve their lot. This stage may be dated from the 1860's or 1870's through the 1930's. The Depressed Classes themselves took the initiative in conversion. Usually a caste brotherhood or a portion of it in a particular village decided to convert and then encouraged their friends and relatives in neighbouring villages to convert as well. This they did because they thought conversion would be good for their people. Recent studies indicate that the primary 'good' converts had in mind was not economic (as economic reprisals far our weighted any economic benefits received) but social and psychological' a chance to acquire helpful friends outside the village, and most important of all, a new sense of ones own worth, dignity and self-respect which came with conversion. (*"From Indian Church to Indian Theology: An attempt at Thelogical Reconstruction"* in Arvind Nirmal editor, A READER IN DALIT THEOLOGY, PP.97f)

It was this deluge of mass conversion that awakened some thinking Hindu reformers to make special efforts to improve the conditions of the Depressed Classes. The initiative during this second phase of the Dalit movement was with caste Hindus led by Gandhi and his Harijan Sevak Sangh. The undisputed leader of the Dalit movement, Dr. B.R. Ambedkar, too, was convinced that a conversion to a religion other then publicly denounced Hinduism its customs and traditions and said, "Even though I am a born Hindu I will not die a Hindu." After his conversion to Buddhism on the 14th October 1956 he said that he felt as if he had been released from hell. He embraced Buddhism and this new religious appeal lay in the fact that it stood for a casteless society.

Religion continues to play a crucial role in the Dalit movement. The continued desperation of the Dalits was underscored in February 1981 when a spate of mass conversions took place in Meenakshipuram and Ramanathapuram in Tamil Nadu. These conversions in the South sent religious and political shock waves among organizations like RSS and VHP.

Our task seems to be two fold. On the one hand every attempt must be made to reconstruct the Pre-Aryan dalit religion through an indepth research and also write reliable histories of mass conversion movements in different regions. Politically, it must be ensured that dalits have a real choice in choosing to follow a religion that they want to. The Presidential order of 1951 is discriminatory in that the economic and other benefits are extended only to the dalits belonging to the Hindu fold and Sikh faith. The V.P. Singh government also included the Neo-Buddhists in this scheme subsequently.

Dalit Sociology : Sociology is the study of the structure and functioning of human society. More broadly, it could be defined as the study of social reality. E. Durkheim has said that "a society is not simply the mass of individuals that comprise it, nor the territory it occupies, nor the things it uses, nor the movement it carries out but above all it is the idea that it has of itself." (*The Elementary Forms of the Religious Life*, P. 618)

How do the dalits then perceive their own social reality? About this the following points could be made. They see themselves as the people discriminated against socially, religiously and economically. Secondly, they see themselves as the people who are dehumanized. Fifthly, they see themselves as a people who have been defeated, dispossessed and deprived by others. Finally, they see themselves as a people on the Periphery of the Indian social life. The 'Periphery' is not only in the literal sense of a geographical location, their existence on the outskirts of the Indian Village, but also in the sense that the rest of the society behaves as if the dalits simply do not matter.

In addition to the above listed characteristics of the dalit social reality, we should also add their segregation and their scatteredness. The net result is that they have developed. What Bishop Azariah calls, "Wounded Phyche".

But perhaps the most serious social handicap of the people is what I call the "Casteism of the outcaste" people. Technically, they are outside the Varna (Four-fold caste system) system, but because of the all-pervading casteism of Hinduism, they are divided into further Sub-divisions. Thus, we see the Malas and the Madigas and the Mahars and Margs going for each other's throats. The "Dalit Scenario" presents a picture of greatly disunited dalits.

Dalit Economics : The economic life of the dalits again presents a depressing scenario. The government's own Sixth Five Years Plan document for 1980-85 admits :

Three decades of development have not had the desired impact on these socially, economically and educationally handicapped groups. Their problems cannot be resolved, through the percolation of general economic growth. The majority of the Scheduled Castes and Scheduled Tribes, who form one-quarter of population, are below the poverty line– Continuing to pursue traditional Occupations, they are unable to participate fully in the process of modernization. The practice of untouchability against Scheduled Castes is a special handicap for them, and even the few educated groups amongst them are unable to compete for job opportunities created while Scheduled Tribes still remain outside the mainstream of development mainly because of their relative isolation and their exploitation by outside agencies. (*Sixth Plan Document* 1980-85, P. 417).

The situation did not change much even in relations to the Seventh Plan. In the context of the Seventh Plan, P.S. Krishnan writes :

The situation of the Scheduled Castes is the result of economic exploitation and deprivation and structured and organized inequality, in their extreme form, over the centuries in our country, particularly in the rural society and economy. (*Development of the Scheduled Castes* in Seventh Plan and Development of weaker sections, ed.J.Kananikal, ISI, P.41)

The "Positive discrimination" policy of the government also has not helped very much because of the persisent prejudice against dalits among the higher castes. The *Economic and political weekly* reports that:

There is an instance in the medical faculty of an SC student accorded a high percentage of marks in the previous exam and failing in the first year MBBS exam, but passing smoothly after he got his surname changed into that of a higher Caste. The same report tells us that some scheduled caste students when they applied through the reservation were told at their faces that they should become sweepers and scavengers not doctors. (I.P. Desai, *Anti-Reservation Agitation and structure of Gujarat Society*, EPW, 2 May, 1981, P.819)

Thus, both in rural and urban situations, dalits are economically handicapped. The most significant characteristic of the dalit people is the disproportionate burden of agricultural labour they carry. The proportion of agricultural labourers among rural made workers of the dalits and dalit converts is 52.55 percent against the corresponding proportion of 12.78 percent of non-dalit population. Even in the spheres other than agriculture, the dalits have to do a good part of hard, hazardous, low-income, low prestige, low-status labour. When we look at the urban occupational pattern of the dalits, it may be seen even the famous modernizing trend of urbanization has by-passed them to a great extent.

Against this economic scenario, some of the following schemes must be tried. Integrated economic development schemes for different occupational groups. Integrated economic development schemes for bringing about occupational mobility. Educational development schemes. Schemes for providing essential needs and continued positive discrimination. (Krishnan, OP. Cit., P.58)

Dalit Politics : Through the initiative of late Dr. B.R. Ambedkar, three different experiments have been tried. They were : (a) Independent Labour Party, (b) Scheduled Castes Federation and finally (c) The Republican party of India. As we know, the Republican party of India has had several factions. It has ceased to be an effective political force. Dr. Ambedkar's vision that the RPI would be a party of all weaker sections has not been realized. There are several reasons for this. The "Casteism of the Outcastes" is one such reason. Then political reservations have ben manipulated by political parties in such a way that the dalit electorate were always divided. Perhaps the earlier dalit demand for separate electorate should be reconsidered in a fresh manner. What is the role of caste in Indian Politics ? Should we accept Rajani Kothari's thesis that both politics and caste are undergoing changes through mutual interaction? (*Caste in Indian Politics*, Introduction, PP. 3-25) Can the caste itself be used creatively for a more dynamic politics? Will such a use be too risky and dangerous ? These are some of the issues that we must consider.

Meanwhile some of the realities the dalits face in their exercise of their political rights should worry us. They are not even allowed to exercise their right to vote freely. Alexandra George writes :

During the last 1980 general elections the chief Election Commissioner received reports from many constituencies about intimidation and assaults on Scheduled Castes and lower Castes. In Katha Village only 30 km from the Capital, New Delhi, Scheduled Castes were chased away from the special polling booth set up for them and told their votes would be cast for them. In Haryana, in thirty villages in Rohtak district, thirty villages in Sonpat district and fourteen villages in Mahendragarh district polling booths were captured and SCs were stopped from voting. (Op. Cit.p.212)

Dalit Movements : Above, I cited John Webster's historical analysis of the phases of the Dalit Movement. The first phase was characterized by the mass conversion movements. The second by the caste Hindu efforts at social reform. According to Webster, the third phase dated from the 1920's to the present is characterized by self-assertion and self-reliance on the part of the dalits. (OP. Cit. P. 100) This, indeed, is the right direction for the dalit movements to take.

No adequate typology of dalit movements has been developed, so far. There are, however, two notable exceptions Ghanshyam Shah classifies dalit movements into (a) Reformative and (b) Alternative. The former tries to reform the caste system to solve the problem of untouchability and the latter attempts to create an alternative socio-cultural structure by conversion to some other religion or by acquiring education, economic status and political power. Shah further divides the Reformative type into (a) Bhakti movements, (b) neo-Vedantic movements and (c) Sanskritization movements. The Alternative movements are divided into (a) Conversion movements (b) Secular Movements. (Ghanshyam Shah, *Social Movements in India*, P. 108)

The second attempt at typology of the dalit movements comes form T.K.O. Oomen, His classification is as follows: (a) Bhakti movements trying to purify Hinduism (b) Movements oriented to a reinterpretation of Hinduism so as to cleanse it of its evil accretions notably neo-Vedantic movements and (c) Movements rejecting Hinduism-conversion movements.

(*Women, Protest and Change: Studies in social movements*, P. 258)

It is obvious from the above two typologies that the reformist types are opted for by caste Hindus and the alternative types are opted for by the dalits themselves. Gandhi and Ambedkar belong to the two types respectively. Perhaps we need both them. The dalits need to assert themselves and their rights and the caste Hindus need a change of heart.

Dalit Literature : Dalit literature or Dalits Sahitya movement originated in Maharashtra in the early 1970's. Its has derived its inspiration from Ambedkar's writings. It seeks to become the voice of the voiceless. From Maharashtra, it has now spread to Karnataka, Tamil Nadu, Uttar Pradesh and other states. The three distinguishing marks of Dalit Sahitya are : a) Pathos, (b) Protest and (c) A search for a better tomorrow.

Most of the dalit writers are actively involved in the actual dalit struggle movements. Dalit literature has raised the question of appropriate alternative literary criteriology. It has enriched the respective languages and made literature more life-oriented and realistic. Most of the Universities now have a separate branch of study for Dalit Literature.

Conclusion : What is presented above is only a rough sketch of the Dalit Scenario. We need these type of studies. The Socio-economic and Political sphere requires a participatory liberative type of research–one which includes Dalits greatly.

These studies will enable us to move in the right direction of realizing our Constitutional ideals of Liberty, Equality and Fraternity.

15

Christian Solidarity with National Dalit Movement

Henry Thiagaraj

This is a remarkable development today in comparison to ten years ago when people in the Churches were shy of using the word "Dalit" and some of the church officials said that we should not bring caste in to the church, without realizing that caste already existed in the Churches in India. Many clergymen then were very critical and were not willing to cooperate to work for Dalit Liberation. At that time a fashion among the liberation theologians was "economic liberation" which emphasized the class differences and avoided the caste discrimination in the Church. Social oppression and discrimination is largely associated with untouchability.

This aspect to some extent was realized by some Church Leaders in August 1993 when I was the Convenor of the Delegation of Church Leaders to call on the President of India, Dr. Shankar Dayal Sharma, to speak about the Dalit Christian's discrimination. There were many Bishops from both Church of North India and Church of South India including the Moderator of CNI and the President of SC & ST Unit of Catholic Bishops Conference of India. This marked a sea change in the attitude of the Church Leaders over a period of seven years.

Yet, the struggles of the Dalits are not decreasing, or being solved as an increasing number of atrocities are being committed on Dalits who have become the victims of violence only show that their struggles will continue in greater vigor. Now we see the attack on Church and the Christians by the Hindu Sangh Pariwar and other Hindu fanatics and reminded us of the famous saying of **Pastor Niemoeller,** a Victim of the Nazis:

First they came for the Jews
and I did not speak out,
because I was not a Jew
Then they came for the Communists
and I did not speak out-
because I was not a communist.
Then they came for the trade unionists
and I did not speak out-
because I was not a trade unionist.
Then they came for me-
and there was no one left
to speak out for me.

When the Hindu Sangh Pariwar demolished mosque in 1992 the Churches in India kept quiet. When the Dalits were attacked and Dalit women were raped, the Christians kept quiet. Now churches are being burnt, we are crying! But we need the support of others. It is in this context I would like to ask all of you when such atrocities are happening what is the church doing? What are you doing? Often Christians as good people keep silent, or want to bear everything silently! The Bible has a tradition of fighting for justice.

The whole prophetic movement of the Old Testament was significantly clear that oppression should be removed and justice established and the Kingdom of God will be filled with justice and righteousness. These sayings came because of the oppression suffered by the Jews in the Old Testament period.

One of the earliest of prophets Amos coming from Rural background conveyed the following God's message to the people:-

I hate, I despise your festivals
And take not delight in your feasts
Though you bring to me burnt-offerings:
I will not accept your gifts
Nor look at the beasts you offer.
Away with the noise of your songs!
I will not hear the strum of your harps!

(Amos)

Amos appealed to the people "to hate evil and do what is good". Again this type of statement spoken by Prophet Isaiah.

- *"When you fast, you make yourselves suffer; you bow your heads low like a blade of grass, and spread out sackcloth and ashes to lie on. Is that what you call fasting? Do you think I will be pleased with that?*
- *The kind of fasting I want is this: Remove the chains of oppression and the yoke of justice and let the oppressed go free.*

- *Share your food with the hungry and open your homes to the homeless poor. Give clothes to those who have nothing to wear, and do not refuse to help your own relatives;*
- *"Then my favour will shine on you like the morning sun, and your wounds will be quickly healed. I will always be with you to save you; my presence will protect you on every side". (Chapter 58: verse 5-9)*

God answers us only if you put an end on oppression then only He will answer your prayer, He will respond to your call to Christ in whose life all the prophesies are fulfilled stood for the liberation of the oppressed. In Nazareth, Christ at his early age has declared His Mission, the purpose of coming to us in this world to set the oppressed free. His famous declaration is well known to all of you.

The Spirit of the Lord is upon me,
Because he hath anointed me to preach the gospel to the poor;
He hath sent me to heal the brokenhearted,
To preach deliverance to the captives,
And recovering of sight to the blind,
To set at liberty them that are bruised,
To preach the acceptable year of the Lord

(St. Luke Ch4, V 18-19)

As Christians it is our task, and we should hear the Call of God to work for Dalit liberation and to work for the justice of the oppressed Dalits. It must be noted that many people who spear headed the Dalit Liberation work in India are Christians. It is the Dalit Christians who were hurt, assaulted, butchered, killed, yet there is, Civil Protection Act to protect them!. This was the case at Tsunduru in Andhra Pradesh or in Southern Districts of Tamil Nadu.

The Churches must fight for the injustices and practises of discrimination. Bishop Liberation of the Christian Dalits is bound with the liberation of the Dalits. It is true, yet very unfortunately now the Hindu fanatic groups are sowing the seeds of division and made Dalits, say things against Dalit Christians. But unless the Church takes it as a major task the Dalit Liberation work will remain weak. Indirectly we will strengthen against those who prosecute us!

The Church is not an impersonal body, Church is a human body which is dynamic transforming society. It is usually the Christians who fight against injustices and create awareness to fight for Human Rights. As we see many (Non-Government Organisations) NGOs are lead by Dalit Christians, even those who in the beginning felt shy are not afraid now to call themselves Dalits.

One of the great weaknesses are even the curse of our people is that because they were dehumanized for thousands of years. They were not made to come together and work together and enjoy human fellowship. They were divided on the basis of occupation like leather workers, sanitation workers and agricultural labourers, etc. It became difficult to unite them with a common factor. The common factors that remain constant are negative like discrimination, oppression, violence, violation on Human Rights. There is no positive factors to unite our people-"who die in the words of Christ like **"sheep without shepherd"**.

As Dalits are divided on the basis of language, occupation, cultural and regional factors, it is difficult to bring them together. It is for this reason Dalit solidarity programmes are promoted. The important task as Babasaheb Dr. Ambedkar said is to make our people to become humanized, that is from dehumanized condition humanize them first. This humanizing process is a great task when they are divided by several factors. Babasaheb Dr. Ambedkar said:

- "Ours is a battle not for wealth or for power. It is a battle for freedom. It is a battle for the reclamation or human personality"

Often caste conflicts are treated as local law and order problem. Even though seven Dalits including the Chairman of Panchayat were butchered like in Melavalavu, worst caste violence had occurred in Southern Districts of Tamil Nadu or Mumbai – these are treated as local law and order problems. When these matters were raised in the Parliament, the Home Ministers would repeat what the bureaucrats tell them. They had said that it is a matter coming under the purview of the State law and order, we are asking the Chief Minister to take necessary action as this is a state subject. If more questions are raised and Members of Parliament demand action, they will appoint a judicial commission whose report will not come out easily or when the report is released, people forget the facts and what happened to question it. The report will distort the facts and realities. In the life of Dalits, we have found that "Justice delayed is justice denied" a reality in our life.

It is in this situation during the 50th Anniversary of the Universal Declaration of Human Rights some of the NGOs who came for a consultation at ISI, Bangalore decided to launch a National Campaign on Dalit Human Rights. It is proposed to collect signatures from ten million people. In the beginning of it we presented 1000 signature to the President of India on 10 December 1998–World Human Rights Day and 50th Anniversary of UDHR.

As Dr. Ambedkar said: "The Hindus practise injustice and tyranny against Untouchables only because they are weak. First Untouchables cannot face social and religious persecution, so long as they remain weak and divided. Secondly, they do not possess enough strength to face the tyranny. With those two conclusions, the third one automatically follows. That is the strength required to face the tyranny needs to be procured from outside."

In my opinion it has to come from Universal Declaration of Human Rights (UDHR). This is why we are asking the UN High Commissioner for Human Rights to give us the right and freedom to choose our belief as assured in the UDHR.

> *Everyone has the right to freedom of thought, conscience and religion; this right includes freedom to change his religion or belief, and freedom, either alone or in community with others and in public or private, to manifest his religion or belief in teaching, practise, worship and observance.*
>
> *UDHR ARTICLE 18*

We have also launched this National Campaign in the Constitution Club with the Union Minister for Health and Family Welfare Mr. Dalit Ezhilmalai, giving us the lead and inaugurating the Campaign on 10th December'98. By 14th April 1999, we wanted to complete the collection of ten million signatures and become more vigorous by representing to Prime Minister, Governor, Chief Minister, President and to the International Forums.

If Churches express solidarity with this national movement and will inform their parent missions of all those church missions with whom they have partnerships, networking connections it will bring the international pressures and the problems of Dalits are likely to be solved. As the aid money that is received by the Government should have a clause that it should reach the poorest of the poor–the Dalits, who are still living in thatched huts, are homeless whose children are still out of school and are half-naked and has large number of school drop-outs. Our people are still living as agricultural labourers, sanitation workers, etc. hardships amidst. Some of you may have read in the Newspaper (New *Indian Express*) that the American Government has a Special Assistant Secretary to study the discrimination on the basis of religion that to impose sanction on Governments.

Unless Churches in India realize their task, their prophetic Mission and takes it up with its prophetic role and spearheads this Dalit Liberation struggle and mobilize the public opinion both in the country and abroad, our struggles may not find easy solutions.

I would like to remind you what a prophetic role Dr. Martin Luther King, Jr., played in leading the Afro-American people towards their liberation. He won the Noble Prize for his services. His struggles for the liberation of the African American people in United States was based on his Christian conviction and Christian faith.

"In a real sense all life is inter-related. All are caught in an inescapable network or mutuality, tied in a single garment of destiny".

Dr. Martin Luther King, Jr.

If Dr. Martin Luther King, Jr., a Christian Pastor can bring deliverance to the African-American people, how much more the powerful Church in India can do by giving a lead to the Christians in India. We all should work towards the Kingdom of God.

Then justice will rule through all the land and out of justice, peace. quietness and confidence will reign for ever more. (Isaiah 32.17)

I know a few pastors have expressed lot of support to Dalit struggles and have opened their church compound for Dalit consultations and organizing the poor Dalits. Yet I know many other pastors and church officials think Dalit liberation is not their business! It is only to remind the words of Pastor Niemoeller, "First they came for the Jews. Then they came for the Dalits and now they are coming for Christians." If you have not raised your voice and condemn the Dalit atrocities and they come for you there may not be anyone to speak for you. So, my friends, wake up, arise and stand against discrimination and injustice.

Footnotes

1. Krishnan, PS: Keynote address delivered at the National seminar on Implementation and Impact of SCs/STs (Prevention of Atrocities) Act, 1989 on the Scheduled Castes organized by Centre for Social system, School of Social Sciences, JNU, March 22-23, 2000
2. Naval, op.cit., p. 4
3. Human Rights Watch, Broken People, Caste Violence against India's untouchables, 1999; p. 25
4. Ghurye, G.S. quoted in Bhopal Document–Chartering a New Course for Dalits for the 21 century,
5. Bhopal Document, op. cit., p. 16
6. Naval, op. cit., p. 10
7. Naval, op. cit., p. 13
8. Naval, op. cit., p. 15
9. Naval, op. cit., p. 16.

16

The Dalit Question : Search for a Human Future

Dr. K. Wilson

For quote sometime all of us have been abundantly using the term "Dalit" with reference to certain particular segregated castes. Dalit problem, too, is viewed and dealt with as a caste problem, and that, too, as the problem of some sub-castes. But in itself, the term Dalit does not denote any caste or sub-castes. If this term is ever used with reference to the "untouchables" sections of India, it is purely on existential grounds only and not on the basis of caste. It is addressed to describe the human condition of particular castes and sub-castes which are subjected to sub-humanity, deprivation, and marginalization. It manifests the culture of the fourth World.

According to the fundamental human rights implemented at the U.N.O., in 1948, "All Human beings are born free and equal in dignity and rights. They are endowed with reason and conscience" (Article-I). But this is not in the case of Dalits in India. The following articles make no meaning to them. Everyone has the right to life, liberty and security of person (Article-3). No one shall be held in slavery or servitude; and the slave trade shall be prohibited in all their forms (Article-4). No one shall be subjected to torture or to cruel, inhuman or degrading treatment or punishment (Article-5). No one shall be subjected to arbitrary interference with his privacy, family, home or correspondence, not to attacks upon his honour and reputation. Everyone has the right to the protection of the law against such interference or attacks. Everyone has the right to freedom of movement and residence within the borders of each state. (Article-13). Men and women of full age, without any limitation due to race, nationality or religion, have the right to marry and to found a family.

(Article-16.1). Everyone has the right to own property alone as well as in association with others. (Article-17.1). No one shall be arbitrarily deprived of his property (Article-17.2). Everyone has the right to freedom to change his religion or belief, and freedom, either alone or in community with others and public or private, to manifest his religion or belief in teaching, practice, worship and observance. (Article-18) Everyone has the right to work, to free choice of employment, to just and favourable conditions of work and to protection against unemployment. (Article-23). Everyone, without any discrimination, has the right to equal pay for equal work. (Article 23.2) Everyone has the right to rest and to leisure, including reasonable limitation of working hours and periodic holidays with pay. (Article-24) Everyone has the right to a standard of living adequate for the health and well-being of himself and of his family, including food, clothing, housing and medical care necessary social services, and the right to security in the event of unemployment, sickness, disability, widowhood, old age or other lack of livelihood in circumstances beyond his control. (Article 25.1). Everyone has the right to education. (Article 26.1). Everyone has the right to education. (Article-26.1). Education shall be directed to the full development of the human personality and to the strengthening of respect for human rights and fundamental freedoms. (Article-26.2). Everyone has the right freely to participate in the cultural life of the community, to enjoy the parts and to share in scientific advancement and its benefits.

(Article-27.1)

But millions of Dalits are not privileged enough to enjoy these rights. They cannot choose their residential areas, cannot vote according to their wishes; they are not privileged to dine along with all the others. They have not the capacity to posses immovable properties. They do not have opportunities, for better education; do not have employment opportunities. They are powerless to participate in the decision making process. They cannot dare to ask for justice or for just wages. For that matter, they cannot exercise their right to claim their human right. This is the reality. In short, they have no right to be human in their own land. They have only one right, i.e., to be servile under and serve the interests of the elites and the privileged. If and when they break this, then, they are considered to have violated their right. This perhaps functions as the Indian model of human right. Their rights to be human is questioned and systematically denied from their birth to death. But such violations have not been focused by organizations such as Amnesty International (AI), the scope of which is limited to things such as tortures, rapes, and deaths in police custody, imprisonment without trial.

The A.I., is dealing with the problem of human rights in terms of State verses the People. But the problem of Dalit human rights is intertwined with the Indian society verses the Dalits. This the A.I. does not seem to be concerned with. Strictly speaking, if there is any community which has the problem of right to be human beings, it is these Dalit sections only. Their sub-human conditions substantiate this. But, on paper, it is as though they have all the rights on the face of the earth. Without their name there are no newspapers, no elections, no foreign aid, no political manifest, no development projects. It come out of the elitistic trap of caste. Instead of raising their rights to be human, they are still grappling with the problem of caste. It is as though their future, their humanity hinges on caste problem. They therefore argue that to regain or resort their humanity, caste must be removed. On the other hand, there are some who treat the problems of caste and humanity as identical.

Caste is an idea; a psyche; a tradition, an inheritance, a unit with certain specific characteristics. It is part of Indian reality. Every Indian inherited a social form such as tribes, castes. At the same time, we are endowed with certain rights to be human by virtue of our inherent humanity. I have a right to be human regardless of my caste. My humanity does not depend upon my caste. Humanity is not the private property or monopoly of any particular caste. One needs to disown his or her caste to attain one's humanity. My prestige or my value does not depend upon my name. I do not have to change or disown my name in order to attain fame and prestige. So, is the case with caste. Let us not look down on our own caste. In the same vein, let us not look on ourselves down. Contemporary Dalits must come our openly and respect, assert and function within their own caste.

Dalit redemption from caste stigma takes place when Dalits learn to respect their own social forms viz: their castes and sub-castes. As long as Black people in the West believed and practiced the Whiteman;s interpretation of their colour, the Black man thundered saying that my very blackness is the source of my beauty; the Black community emerged as authentic human beings. It is this which should happen in the Indian context also. To accomplish this, a team of Dalit Youth must dedicate itself for the cause of human rights, education to the Dalits, particularly at the grass root level. Human rights can be asserted in terms of two things. The one is one's consciousness of himself or herself; i.e. in one's undiluted confidence of himself or herself as a human being. The second is one's own being i.e., in one's objective life. This has to do with his material standing and the concomitant relations his or her human right standing without inhibitions. A conscientized poor man finds it an uphill task to realize his human standing. Unless a person is materially developed, it will be difficult for one to exercise one's human rights. Hence, the term human right must, in the Indian context, be interpreted as "Human Development". Right without development is a contradiction in terms.

Dalit youth must engage themselves in communicating two kinds of education: (1) Consciousness education (2) Development education. The former is aimed at unfolding the undiluted humanity of Dalit, inspite of their poverty. The second seeks to create an urgency among the Dalits to improve their material conditions. Dalit youth must shoulder this responsibility for educational movements. By doing so they will be creating a new history in the life of Dalits. It is imperative that a clear-cut action programme on human rights education is drawn and implemented to Dalits in all the State, District and Gram Panchayat levels. A national programme for human rights education must be launched forthwith. This task can be undertaken only by Dalit Youth.

"A new man is emerging. He is the man of the Fourth World. His World is going to be found neither on the power of capital nor on the forced ideology, but a World based on the knowledge of what it means to be human. Let the Dalit Indian become partners of this human future by working as the agents of its concretization."

Dr. K. Wilson is the Emeritus Professor of Philosophy of Osmania University, Hyderabad, and a Dalit Intellectual known for his innovative thinking.

17

The Law Against Atrocities

Bhagwan Das

There are two kinds of religion in the world. Organized religions have a founder, scriptures containing the teaching of the founder, and rituals, festivals and ceremonies approved by the founder or introduced by devout successors. Unorganized religions have developed according to the wisdom, knowledge, social and religious needs of the people. Judaism, Buddhism, Christianity, and Islam are organized category. It is difficult to define Hinduism. For the purpose of making marriage succession law, the law makers chose to use a very broad definition. Sir Hari Singh Gour wrote in The Hindu Code (p.86) "When we think of Hindu religion, we find it difficult if not impossible to define Hindu religion or even adequately describe it. Unlike other religions in the world, the Hindu religion does not claim any one prophet; it does not worship any one God; it does not subscribe to any one dogma; it does not believe in any one philosophic concept; it does not follow any one set of religious rites or performances; in fact it does not appear to satisfy the narrow traditional features of any religion or creed. It may broadly be described as a way of life and nothing more".

> "Even if a Dalit mustered up the courage to approach the police when his or her civil rights were violated, the police officers rarely registered the complaint. . . "

Essential features of Hinduism are caste, the practice of untouchability, as well as belief in Karma and rebirth. All Hindus follow

Courtesy: Dalit International News letter, USA.

the law framed by the Brahmins, especially in the matter of naming children, the performance of marriage ceremonies, and cremation. Dalits and other lower caste people did not follow these customs until the final decades of the 19th century. Their mass conversion to Christianity frightened Hindus because numerical strength had become politically and economically important. They began to own the low castes as long lost brethren and vigorously promoted their Hinduization. As a result, many among the deprived, oppressed and exploited began to imitate upper caste Hindus in such matter as festivals, rituals and ceremonies.

Hindu society is now divided into more than five thousand castes and Dalits (Untouchables), who were counted under the Scheduled Castes Order appended to the Constitution in 1950 as Scheduled Castes are divided into more than nine hundred castes. The caste system has sustained Hinduism and is based on "graded inequality," one caste above the other.

Early Legislation

Untouchability was abolished under Article 17 of the constitution which was adopted on November 26, 1949. Some six years after the adoption of the constitution, a law was enacted known as the Untouchability Offenses Act 1955, which contained very mild punishments against offenders and thus served neither a corrective nor deterrent purpose. It was amended in 1976. Its title was changed to the Protection of Civil Rights Act 1976 and more deterrent punishment was added. The law did not define Untouchability because the Honorable Law Minister said, "There is no need to define 'Untouchability'; everybody knows it."

The promotion of education; urbanization; provision like the reservation of seats for Scheduled Castes and Scheduled Tribes in legislative bodies and public services the general awakening among Dalit people; and Hindu propaganda to own the Untouchables to prevent their conversion to Christianity, Islam, Buddhism or Sikhism have all contributed towards the abolition of untouchability in the cities to some extent. However, more than 70% of the Indian populations live in villages where untouchability is practiced rigidly. The law does not help partly because the majority of the people do not know about this law. Even if a Dalit mustered up the courage to approach the police when his or her civil rights were violated, the police officers rarely registered the complaint under the Protection of Civil Rights Act. The majority of cases were dropped or ended up in acquittals for want of "evidence".

Whenever the Scheduled Castes or Scheduled Tribes people tried to assert their rights granted by the constitution or subsequent legislation, the dominating castes, such as the land holding upper castes in the rural areas, use violence and other methods to terrorize the Dalits and silence the people belonging to the deprived and oppressed sections of society. These powerful, well-to-do land holding castes have no fear or respect for the law. The usual methods they employ to terrorize include raping the women, striping them and parading them through the village streets naked, killing leaders of organizations demanding the wages set by Government, burning the houses of Scheduled Castes and Scheduled Tribes people, and denying them passage through the fields or water rights. These acts have been treated as "acts of atrocities". As the number of such acts increased, a law known as the Scheduled Castes and Scheduled Tribes Prevention of Atrocities Act was passed in 1989. In order to enforce it, rules had to be framed. It took the Government six years to draw up and publish those rules. They were finally published in the Gazette of India on March 31, 1995.

Some Reflections

Both untouchability and atrocities have the sanction of religion and tradition. In the famous epic poem, the Ramayana, Rama had beheaded the Shudra, Sambukh, who, because of the fact that he was a Shudra by birth, had violated the law by worshipping the God to attain "Devlok". Similarly in the Mahabharata, Eklaviya, a low caste man, was denied admission to archery classes by a Brahmin teacher and was asked to cut off his thumb because he had acquired proficiency in the art of archery without paying a "Gurudakshana" fee to the teacher. In the Hindu law books provisions were made to keep the Untouchables poor, ignorant, illiterate, divided, deprived and disunited. they were required to pay higher rates of interest and were permitted o retain only a fraction of any money they found on the roads or in other places.

It is easy to frame laws to abolish atrocities arising from untouchability and put them on the statute books. However, given the background described above, it is difficult to enforce those laws in favor of the poor, helpless Untouchables. The bureaucracy, the police and the judiciary are dominated by the upper caste Hindus who have been enjoying power for centuries.

There is a growing awareness among the Dalit masses. They are discussing issues like globalization, privatization, abolition of reservations in the public services, changes in educational policies, the non-enforcement of laws against atrocities, the exclusion of Dalits from the Planning Commission, the role of the judiciary, the emergence of private armies to terrorize Dalits, and the promotion of Hindutva in conferences and seminars throughout the country. Soon mass movements may emerge to fight caste and to organize people for brining about real changes. The Dalit Problem is gradually being internationalized.

18

Non-Governmental Organizations and the United Nations System

Ibrahim Fall

We have now reached the end of a long and arduous road which began some three years ago with the General assembly's decision to convene a World Conference on Human Rights.

From the beginning, the World Conference was seen as a dynamic process aimed at involving ever larger sectors of society in our quest for effective protection of human dignity. Here I think we can claim success. Our meetings here in Vienna have been a "World" Conference in the true in the sense of the term. People from every corner of the earth were represented and the subjects dealt with are the daily preoccupations of all our fellow human beings.

Never before have so many Governments representing so many diverse cultures and peoples given such indepth attention to human rights. Throughout the preparatory process in the NGO activities, intense debate and reflection by Governments in dialogue with other Governments, International organizations, national institution, the NGO community and human rights experts have dissipated many misconceptions and made real progress in mutual understanding. Common views and strategies have evolved from this growing consultation.

This mobilization for and participation in the Conference may well be one of its most significant outcomes, especially if it is enhanced in the future by more cooperation and coordination among the institutions

Mr. Ibrahim Fall, Secretary General of the World Conference on Human Rights held at Vienna on 25th June 1993, in a closing statements made at the conference.

and organizations active in the field of human rights and / or development.

I would also like to underline here the direct participation of the people concerned in the Conference itself. Children spoke directly to the plenary on the violations of their rights and their hopes for the futures. Women also told us of the issues directly concerning them, as did indigenous people from all over the world. This Conference also benefited from the substantive contribution of the United Nations treaty bodies, our special rapporteurs and working groups, United Nations specialized agencies and bodies and regional human rights organisations.

Governments were, of course, at the centre, for only Governments can undertake international obligations and only Governments are ultimately responsible for human rights protection.

The Conference itself was an act of reaffirmation and strengthening of the international standards proclaimed by United Nations since its creation and the validity and importance of enhancement of the methods of implementation developed since then.

This must be understood to extend not only to the rights themselves, but also to the protection of those rights. We must act as energetically and with equal determination to protect the human rights of victims-especially of massive voilations-no matter where they live, and regardless of their culture or religion. It is their right to protection, not our option to act or not. And I understand the concerns of those who see a lack of consistency in this matter.

We also have reaffirmed the crucial principle of equality and the need to fight all forms of discrimination, xenophobia, and intolerence. One of the greatest dangers to human rights is racism, racial discrimination and exclusion. These are cancers, which begin by attacking the weakest members of the community, minorities, immigrants, refugees, indigenous people, and which can soon spread to destroy a whole society. It is vain to look for long-term economic progress in a society of exclusion and I wish to solemnly warn against the temptation of seeking short-term political gain through the language of exclusion.

The Conference's recognition of the interdependence and mutually reinforcing relationship between democracy, development and human rights is important. It will provide the foundation for future convergent action by international organization and national agencies to promote all aspects of human rights. Further, the recognitions by this conference of the right to development as a human right means that we can now turn from theoretical debates to seeking ways of giving reality to the development.

Mr.President, there are a number of the areas of progress which can be mentioned, such as:

Women

On the issue of women's human rights, in response to the unprecedented call from a worldwide movement, the World Conference took historic new steps.

The main policy message of the Conference is that equal status of women and the human rights of women should be integrated into the mainstream of United Nations system-wide activity. All the human rights treaty bodies and the monitoring special Rapporteurs and Working Groups of the Commission of Human Rights should incorporate women's human rights concerns in their work. The role of Governments, NGO's and the United Nations Secretariat is very important in that respect. The Conference also calls for increased cooperation between the Commission on the Status of Women, the Commission on Human Rights, the Committee against the Discrimination of Women, UNIFEM, UNDP and other United nations agencies.

At the normative level, the Conference calls for the universal ratification of the Convention against the Discrimination of women by the year 2000, and the preparation of an optional protocol to this Convention introducing the right of petition.

The Conference clearly saw violence against women as a human rights concern, as affecting women's fundamental human dignity. It calls for the elimination of all forms of sexual harrassment, exploitation and trafficking in women, the elimination of gender bias in the administration of justice and the eradication of any conflicts between the rights of women and the harmful effects of certain traditional practices, cultural prejudices and religious extremism. It also gave its support for the creation of a new mechanism, a Special Rapporteur on Violence against Women at the Commisssion on Human Rights and called for the adoption of the Declaration on Violence against Women by the General; Assembly.

Finally the full integration of women at the policy-making level, both within the Secretariat of the United Nations and within the decision-making and experts bodies of the Organization has also been called as well as training for United Nations human rights and humanitarian relief personnel so that they are assisted to recognize and deal with human rights abuses particular to women and to carry out their work without gender bias.

Children

Children's rights have also been given specific attention.

The World Conference stressed that:

States should ratify universally by the year 1995 the Convention on the rights of the Child and integrate it in their national action plans.

Laws, regulations and customs harmful to the girl child should be eliminated.

The Conference strongly supports the proposal of the Committee on the Rights of the Child for a study into means of improving the protection of children in armed conflicts and calls on the Committee to study the question of raising the minimum age of recruitment into the armed forces.

Here, Mr.President, we must remember the devastating effect on children of illicit drugs especially on the eve of the International Day against Drug Abuse and Trafficking.

Indigenous Peoples

The World Conference agreed to recommend to the General Assembly that it proclaim an international decade of the World's indigenous peoples. This will allow the United Nations to build on the measures taken in 1993 during the International Year and open a new chapter of partnership between indigenous peoples and Governments.

The World Conference also agreed to recommend that a voluntary fund be established to finance the activities of the international decade and it also supports the strengthening of the office dealing with indigenous people in the United Nations.

Monitoring

In the area of monitoring,

- The World Conference has underlined the importance of preserving and strengthening the system of Special Procedure rapporteurs/Representatives/Experts and Working Groups of the Commission on Human Rights and has asked that they be provided with the necessary human and financial resources.
- The procedure and mechanisms should be enabled to harmonize and rationalize their work through periodic meetings and all States are asked to co-operate fully with them.
- In addition to the above-mentioned central provision, the final declaration stresses repeatedly the need for protection of all human rights as a priority objectives of the United Nations and consequently the strengthening of national and international mechanisms.
- The call for additional resources for the Centre for Human Rights also includes special procedures and mechanism and the final document specially mentions that the Centre should be assured adequate means for this purpose.
- The existing Special rapporteurs on torture and on racism, racial discrimination, xenophobia and related intolerance have

been specially referred to and the decision of the Commission to consider the appointment of a Special Rapporteur on violence against women at its next session has been welcomed.

Ratification and Reservations

- The World Conference has demanded, not only for the universal ratification of the Convention on the Rights of the Child and the speedy ratification of the other human rights instruments, but
- The Secretary-General and the treaty bodies should pursue a dialogue with states to identify possible obstacles to ratification and show such obstacles could be removed.
- Call for special attention to be paid in the 1998 review of progress achieved towards universal ratification of the treaties and their protocols.
- States should be encouraged to limit the number and scope of their reservations to human rights instruments and ensure that such reservations are not imcompatible with the object and purpose of a treaty.
- States are invited to consider ratification of the International Convention on the Rights of all Migrant Workers and Members of their Families as soon as possible.

Economic, Social and Cultural Rights

- The World Conference welcomed the appointment by the commission on Human Rights of a thematic Working Group on the right to develop with the urgent task to look into measures to eliminate obstacles to the Declaration on the right to development, and recommended that the possibility of elaborating an optional protocol to the Covenant on Economic, Social and Cultural Rights should be given further consideration by the Commission in Human Rights.

Technical Assistances

One major theme which runs throughout the Declaration and Programme of Action is the need to strengthen the enjoyment of human rights through technical assistance should be made available were pointed out including in strengthening the institutions of democracy and human rights, the judiciary, in the protection of minorities, indigenous peoples and in promoting human rights education.

High Commissioner

The World Conference recommended the General Assembly to give consideration at its 48th session to the question of the establishment of a High Commissioner for Human Rights for the promotion and protection of human rights.

Resources

In terms of strengthening the resources of the Centre for Human Rights the Conference expressed its concerns at the growing disparity between activities of the Centre and the human, financial and other sources available to carry them out, and requested the Secretary-General to take immediate steps, to substantially increase the resources for the human rights programmes from the regular budget and to take urgent steps to seek increased extra-budgetary resources.

Within this framework, an increased proportion of the regular budget is called for to be allocated directly to the Centre for Human Rights so as to enable it to carry out its activities effectively, efficiently and expeditiously.

Moreover, the Secretary-General and Member States are urged to adopt a coherent approach aimed at securing resources commensurate to the increased mandates.

Follow-up to the World Conference

Three main recommendations have been made: that the General Assembly considers ways means for the full implementation, without delay, of the recommendations contained in the Declaration of this Conference; that the Commission on Human Rights annually review the progress towards this end; and that the Secretary-General of the United Nations invite on the occasion of the Fiftieth Anniversary of the Universal Declaration of Human Rights all States, all organs and agencies of the United nations system related to human rights, to report to him on the progress made in the implementation of the Declaration of this Conference.

The Conference also dealt with increased coordination on human rights within the United Nation system; persons belonging to national or ethnic, religions; the rights of the disable persons; strengthening of human rights; and human rights education. The Conference also placed special emphasis on the elimination of torture urging all States to put an immediate end to torture and to adopt the measures of prevention.

Mr. President,

We have come to the end of the World Conference road and are about to begin on another, that of putting into practice the Conference's decisions.

The Declaration has set out for us a programme of Action for Human Rights based on the principle of cooperation, the need to adopt a holistic approach to promoting human rights and the necessity of involving actors at all levels, international, national and local.

Cooperation is essential to the identification of problems, to finding appropriate solutions and the resources necessary for their implementation. But cooperation will only be viable if its based on the reaffirmation of the principles and rules of human rights and rules of human rights and a commitment not to tolerate violations.

A key lesson of the World Conference is that we must adopt a holistic and coordinated approach to promoting human rights. For examples, in protecting the rights of the child we must look at the wide range of factors affecting the child's daily life; health, education, food, shelter, parental employment and remuneration, legal protection, protection from exploitative labour, treatment in the judicial system, etc. Progress in one area can depend on advances in another. Without such a coordinated approach many well intentioned programmes could prove fruitless. Thus, the whole United Nations system is potentially involved. As this is true for children, it is so far extreme poverty, migrant workers, women, persons with disability, among others.

The Declaration is in fact very rich in content and even a summary description of its different aspects would but be possible here. However, it does suggest a way of bringing all the various elements together so that they may have a positive impact on the enjoyment of human rights. Internationally, it recommends a comprehensive United Nations programme to help State build and strengthen their human rights infrastructure. That programme, coordinate by the Centre for Human rights should provide at government request a large number of services.

The World Conference also recommended the drafting of coherent and comprehensive plans of action for human rights assistance in a wide number of areas. And the Conference recommended that each State considers the desirability of adopting national plans of action for human rights.

I believe that these suggestions could provide a framework of planning dialogue and cooperation and enable us to measure progress as we have never been able to do before.

Mr. President,

The new approach to promoting and protecting human rights together with the detailed programmes and targets contained in the Declaration will require some very significant changes in how we work in the United Nations. A close collaboration based on shared information, respect for specific competence and mutual confidence will have to be built up between the Centre for Human rights and the various United Nations agencies and programmes.

But we will have to go beyond and incorporate into our thinking and planning the expertise, experience and resources of regional inter-governmental bodies, national institutions, universities and non-governmental organizations. In this regard, the world Conference has forseen, a great role for non-governmental organizations, as well as international financial institutions, developement agencies and the media in the implementation of the program of action.

The undeniable achievements of this Conference are due to the work and dedication of all who took part in this Conference and its preparation; you can be proud of your achievements.

I wish to thank all those who from near and far made their contributions, often in difficult circumstances, to the success of this Conference; and here, I thank especially our interpreters. May I wish you all a safe journey home.

Mr. President, I wish to turn to you and to extend our deepest thanks to the People of Austria and their government and the City of Vienna for having provided the hospitality and conditions of work which have contributed so much to our success.

We can leave Vienna with a sense, of accomplishment and hope and with the knowledge that a solid foundation of principles, understanding and commitment has been laid for future progress. Human rights is becoming a common language of humanity. It is a slow process, especially for those who suffer violations or those who work for respect for human rights often at their own personal risk; and here I want to honor the courage and dedication of human rights workers throughout the world. They are essential to progress.

Finally, Mr.President, today, in adopting this Declaration, the Member States of the United Nations have solemnly pledged to respect human rights and fundamental freedoms and to undertake.

Individually and collectively actions and programmes to make the enjoyment of human rights a reality for every human beings. Our undertaking here has been made in front of the eyes of the World and history will judge us, not by the words on the pages of this Declaration, but by the sincerity of our efforts and the success we achieve in bringing about changes in the way people live.

We must not fail. For the credibility of the whole United Nations is at stake.

Thank you for your attention.

19

Dalits at Durban – World Conference Against Racism

A.X.J. Bosco

The *World Conference Against Racism*, Racial Discrimination, Xenophobia and Related Intolerance, was held in Durban, South Africa, from the 26th of August to 7th September,2001, It was a gathering of discriminated and exploited peoples, as well as of activists involved in promoting their cause, from all over the world.

Three groups were highlighted. (1) The Africans who have suffered severe slavery and colonization. They demanded an apology, compensation and reparations from those who had exploited them. (2) The Palestinians who have been driven out of their homes. They demanded back the territories taken from them by Israel. (3) The Dalits from South Asia who have been segregated on the basis of the caste system and have been treated as untouchables and outcastes. They demanded dignity, respect and an equitable distribution of land and resources. Besides these three groups, there were the Roma gypsies, the Sri Lankan Tamils, the migrant workers, the refugees, people infected with HIV/AIDS, Mexicans living in USA, the Dalits of other countries like Japan and Nigeria, and other marginalized groups.

> "A unique and special Dalit attraction were the men and women drummers from different states"

There were three conferences that took place in Durban. A Youth Conference was held on the 25th and 26th August), a Forum for NGOs (Non-Governmental Organizations) followed on the 27th August to 1st September, and finally the Inter-Governmental Conference was held on the 1st to 7th September.

Courtesy : Dalit International Newsletter USA.

The Dalit Presence at Durban

One of the diplomats from Europe, commenting on the Dalit group, said "I had never seen such an expression of solidarity from the grassroots in my 20 years of experience". For the first time, members of most of the international communities came to know the Dalits, the so-called untouchables, the 260 million discriminated and marginalized people in South Asia and other countries. This is because the WCAR in Durban was first time that Dalits had participated in a world conference in large numbers and had voiced their grievances.

Dalits made themselves very visible, not only by providing posters and handouts but also by wearing headbands with the words "Dalit Rights are Human Rights" on them, black jackets on the back of which were printed "Include Caste in WCAR," and different kinds of badges.

A unique and special Dalit attraction were the men and women drummers from different states of India. Wherever the drummers started beating their drums, the crowds gathered. The African women who seem to have dancing in their blood spontaneously started dancing with great joy. The drum artists performed during the rallies and gave an hour-long cultural program with street plays which was very much appreciated.

About 200 Indian Dalits from various walks of life-Dalit activist, victims, lawyers artists, politicians media personnel, bishops, pastors, nuns and many others–participated in the NGO Conference and stayed on for the Inter-Governmental Conference. The Indian Government sent its own people to the NGO Conference to make propaganda against the Dalits. The Brahma Kumaris, a congregation of Hindu nuns, the disciples of Swami Ravi Shankar, and others like them distributed books and pamphlets and spoke against the Dalit cause.

There was a big rally from the Natal Technicon grounds to the Kingsmead stadium. It was an impressive rally of thousands of people through Durban, led by the South Africans. People carried banners and posters, sang, danced and shouted slogans. The Dalits drummers led the Dalits of different countries. Many Africans and Afro-Indians joined in the dance. At the end of the rally the Muslims lined themselves up and had their 'namas'.

The person who sat next to me in Kingsmead Stadium at the inaugural session was Jennie Mari Luna, young Mexican American woman from New York, who along with her companions had came to know for the first time about Dalits. Some of the South African youth asked for our "Dalits Rights are Human Rights" headbands, tied them around their heads, and went around supporting us. Among the world leaders who spoke about the Dalits and expressed solidarity with us throughout the conference were Thabo Mbeki, the South African president, and Mrs. Marry Robinson, High Commissioner of United Nations Human Rights Commission.

FROM THE GOVERNMENT OF INDIA

"In the run up to the World Conference, there has been propaganda, highly exaggerated and misleading, often based on anecdotal evidence, regarding caste-based discrimination in India. We in India have faced this evil squarely. We unequivocally condemn this and, indeed, any other form of discrimination. The issue has remained at the top of our national agenda. I have just spoken of our Constitution, legislative and administrative framework; of our affirmative action programmes for the uplift of the members of the historically disadvantaged castes. We are proud of the positive difference these measures have made. The institutions of our democratic polity, the progressive removal of poverty and the spread of literacy have empowered and given a voice to millions of the weaker sections of our society. We are determined to continue this national endeavour.

"Madame President, we are firmly of the view that the issue of caste is not an appropriate subject for discussion at this Conference. We are here to ensure that there is no stat-sponsored, institutionalized, discrimination against any individual citizen or groups of citizens. We are here to ensure that states do not condone or encourage regressive social attitudes. We are not here to engage in social engineering within member states. It is neither legitimate nor feasible nor practical for this World Conference or for that matter, even the U.N. to legislate, let alone police, individual behaviour within our respective societies to change thoughts, processes and attitudes; indeed, the hearts and souls of our peoples. This is the task we pledge ourselves to remain engaged in."

Statement of Mr. Omar Abdullah, Minister of State for External Affairs, Government of India, to the World Conference on 2 September, 2001.

Caste Outside India

We know that Dalits are present in South Asia i.e., in India, Nepal, Bangladesh, Sri Lanka and Pakistan as well as in the Indian diaspora i.e., Burma, Malaysia, south Africa, East Africa, the Caribbean, United Kingdom, Canada and United Nations . But we came to know about the caste system existing in other countries as well. In a meeting organized by the Robert F. Kennedy Center for Human Rights in Washington D.C., held at the Seaboard Hotel in Durban, we met Buraku people from Japan, Osu people from Nigeria and the Mitgan of Somalia. There are 3 million Buraku people in Japan: they spoke about the discrimination meted out to them. Ibu Sebastian, an Anglican pastor from Nigeria, spoke of the severe caste discrimination in Nigeria. The low caste people are called Osu. Although 90 percent of the Osu people are Christians, so far there has been no bishop from among them. Recently a few Osu priests have been ordained. There are 2 million Osus in Nigeria and 1 million outside Nigeria who ran away from the country to escape the rigors of the caste system. Asha from Somalia told us that the Mitgans, the low caste, is considered impure, unclean, and thus untouchable. These outcastes are not allowed to organize themselves. A popular proverb goes, "The world will come to an end when the noble caste starts drinking and the Mitgans start praying".

Physical and social segregation, prevention of inter-caste marriages, the language used to make them feel like outcastes, illiteracy, poverty, landlessness, impunity for perpetrators of crimes, and non-implementation of existing legislation are the common features and limitations shared by all these Dalits.

Dalits at the NGO Forum

Two Dalits women victims exposed the atrocities meted out to them. One of them, Hajamma from Andhra Pradesh, belongs to the community of Jogins who are a part of the Dalit community. The Jogin women are supposed to be dedicated to God. What this means in actual practice is that they are not allowed to marry; they are the property of the dominant caste. A dominant caste man can take a Jogin, marry and make use of her for as long as he likes. Later he can hand her over to another dominant caste man, or simply send her away whenever he wants. It is an institutionalized system of prostitution. During the NGO Forum she spoke of the injustices she and other members of her community had suffered.

The other victim was Mani Mekalai from Tamil Nadu. The Dalit community in her village had requested her husband to stand in the election for Village President and he won. The dominant caste people could not accept him as the leader of the village. Before he could take office as president and exercise his responsibilities, the dominant caste people waylaid a bus in which he was traveling. They caught hold of him and stabbed him. He pleaded that they not kill the five other Dalits who were traveling with him. However, they not only killed all the five Dalits before his eyes, but they also severed his head, took it away, and threw it into a well. Mani Mekalai herself has finished only elementary school studies and now has four children to care for. Many wept during her speech, which was translated into English and other languages. These and other sharings of victims moved and touched many hearts.

20

Human Rights Education for Prevention of Violence

Dr. Justice K. Ramaswamy

The cultural ethos and sustained equal respect the society gives to fellow individuals of all hues are measured as symbols of its civilisation at a given time. Their social relations reflect the level of prevailing culture. Every individual has inherent right to dignity of person, equality of status and freedom to enjoy all the rights in equal measure as also has a duty to ensure that others too enjoy the human rights individually as well as collectively. Education fosters human rights and fundamental freedoms for human development to satisfy one's spiritual and material needs. Discrimination and denial of human rights and fundamental freedoms had, in the past, led to social unrest and political revolution, bred violence and upset the even keel of peace and order within and between the societies and nations. This was manifested in the two world wars.

The United Nations Organisation, resultantly, had adopted and given to the world family a charter of human rights declared on December 10, 1948 – otherwise known as 'Universal Declaration of Human Rights'. Its Preamble recognises these inalienable human rights treating them as everyone has been born free and entitled to all the rights and freedoms without distinction of any kind, such as race, colour, sex, social origin, birth, property, status, etc. Recognition and respect for human rights is the foundation of freedom, peace and justice in the world, as stated are

---

Dr. Justice K. Ramaswamy, Member National Human Right Commision.

inalienable rights of all the members of the human family. Education is the key to realise human rights and concomitantly, imposes duty to respect equally the rights of fellow individuals. The importance of education needs hardly to be emphasised.

Education strengthens self-confidence and imparts respect for fundamental freedoms. Education infuses awakening and ignites social consciousness. Education helps to equip knowledge, remove quagmire of ignorance, kindles the lamp of new vistas for aspirations and hopes for better for future. It equips human mind with a new vision, vistas and promotes social mobility. It inculcates tolerance and enhances ability to think amidst diversity for adjustment and accommodation and brings harmony in social relations. Education raises higher levels of consciousness against exploitation. Education is a channel to improve excellence in all spheres of individual and collective activity.

In a multi-religious, linguistic and hierarchical caste based pluralist society of India, the right type of education imbued with human rights culture and spirit would foster unity in diversity as single human family and integrated nation. Even after 53 years of our independence, we are yet to be a united Republic.

The Universal Declaration of Human Rights containing 30 articles has given basic and fundamental, civil, political, socio economic and cultural rights and freedom to all individuals in world human family without discrimination of any kind. Article 26(2) of UDHR says that education shall be directed for the full development of the human personality and to strengthen respect for human rights and fundamental freedoms. Its importance is implicit that those who are aware of their rights, must ensure that the equal rights of others will not be trampled upon. Realisation of one's own human rights imposes correlative duty to respect others' rights for peaceful, social transformation and order in the society. The Paris Conference of UNESCO held in October 1974, recommended that "education should be directed for the full development of the human personality and to the strengthening of respect for human rights and fundamental freedoms. It shall promote understanding, tolerance and friendship among all nations, racial or religious groups and shall further the activities of the United Nations for the sake of peace."

The International Covenant on Economic, Social and Cultural Rights, in particular, Article 14 thereof, enjoins the State's responsibility to offer compulsory primary education to all free of charge. It emphasises action plan and demands its progressive implementation by every State.

Article 13 recognises right of everyone to education which shall be directed to the full development of human personality and the sense of its dignity. It shall strengthen the respect for human rights and fundamental freedoms; education shall promote understanding, tolerance and friendship among all racial, ethnic or religious groups and enable all people to participate effectively in a free society. Teheran Conference on Human Rights (1968) calls upon the member States "to ensure that all (means of education) should be used to stimulate interest in the problems of Human Rights in the changing world." Human Rights education strives to promote respect for the Human Rights and freedom. Therefore, diverse need based realistic measures require to be taken up for their realization. Human Rights education frees those affected by the shackles of superstitutions, ignorance and illiteracy. The United Nations, therefore, adopted a world plan of action in Montreal in March, 1993 aiming to foster an attitude of tolerance, respect and solidarity inherent in human rights. The Montreal Convention, therefore, emphasizes to educate individuals and groups about human rights so that untoward conduct leading to denial of human rights is changed. Learning of human rights is not an end in itself, but is a means to end violation of human rights and to build a culture of peace, change of mindset based on democracy, development, tolerance, humane conduct and human respect.

How the human rights education be disseminated among the people, and the student community, is an on-going intense debate. Some experts are of the view that human rights should be a subject of study in the same way as other humanities. Then only human rights education acquires due status in the curriculum. The other school of thought is that the contents of the human rights should be included in every subject which would pervade at all levels–schools and colleges. Jose Ayala Lasso, the former High Commissioner, U.N.O., said, "The objective of all human rights educational activity should be to teach the common language of humanity. Human Rights should not be one subject of education, but should permeate all aspects of education in all forms."

In India, the number of illiterates is more than the population on the eve of Independence of India. A vast 48 per cent are illiterates. Education in human rights cannot succeed unless the level of literacy is satisfactorily raised. Though Article 45 of the Constitution of India lays emphasis on compulsory education upto the age of 14 years, within ten years, from January 26, 1950, but unfortunately, it is a neglected constitutional duty of the State. Even till date, though the Supreme Court had held that right to elementary education is a fundamental right and has said Article 27 of the UDHR and Article 14 of the International Convention of Social, Economic and Cultural Rights, it is a far cry in India. Massive illiteracy is a major contributory factor for superstition, unfounded hierarchical caste pride and prejudice, perpetration of untouchability, denigration of majority poor as unequal and denied dignity of person to vast majority, in particular, to the Dalits and Adivasis in flagrant violations of human rights.

The Human Rights teaching must be conditioned by the values and ethos of the society and patterned on the culture and genius of our society. The human rights culture is not alien to our Indian civilization and culture. The Westerners, by dint of education, enriched their culture adopting Indian cultural ethos. An American author, Charles Norchi, in this behalf has said thus "Human Rights is really about human dignity, a notion familiar to India's civilization centuries before the West was even born." His article was published in SPAN, September, 1995 issue.

As stated eariier, multi-religious and linguistic diversities and hierarchical caste-structure brought about vertical division in the society. Unity among Indians and fraternity became fragile. Illiteracy breeds their perpetuation. Therefore, multi-pronged programme of action is necessary to disseminate human rights education which brings about change in the mindset of the unfounded prejudices, misunderstanding, and denigration of each other. Therefore, teaching of human rights should be an inter-individual and inter-societal duty. The rights and duties should be laid equal emphasis on. If one performs his duty to respect the human rights of others, his own human rights and others' automatically get respected. Gandhiji, the Father of the Nation, therefore, laid emphasis on duty consciousness thus : "I learnt from my illiterate but wise mother that all rights to be deserved and preserved come from duty well done. Thus, the very right to live accrues to us when we do the duty of citizenship of the world". Therefore, before claiming for the right, it is the corresponding duty to be performed first. The spirit of inter-related right and duty be emphasised in imparting human right education.

Justice S.M. Sikri committee constituted way back in 1980 promoting human rights education in India, suggested different approaches at different levels of education. It suggested that at schools and upto +2 level, human rights values could be best inculcated through stories, poems, biographies and other similar literature. School children should not be over-burdened with human rights teachings for the purpose of securing marks at the examinations. Emphasis should be placed only on inculcating human rights values on the impressionable minds. Therefore, for its success, it should not be confined to open curriculum of the school. It must be reflected in the "hidden curriculum creating the school atmosphere to display respect for human right and inculcation of the spirit of human values."

Children at the elementary school stage should be developed in their impressionable minds positive attitudes and values which could be secure by providing democratic environment, enable them to enjoy their rights and simultaneously, learn respect for the rights of others and to treat others as equals of caste or religious discrimination. Development of this broad outlook and constructive attitude formed in the childhood would enable children to grow into responsible and responsive mature citizens with constant concern for human rights of others. At the secondary school level, human rights knowledge is to be imparted more systematically. Students should be encouraged to develop capacity for action and with greater intellectual maturity of students, there is a scope for shaping curricular subjects in a more imaginative and interactive manner. Resources like libraries, museums, press, media–printing as well as electronic and radio–should be exploited to converge correctly the message of human rights and disseminate the spirit of human culture, human values and humane behaviour and relationship towards one another. At the college and university levels, the Sikri Committee recommended that the values and concepts of human rights can be taught through books and other regular courses. Even the students in the stream of Science, Medicine, Commerce and Technology, should also be exposed to the perspectives of human rights which are inter-related to disciplines. At post-graduate level, the concerned department should introduce regular course and diploma course also on Human Rights.

Human Rights education imparted to the adults would contain its substance and effective application. While emphasising diverse aspect of human rights, the goal orientation is to ignite in their talk and deed the need to defend human rights, fight against their abuse and duty to observe the human rights of others in equal measure. It should be among individuals and groups of people. they should also be activated for being vigilant about their protection and defence and dutifully abide by the spirit and content of the human rights. the constitution (42nd Amendment) Act, 1976 brought Chapter IV-A, 10 commandments of fundamental duties of every Indian citizen). The thrust thereof is to infuse in every citizen of India the duty to abide by and respect the ideals and institutions of the Constitution, the national flag and the National anthem; to protect sovereignty, unity and integrity of India; to promote harmony and spirit of common brotherhood among people, transcending religious, linguistic, regional barriers or sectional diversities, renounce derogatory practices belittling the dignity of women, to preserve and value rich and composite heritage and culture; to protect environment, to develop humanism, scientific temper, spirit of inquiry and reform, to abjure violence, protect public property, to improve excellence, individual and collective, so as to take the nation to the course of higher levels of endeavour and achievement etc.

The secular content of the Preamble, a basic feature of the Constitution, is to eradicate all prejudicial attitudes or practices, derived from or connected with religious or social beliefs which impede development and retard integration of the nation. Secularization, in accordance with its wide concept, stabilizes our democracy and establishes unity and fraternity among our plural society. Even after 50 years operation of the Constitution, instead of unity and integrity taking place among the people, caste-orientation and sectional division are gaining intensity, dividing the people on caste lines, fundamentalism, distrust, disharmony and mutual antagonism among various religious groups and standing as walls of separation among the people. The cultural, social and moral values, are getting degenerated and eroded. Every citizen lays emphasis only on his/her rights, disregards correlative duty towards his fellow individuals and societal interests.

Fundamental duties and the ideals of the Constitution envisioned in the Preamble of the Constitution, a basic structure, are to promote socio-economic justice, dignity of the individual, equality of status and of opportunity, fraternity and unity among the people which would really be achieved only when human rights culture and spirit become a part of life of the citizens through formal and informal education.

The Government of India appointed Justice J.S. Verma Committee, former Chief Justice of India and presently Chairman of the NHRC, to suggest operation methods for teaching fundamental duties to the citizens of this country. After elaborate study, discussion and consultations with various interests, it has submitted a report consisting of two volumes to the Human Resource Development Department of the Government of India. The Committee identified the Indian way as the tool through which the human rights education and fundamental duties are integrated as part of the attitude and spirit of human behaviour of every citizen in India so as to bring about harmony of religions, unity among the people transcending religious, regional, sectional, casteist prejudices and disunity. It suggested to make the inner life of the man more humane to realize positive social and cultural values of diversity, human rights and human responsibilities emphasising that the rights and duties are two sides of the same coin. It touched the root cause that "For centuries, there has been inequality in the social structure, resulting in the exploitation of a cast segment of our population, whether it be the socially deprived sections, women or minorities, in a caste-based hierarchical society with a feudal politico-economic system, an inevitable reality". Indian leadership recognized this reality. The framers of the Constitution emphasized social justice, equality, respect for pluralism and secularism, human dignity and equality in participation through a democratic social structure. Therefore, "one has to stress, both rights of the deprived as much as emphasizing the duties of the citizens." While Sensitizing students to the rights of the dispossessed teach them their duties as persons belonging to relatively more advantageous groups, organize the dispossessed by empowerment. Inculcation of fundamental duties would enhance societal values which would keep a check on the derogatory practices of younger generations and would guide them effectively with compassion and empathy. Societal approbation is always much stronger than legal sanctions. Take the children through the right curriculum of fundamental duties and effective preparation of teachers to handle these curricula through well-designed teaching educational programmes, play a very significant role to ensure understanding and internalization of fundamental duties in the educational institutions and communities.

As was mentioned earlier, Justice Verma Committee also laid emphasis on the role of media–print electronic and radio–apart from schools, colleges and universities, to educate the human rights, their content and spirit to create an impact on the minds of the citizens to nurture fundamental duties in their daily lives.

After the constitution of the National Human Rights Commission in 1994, it has taken, as its programme of action, dissemination of human rights education, human rights culture and spirit among the student community and citizenry. By its interaction with the University Grants Commission, in several universities and colleges, it has started human rights education courses, which are now becoming a part of the curriculum. Degree and certificate courses are now being conferred. As recommended by Justice Verma Committee, if they are made part of the curriculum and, as was recommended by Justice Sikri Committee, even preliminary stage onwards, different imaginative, practical content courses are adopted and articulated. The impressionable minds of the children get used to the human rights value, culture and spirit as part of life. Adults, when taught the rights and the duties, protection and prevention of the human rights violations and defend the violation of the human rights of vulnerable sections, it creates harmony and fraternity, in the society, thereby remove misunderstanding, misgivings and mutual acrimony. Thus, fraternity stands to gain, unity among the people is secured and integrity of the nation established.

21

Human Rights Education – India's Heritage

Dr. R.M. Pal

Indian scholars and human rights intellectuals have been talking and writing, apropos of human rights violations, about India's glorious past of 5000 years, written in gold, and pleading that the past must be revived to usher in a new India where the values of tolerance, non-violence, friendship for all, equality, respect for all persons, human dignity and rights, and freedom will be respected and cherished. They, however, leave us in dark as to which past is to be revived/reborn, of which we can be proud; and which one needs to be buried. Obviously, we want to revive that past which will help India come into the inheritance of the blessings of modern civilization. Which means that we have to resist the temptation of reviving an imaginary Golden Age of India's past.

Furthermore, as professor Romila Thapar puts it, "The supposed perfection of the past has hampered our understanding not only of the social processes, but also of our own cultural identity. An analysis of the totality of Indian society today has to account for a variety of transitions taking place and involving tribal groups, peasant groups, and at the most articulate level, the change to industrialization. The nature of these changes will often involve a basic change of social values. The confrontation can no longer be evaded as it once was by recourse to the theory that our concern has always been only with things spiritual, or by an escape into the past. But the process can be facilitated by an awareness of the past, deriving from a realistic assessment... It is only the awareness that history is made by an entire people into its total activity, which can bring us nearer to explaining the past in its concrete actuality. And, this, after all, is the ultimate purpose of historical investigation".[1]

At the fag end of the 20th century we cannot afford to go round in circles of ideological confusion. We need to raise our voice of reason and wisdom, discover our old literature, philosophy, and civilization to make us wiser and constantly remind us of our journey forward. This is how Europe recovered from the savagery of the Dark Age and many of the crudities of the Middle Ages. The idea behind revivalism rebirth (I use these two words interchangeably, for the sake of convenience, even though they mean different things) is to look at our past, that past which can guide us to respect the individual's dignity, and to build a future of which we can be proud. In the process we should have no hesitation, indeed, we must be brave, in discarding those aspects which hamper our progress, like, for example, the theories of *Karma*, Transmigration of Soul, *Maya*, the principle of division of society into castes, the form which the system of exploitation assumed in by-gone days that was declared to be the creation of God, the 'spiritualist' culture that seeks to persuade the poor, the depressed, the oppressed, and the exploited to reconcile their lot to suffering, sacrifice, love, and voluntary poverty–all that signify complete surrender, and absence of the spirit of revolt. We must be brave to discard these even if they are backed by scriptures–indeed, we must bury such scriptures.

The highest appreciation of our past would be to find out how it could generate in us the spirit of revolt against social injustice and human rights violations. Indeed, a very large canvas, and a huge agenda for our historians in the above context, to proper a course of study based on our heritage for human rights education to be taught in schools, colleges, and universities.

As regards to tolerance, respect for human rights, dignity of and respect for the individual and his/her freedom, that have been part of our heritage, and need not be a great sophisticated scholar or historian to know that even the philosophies of religious movements in the not-too-distant past, not to speak of the materialist philosophy of ancient India[2], incorporated such values. Regrettably, the human rights intellectuals and activists have hardly taken note of these movements, possibly because of the fact that most of these originated from, and inspired by, the lower strata of society. And also that, to quote Romila Thapar again: "The cultural identity which we have forged in recent times has been that of a Sanskritic upper caste, or else its equivalent in a Persian upper caste. Yet these identities are as elitist as the English speaking identity of contemporary Indians.... (The fact remains that) the common features of religion for the majority of Indians lie in the worship of the Mother Goddess and fertility cults and in the teachings of what have come to be called the devotional or *bhakti* sects and the 'saint' and the 'pir'. Emphasis is continually given by historians to the spread of Islam symbolized by the Quran. Yet so little recognition is given to the fact that in the practice of religion it is local cult, the non-Sanskritic tradition which is often predominant."[3]

It is in this context that I have given below a summary account of this non-Sanskritic tradition with special reference to the medieval age (this period should not be confused with what is known as the Middle Ages in Europe), that is, before the advent of European learning which came to India with the British. I suggest that contributions made in this period can inspire human rights activitists in their work, and also scholars and educationists including the Government of India appointed National Human Rights Commission (NHRC), and the National Council of Educational Research and Training (NCERT), involved in the task of framing courses of study for human rights education.

The NCERT with the active support of the NHRC has brought out a Source Book on Human Rights Education which contains summaries/ excerpts from various UN Charters and Covenants and also from our own Constitution. One wonders, however, if a mere textbook reading of constitutional provisions and UN Charters can develop a human rights culture which is what the NHRC's stated objective is. Furthermore, aren't these already taught in the Civics, Political Science, and Law Courses?

During the Buddhist period, interest in man, man in his own image, and man's affairs on this earth, unlike interest in gods and goddesses and good life in heaven after death, this earth being a vale of tears, became the primary concern of thoughtful men and women. Buddha rejected the caste system. Human sufferings made Prince Gautam Siddhartha restless and he left all luxuries and comforts of the King's palace in search of remedies for all human miseries on this earth. The basic tenets of Buddhism are non-violence, non-hatred, and friendliness to all. Emperor Asoka who became a devoted follower of the Buddha took to the non-violent, humanitarian and humanist philosophy of Buddhism. Also, he became a great champion of freedom and tolerance. He pleaded for universal tolerance. One of the Most significant contributions of Buddhism was the introduction and spread of secular education–education for all. Organised universities came to be established under the direct influence of Buddhism.

There were other aspects–non-Vedic–like the Nath, Yoga Siddharcara who, too, like the Buddhists, found the key to all religious mysteries in the human body itself. "The position of the Nath-Panthi siddhas and jogis in Hindu society needs to be understood. Most of the nath-panthi siddhas and jogies belonged to the low castes, opposed the caste-based inequalities, denounced the religion of works favoured by the *Brahmins,* and did not favour image worship"[6] Women played an important part in these sects, particularly in the Tantra.

There are other folk religious / sects which came into prominence in the medieval period : the well-known *Bhakti* movement, and the Baul movement in Bengal. They are remarkable for their simplicity, directness, and for preaching and practicing tolerance, love, and friendliness. Bhakti, the path of devotion, implies, belief in the Supreme Person not a Supreme Abstraction. It is, therefore, a very straightforward and unsophisticated belief. This movement has non-Aryan roots; in fact, according to some scholars, it originated in the Dravida country. It was opposed by the *Brahmins* for a long time because of its utter disregard for caste divisions, religious rituals and ceremonies.

The tradition of *Bhakti* has played an important part among the Tamils as mentioned in the works of the Alvar saints, most of whom came from low castes. In the beginning, the movement was restricted to the lower strata of society who were oppressed by the Brahmanical religion. At a later stage, Vaishnavas of even higher castes hailed their literature. One Alvar saint, Andal belonged to a low caste; she was accepted as a religious leader by the society in general. This is an indication of the popularity of the *Bhakti* movement. The great scholar Ramanuja, the best known exponent of this movement, was influenced and inspired by the "works of the Alvars, which were collected by the disciples of Ramanuja at his special request, and from which Ramanuja himself drew much inspiration and pabulum for this system of thought".

At this point, a brief look at the advent of Islam in India is necessary. In India, Islam led to a series of responses. We can ill afford to ignore them as also the creative influence of Islam. An analysis of the Muslims conquest of India is of practical value today, and will help Indians–both Hindus and Muslims–appreciate the positive results of Muslims conquest of India. (This is necessary, among other reasons, for a solution of the communal question which has been one of the major sources, along with the caste system, of human rights violations.)

It may be noted in this context that Europe came out of the shackles of the Dark Age and the middle ages, and entered the civilized era by learning from the Muslims. It is equally true that a large number of Hindu reformers, largely in the Bhakti movement in medieval India, who revolted against orthodoxy, were considerably influenced by the Muslims conquest and its social effects. The devotional Bhakti and the Islamic Sufis (the Sufi teacher, Khwaja Moinuddin Chisti came to India in 1193) have much in common. In medieval times north India mysticism was the product of both the Bhakti movement and the tradition of the Sufis. One important aspect of this mysticism is its complete independence from orthodox scriptures. These teachers practised and taught tolerance.

The interaction of Bhakti and Islam, specially the Sufi idea, gave rise to a number of progressive movements with the core philosophy of tolerance. Human rights educationists should give the utmost importance to this aspect. It is regrettable that it has, with some notable exceptions, been generally studied in isolation. It should, therefore, be emphasized in our text books that "relations between Islam and the religions of the area (South Asia) were marked by mutual understanding and tolerance. This spirit of mutual understanding, tolerance and cooperation were, to a large extent promoted by the rise and spread of Sufi and Bhakti ideas."

Our students must be reminded over and over again of what Rabindranath Tagore said, "the Sakas, the Hunas, the pathans and the Mughals, all have been merged into one body." With a view to combating the religious frenzy that has been playing havoc in our country. We must remind ourselves of the forgotten fact of history that "a distinctive feature of the thought and life the people of South Asian region is their adherence to the tradition of tolerance, syncretism and co-existence, (and in this context) the coming of Islam was an event of outstanding significance for the history of this subcontinent. This syncretic and humanist tradition in South Asian society and social thought is remarkably portrayed in the following poem of Kazi Nazrul Islam:

I sing the song of equality/where all barriers have crumbled/All differences have faded,/and Hindus-Buddhists-Muslims-Christians.

Have come together and have merged./I sing the song of equality".

In short, we must remind ourselves over and over again that a pluralistic society can flourish only if its basic value remains tolerance.

Namdeva and Tukaram from Maharashtra, the former a tailor, and the latter a peasant, made the *Bhakti* movement increasingly acceptable to the people. Namdeva taught: "The stone image speaks not, see the lord within. the Tirthas (holy pilgrimage) cannot wash away sins: clean your heart instead. Fasting and other observances are futile, unless your being is purified. What can ceremonies do if love awakes not in your heart?"

In Bengal, the well-known Vaishnava poets Jaidev, Vidyapati, and Chandidas, as also Chaitanaya popularized the movement. The *Bhakti* movement during this period spread to almost all parts of India.

Though the movement did not succeed in breaking through caste barriers, the very fact that many of its leaders belonged to lower castes, and also that it believed in the equality of men, must be taken note of by the human rights educationists.

In the fourteenth century, Swami Ramananda (1370-1440) challenged caste divisions, revolted against traditional religious rituals and started preaching in Hindi, and not in Sanskrit which was the preserve of the upper castes. His thought is well-reflected in the following words: "Wherever I go, I see water and stone; but it is you who had filled them all with your presence. In vain do they seek you in the Vedas... (Granth saaheb). Ramananda had 12 important disciples. They all belonged to low castes. One of them Ravidas was a cobbler. "The recitation of the Vedic Mantras, even for many millions of times, will not satisfy the pangs of the longing (to see you)", sang Ravidas ((Granth saaheb). The most famous disciple was Kabir, a Muslim weaver. The Sufi and Bhakti traditions of the Islamic and Hindu religions blended in his teachings. He struck at the very roots of ritualism and superstition. "O God, whether Allah or Rama, I live by thy name", sang Kabir. Since Kabir composed songs for the common people he chose Hindi. "Sanskrit is like water in a well; the language of the people is a flowing stream", said Kabir. A married man, with a son and daughter, Kabir did not practise celibacy and asceticism. He practised and preached the gospel of universal tolerance and was one of the exponents of utmost importance to human equality and denounced inequality based on caste, station, and wealth.

The founder of the great Sikh religion Guru Nanak was greatly influenced, by Islamic and Sufi ideas. Sikhism is known for its simplicity, and this was derived from Kabir's teaching. Both Kabir and Guru Nanak found a common link between Hinduism and Islam. "The Supreme significance of Nanak was that he was the harbinger of Hindu-Muslim unity, for he sought sincerely to reconcile Islam with Hinduism as the following verse will show : *Guru Nanak Shah faquire/Hindu Ka Guru aur/ Musalman Ka pir*"[11]

Dadu, a cotton-curder was another of Kabir's outstanding followers. "When I look upon the beauty of this universe, I cannot help asking, "How, O Lord, did you come to create it? What sudden wave of joy coursing through your being compelled its own manifestations? Was it really due to a desire for self-expression, or simply on the impulse of emotion? . . . That is why your Universe. . . has charmed me so . . . Dadu has no desire to know; he is satisfied to remain enraptured with all this beauty of yours', and to rejoice in it with you, so sang Dadu–so very different from the hair-splitting and complicated intellectualism of *Jnana* and *Karma*.

The story of such mystics of the *Bhakti* movement is long. I have given a very brief introduction to this movement in the foregoing with a view to bringing before human rights activists and educationists the positive aspects of our past.

Bauls are not known outside Bengal. The philosophy of the Baul movement lies in the simple man's (Sahaj) search for the "Man of his heart"-his God. The movement traces its origin to the fall of Buddhism and Vaishnavism.

Bauls are like the wind (Baul means wind, vayu)-always free, not tied to any religious traditions. They accept no caste division; they do not worship any special deity or do they accept any temple or mosque. Baul devotees belong to the lowest strata of both Hindus and Muslims. "What need have we of other temples, when our body is the temple where our spirit has its abode?" they sing. They do not observe asceticism, or do they believe in celibacy. Earthly love, they maintain, helps them to feel Divine love, and harmony between material and spiritual needs. The following Baul song contains the core philosophy of the Baul movement:

This is why, brother, I became a madcap Baul. / No master I obey, or injunctions, canons, or customs / Manmade distinctions have no hold on me now. / I rejoice in the gladness of the love that dwells out of my own being. / In love there is no separation, but a meeting of hearts for ever. / So, I rejoice in one and I dance with each and all. / That is why, brother, I became a madcap Baul.

One of the most famous Bauls, Faqir Lalon Shah sang thus :

Everyone asks Lalon what is your religion: / Lalon says, I know he is a Musalman; / But how would you identify the religion of a female? / A Brahmin male is identified by his poita (sacred thread); / But how would you identify a Brahmin female? / One holds rosary in hand, theother wears tasbi)bead) in his neck, / That is how one's religion is known; / But at moments of birth and death do these signs remain? People everywhere talk and gossip about religious differences. / Lalon says, I have dropped all polemics about religions in free market.

I may add that Rabindranath Tagore was greatly influenced by Kabir and translated many of Kabir's poems into English in collaboration with Evalyn U derhill. Guru Nanak, too, left a lasting impression on Tagore's mind. Tagore was also greatly influenced by Bauls like Lalon Faqir and Gagan Harkarai. He composed many songs under their influence.

Notes

1. The Past and Prejudice, by professor Romils Thapar, National Book Trust, New Delhi, 1975, pp. 60-63.
2. The school of philosophy, *Lokayata* considered physical sense data to be the only source of knowledge. It challenged the whole of Hindu metaphysics, and rejected after-life and reincarnation. This rejection is found elsewhere too. In the Ramayana a Brahmin, *Javali* advises Rama thus: "I grieve for those who, abandoning the pleasures of the world, seek to acquire merit for felicity hereafter and sink to an untimely death, I do not grieve for others. Men

waste food and other precious things by offering them by yearly, as sacrifices in honour of their departed ancestors. O Rama, has a dead man ever partaken of food? If food that is eaten by one, nourishes another, then those who journey need never carry provision on the way. Relatives might feed a Brahmin, in his name, at home. O Ramachandran, these scriptural injunctions were laid down by learned men, skilled in inducing others to give, and finding other means of obtaining wealth, thus subjugating the simple-minded. Their doctrine is 'Sacrifice, give in charity, consecrate yourselves, undergo austerities, and become ascetics'. O Rama, be wise, there exists no world but this, that is certain. Enjoy that which is present and cast behind thee that which is unpleasant. Adopting the principles acceptable to all, do thou receive the kingdom offered thee by Bharata" Ayodhya Kand). (Quoted by K.M. Sen in his book Hinduism, Penguin, 1961, pp. 63-64).

3. Romila Thapar, cited above. P.6.
4. I have not dealt in this essay with the short-lived Renaissance that was ushered in India, specially in Bengal and Maharashtra, under the direct influence of European learning and philosophy and which gave rise to a large number of reformers and reformist movements, intellectual activists, and political thinkers whose contributions have been recorded and acknowledged by most historians. Contributions made by European learning and philosophies in the field of human rights, civil liberties, and individual liberty have been significant, and they find elaborate mention in text books.
5. The Hindu caste system, in the context of human rights, must be dealt with in great detail, for it represents inequality and has played an important role in stratification of Indian society–particularly because of its so called 'divine' origin. The caste system by its very nature, goes against respect for an individual's dignity and freedom to express himself. Further, the caste system had a racial origin in its association of castes and colour, for example, an important verse in the Mahabharata: Bhirgu explains the nature of castes to Bharadvaja, "*Brahmins* are fair, *Kshatriyas* are reddish, Vaishas are Yellowish, and the Sudras are black". What should be of interest for human rights education affected by desire, anger, fear, sorrow, worry, hunger and labour' how do we have caste differences then? (Santi Parva). (Quoted by K.M. Sen in his book, Hinduism, Penguin, 1961, p.28)
6. That in ancient India, the caste system was repudiated is also illusrated by a number of characters in the Mahabharata: (1) the story of kind Yayati and Devayani–Devayani, a Brahmin marries Yayati who is a Kshtriya with the consent of her father, Guru Sukracharys, (ii) Vidura, one of the wisest men in the Mahabharata and also described as the very incarnation of Dharma was the son

of a Sudra Raman, (iii) Rishi Vaisishtha was born of a prostitute, (iv) Parashara was born of a Chandala woman. Another example of argument was born of a Chandala woman. Another example of argument against caste divisions, from the *Bhavishya Purana*, "All human beings have the same Father, and children of the same Father cannot have different castes".

7. Professor Satish Chandra in Cultural Interaction in South Asia, edited by S.A.I. Tirmizi, Hamdard Institute of Historical Research, New Delhi, 1993, p.103.
8. Human Rights Educationists should find this book useful preparing reading material for school students. It is a collection of papers written by scholars from South Asia, presented before a Colloquium organized by Jawharlal Nehru University, New Delhi, Hamdard Institute of Historical Research, New Delhi, and Jmia Hamdard, New Delhi, in 1991. Their papers, "Aspects of Society and Social Thought in South Asia: The Syncretic and Humanist Tradition" by professor Salahuddin Ahmad of Dhaka University, "South Asian Sufis and their Social Linkage" by professor Riazul Islam, professor Emeritus at Karachi University, and "Interaction of Bhakti and Sufi Movements in South Asia" by professor Satish Chandra of Jawharlal Nehru University of New Delhi, deserve special mention in the context of human rights education.
9. S.N. Dasgupta, A History of Indian Philosophy, Vol.III, 1940.
10. In spite of the fact that Islam had played out its progressive role before it penetrated India, Islam was welcomed as a message of hope and freedom by victims of the Brahmanical reaction which had overthrown the Buddhist revolution resulting in a state of chaos in Indian society. How is it that the Mohammedans, though not large in numbers, managed to rule a vast country for such a long time, and millions of people converted themselves to the new faith? The fact remains that the Mohammedans satisfied certain objective requirements of Indian society. The historian Havell (not an admirer of Islam, he is a great admirer of ancient Hindu culture) in his book, Aryan Rule in India writes" "It was not the philosophy of Islam, but its sociological programme which won so many converts for it in India. The victorious progress of Islam in India is not to be accounted for by external reasons. It was mainly due to the political degeneration of Aryavarta which set in after the death of Harsha. The effect of the Musalman political creed upon Hindu social life was two-fold: It increased the rigour of the caste system and aroused a revolt against it. Islam made the Sudra a free man and potentially a Lord of the *Brahmins*. Like the Renaissance of Europe, it stirred up the intellectual waters, produced many strong men, and some men of striking originally of genius. Like the Renaissance also, it was essentially a city cult; it made the nomad leave his tent and the Sudra abandon his Village. It developed a type of humanity full of joie de vivre". (quoted by

M.N. Roy in his book, Historical Role of Islam, Ajanta, 1990 reprint, Delhi, pp.84-85. M.N. Roy wrote this book in jail during the period 1930-36 to indicate the way to a solution of the Hindu-Muslim problem in India. This book deserves to be read by human rights educationists as also by members and officials of the National Human Rights Commissions).

11. Satish Chandra, cited above, P 100. What professor Satish Chandra writes with special reference to Tulsidas, the chief exponent of one trend of the Bhakti movement which was devoted to Rama, should be specifically noted by human rights educationists even though Hinduvtavadis will take objection to Professor Chandra's Comments and views: "Tulsidas laid considerable stress on the need for social and political stability with the framework of which alone religious duties could be properly performed. The basis of this was his belief that the overwhelming sections in society consisted of people with wicked and evil propensities. . . . Social control implied the maintenance of a reformed caste system in which people did not transgress their prescribed duties. . . Tulsi's own approach was fundamentalist or traditionalist in the sense that he based his teaching on the scriptures which, along with the *Brahmins,* were to be respected and were to be regarded as the bedrock of religion. He also strengthened and revived the tradition of image worship, the deity being worshipped and treated with the deference due to a person of high status. The tradition of reincarnation was automatically reaffirmed". Pp. 109-110.
12. Professor Salahuddin Ahmad of Dhaka University in Cultural Interaction in South Asia, cited above, p. 87.
13. J.N. Sarkar, Thoughts on Trends of Cultural Contracts in Medieval India, Calcutta, 1984, p. 102.

22

Human Rights in Education and the Schooling of Dalit Children

Dr. Geetha B. Nambissan

In the broadest sense, Human Rights is the right of every citizen in this country to be treated with dignity regardless of caste, community, gender and thereby realize their own capabilities and capacities. Access to education is, but a part to this right to a life of dignity.

There can be two ways in which the question of human rights can be dealt with in the context of education. One is to state that the education system should facilitate the spreading of an awareness of high importance of human rights and an understanding of human rights and an understanding of the premises on which they are based as well as the safeguards that are available for the protection of these rights. This can be broadly referred to as Human Rights Education (HRE), and NCERT and UGC documents broadly refer to this. The second is to critically look at the practice of human rights within the education system.

There can be no quarrel with the objective of wanting to strengthen the subject content in relation to human rights wherever it is appropriate in subject areas such as social studies, civics and so on. In this context it is probably adequate to integrate the teaching of human rights within the content of what is already being taught, rather than introduce an additional subject at the school stage and thereby increase the load of an already burdened school curriculum. There is considerable potential within existing content areas to do so and it is a matter of how effectively and sensitively this is done.

Of crucial importance to the issue of (in relation to education is the practice of (within the education system itself. In other words we probably need to first understand the concrete practice of (within the education system (and the manner in which the experience of different social groups varies in this context), before we can speak in general of (the content of this education, whom it should focus upon and so on.

Anyone who looks at the schooling statistics in government document will be struck by the extent to which certain social groups lack even the minimal access to opportunities where they can acquire basic skills of literacy and numeracy, i.e. to primary stage of education. I am specifically referring to the relatively low enrolment and high drop-out rates from school of children form Dalit communities, officially called the Scheduled Castes. What is, however, important is that these are social groups that have also been traditionally denied a life of dignity in society. Today when we are discussing the role of education in human rights literacy it becomes important to see whether children from communities whose human rights continue to be trampled upon are able to receive education with dignity from schools. The school is of particular importance as these are institutions that occupy public space and profess aims of equity ensuring equality of educational opportunity with social justice.

There are two points of importance that need to be remembered in the context of the education of Dalit children. One is that these children come from communities for education. The lack of exposure of generation of skill of literacy, numeracy, literature and other forms of knowledge considered desirable is likely to put them at a disadvantage where access to school knowledge is concerned. This would imply that such children are likely to require specific pedagogic support from the school system. This is integral to their rights to education. The other point is that Dalit communities have been denied learning in the past specially because of the caste to which they belong. There is hence need for special vigilance to see that they do not continue to face social discrimination within the school.

A majority of Dalit children in both rural and urban areas do not attend schools. Though education documents assure that school are available within walking distance to all children in rural areas, this does not even hold if one looks more closely official statics. Further, given the special segregation of Dalit communities in villages and among them specially those who traditionally remove nightsoil and the fact that schools are located within the upper caste areas, the question of how socially accessible schools are, is also relevant.

Coming to the school themselves what need to be seen is the quality of facilities that are available to Dalit children. One knows that the generally quality of primary schools in rural areas is poor. What is the condition of school that cater primarily to Dalit children by virtue of being located in their habitations ? Passing reference in a few studies and reports give rise to the suspicion that school where Dalit children predominate may be in poorer condition than the average rural school to ensure that education is received in conditions that maintain the dignity of the individual child. Inadequate inputs in schooling, the poor quality of teaching, and so on likely to be particularly detrimental to the education of children from these communities are relatively less exposed to the kind of skills required in the class room.

Equally important particularly for Dalit communities are the social processes within school and classroom that influence the learning environment provided for children. There is not much research evidence on what it means to be a Dalit child within the Indian classroom, specially in the rural areas where the majority of Dalit school children are to be found. Scattered references in a number of studies do indicate that the education of Scheduled castes may still not be looked upon with favour by upper and dominated castes in many parts of India.

Within the school it appears that Dalit students continue to experience social discrimination and this can be seen both in the official curriculum, i.e. in the approved content of education and the hidden curriculum of schooling. Scheduled Caste communities and the experience of untouchability rarely form part of school knowledge. Textbooks are silent about Dalit communities, even in stages where these communities form a significant section of the population. Though untouchability and the maintenance of social distance from certain communities still persists in most parts of India, such practices are rarely mentioned in school books or discussed in the classroom.

Dalits who look back upon their often painful experiences in school refer not to their invisibility in text books, but to the distinct message of social inferiority that is conveyed to them by their teachers (the majority of teachers continue to come from middle and upper castes) and peers. Personal experiences of Dalits educated in the post-independence period mention instances of Dalit children being asked to sit separately from their classmates, of being refused drinking water and served in broken teacups, made to dine separately and so on. A number of observers have noted the fact that teachers refuse to touch their slates or copies, or even resort to physical punishment for fear of pollution. Discouragement from teachers and indifference on their part to the academic needs of Dalit students is also reported in a few studies. Passing reference is also made to friendship patterns tending to remain within caste boundaries in schools.

The point being made here is that children belonging to the lowest castes continue to be discriminated within the school and classroom and blatant malpractices particularly in the attitudes of teachers and school authorities as well as in peer behaviour continue. The inadequate academic support given to Dalit children, the prevailing attitudes regarding these communities and the stereotypes that teachers and other members of the school community hold regarding their educability and their destiny impinges on the right of the child to education with dignity.

Given the scenario that exists regarding social groups that suffer from the backlash of caste in society at large, it is unlikely that human rights education in the abstract will bring about any significant change in the education environment provided for children belonging to these communities. What is required is that school practices in relation to discrimination, or the need for social justice within schools, is directly addressed. How this needs to be done is a matter of democratic debate and discussion but one can point to a few areas of intervention.

One is the official content of school education where a conscious effort should be made to critically analyse the manner in which school text books portray socially vulnerable communities both in terms of their visibility as well as the kind of roles they are seen to lay if represented. In the context of what is called the hidden curriculum there is need for a multi-pronged strategy. One is the need to ensure that access to facilities within educational institutions and the meting of stringent punishment where there is any form of discrimination. The other is in the context of programmes to sensitize and create awareness among teacher educators, teachers and school administrators not only of human rights where these children are concerned, but also of the negative impact that social discrimination can have for the development of children and the realizing of their full potential. The special role that the schools can play in reinforcing academic inputs for these children need to be stressed. Similarly, within the classroom the raising of awareness of human rights requires that such awareness is linked to critical consciouness of school practices including peer group behaviour in as sensitive a manner as possible. For both teachers and students this can be done more effectively through dialogue and discussion rather than in a didactic manner. Group projects can offer opportunities both for the recognition of underlying attitudes and critically looking at them.

Children especially those from Dalit and Minority communities are in an extremely vulnerable position in the classroom. Protection and support to children in order that they can exercise their rights will be important in efforts to create and educational environment conducive to learning with dignity. In this context the links that democratic and civil liberties organization forge with schools will be critical.

23

Education for Liberation of Dalits

Dr. Henry Thiagaraj, Julie Thomas

The sheer magnitude of the people suffering discrimination over 2000 years touches one's conscience! About 200 million people still continue to live with violence based on discrimination. They had lost their land rights. Their spiritual heritage was crushed to an extent that it become extinct. They live in dehumanising conditions. Dr.Ambedkar, the greatest of Dalit leaders said, "Our battle is not for wealth or for power. It is a battle for freedom. It is a battle for the reclamation of human personality." It is the *Hindu* social system of "Caste" which condemned the Dalits to live in dehumanising conditions denying the growth of the human personality. Therefore, the humanising process becomes crucial to liberation work among Dalits. Humanising process work in the area of consciousness where there are many dynamic layers.

Similar to the ancient Hindu caste system, the modern science and technology promote living mechanically, and create dehumanising conditions. Intelligence and rationalism breed inhumanity among people. State capitalism, the government bureaucracy, and regimentation control society and people contributing dehumanising people. There is growing trend among educated people to reject traditional religion and to go for searching new forms of spirituality to fill the vacuum in human life. Psycholgists observe that most of the worship and religious practises remain at a cerebral level, reflecting mechanical behaviour conditioned by a stimulus response. When many international visitors and scholars visit India they seek some spiritual insights which can help them in their life. When we encounter such visits, we share our educational experience to enable people to be in touch with their humanity or the humanising process through the meditation and actual human encounters. We observed that when strangers like Americans go to a Dalit village, meet the people at a human level, the human experiences shared produce transformation. Almost all the the young visitors have been profoundly influenced.

The Dalit Liberation Education Trust, which was founded by me in 1985 committed for social change, justice and liberation of the oppressed has broad vision of reaching out to all people and making its work secular through educational programmes like providing awareness education, human rights education, health education, etc. – all of which touch the life of the people. In the process, we have combined a spiritual dimension to raise the consciousness of the people. Thus, we have realised the importance of holistic view of the human beings. It is said that incarnation means when a person become truly human then he discovers the divine in that person. Thereby one moves in to the area of consciousness which unfold spiritual insights and move people to service, commitments and turn their life.

Deep in our human self, whatever is our physical condition there is a vast source of human heritage which provides us the strength of life. In this deeper self of our being it is possible to experience motivation, commitment for service, social change and personal growth. Any experience which touches our humanity within ourself brings a transcending influence to overcome the barriers and divisive factors. The human beings alone have the ability to become aware of their self and to observe their behaviour and to shift their attitudes, thinking and behaviour. This human experience is cross cultural, binds people and has power of transcendence as we had seen in our liberation education work in the last 15 years. As a pioneering experiment, for the first time in India, the Dalit Liberation Education Trust initiated process of liberation education through the method of interacting with educated youth from the oppressed communities. It is a creation of awareness education, based on questions of their living conditions, which stimulate their thinking process. Discussions are focused on their basic attitudes to life and how they are accepted. This interaction which is experience oriented, in an intensive camp life for about 5 days, providing 'education for living'. It is to find a remedy to the existing unjust and unequal social situations, the camps are organised. Dalit youth leadership camp enables its participants to become aware of their self, who they are, and in that process, they gain human dignity and worth of the self. An expanding self includes others–the community–leading to social awareness. This growth of self often results in social commitment to serve fellow beings.

This experiment by a team of committed personnel in organising youth camps for Dalits resulted in greater satisfaction and a rewarding experience as participants reported gaining insights to manage their life. They gained confidence to tackle social problems and became responsible for social transformation. They came forward to organise local people to voice their needs and to express their legitimate grievances.

Now they 'hear' the truth and question false beliefs which conditioned their life. Now they 'speak' instead of silently suffering oppression. They 'see' a newness of life and freshness of approaching problems. They gain insights to see their emotional thought patterns. Now they 'know' what is the reality of life. They experience the best in their human life emerging. They become more integrated in their personality. They acquire integrity in life. As a result of the new awakening described above, they find motivation to serve their fellow human beings. Their life becomes enriched. They are provided counselling to enable them to tackle the problems of life and society. New ideas are like seeds sowed in the hearts and minds of young people. They sprout possibilities for creating a just and new social order in India, to remove extreme inequalities which haunt our society.

Organising Dalit Youth through sports and culture activities becomes easier–an entry point. It was found in the Centre's experience of working with youth from oppressed communities that the component of "recreation" plays a vital part and draws them to community activities. This has to be understood in the context of their hard work and the mental and physical burden with which they live and work. Recreation in the form of games, and entertainment through music and group dance are very popular, similar to the traits observed among the tribal people and African communities. This aspect of life reinforces the belief that Dalits are the oldest people of the Indian Continent. Dalits are tribal communities living on the plains possessing a natural and historical heritage of music, dance and valour in sports. However, these natural instinctive abilities were suppressed by upper caste people. Given an opportunity, these abilities come out very naturally. This opens up the possibility of organising the Dalit people and providing liberation education through recreational medium, designed specially with a purpose of creating awareness and initiating a process of liberation.

We have, during our tours in Ramanathapuram region, found that Dalits are still musicians, good drummers, who are in possession of ancient musical instruments. It is maintained that this cultural heritage has been taken over from the Dalits by upper caste people. Dalits who were the musicians of the Royal Courts were condemned as untouchables and landless labourers and were forced to play for funeral procession. During the youth camps the participants are encouraged to express freely their musical talents. They experience liberation through music and dance.

Comments from Foreign Scholars

Dr. Archie Nations of USA, has observed "Employing an unusual approach to helping the Dalits, Henry Thiagaraj, a Dalit, who founded the Dalit Liberation Education Trust in Madras, his Dalit Liberation Education Centre staffed by a small group of young Dalits whom he trained, does not dispense financial aid to the under privileged nor does it merely arouse hopes for deliverance that are thwarted by institutional imprisonment in the caste system. Instead it pursues the deepest need of untouchables: the repairing of their wounded psyche and the restoration of a sense of dignity, self-worth and personal initiative".

Dr. John Webster's: I first became acquainted with the Dalit Liberation Education Trust and Mr. Henry Thiagaraj during a visit to India in 1987. Since then and during my annual visits to India, I have spent time with him discussing and observing the work of the Trust. It is by all accounts one of the oldest NGOs devoted to the development of the Dalit people and I still think it is one of the most effective.

What struck me so forcefully at the outset was the innovative nature of their youth camps. Instead of just lecturing at the youth and then giving them some recreational time off to enjoy themselves, the whole program was aimed at building self-confidence through introducing subtle but significant modifications of behavior.

Emphasis was also placed upon learning through doing and this became a process not only of self-discovery but also of discovering a new self struggling to find expression. It would be difficult to document the contribution of these youth camps either to the youth themselves or to the subsequent expanded work of the Trust. I myself have drawn upon it a bit in the training of pastors who both are Dalits and serve Dalits.

I am strongly of the opinion that these youth camps and related youth activities should continue. While many programs focus on trying to improve the outward circumstances of Dalit lives, these have been based on the premise that first at least a partial inner transformation needs to occur before Dalits can take full advantage of the opportunities that come their way. Increased information and skill development by

---

Editor, Dalit International letter USA.

themselves are not enough; a new self-image and self-confidence must also be developed as well.

Evolution of Identity

Dalit Youth Camp – An Experience

Note by Editor

I. At registration
we are still forms and name tags,
surfaces and labels.
Soon each name becomes a face, a voice, a goal.
The introductions give only a glimpse
of who we are and who we want to be–
My name is Ruth,
or I am in tenth standard,
or I want to teach dance.
Gathered in the large classroom
we form a circle,
tied by the threads of proximity and a common program,
by the nervous newness of the camp and the anticipation of days to come.

II. As slides dance on the wall
Showing brains and hearts and muscles,
the message is clear:
whatever lies we have been told by society
about "difference" or "untouchability"
we are all the same on the inside.
We confront our fears about our appearances–
I am too dark
or too short
or too lean.
and learn to look at the beauty in ourselves.

III. Each name, each body,
houses a person in the truer sense:

the emotions and spirit,
hopes and fears of individuals.
We look into ourselves in silent meditation–
Understanding our weaknesses,
Recognising our strengths
Discovering our blessed humanity.
In sharing our thoughts and experiences,
we find that we are not alone
and the voices addressing the group grow stronger
As the drawstrings of the camp
pull our small community closer,
we also begin to see more clearly
the larger family to which we belong–
the vast and diverse community of the Dalit people's
From a common history of oppression and struggle,
we find strength–in the words of Ambedkar,
in our cultural songs and dances,
in our knowledge of the truth.
Gathered on the rocks of a tribal village,
we form a circle, cemented by the melted divisions of SC and ST, by the shared burden of pain and the common joy of laughter.
The identities of our ancestors
were shaped by those with the power to enslave,
those who made the Dalits a broken people,
They try hold us down today
with political propaganda and slanted news;
they try to force us down with violence.
But we are learning to assert our rights–
to education and employment,
to fair treatment by the police,
to freedom from fear and assault.
We are claiming our human rights.

Gone are the bashful hands
that once covered the mouths
of those called on to speak.
We trust each other and believe in ourselves.
Through dramas and songs, writings and speeches,
we will tell the world who we are and what we've learned
We will be heard–in the government and business, in the media, in our local communities and
around the globe.
We will not be silenced.

At the closing ceremony,
we are people, we are friends,
with a deeper understanding of
ourselves and others.
Together we burn the evils of society–
superstition, dowry, caste prejudice–
and light lamps of hope.
Gathered in the large classroom
we form a circle bound by the
experiences shared here and at home,
by our vision and commitment to a new society,
by the clap of our hands and the shared sorrow of saying goodbye.

24

International Educational Encounters with Dalit People

Semester at Sea Students Experience a Dalit Village

Patrica Nickels

Humankind's pursuit of knowledge has been intricately linked to ships and the sea. From early civilizations to the modern era, the exploration of distant lands, the exchange of ideas and commodities, and the search for knowledge have occurred in this manner. The Institute for Shipboard Education exits out of the recognition that, in an increasingly interdependent world, there is a vital need to advance the exchange of knowledge and understanding between cultures. The Institute is defined by its on-going commitment to combine academic excellence with challenging experiential programming in order to remain at the forefront of global education.

Semester at Sea

Semester at Sea is an academic program sponsored by the Institute for Shipboard Education and the University of Pittsburgh. This program offers university students an unusual international and comparative studies experience by offering programs that incorporate direct contact with people and their cultures. These programs afford the opportunities to develop cross-cultural understanding of human commonalities and global interdependence, while simultaneously recognizing, defining and

---

Patricia Nickels, International Field Program Coordinator for the Institute for Shipboard Education, University of Piitsburgh observed in an article:

respecting individual potential cultural diversities. The Institute's approach to international and cultural education provides the framework for a lifetime of learning, concern and commitment to others.

Approximately 600 university students (plus faculty, staff and adult passengers) participate in each voyage. Students undertake academic course work while traveling around the world aboard a ship and studying in ten countries. The 100-day semester includes roughly 55 days of class at sea aboard the S.S. Universe Explorer and 45 days in ports allowing four to six days per port. A typical Fall itinerary includes Japan, Hong Kong, Vietnam, Malaysia, India, Egypt, Turkey, Croatia, Italy and Morocco. A typical Spring itinerary includes Cuba, Brazil, South Africa, Kenya, Malaysia, Vietnam, Hong Kong and Japan.

The Field Program is an integral part of Semester at Sea. Field experiences become the "laboratory" component of each course in our liberal arts curriculum. Educational activities on land are designed to complement classroom instruction, and field work provides 20% of the contact hours for course credit. Semester at Sea's Field Program contains a variety of structured activities to enable students to fulfill academic requirements while accommodating a diverse range of interest, travel experiences, and budgets. Faculty-Directed Practica are designed to meet the specific needs of the course and are led by faculty members drawing on their own international experience.

Field experiences include diverse activities such as home stay opportunities, attendance at a Afro-Brazlian Drum Workshop; meeting university students through welcome receptions, home stays, sports competitions, and lectures / discussions held on nearby campuses; visits which afford time to interact with peers; visits to an African Township or Robben Island in Cape Town, South Africa; volunteering time to interact with orphans in various ports, or experiencing an indigenous group and staying at a longhouse in Vietnam or Malaysia. Students have an opportunity to talk with the street children in Brazil, members of the Congress of South African Writers, leaders of environmental organizations in India, housing authorities in Hong Kong, attend a Sufi Dervish Brotherhood Meeting in Turkey, or corporate officials of Toshiba or Sanyo in Japan. Other field activities provide opportunities for travel to places of significant cultural, historical and political interests. Opportunities are provided for visits to the Great Wall in China, the Taj Mahal in India or the Great Pyramids in Egypt. Students learn about wildlife ecological issues, and the life of the Maasai while on safari in Kenya. Studies are made of the flora and fauna tropical rain forest destruction while canoeing down the Amazon River. This is just a sampling of the many field activities available during a voyage. These international field experiences, coupled with a stimulating on-board classroom environment, make Semester at Sea an exceptional opportunity for learning.

Why the Dalits are Included

One field experience which has profoundly effected Semester at Sea students is an overnight stay in a Dalit Village. When Dr.Walton Johnson began to prepare field experiences for the students of his Dynamics of Ethnicity course for the Semester at Sea Fall 1989 voyage, he had no idea he would be establishing a relationship which would endure for years to come.

Professor Johnson wanted to provide unique insight for his students into the problems of inter-groups conflict. When asked why he looked to India for this insight, he indicated "the caste system is regarded by many scholars as the archetypal and most perfected system of domination. I taught about caste, therefore, as a way of teaching about the main elements in all systems of domination."

Professor Johnson's search for a 'civil rights' organisation working on behalf of the Dalits led him to Mr.Henry Thiagaraj of the Dalit Liberation Education Trust, in Chennai, India. who agreed to arrange for the regular group of Semester at Sea students to visit and spend the night within an 'Untouchables' village. The first visit during the Fall of 1989 was tremendously successful. So, successful that visits have been arranged since then for more than 500 Semester at Sea students over the past 10 years who have gained lifelong impressions of the plight which occurs within caste system.

Visiting the Villages

Although the Dalit village visits have followed a similar schedule, to each student the experience is unique and of great impact. Each semester currently provides opportunity for 60 students to experience a Dalit Village. Upon arrival at the Dalit Liberation Education Trust headquarters, the students are greeted by beautiful and elaborate rice designs of welcome ceremony which prepares them mentally and emotionally for what they will be experiencing. A large welcome design in the center of the assembly room floor is lit by clay lamps. Each is handed a small, shallow clay vessel filled with oil and a wick as they step forward to light their candle. Standing in a silent meditation circle, some might share a thought reflection on their upcoming experience. From this moment on, a bond is created among the students and the Dalit people. A welcome song is often performed prepared specially for the Semester at Sea students.

The students are then separated into groups of 10 with each group going to a different villages accompanied by a Dalit guide. Dr.Larry Glasco Professor of History at Pittsburgh University accompanied a group of Semester at Sea students on a visit during a Spring 1993 voyage, Dr.Glasco reflected on the welcome the group received to the village in great detail. "The welcome we received was incredible. One group of women came forward to place garland of white jasmine around our necks. Another group of women came forward with pans of red dye (kungam) which is applied in a round dot on our foreheads. This was followed by pans of yellow dye-sandalwood paste applied in horizontal strips on either cheek and the front of the throat. The men gathered small piles of leaves and twigs in the center of the settlement's lone dirt road, which they lit. They passed drums through he fire and then began a spirited drumming and dancing. The warming of the drum was repeated every 10-20 yards followed by more dancing. Villagers gathered and smiled and spoke what English phrases they knew. The children desired greatly to touch us. People warmly invited us into their back yards to see their goat or cow and into their humble homes. The atmosphere was like a festival. There was no begging, no hostility or resentment. At first their stares, even though accompanied by smiles, were unsettling and made us self-conscious, but as the evening wore on we became more relaxed and felt at home. During a beautiful sunset, the group was led in a procession down the road to another Dalit settlement where a similar welcoming was held. It seemed the dancing and drumming would never stop."

Accommodations at the villages are quite different from what the Semester at Sea students experience on a daily basis. There is no running water; like the locals, students use a nearby field to go to the bathroom, careful not to leave toilet paper; students sleep on thin straw mats on the floor of a concrete building; dinner is brought from the ship and is typically a peanut butter-and-jelly sandwich so as not to spoil in the heat during the many hours before they will actually eat it. And yet, none of these inconveniences are ever mentioned by the students. The overwhelming majority see the Dalit people in ways similar to that which was expressed by Jennifer Kirsch, "I know that they suffer from serious prejudice, but they still managed to be so free, open and happy. Somehow I could just feel the peace in the air of the village. I had an amazing time with my new friends and hope the future holds great things for them."

The Dalit Village Visits are often cited by Dr. John Tymitz (Chief Executive Officer), Dr. Max Brandt (Chief Academic Officer), Dr. Les McCabe (Chief Operations Officer), myself, and others at ISE as a model for what Semester at Sea hopes to accomplish with its field program. We believe that these visits are an invaluable first-hand experience with the people of India that changes our students' lives. Our students learn about the problems and challenges facing the Dalits; they also learn about their progress and successes. Most of all, they meet members of a Dalit community–visit their homes, laugh with them, communicate with them, and share with them. The Dalit Village Visits continue to be one of the most highly-rated port experiences that we offer. Students as well as faculty and staff often make the comment that their overnight visit to a Dalit village was one of the highlights of their Semester at Sea voyage.

PERSPECTIVES: According to Dr.Les McCabe, Chief Operating Officer at the Institute for Shipboard Education, his research on The Development of a Global Perspective During Participation in Semester at Sea: a comparative global education program, indicates that Semester at Sea students are profoundly impacted by their in-port experiences, particularly in India. Dr.McCabe reports that during the course of port experiences, some dramatic events occur which at times challenge existing ways of thinking for the participants, and caused them to change on the cross-cultural knowledge dimension. These periods of culture shock are important contributors to global perspective development. The extreme contrasts serve as a catalyst for deeper understanding of the similarities and differences of the cultures and people of the countries visited. One student commented, "India represented the furthest culture from the US. I was totally astonished with the way things were and I could actually empathize with the people."

Students often find themselves overwhelmed by the beauty of the people and the warm welcome they receive when they visit the Dalit village. Most have never had an experience of this type before. Prior to the visit, they might have preconceptions that the people would be sad or dirty or rude. Confronting the exact opposite causing the individual to pause and see the people for who they are. Dr.Larry Glasco summarized his visit in this way. "This experience left me with two questions. How can people treated so miserably be so beautiful and joyful? How can people so beautiful and joyful be treated so miserably?" Nedra Pickler visited a Dalit village during the Spring 1998 voyage and reflected on her visit with the following poem:

I KNOW HOW IT FEELS

I know how it feels to be the new kid in the class
where everyone looks, and points, and then
wants to meet you.
I know how it feels to be the president of the
United States,
where people line up just to shake your hand.
I know how it feels to be Desmond Tutu, aboard
Semester at Sea,
where everybody comes out of their hiding
Places to catch a glimpse of you, and to
savour your words.
I know how it feels to be Maya Angelow
where when the crowd wants you to sing and
dance, you give them everything you've
got, plus a piece of yourself.
I know, of course, how it feels to be me,
to come to a far away land, to open myself to a
world I have never seen.
I don't know how it feels to be an "untouchable".
or why they are given that name because
I know how it feels to be touched by one
touched by a Dalit Forever

I would like to share with you some comments from participants in recent Dalit Village Visits:

"This practicum was amazing! We were able to witness first hand how the Untouchables live and what little bit of their lives is like. It helped us see the educational and economic and social gap between different elements of Indian society. It was good a way to see how people were challenging the tradition of caste and helping others. I enjoyed seeing the work and dedication of the Dalit Education Trust. This was by far the best SAS practicum I have been on in terms of contact with the local people and really getting to experience their hospitality and spend time with them. I like the personal contact with the people the most." (Student, Spring 1998).

"I learned that there is a human face to what we learn in books. Strategies for development, malnutrition, income distribution inequalities, and other such topics begin to take on true meaning when you see the object of discussion first hand." (Student Spring 1998)

"I came away with more insight into a close community that appeared to have so little but yet presented themselves as a happy, healthy community. My favorite part of the visit of parading in the streets with the people as they welcomed us into their homes to show off all they had and be so proud of it. It made by heart and soul smile." (Student Spring 1998)

"I loved it. Incredible. The people are just like everyone else in the world." (Student, Fall 1997)

"On this trip, I learned a little more about humanity, about generosity, about humility and humbleness. What makes me better than them? Nothing. The sense of community they display is beautiful and encouraging. It was a very enriching trip.' (Student Fall 1997)

"The academic objectives of introducing students to rural social and economic structures in India is superbly met by this practicum. Students learn about the caste structure-first-hand-and about the daily lives of rural residents. This trip is a must in India! I wish more students could experience it," (Faculty member, Fall 1997)

"Happiness is not found in material wealth for these people. It was an excellent trip. I enjoyed the one-on-one immersion into untouchable culture." (Student, Fall 1996)

"This was an absolutely moving, powerful, amazing experience that I am just beginning to understand. This was ultimate in experiential education." (Student, Spring 1996)

"I can not even express in words What I have learned. This visit covered so many topics. I learned that the Dalit people are a beautiful group of people filled with love to share. They are hard-working and very proud of their community. This was the most moving experience of my life." (Student Spring 1996)

"I learned that these Dalit people have a wealth that far exceeds that of many people in the U.S.-their relationships with each other, hard work, hope, and the ability to take care of each other. The people were so welcoming. They didn't ask for anything; they wanted us to be happy and they kept giving. They are beautiful people. Although we didn't speak the same language, we could still communicate through a smile and "sign language." (Student Spring 1996)

In commemoration of the 10 year anniversary of Semester at Sea's relationship with Mr.Henry Thiagaraj and the Dalit Liberation Education Trust, we are truly indebted to Mr.Thiagaraj for his tireless efforts to provide this unforgettable experience to the students of Semester at Sea.

25

Christian Perspective of Human Rights and Dr. Martin Luther King, Jr.

Dr. Henry Thiagaraj

Human Rights are usually viewed as a modern subject which arose out of the treatment of prisoners of the World Wars. The Declaration of Human Rights by the United Nations of 10" December 1948 is a land mark in the history of human kind, which lifted humanity to a new level. It codified the fundamental rights of a person and became the basis for the constitutions of many countries and their governments. Some Asian Countries view human rights as a movement of the Western culture, which is not applicable to the Asian culture. The United Nations have reiterated the universality of the Human Rights - applicable to all countries.

As culture has a close bearing on the religious beliefs of the people, it becomes necessary to examine the impact of the religious beliefs on the cultural values. Dr Baba Saheb Ambedkar has pointed out that in world history; religious reformation precedes political and social reforms. He, therefore, thought that annihilation of caste system is necessary in Hindu religion to make the modern democratic movement a success and to ensure equal rights by removing untouchability from Indian soil (Annihilation of Castes p. 43-44). Students of Indian philosophy and Religion observe that in Indian thought, the individual human being does not occupy a pivotal position. The denial of the individual dignity and rights reflect in the oppressive social system prevalent in India and practiced in the predominant Hindu social system like the taboos of caste and taboos on women.

The Jewish and the Christian heritage provide a basis for an egalitarian society in which each human being is respected and equally treated. In the book of Genesis, it is recorded: Then God said, "Let us make man in our image, after our likeness..." So God created man in His own image... male and female He created them. (Gen. 1:26-27)

An excellent interpretation of the above verse was given by Dr. Martin Luther King Jr., the Liberator of the Afro - American people, who says in his book "Man in a Revolutionary World': "Deeply rooted in our religious heritage is the conviction that every man is an heir to a legacy of dignity and worth. Our Judaeo - Christian tradition refers to this inherent dignity of man in the Biblical terms as the image of God. The innate worth referred to in the phrase, the image of God, is universally shared in equal portions by all men. There is no graded scale of essential worth. There is no divine right of one race which differs from the divine right of another. Every human being has etched in his personality the indelible stamp of the creator. Every man must be respected because God loves him. The worth of an individual does not he in the measure of his intellect, his racial origin, or his social position. Human worth lies in relatedness to God. An individual has value because he has value to God. Whenever this is recognized, "Whiteness" and "Blackness" pass away as determinants in a relationship, and "Son" and "Brother" are substituted'.

The Ten Commandments provide a basic structure for human rights, recognize individual liberties and prohibits killing a human being, stealing another's property, coveting neighbour's wife, etc. The earliest of the prophets, Amos in 81 century B.C. condemns perversion of justice by the rich exploiters. He says that the Lord "will certainly punish them. They sell into slavery honest men who cannot repay even the price of a pair of sandals. They trample down the weak and the helpless and push the poor out of the way... so profane my holy name." (Amos 2:6 - 7)

"You people hate anyone who challenges injustice and speaks the whole truth in court You have oppressed the poor and robbed them of their grain ... You persecute good men, take bribes and prevent the poor from getting justice in the courts" (Amos 2: 10-12)

"The Lord says, 'I hate your religious festivals; I cannot stand them! When you bring me your burnt-offerings and grainofferings, I will not accept them;... Stop your noisy songs; I do not want to listen to your harps. Instead let justice flow like.a stream, and righteousness like a river that never goes dry." (Amos 5:21- 24)

"Hate what is evil, love what is right, and see that justice prevails in the courts" (Amos 5:15)

Again this type of message was delivered by Prophet Isaiah.

- When you fast, you make yourselves suffer; you bow your heads low like a blade of grass, and spread out sackcloth and ashes to lie on. Is that what you call fasting? Do you think I will be pleased with that?
- The kind of fasting I want is this.- Remove the chains of oppression and the yoke of justice and let the oppressed go free.
- Share your food with the hungry and open your homes to the homeless poor. Give clothes to those who have nothing to wear, and do not refuse to help your own relatives;
- "Then my favour will shine on you like the morning sun, and your wounds will be quickly healed. I will always be with you to save you; my presence will protect you on every side".

(Isaiah Chapter 58: verse 5-9)

God answers us only if you put an end on oppression then only He will answer your prayer. Thus historically in the Jewish religious heritage championing the cause of the poor and the oppressed is both a religious and moral obligation. All the prophets of the Old Testament championed the cause of justice and spoke of liberating the captives and the power required in our spiritual and religious life by living a sinless life.

Christ was born during the time of the expansion of Roman Empire when Caesar Augustus was ruling Rome. During the same period the Greek civilization with all its intellectual greatness was deteriorating and the materialistic Roman Empire was rising. While the Greeks appreciated the intellectual and aesthetic pursuits, their morals were deficient in that they had slaves who were denied human rights. Mere intellectualism was a failure as it could not fulfill the spiritual aspirations of the people. The material wealth of Rome and the great conquests of lands by Roman Empire resulted in territorial expansion but failed to fulfill the inner - human longings of the spirit of man. Roman emperors driven by the craze of wealth and power headed towards destruction. It was in this context Christ was born and Christian spirituality commenced. God will respond to your call to Christ in whose life all the prophesies are fulfilled, as Christ stood for the liberation of the oppressed. In Nazareth, Christ at his early age has declared His Mission: the purpose of coming to us in this world is to set the oppressed free. His famous declaration is well known:

The Spirit of the Lord is upon me,
Because he hath anointed me to preach the gospel to the poor;

He hath sent me to heal the brokenhearted
To preach deliverance to the captives,
And recovering of sight to the blind,
To set at liberty them that are bruised,
To preach the acceptable year of the Lord (St. Luke Ch. 4, V 18-19)

Dr. Albert Schweitzer observes that "Civilisation collapses even when in other directions creative and intellectual forces of the strongest nature are at work, when ethical foundation is lacking". Similarly religion without ethical values becomes immoral religion just as morals without religion become irreligious morality. These contradictions are resolved in the paradigm of human rights, which combine the spiritual and the moral they indeed become inseparable. Again Dr. Schweitzer points out that, 'it is only in his struggle to become ethical that man comes to possess real value as a personality". In order to have authentic civilization, ethical values are essential. Ethics of human beings start with the premises of an individual personality. When individual persons become spiritual that person acquires a new dimension in evolving humanity - in shaping the future of the world. In a secular democracy materialistic forces have their fun freedom. With the loss of spiritual values democracies have decayed and civilizations have fallen. Human rights can be mere rhetoric, useless words, when people are suffering. A human being should be capable of enjoying human rights for which the spiritual dimension is essential. It was during this period when Greek and Roman civilizations collapsed without spiritual content; the good news of Christ really saved human beings and gave them sanctity. Human rights then became meaningful and valuable.

In Christ human life acquired divine dignity and became sanctified. The respect for human life was strengthened and exalted and the divinity in everyone was recognized. God became human and thus lifted up humanity to the level of the divine. This incarnation of God in human body is the spiritual basis for human rights. "For God so loved the world that He gave His only son, so that every one who believes in him shall not perish but have everlasting life" (John. 3:16). Thus human beings and their rights acquired a divine sanctity, hitherto unknown in history. 'Man is rather an understanding human being whose vision has been impaired by the cataracts of sin and whose soul has been weakened by the virus of pride, but there is sufficient vision left for him to lift his eyes unto the hills, and there remains enough of God's image for him to turn his weak and sinbattered life towards the Great physician, the curer of the ravages of sin", says Dr. Martin Luther King Jr. in his book: "The strength to Love".

"THY KINGDOM COME" WITH HUMAN RIGHTS

Religion has two streams of moving people. One is concerned with life in the mundane world- the 'here' and 'now' of our present life the existential world. The other is 'the other - worldliness' being concerned with things pertaining to heaven and do not have anything to do with the present world. So there are religious people preparing their present life for the other world, the future heaven. Then there are people much concerned about problems of this world like poverty, injustice, ignorance, disease etc. They are devoted to find heaven on earth. Their life is dedicated to serve humanity to solve the problems of the society. In this stream of religious life which is concerned with bringing the kingdom of God on earth, people are concerned with establishing a just rule, a just society and removal of discriminations, and removal of inequalities, Prof. Harold Dewolf writing in "A Theology of the Living Church" points out: "The Christian needs to know what is meant by the kingdom of God. For him the kingdom is the summum bonum, "the pearl of great value" for which everything else ought to be willingly sacrificed. Its supreme uniting principle is love ...."Christ told us that "the kingdom of God is within you". (John. 14:5) that is in every human being. When we say the Lord's Prayer, "Thy Kingdom Come" we are actually asking God to open our eyes to his kingdom within us - to become conscious of his divine rule within us. His seeking justice and equality within his peace and love dwelling within our hearts is manifestation of the Holy Spirit with each Christian establishing the divine kingdom of human rights on earth through our service to people in our society.

A Christian who really seeks and serves the kingdom of God on earth, respects human beings and works for their liberation, does an authentic spiritual service. Hence it is imperative for every Christian to know the human rights of every person, to read the declaration of human rights and to work for its implementation. It provides a good basis for establishing God's kingdom on earth

In God's kingdom certainly there would be no distinction between Jews and Gentiles, man and woman among different castes. In his kingdom the weak will be cared for, the neglected will be exalted. It is our divine duty to be engaged in service of restoring human dignity to the people who are dehumanized, who have been victims of injustice for centuries and to work for the human rights of our people, as a divine task commanded by our Lord. In this service to humanity, we follow the example of Lord Jesus Christ. Christ did not condemn the woman taken in adultery and empowered her to sin no more. He did not insult the publican. He cared for the sinners and saved their lives. He showed the value of service by washing his disciple's feet and broke the distinction between servant and master. He loved the children and recognised their worth in society, a basis for children's rights. The sacred command "to love your neighbour as yourself' recognizes the divinity in every human being and one's rights. The sacred personality of human being is distinctly respected by Christ in moving with the sick, the handicapped and the people injured and insulted by the society. Christ exalted the widow's mite, dined with the outcastes and mixed with neglected humanity. In the process he gave them real salvation, an opportunity to discover their real human worth. There can be no better basis for human rights than the Christian Gospel - the good news which emancipates the people in bondage. In recent times the liberation of the Afro-American people was accomplished by Dr. Martin Luther King. Jr., who was a Christian pastor and was inspired by the power of Christ, The white Americans recognizing this Black leader's power of Christ and the following he had, bowed to his demands to remove discriminatory laws. In a secular democracy, materialistic forces have their full freedom. With the loss of spiritual values, democracies have decayed and civilizations have fallen. Human Rights can be mere rhetoric, useless words, when people are suffering.

In the Kingdom of God, there is both justice and love. Christ combines the justice of the Old Testament prophets and the personal love of God for human beings. Christ demonstrated in his life what it is to lift up humanity which was neglected. A king or a ruler is symbolic of the power to rule, and power to administer justice. He has power over people, but when the power is abused it results in denial of human rights. Power when used appropriately empowers people. Regarding the use of power and love, Dr. Martin Luther King Jr. explained:

> *"Power, properly understood, is the ability to achieve purpose. It is the strength required to bring about social, political or economic changes. In this sense power is not only desirable but necessary in order to implement the demands of love and justice. One of the greatest problems of history is that the concepts of love and power are usually contrasted as polar opposites. Love is identified with a resignation of power and power with a denial of love" ... "What is*

needed is a realization that power without love is reckless and abusive and that love without power is sentimental and anaemic. Power at its best is love implementing the demands of justice. Justice at its best is love correcting everything that stands against love" (Where do we go from here?' p. 37)

How will the kingdom of God be? It will be a place of freedom, where people, who are free, work in joy. It will be inhabited by people who are free and enjoy freedom. The Kingdom of God speaks of a spirituality which affirms life on earth. It protects life because life has dignity and is accorded a divine status. This new spirituality provides us with a vision of an open society where the whole world is embraced by our love.

If we work and serve for the kingdom of God as Dr. Martin Luther King says, there will be no conflicts and dashes in India. 'We have inherited a large house, a great "World House" in which we have to live together black and white, Easterner and Westerner, Gentile and Jew, Catholic and protestant, Muslim and Hindu - a family unduly separated in ideas, culture and interest. Learn to live with each other in peace".

A Christian's experience of the Kingdom of God has a vision in which, "When we allow freedom to ring, when we let it ring from every village and every hamlet, from every state and every city, we will be able to speed up that day when all God's children, black men and white men, Jews and Gentiles, Protestants and Catholics, will be able to join hands and sing in the words of the old Negro Spiritual: "Free at last, Free at last, Thank God Almighty, we are free at last", cried Dr. Martin Luther King, Jr. who won the Noble Prize for Peace in 1964.

The people who are busy with the other world, the future of life in the other world, which exists out somewhere or up in the heaven, go to the extent of negating life on this earth. In the process, human values and the human rights are violated. Often this stream of thought is identified with extremism, fundamentalism, and diverting our life energy to somewhere else. Instead of solving our problems, extremism and negation of life create more problems; for example, people who practice discrimination in the name of religion are living an immoral and irreligious life.

It is *Un-Christian* to practice casteism. When we open the matrimonial columns advertised in the leading newspapers in India, we can find a number of Christians who seek caste and communal identities, even though they practice Christian faith. It then becomes a big contradiction: How can a Christian have caste prejudices and still worship Christ who by his death broke all distinctions within the human family? Caste discriminations like colour prejudices, are fundamentally opposed to.

Christian teachings and to the Kingdom of God. For an authentic Christian spiritual experience, it is essential to work for the realization of human rights. One has to be really free from discrimination and caste prejudices to embrace humanity with the divine love of agape - which is universal but actually experienced in our particular individual life.

The source of human rights is Christ and His love. In the experience of Martin Luther King, whose deep spiritual experience of Christ moved him to lead the oppressed black people: "The cross is the eternal expression of the length to which God will go in order to restore broken community. The resurrection is a symbol of God's triumph over all the forces that seek to black community. The Holy Spirit is the continuing community reality that moves through history". Caste discriminations have crucified Christ. We practice caste differences within the Church and deny justice to the oppressed Dalits. Our inhumanity which refuses the rural poor Dalits to enjoy their legitimate human rights crucifies Christ every day. Is our blood boiling whenever we hear an act of injustice or when a Dalit woman is raped, a Dalit hurt, Dalit houses burnt? Our social record: every hour two Dalits are assaulted! Every day three Dalit women are raped! Two Dalits are murdered! Two Dalit houses are burnt in India! - as per the Govt. statistics.

Ten years ago people in the Churches were shy of using the word "Dalit" and some of the church officials said that we should not bring caste in to the church, without realizing that caste system already existed in the Churches in India. Many clergymen then were very critical and were not willing to cooperate to work for Dalit Liberation. At that time a fashion among the liberation theologians was "economic liberation" which emphasized the class differences and avoided the caste discrimination in the Church.

Social oppression and discrimination is largely associated with untouchability. This aspect to some extent was realized by some Church Leaders in August 1993 when I was the Convener of the Delegation of Church Leaders to call on the President of India, Dr. Shankar Dayal Sharma, to speak about the Dalit Christian's discrimination. There were many Bishops from both Church of North India and Church of South India including the Moderator of CNI and the President of SC & ST Unit of Catholic Bishops Conference of India. This marked a sea change in the attitude of the Church Leaders over a period of ten years.

Yet, the struggles of the Dalits are not decreasing, or being solved as an increasing number of atrocities are being committed on Dalits who have become the victims of violence only show that their struggles will continue in greater vigor. Now we see the attack on the Church and Christians by the Hindu Sangh Pariwar and other Hindu fanatics. Pastor Niemoeller, a Victim of the Nazis is often quoted for this famous saying:

First they came for the Jews

and I did not speak out,

because I was not a Jew

Then they came for the Communists

and I did not speak out

because I was not a communist.

Then they came for the trade unionists

and I did not speak out

because I was not a trade unionist.

Then they came for me

and there was no one left

to speak out for me.

When the Hindu Sangh Pariwar demolished the Babri Masjid (mosque) in 1992 the Churches in India kept quiet. When the Dalits were attacked and Dalit women were raped, the Christians kept quiet. Now churches are being burnt, we are crying! But we need the support of others. It is in this context I would like to ask all of you when such atrocities were happening what were the churches doing? What are you doing? Often Christians as good people keep silent, or want to bear everything silently! The Bible has a tradition of fighting for justice.

As Christians, it is our task, and we should hear the Call of God to work for Dalit liberation and to work for the justice of the oppressed Dalits. It must be noted that many people who spear headed the Dalit Liberation work in India are Christians. It is the Dalit Christians who were hurt, assaulted, butchered, killed, yet there is, Civil Protection Act to protect them! This was the case at Tsunduru in Andhra Pradesh or in Southern Districts of Tamil Nadu.

The Churches must fight for the injustices and practices of discrimination. It is unfortunately very true that the Hindu fanatic groups are sowing the seeds of division and made Dalits, say things against Dalit Christians. But unless the Church takes it as a major task, the Dalit Liberation work will remain weak. Indirectly we will strengthen against those who persecute us!

The Church is not an impersonal body; Church is a human body which is dynamic transforming society. It is usually the Christians who fight against injustices and create awareness to fight for Human Rights. As we see many Non-Government Organisations (NGOs) are led by Dalit Christians, even those who in the beginning felt shy are not afraid now to call themselves Dalits.

One of the great weaknesses or even the curse of our people is that because we were dehumanized for thousands of years, we were not made to come together and work together and enjoy human fellowship. We were divided on the basis of occupation like agricultural labourers, leather workers, sanitation workers, etc.

As Dr. Ambedkar said: "My Hindus practice injustice and tyranny against Untouchables only because they are weak. First Untouchables cannot face social and religious persecution, so long as they remain weak and divided. Secondly, they do not possess enough strength to face the tyranny. With those two conclusions, the third one automatically follows. That is the strength required to face the tyranny needs to be procured from outside.

In my opinion it has to come from Universal Declaration of Human Rights (UDHR). This is why we are asking the UN High Commissioner for Human Rights to give us the right and freedom to choose our belief as assured in the UDHR.

> *Everyone has the right to freedom of thought, conscience and religion; this right includes freedom to change his religion or belief, and freedom, either alone or in community with others and in public or private, to manifest his religion or belief in teaching, practice, worship and observance. UDHR: ARTICLE 18*

If Churches express solidarity with this national movement and will inform their parent missions of all those church missions with whom they have partnerships, networking connections it will bring the international pressures and the problems of Dalits are likely to be solved.

As the aid money that is received by the Government should have a clause that it should reach the poorest of the poor-the Dalits, who are still living in thatched huts, are homeless whose children are still out of school and are half-naked and has large number of school drop -outs. Our people are still living as agricultural labourers, sanitation workers, etc. hardships amidst. Unless Churches in India realize their task, their prophetic Mission and takes it up with its prophetic role and spearheads this Dalit Liberation struggle and mobilize the public opinion both in the country and abroad, our struggles may not find easy solutions.

I would like to remind you what a prophetic role Dr. Martin Luther King, Jr., played in leading the Afro-American people towards their liberation. He won the Noble Prize for his services. His struggles for the liberation of the African American people in United States were based on his Christian conviction and Christian faith.

> *"In a real sense all life is inter-related. All are caught in an inescapable network or mutuality, tied in a single garment of destiny".*
>
> Dr. Martin Luther King, Jr.

If Dr. Martin Luther King, Jr., a Christian Pastor can bring deliverance to the African-American people, how much more the powerful Church in India can do by giving a lead to the Christians in India. We all should work towards the Kingdom of God.

> *Then justice will rule through all the land and out of justice, peace. quietness and confidence will reign for ever more. (Isaiah 32.17)*

I know a few pastors have expressed lot of support to Dalit struggles and have opened their church compound for Dalit consultations and organizing the poor Dalits. Yet I know many other pastors and church officials think Dalit liberation is not their business! It is only to remind the words of Pastor Niemoeller, "First they came for the Jews. Then they came for the Dalits and now they are coming for Christians." If you have not raised your voice and condemn the Dalit atrocities and they come for you there may not be anyone to speak for you. So, my friends, wake up, arise and stand against discrimination and injustice.

In India the Christian Church has to walk a long way to realise the importance of human rights in our society and towards the real life of the risen Lord whose power has to be manifested in liberating the oppressed in India. Realisation of human rights in our society and to our people can be an in-depth spiritual experience and an authentic Christian service if we are spiritually awakened to see the realities of life.

Bibliography

1. The decay and the Restoration of Civilization - Albert Schweitzer.
2. The making of a Mind - Dr. Martin Luther King. Jr.
3. Where do we go form here? Dr. Martin Luther King. Jr.
4. Annihilation of Caste - Dr. B.R. Ambedkar.

Human rights has become today one of the central challenges of civilization. People, no matter where they live, increasingly demand respect for their human rights and judge the institutions of society by how well they respond to demands. Food, shelter, employment, education and access to health - care go hand in hand with demands for respect for culture, equitable and effective justice, the right to participate in government, to express one's thoughts freely and to live one's own moral and spiritual convictions.

The challenge is not only felt on the national level where the institutions of society are more fully developed. The international community also has to face the issue of how well it contributes to the effective enjoyment of human rights. Dr. Boutros Boutros - Ghali Secretary General, United Nations.

26

Human Rights Education for Social Transformation

Dr. Henry Thiagaraj

This chapter deals with my reflections and experiences of working with grassroots communities and the Dalits. Now I look at my life and this world in which I live. I reflect on this life experience as the new horizons of 21st century create new opportunities. I propose to present this chapter in three sections: First, the global situation vis-a-vis Human Rights, including the Indian situation. Secondly Experiences obtained in the field, working among grassroots Dalit communities, and thirdly inter-connections between human rights the social transformations.

The World Crisis

We live at a crisis point in history. Since 1991, we witnessed changes sweeping this planet beginning with the dissolution of the Soviet Union and the end of an era of cold war. Now we live in a world which is threatened with terrorism, glaring violations of justice and peace. The conflicts around the world, violence inflicted on innocent human beings and man-made disasters prove that the human society is sick, what Sigmund Freud called "the social neuroses". What the 21st Century has in store was shown in a very dramatic TV news, on the morning of September 11th 2001 in New York, as passenger planes crashed on the World Trade Center towers. It was aimed to smash the economic might of America in a symbolic manner. This is unbelievable yet happened to the mighty country of America, which has all the defense technology,

---

This Chapter is based on the 15th Academic Public Lecture delivered on 12th January 2002 at Gurukul Lutheran Theological College Auditorium, Chennai.

scientific tools, "intelligence" resources and "crime mapping devices" at its disposal to detect such attacks.

This devastating incident was an unpredictable product of the human mind, an expression of the social neurosis, which challenges our sanity and humanity.[1] An aftermath of this terrorist attack on Sept. 11, is the entry of Coalition Forces led by USA in Iraq which has been well covered in the media that there is no need to repeat except to express the feeling of anguish, pain and depression that the world is moving in a path of regression.

Louis Mumford, criticizing our modern civilization says:

> "Now this mechanical chaos is plainly not self-perpetuating, for it affronts and humiliates the human spirit; and the tighter and more efficient it becomes as a mechanical system, the more stubborn will be the human reaction against it. Eventually, it must drive modern man to blind rebellion, to suicide, or to renewal: and so far it has worked in the first two ways. On this analysis, the crises we now face would be inherent in our culture even if it had not, be some miracle, also unleashed the more active disintegration that have taken place in recent history."[1]

Some of us in the NGO community who participated in the UN World Conference on Racism at Durban in Sept. 2001, thought that though we could not achieve all that we wanted against discrimination, we were reasonably satisfied that the mandate to end racism was renewed. We left Durban around the 8th of September 2001*. A few days later, my dreams of an ideal world collapsed, as the world was in gloom over the terrible air attacks on the buildings in the United States. The human values and the human rights cause to which I am committed seemed to vanish. I was deeply depressed and disappointed. I asked the question where is the world heading? I saw anarchy, chaos, pain and anguish and people dying. Ultimately I saw war declared. All of these tragedies dramatically raised the question of Human Rights. The reaction of September 11, 2001 was that many nations enacted repressive laws and security measures which hamper the realization of human rights. After a while it was clear to me that Human Rights Education, as a programme of prevention of violence and violations, is urgently required to remedy the situation into which our world has plunged. Human Rights Education is crucial, essential and must be integrated into the education of people all over the world. Clearing the doubts that some of us had, Mrs. Mary Robinson, who was in 2001 the UN High Commissioner for Human Rights said:[2]

"The relevance and importance of human rights during conflict should never be underestimated. Of course humanitarian law–the law of war–operates in conflict serving as a bulwark against the worst violations of rights. But side-by-side with that body of law the core of the human rights agenda also remains in operation.

"Human Rights is an important element also in the settlement of conflict. It is vital to ensure that settlements are ethical agreements, which will promote and protect human rights rather than abridge them. It is something of a truism that the seeds of new battle are often sown in the unfair settlement of the old. Application of human rights principles and values to the settlement stage of the process is one method of countering that risk. "Essentially the human rights goal must be to attempt to break the cycle of hatred of intolerance and of violence. Human Rights Education is a powerful tool in this regard. It can serve as a counter to a culture of ignorance and intolerance. It provides and develops a space for participation: it drives a demand for responsive institutions of State which in turn provide alternatives to conflict."

"However this is not the complete story: True equality–both material and in terms of parity of esteem–must also be sought if conflict is to be prevented. This is where, once more, the nexus between peace, human rights and development comes into focus. There can be no enjoyment of human rights by all where some are excluded by disadvantage, discrimination and prejudice. For human rights development and the rule of law act as the counter-force to the destructive ideologies of hate that inevitably spiral into conflict and violence."[4]

Again to quote Mrs. Robinson

"Never has this point been more clearly evident than now. In the current international crisis, there may be some who suggest that human rights, including the issue of racial discrimination, must take less priority. It is sometimes claimed that concern with human rights gets in the way of winning the peace or defeating terrorism. Experience throughout the world, including in the case of the island of Ireland, demonstrates that this is wrong thinking. We must condemn and combat terrorism. But there can be no stable peace, no true human security without human rights and real public participation."[5] Mrs. Robinson was the President of Ireland and knows more about terrorism than some other world leaders.

In his Annual Report presented to the General Assembly of the UN last September (2001), the Secretary General of the UN stated: "Bridging the gap between human rights norms and their implementation continues to pose a substantial challenge for the United Nations. The Commission on Human Rights plays a crucial role in meeting this challenge by providing a forum for discussion. Forty-two special rapporteurs, independent experts, and chairpersons of bodies and groups submitted country and thematic reports. Those reports painted a bleak picture of the status of the human rights in the world today."[6] The UN has declared 1995-2004 as the UN Decade for Human Rights Education. The United Nations reminds us that we are living in the Third Decade of Combating Racism.

Twelve Global conferences were organized by the United Nations between 1990-2002 to renew the commitment of the UN for a social transformation of people around the world. They are:

1. The World Summit for Children held in September 1990, New York.
2. The World Summit on Earth (Environment and Development) held in June, 1992 at Rio de Janeiro, Brazil.
3. The World Conference on Human Rights held in June 1993 in Vienna, Austria.
4. The World Conference on Population held in Cairo, Egypt in September, 1994.
5. The World Summit on Social Development held in Copenhagen in March, 1995
6. The Women's Summit The Fourth World Conference on Women–held at Beijing in September, 1995.
7. Second United Nations Conference on Human Settlements (Habitat II, June 1996, Istanbul).
8. The Earth Summit 5 (Sustainable Development) at the UN Headquarters in New York in September, 1997.
9. The Millennium Summit–September, 2000 at the UN in New York.
10. UN Conference on the Least Developed Countries–LDC at Brussels in May 2001.
11. World Conference on Racism in Durban September 2001.
12. World Summit on Sustainable Development in Johannesburg, South Africa from 2-4 September 2002.

Though these global Conferences attracted participation of NGO's representing people all over the world, there is a criticism that these conferences were inter-governmental in character and did not include the views of "the people of the United Nations". The increasing segregation of NGO's in these global conferences for security purposes makes these conferences more of an inter-governmental show, devoid of the voices of the people making the Preamble of the UN–"We the people of the UN" becomes a farce increasingly. However, it cannot be denied that they have become a turning point in providing guidelines to Governmental and Non-governmental organizations to move into the 21st Century. The presence of NGO's as the voice of the poor, the oppressed and the discriminated was felt at all these world events. NGO's were able to bring massive materials and evidence to correct the imbalances and distortions taking place within government and social structures. These world conferences seem to point to a new paradigm for development in the new age, for the 21st Century. In November, 2000 at New Delhi a global colloquium was held "in search for the missing ingredient in international development". Specialists from the three fields of Science, Religion and Development gathered to consider integrating spirituality into efforts to eliminate poverty and achieve social justice. But for the present let us leave this topic for greater research.

A Challenge for Development

The nexus is between peace, human rights and development scenario. As we tackle terrorism, combat cross-border terrorism, and strive to capture terrorists, and militants, all these efforts add to a heavy cost to us, both in mental agony and material terms. The world economy, already affected by the September 11 attacks, slows the progress of poor people and the growth process of developing nations. Unresolved conflicts, violence and man-made disasters make us pay a heavy price! The gap widens between the rich and poor, as the funds earmarked for development are diverted for security and defense. Military contractors and manufacturer of weapons are thriving; as problems of poverty, illiteracy and disease remain unsolved.

After 50 years of the founding of the United Nations, it is said that there has been unprecedented material progress in the world–and "deepening despair for millions of people." Poverty and prosperity have become globalized. In the last four decades the United Nations Development Programme, (UNDP) accomplished some results like greater literacy, better nutrition and increase in life expectancy. Yet UNDP has reported a widening gap between rich and poor. The UN could not eradicate global poverty, nor hunger in the world. World Bank experts thought that a few doses of capital would cure the ailments of poor countries. It did not work. Many developing countries witnessed political turmoil, became indebted, and suffered much. A classic example is the political fiasco of Argentina. It is apparent that material input like capital inflow alone is not sufficient. There is now greater doubt about traditional economic measures:

- Currently over 1.3 billion people live on less than $1 a day, a number which grows by 25 million people every year. The daily income for people in LDCs in the lowest in the world; average per capita GDP was $235 in 1997, compared to $24, 522 in developed countries. [7]
- Ordinary people are facing terrible poverty every day; most have no power to change the situation, and become increasingly marginalized from the political process.[8]
- A World Bank Report states that 1.3 billion absolute poor live in conditions "limited by malnutrition, illiteracy, disease, squalid surroundings, high infant mortality, and low life expectancy as to be beneath any reasonable definition of human decency".
- Among all poor people, 1.5 billion have no sources of clean drinking water or access to sanitation.
- Most poor go to bed hungry.
- The poor are particularly vulnerable to natural disasters such as drought, floods and storms, having little or no margin for survival when their housing, possessions and means of production are destroyed.
- Out of the world labour force of 2.8 billion, there are 120 million people who are actively looking for work, but without success.
- The vast majority of the absolute poor-700 million people-are classified as under employed, working long hours, often at back-breaking jobs that don't come close to covering their most basic needs. A startlingly disproportionate number of these people are women. The largest numbers of poor people—about half of the total—eke out a bare existence in the countries of South Asia.
- One quarter of the world's poor live in East Asia.
- Eighty per cent of the world's poor live in rural areas, with the great majority in Asia and Africa. But the rural poor are mostly landless, or have farms that are too small to yield an adequate income.
- Poverty has increased in recent years, in both relative and absolute terms, in Africa, Latin America and the industrialized countries, while decreasing in Asia.
- Poverty's impact is heaviest on women, followed by the elderly and children.

The statement that one billion people worldwide struggle to survive on less than one dollar a day and therefore live in poverty (World Bank 1995, v, ix) is "the big lie" according to NGOs present at the World Summit for Social Development in Copenhagen in March 1995. The NGOs felt that the World Bank created a false measure of "poor" which serves to distort the true level of destitution confronting the millions. The true figure of global poverty,[9] is truly astounding, probably well over three billion as per the evaluation of the NGOs. "The majority of humanity is thus made up of a combination of the poorest and those slightly better off; all of whom, regardless of ethnicity, race, or, gender, raise questions of equity and justice. Many nations today confront social disintegration, to a large degree the result of the unequal distribution of wealth. The persistent, day-to-day tragedy of absolute poverty and its consequences is staggering....One finds a deep tragedy of economic and political power has led to an international system that produces massive suffering."[10]

"The torture of a single individual rightly raises public outrage. Yet the deaths of more than 30, 000 children every day from mainly preventable causes go unnoticed. Why? Because these children are invisible in poverty. Poverty eradication is a major human rights challenge of the 21st century. Decent work and protection against calamities are not just development goals, they are also human rights"[11]

The Human Development Report of 1994 states, that "India alone accounts for nearly 27 percent of the world's poorest, which is about 350 million people, the largest such grouping anywhere in human history. 70% of India's population of 800 million people live in villages; 52% are illiterate, 38% do not have access to safe drinking water, 57% have no access to electricity, and 59% do not even have proper houses to live in. [12]Nearly half the world's illiterates are in India and almost two-thirds of India's female population is illiterate. With the status of primary and secondary education in shambles throughout the country, the base of human development has been completely eroded. The Primary Health Care system in the rural areas has become a farce; sanitation and hygiene in urban localities are hopelessly inadequate; and the public hospitals, the only medical care to which the poor have any access, are in a state of deprivation.

More than fifty-five years of planning and money spent on development in India has brought several distortions like the rich becoming richer and the poor remaining poor. The enigma of poverty remains unsolved. Even after economic liberalization introduced several years ago, a senior statesman observed, "We should realize that the existing policies and programmes for eradicating poverty and to generate employment in the country have proved to be a failure."[13]

The *Human Development Report 2000* recommends, "Poor countries need faster growth to generate the resources needed to finance the eradication of poverty and the realization of human rights. But economic growth alone is not enough. It needs to be accompanied by policy reforms that channel funds into poverty eradication and human development and into building institutions, shaping norms and reforming laws to promote human rights."

Increasing economic marginalization of large sections of the community has led to social tensions, social disintegration and a steep sense of insecurity among the population. Added to this list of woes is the plight of 200 million Dalits, who as untouchables live separately, segregated from the caste Hindu communities. Villages are divided into a Hindu caste village and a Dalit colony. In some of these Dalit (untouchable) villages, women have to walk one kilometer or more to get drinking water, as they cannot have access to the drinking water in the caste village.

Among the NGO's, those who speak on economic disadvantages often ignore social disparities. The concept of social justice is not very palatable to many NGOs, especially the elitist academic scholars. In these circumstances, there is a danger that the dominant NGOs may permit and perpetuate existing social disparities. It is in this context that the World Conference on Racism's attention was drawn to the question of untouchability and the plight of Dalits in India, Dalit discrimination. We are reminded of the clarion call of Late Dr. B. R. Ambedkar, the architect of the Indian Constitution:

> "The world owes a duty to the untouchables, as it does to all oppressed people to break their shackles and to set them free"

The world leaders have not woken up to notice the discrimination suffered by 200 million untouchable people living in India. As apartheid was visible, based on colour, it was able to easily attract the attention of the world, whereas caste discrimination which is worse than apartheid remained invisible and concealed to the eyes of the world. It was only ten years ago, the Dalit discrimination issues were brought to the attention of the UN Human Rights Commission and highlighted during the *World Conference Against Racism* at Durban in 2001.

The Hindu belief system of caste which discriminates Dalits is based on one's place of birth in society, outside the caste village. It is also based on descent of occupation, which has been practised for more than 2000 years. Dalits are the native people, indigenous to Indian sub-continent. According to one theory of Indian history the Hindu Aryans who came to India took away the lands of the indigenous people, the ancient Dravidians (*Adi Dravidars*) and enslaved them, drove them to colonies subject to discriminatory laws and kept them as bonded labourers.

One fifth of the Indian population belong to the *untouchable communities, the Dalits,* most of whom live in poverty and squalor, in addition to the social discrimination imposed on them by religion for the past 2000 years. 'Dal' is the Sanskrit root meaning 'to oppress', to break, to put aside. Dalit therefore means those who are oppressed, particularly the discriminated "Untouchables". In the present Indian context, the Dalits are the so-called "Panchamas" the fifth class people, the outcasts, who literally live outside the caste system of *Varnashrama Dharma,* the four fold caste system in Hindu sociological hierarchy. At present they are called the enumerated in the Government list of Scheduled Castes and Tribes (SCs and STs) of the Indian Constitution. The caste system through Hindu religious indoctrination of the Karma and sins of past birth, has perpetuated poverty and servitude in India, the basis for economic inequalities and social disparities through a rigid social hierarchy.

Mr. H.Hanumanthappa, Ex-Member of Parliament and the Chairman of National Commission for Scheduled Castes and Scheduled Tribes 1995, describes the conditions of Dalits as follows:

> "The Dalits are in different stages of socio-economic development and are engaged in divergent forms of work for their living. The practise of such traditional unclean occupations as scavenging, carrying night-soil, removing dead animals, leather work, beating of drums, etc. gave them a low position in the traditional caste hierarchy and they are viewed as occupying the lowest rung of the social ladder. The vast majority of Dalits are landless and work as agricultural laborers and wage earners to eke out their livelihood. Dependence on upper-caste landowners for agricultural labor and perpetual subjugation forces many of them to live as bonded laborers. On the educational front the Scheduled Castes lag far behind the general population of India. The general literacy rate in 1991 was 52.19% while the literacy among the Scheduled castes was only 37.41%. The condition of the Dalit women is particularly deplorable. They are doubly under-privileged being women belonging to the Scheduled Castes. They constitute the major work force doing hard manual labor and engaged in agricultural operations and their exposure to outdoor work and interaction with the cunning employers make them vulnerable to sexual exploitation. Abject poverty forces Dalit women to become

victims of Devadasi, the institutionalized prostitution system prevalent...." "The Dalits constitute the weakest of the weaker sections of the society. Landlessness, a low level of literacy, and social discrimination arising out of the practise of untouchability not only account for their miseries but are also factors contributing to perpetration of atrocities against them. They are victims of atrocities, which include heinous crimes like murder, grievous hurt, rape, arson, etc."

India has a terrible human rights record in regard to Dalits. Since 1996 increasing political awareness among Dalits, and any visible improvement in their living conditions increases intolerance, and unleashes violence on Dalits by caste people. A TV documentary "60 Minutes" by the CNN in the US telecast on (March 21, 1999) with Christian Amanpour's commentary portrays the caste discrimination in India. The report of the Human Rights Watch, USA, on India under the title Broken People–*Caste Violence Against India's "Untouchables"* (April 1999) records the violence inflicted on the untouchable people. The societal violence has not diminished.

India's leading national daily, The Hindu dated 20th July 2004 reported that the crimes against the Scheduled Castes and the Scheduled Tribes showed a steady increase between 1998 and 2002 with Uttar Pradesh and Madhya Pradesh topping the list. While the number of cases of atrocities against SCs rose from 7, 445 in 1998 to 33, 507 in 2002, the cases against STs went up from 725 to 6, 774 in the same period. Figures available with the National Crime Records Bureau (NCRB) show that the cases in Uttar Pradesh stood at 2, 737 in 1998 and in 2002 it was 7, 927. Madhya Pradesh reported just 85 cases against STs in 1998 and it rose to 2, 504 in 2002.

Statistics available with the Scheduled Castes and the Scheduled Tribes Commissions indicate that Maharashtra, Rajasthan, Uttar Pradesh, Andhra Pradesh and Tamil Nadu recorded high incidence of atrocities against SC/ST between 1996-2000. Uttar Pradesh, Madhya Pradesh and Bihar reported the maximum number of serious crimes against SC/STs.

Highlighting the social disadvantages faced by the Scheduled Castes with particular reference to the practise of untouchability, discrimination in public spheres and atrocities covered under the Protection of Civil Rights Act, 1955 and the Prevention of Atrocities Act 1989 Professor S.K Thorat of Jawaharlal Nehru University says: "The violation of civil rights includes prohibition of Scheduled Castes to use public water bodies such as wells, water taps, temples, tea stalls, restaurants, community baths, roads, and other social services (Table

14). Despite the prohibition of the practise of untouchability under Article 17 of the Constitution, untouchability is still widely practised across the country. During the period 1981 to 2000 a total of 3, 57, 945 cases of crimes committed against the Scheduled Castes were registered. Thus, annually an average of about 22, 371 cases of general crimes and atrocities were committed against the Scheduled Castes. The break-up of the atrocities and violence for the year 2000 include 486 cases of murder, 3298 cases of grievous hurt and injury, 260 cases of arson, 1034 cases of rape, and 118664 cases involving other offences." The former Prime Minster of India, Mr. Atal Behari Vajpayee speaking at a Dalit MP's Conference on 16th May 2002, regretted that atrocities were still being committed against Dalits and the situation called for a transformation of society. If the Prime Minister of a Country cannot bring transformation with all the resources he commands, it is an indication of lack of political will among the leaders of the country. It leaves the door open for NGO's to work for social change.

Human Rights in India has been the pre-occupation of caste Hindu lawyers and urban elite scholars who are concerned with civil liberties. Till recently the societal violence inflicted on Dalits has not attracted the attention of the people dealing with civil liberties. In 1996 Justice Mr. Ranganath Mishra, the then Chairperson of National Human Rights Commission (NHRC) asked me to organize jointly (with NHRC) a historically significant National Conference on Societal Violence on Dalits, which was inaugurated by the then Speaker of Lok Sabha, Mr. P.A. Sangma. Several distinguished scholars all over India participated in it. The proceedings of this National Conference are now available in a book form; entitled *Human Rights of Dalits Societal Violence* brought out by Gyan Publishing House, Delhi. It was perhaps for the first time in India, Human Rights experts and people saw the violence on Dalits in the new context as violation of Human Rights. After this National Consultation, the National Human Rights Commission called the Ministry of Welfare for consultation and started including its views on the Dalit situation in its Annual Reports. The National Human Rights Commission has undertaken a large research project on Dalit atrocities and a report: "Edifice of Violence" by Mr. K. B. Saxena IAS (Retd.) has been published now.

It is always difficult to do this bit of pioneering work, foundation work. This is like getting electricity connection to a multistorey building where several families are living. Once the connection is provided, the end users can be many tenants, people of different kinds! The basic research and material we produced during 1985-1995 are now widely used for Human Rights Work among the Dalits.

The number of Dalit NGÓ's participating in the *World Conference Against Racism* is like a tree yielding many fruits from the roots of making Dalit discrimination a Human Rights issue. Better still is the beautiful saying "let thousand flowers bloom "among Dalit people. Yes these thousand flowers bloomed should not fade away but become radiant flowers, should yield fruits with seeds and useful plants of liberation.

Babasaheb Dr. Ambedkar pointed out our strength has to come from outside oppressive system of Hinduism:

> "The Hindus practise injustice and tyranny against Untouchables only because they are weak. Firstly Untouchables cannot face social and religious persecution, so long as they remain weak and divided. Secondly, they do not possess enough strength to face the tyranny. With those two conclusions, the third one automatically follows: That is the strength required to face the tyranny needs to be procured from outside." [18]

In my view, the strength required to face the tyranny of Hindu casteism comes from the Universal Declaration of Human Rights. It is imperative to build a strong international network to support the Human Rights Education Movement among Dalit people of different cultural, political, religious and linguistic groups through education on Human Rights. By being united for Human Rights, we can organize Dalits. This should be a priority declaration to empower people to gain their legitimate rights through Human Rights Movement. By liberating the Dalits from the clutches of poverty and social discrimination, we are actually contributing to a new social order based on human dignity, which will in turn create better prospects for National Integration and progress to our country.

Development and Human Rights Realities

Development must always serve the needs of the people, and in the first place those who have less. Several decades ago, reflecting broad disillusionment with growth centered measures of development, there was much talk of a basic needs-oriented approach to development, and some interesting theoretical work was produced on this topic. The concept of basic needs, however, was criticized by scholars from poorer countries, who suggested that it was being used to lock the Third world into persistent poverty, while allowing richer countries to continue on a growth oriented track.[19] Human development, which is elevated by the accomplishment of the human needs, should not be confused with economic growth.[20] Because, there can be growth without development and, there can also be development without growth. For instance, the

United States has a high rate of human development but also a high rate of domestic violence and marital abuse. Every 18 minutes a woman is battered in the US; that means between 3-4 million battered women each year.[21] Also, there were more than 150, 000 reported rapes in 1993 alone.[22] This forces us to rethink the definition of development to include the concept of collective good.

The General Assembly of the United Nations proclaimed the Universal Declaration of Human Rights as a common standard of achievement for all peoples and all nations, to the end that every individual and every organ of society, keeping this Declaration constantly in mind, shall strive by teaching and education to promote respect for these rights and freedoms.[23]

The Expanded Bill of Rights for the 21st Century, approved at the 21st Century Convention in 1992, and organized by the National Organization of Women (NOW) and other groups, clearly articulates the emerging importance of collective human rights. Asserted rights include:[24]

- The right to freedom from sex discrimination.
- The right to freedom from racial and ethnic discrimination.
- The right of all women to freedom from government interference in abortion, birth control, and prenatal and pregnancy services.
- The right to freedom from discrimination on the basis of sexual orientation.
- The right to freedom from discrimination based on religion, age, size, economic status, health condition, parenthood, marital status, or a person's disability.
- The right to a decent standard of living, including adequate food, housing, health care, education and jobs.
- The right to clean air, clean water, safe waste disposal and environmental protection.
- The right to be free from violence, including the threat of war between nations and the threat of violence at home, especially by men against women, by the rich against the poor, by adults against children, by majorities against minorities, by straights against lesbians and gays, and among races and ethnic groups.
- The right of working people to join together in unions, to bargain collectively and use economic sanctions, such as strikes and boycotts.
- The right of all to participate in and have representation in our government.

The provisions listed above are an effort to move beyond the individualist liberal approach to rights, and grapple with group issues of ethnicity, gender, sexual orientation, and subsistence. Writing on this matter, William Felice in his book *Taking Suffering Seriously* says, "This approach thus addresses a major weakness of the human rights dialogue, which too often takes place solely within the realm of elite behavior and, subsequently, nation-state preferences. The assertion of collective human rights, independent of elite and nation states, begins to examine the societal relations within the structures of modern society causing human suffering. These relations and processes result in the denial of many rights to probably the majority of individuals on the planet. There is a moral imperative that we pursue this promising direction and not limit our framework of analysis to that of a privileged worldview."[25]

"As we enter the twenty-first century, it is clear now that such a vision must include rights of gender, sexuality, ethnicity, and race within a dialectical framework of class analysis, to create a society based upon ideals of freedom, justice, and equality."

Human Development Report 2000 Proclaims

Any society committed to improving the lives of its people must also be committed to full and equal rights for all.

- The mark of all civilizations is the respect they accord to human dignity and freedom.
- In short, human development is essential for realizing human rights, and human rights are essential for full human development.
- Polarized by the cold war, the rhetoric of human rights was reduced to a weapon in the propaganda for geopolitical interests.
- A decent standard of living, adequate nutrition, health care, education, decent work and protection against calamities are not just development goals–they are also human rights.

Three priorities and development policies

- Ensuring civil and political rights–freedom of speech, association and participation–to empower poor people to claim their causal links among the many human rights, they can be mutually reinforcing and can empower poor people to fight poverty. Guaranteeing civil and political rights is not only an end in itself it is a good means to poverty eradication. Ensuring freedom for NGOs, the media and workers organizations can do much to give poor people the political space to participate in decision–making on policies that affect their lives.

Major development of the 1990s was the flourishing of NGOs and their global networks rising in number from 23, 600 in 1991 to 44, 000 in 1999. From Guyana to Zambia, from India to Russia, people are organizing civil society groups and NGOs, getting experience defending people's rights against evictions, holding government accountable for building schools, for community development and for human rights education and engaging in countless other struggles.

For the state, meeting its human rights obligations to implement policies and policy making processes that do the most to secure economic, social and cultural rights for the most deprived and to ensure their participation in decision-making. Rights to housing, health care and the like do not mean a claim to free services or a state handout.

Instead, they are claims to social arrangements and policies that promote access to these rights through both the market (housing) and the state (free primary education).

Investing economic resources in promoting human rights. Human rights measures range from the virtually cost-free to those demanding substantial resources for public budgets to provide schools, teachers and judges, for corporations to put in place working conditions that respect core labour standards. There is no automatic link between resources and rights. High incomes do not guarantee that rich countries are free of serious human rights violations any more than low incomes prevent poor countries from making impressive progress for human rights.

Worldwide, public spending on economic and social rights is inadequate and badly distributed. Poor countries need faster growth to generate the resources of finance the eradication of poverty and the realization of human rights. But economic growth alone is not enough. It needs to be accompanied by policy reforms that channel funds into poverty eradication and human development and into building institutions, shaping norms and reforming laws to promote human rights.

The neglect of economic and social rights can undermine civil and political liberties, just as the neglect of civil and political rights can undermine economic and social rights in times of calamities and threats.

Human Rights–in an integrated world–require global justice. The state-centered model of accountability must be extended to the obligations of non-state actors and to the state's obligations beyond national borders.

The Right to Development

The UN General Assembly has passed resolution in 1986 on the Right to Development, however, it took nearly a decade for the UN to emphasize and give priority to this idea of Right to Development. It is the new UN High Commissioner for Human Rights. Mrs. Mary Robinson, who high lighted the importance of this resolution on the Right to Development and asked the member States to implement it in all seriousness.

The Right to Development, of course, includes the Right to Food, Right to Housing, Right to Employment which are the basic necessities for a human being to live with human dignity. When we have nearly one-third of the population living in poverty, realization of the human rights for nearly 300 million people becomes a big task and has been a challenge for policy-makers and development-planners.

The right to progress, to come up in life, to get rid of poverty are aspirations of a human person and are inalienable human rights of that person. We need freedom from hunger and thirst. We want to live free from discrimination and injustice whatsoever, realizing our full human right. Though in India we have the ideals and constitutional provisions, they are not implemented and, therefore, we are asking what can the United Nations really do when it comes to a specific question of untouchability and development benefits reaching the lower strata of society.

We see in the newspapers big advertisements given by the Government: how they provide drinking water and housing for the rural poor. But as NGOs working in rural poor areas, we have found that often these developments exist only on paper, for publicity, but the benefits do not reach the rural poor. This has to be investigated properly. The National Human Rights Commission (NHRC) should bring under its purview implementing the UN resolution on the Right to Development in our country and check on the Govt. Ministries, which are spending large amounts of money. These Government Departments and Ministries need to produce statements of accountability on how the funds are actually utilized. We also know that in many Ministries funds allotted to the uplift of the oppressed people were unutilized. Ms.Veena Nayyar, Member, National Commission for SCs and STs in Delhi (2001) has estimated that several crores of rupees in different Govt. Departments and Ministries have not been utilized to uplift the downtrodden. In 1988, the late Prime Minister Rajiv Gandhi said that out of ten rupees spent on development and poverty eradication not even three rupees finds its way to the actual beneficiaries.[27] It is my plea that the NHRC should take up the responsibility of overseeing the implementation of the right to development to ensure efficient governance and an effective implementation of poverty eradication programmes. Thus, the NHRC can prevent dehumanizing conditions of the people and contain poverty.

The UNDP's Report 1999 Human Development Report (Item 7, Page 12) stresses the need to "build a more coherent and more democratic architecture for global governance in the 21st century". "Just as the nineteenth–century mechanisms of national government were inadequate for the challenges of the post-war era, so today's institutions of international governance are inadequate for the challenges of the 21st century. Many of the basic elements of national governance will be needed in a more robust structure of global governance. An essential aspect of global governance, as of national governance, is responsibility to people-to equity, to justice, to enlarging the choices of all." A policy document of UNDP speaks of integrating Human Rights with sustainable human development for which the paradigm of Human Rights is crucial. Poverty Eradication is not only a development goal–it is a central challenge for human rights in the 21st century.

Human Rights and Development

It is encouraging for NGO's, to see that our labour in the last one decade is reflected in documents of UNESCO, UNDP, etc. UNDP has now acknowledged the importance of "integrating human rights with sustainable development". the UNDP's Annual Report for the year 2004 has the theme: "Cultural Liberty in Today's Diverse World" Respecting Cultural pluralism and multi-cultural education have become important components of democracy, development, and justice necessary for the survival of humanity. Here are a few highlights of UNDP's latest policy:

In order to achieve the Millennium Development Goals set by world leaders in the Millennium Declaration of September 2000, human rights need to be integrated with sustainable human development.

Mainstreaming or integrating human rights into development activities is essential if it is to contribute to the fulfillment of the inherent dignity and worth of the human person. UNDP has played a leading role in applying a rights-based approach to development, in close cooperation with other development actors within and beyond the UN system. UNDP's human rights activities are aimed at achieving the following three objectives:

- Strengthening the UN-led international human rights system;
- Strengthening regional and national human rights capacities as part of the enabling environment for sustainable human development;
- Bringing in mainstream human rights in all of the organization's practise areas: democratic governance, poverty-reduction, energy and environment, crisis-prevention and recovery, HIV/AIDS, and IT for Development.

Key features of UNDP's work in the area of human rights include:

- Support to the development of national human rights action plans;
- Application of the rights-based approach to programming;
- Assistance for human rights initiatives involving civic education, awareness-raising campaigns, strengthening or creation of ombudsman offices and extension of human rights institutions to the sub-national level.

A number of global documents, programmes and resources provide a common conceptual and operational framework for human rights initiatives throughout UNDP. They include: the 1998 policy document on integrating human rights with sustainable human development, the UNDP/OHCHR memorandum of understanding of 1998, the Administrator's September 2000 note on implementing UNDP policy on human rights in the new millennium, the training manual on human rights and sustainable human development, the global programme on human rights strengthening (HURIST) and the democratic governance thematic trust fund.

Education: A Tool for the Elimination of Human Rights Violations

The United Nations prior to the fiftieth anniversary of the Universal Declaration of Human Rights started devoting much of its energy to promoting education to prevent human rights abuses. The need for human rights education has been emphasized in the Universal Declaration of Human Rights and other international documents and treaties. Provisions from these instruments state that human rights education consists of efforts to build a universal culture of human rights through the imparting of knowledge and skills and the moulding of attitudes. Such education should be directed towards:

- Strengthening respect for human rights and fundamental freedoms;
- Fully developing the human personality and its sense of dignity;
- Promoting understanding, tolerance, gender equality and friendship among all nations, indigenous peoples and racial, national, ethnic, religious and linguistic groups;
- Enabling everyone to participate effectively in a free society;
- Furthering United Nations' activities for maintaining peace.

Education Objectives come into Focus

A growing consensus holds that human rights education can both help reduce human rights violations and contribute to building of free, just and peaceful societies. Human rights, as inscribed in the Universal Declaration, form the common language of humanity.

The objects of the United Nations in its human rights educational efforts are to teach the "common language of humanity" to people everywhere. The Organization strives to make humankind fluent in the vocabulary of human rights, and to enable people everywhere – student and farmer, police officer and soldier, cabinet minister and teacher – to apply that vocabulary and meaning to their daily conduct. Through education, the United Nations proposes to build a universal culture of human rights. To quote Mr. Kofi Annan, UN Secretary-General:

"We began the United Nations Decade for Human Rights Education. The idea was to encourage everyone–Governments, international organization, public and private groups professional associates, school and colleges, and ordinary people–to work together in making human rights better known and understood."

"Today, we still have a long way to go. Only a few countries have developed effective national strategies for human rights education. There is a big gap between the promises made under the Decade and the resources actually committed. But non-governmental organizations are doing a lot. Clearly governments need to work more closely with them, and learn from them."

Why is Human Rights Education so important? Because, as it says in the Constitution of UNESCO, "since wars begin in the minds of men', it is in the minds of men that the defences of peace must be constructed. The more people know their own rights, and the more they respect those of others, the better the chance that they will live together in peace. Only when people are educated about human rights can we hope to prevent human rights violations, and thus prevent conflict as well".[28]

Through the years, United Nations efforts to promote and encourage respect for human rights and fundamental freedoms, without regard to race, sex, language or religion, have ranged from standard setting to monitoring, from facilitating international dialogue and cooperation to providing technical assistance, from commissioning technical studies to deploying large-scale peacekeeping missions. The universal language of human rights is the basis of universal standards, international mechanisms, and an ethical and legal foundation of rights and responsibilities of nations and peoples.

There are three dimensions to the promotion of human rights through education:

- Knowledge–providing information about human rights and the mechanisms that exist to protect those rights;
- Values, beliefs and attitudes–promoting a human rights culture through the development of these processes, and

- Action–encouraging people to defend human rights and prevent human rights abuses.

United Nations Secretary-General Kofi Annan says, "Without education, we cannot see beyond ourselves and our narrow surroundings to the reality of global inter-dependence. Without education, we cannot realize how peoples of other races and religious share the same dreams, the same hopes. Without education, we cannot recognize the universality of human aims and aspirations." [29]

Imputs and Action: What emerged from Vienna

The 1993 World conference on Human Rights produced the Vienna Declaration and Programme of Action. It reaffirmed that States were duty-bound to ensure that education was aimed at strengthening respect for human rights and fundamental freedoms. The Declaration and Programme of Action declared that human rights education, training and public information were essential tools to promote mutual understanding, tolerance, friendly relations and peace among nations and all racial or religious groups.

The Conference called on States to strive to eradicate illiteracy and to direct education towards the full development of the human personality and the strengthening of respect for human rights and fundamental freedoms. It called on States and institutions to include human rights, humanitarian law, democracy and the rule of law as subjects in the curricula of all centres of learning, in both formal and informal settings.

UN Decade for Human Rights Education

Based on a broad partnership between Governments, inter-governmental organizations, professional associations and individuals, the Plan has five objectives:

- To assess needs and formulate strategies for the furtherance of human rights education;
- To build and strengthen programmes and capacities for human rights education at international, regional, national and local levels;
- To coordinate the development of effective human rights education materials;
- To strengthen the role and capacity of mass media in the furtherance of human rights education; and
- To disseminate globally the Universal Declaration of Human Rights.

Human Rights education incorporates much more than learning about human rights declarations The single most pressing issue is the creation of an awareness of the worth and dignity of each person. Ultimately, the responsibility for teaching about human rights rests with everyone. It starts with the way we treat one another.

Transformation on a personal level, growth of self, and spirituality become essential criteria for global world order. In the new world order, everyone has to contribute: we should see conflicts really end. NGO's can play a greater role in bringing the social change for the 21st century. For many NGO's it will not be an easy task. Small action groups have a tendency to get stuck with local problems without the advantages of the vision for the people and humanity. Some social activists ignore spiritual dimensions of human nature. It is therefore important to examine the relevance of stereotype concepts to the emerging new issues.

Calling the youth to end racism, in a remarkable speech in Durban Conference on Racism, Dr. Kofi Annan the UN-Secretary General, pleaded for an attitudinal change:

"Our greatest hope of change lies in the rise of a new generation, free from the fears and prejudices of the old. So, the biggest responsibility falls on parents and teachers, and on those who write textbooks, or plan school curricula. They must see to it that children are taught to take pride and pleasure in diversity, and not to recoil whenever they see someone whose habits or appearance are different from their own. And you young people yourselves must take the lead in forming the attitudes of your peers. Yes, my friends, it is people's attitudes, and the way we treat each other, that needs to change, in every country, and whether that happens depends above all on you."[30]

India's population has reached 102.8 crores with 53.2 crore males and 49.6 crore females at an annual growth rate of 1.94. On the eve of Population Day, the Registrar-General of India, J.K. Banthia, declared that India's population was all set to exceed China's by 2035 when it would touch 146 crores. India turned 100 crores in May 2000. The 2001 census shows Uttar Pradesh to be the most populous State with a population of 166 million, followed by Maharashtra (97 million), Bihar (83 million) and West Bengal (80 million). Lakshadweep has the lowest population of 61, 000.

The Scheduled Caste population has touched 16.6 crores (16.2 per cent) and the Scheduled Tribes 8.4 crores (8.2 per cent). The child sex ratio (0-6) slipped from 945 females per 1000 males in 1991 to 927 in 2001. The average literacy rate for above seven population stood at 64.8 against 52.2 in 1991. The census said 75.2 per cent of the male population against 53.6 per cent of females are literate according to *The Hindu* dated 11th July 2004 Chennai Edition.

India continues to languish in the Human Development Index (HDI) rankings at 127 out of 177 countries, unchanged from last year, according to the Human Development Report 2004, though India's performance in terms of preserving the cultural freedom of its diverse population is impressive even when compared with long-standing and wealthier democracies. The report which has "Cultural Liberty in Today's Diverse World" as its theme, highlights India as a successful example of a diverse and highly stratified country. However, a warning about the need to reinvigorate India's commitment to practises of pluralism and conflict resolution in the future, given the recent record. The record being referred to include the Gujarat incidents of 2002 and the "rise of groups that seek to impose a singular Hindu identity on the country". The HDR points out in this context that 36.2% of all casualties in India are communal clashes since 1954 have occurred between 1990 and 2002.

The HDR also takes specific note of the debate on building a uniform civil code in India. While recognizing the desirability of such a development, the report warns that "implementing equality is not the same as implementing uniformity" and advocates an internal reform of all customary laws rather than imposing identical laws across communities.

The report emphasizes the need for empowerment of minorities and says that human development is as much about politics as it is about economics. It traces a history of violence and suppression of cultures and identities the world over including a mention of the sectarian violence in Gujarat. It talks about how we need to recognize and accommodate diverse ethnicities, religions, languages and values – themes that are an inescapable feature of the landscape of politics in the world today. (Times News Network Thursday, July 15, 2004)

The final figures and details of the 2001 Census are out. Tamil Nadu's population as of March 1, 2001, was 6, 24, 05, 679. Of them, 3, 14, 00, 909 were men and 3, 10, 04, 770 women. The sex ratio was 987. The ratio was higher in rural areas at 992, whereas in urban locations it was 982. Children aged below six numbered 72, 35, 160 and the sex ratio in this category was 942. The total literacy rate stood at 73.45 per cent, while the work participation rate, an indicator of the number of workers, was 44.67 per cent of the population. (*The Hindu*, dated 11th July 2004 Chennai Edition).

The State Government machinery in Tamil Nadu professes to protect the constitutional guarantees of the Dalit people in Tamil Nadu. Yet the caste violence and riots are on the increase in Tamil Nadu, which depicts the plight of Dalits in South India. The increasing collusion of the caste politicians with bureaucrats, police personnel and judiciary contributes to violation of human rights of Dalits. Their right to protest against injustices is met with police firing, shooting to death, and arresting innocent people who are languishing in prison. A commonly prevailing Police prosecution pattern during a "communal class" as it is reported where atrocities on Dalits are committed is to ignore the *de facto* First Information Reports (FIRs) of Dalit persons, the real victims, in the villages but only record the FIRs of Caste Hindu leaders and take Dalits to Magistrate Courts for judicial custody as the presence of the falsely charge-sheeted Dalits contribute to violent situation in a local area. In this judicial process, the Magistrate usually ignores the *de facto* situation and take cognizance of the *de jure* papers filed by the Police and orders the Dalits to live 50 kilometers away from their own village–which meant all able-bodied, bread-winning males, earning members of the families are taken away from their homes leaving their wives and children exposing them to more dangers and vulnerability of terror and violence. In these cases, it is left to NGO's, Dalit leaders, etc to collect money and feed both the male members ordered to live 50 miles away from their homes, and to feed their families!

Empowering Dalit Youth-A Pioneering Achievement

From arm-chair philosophy, ideology, and theology of liberation, which is freely given in lectures, the need for practical application of work and pragmatic implementation of plan of action for uplift of Dalit people is urgently required. To fill this need, I established in 1985 the Dalit Liberation Education Trust to uplift our Dalit people through a programme of liberation education. The object is to create a core team of people in rural areas who can work effectively to bring about social change through human rights education. The thrust then was to work with Dalit youth by organising youth leadership camps. Coming from the discriminated and disadvantaged social background, only a very small number of youth finish school and make it to college. A lot depends on these youth as the whole village looks up to these youngsters. But they face a different type of problem. Having been taught in local languages like Tamil in rural areas, they are unable to socially mix with the general stream of students because of lingering caste prejudices inherited in their minds. This leads to frustration and they easily fall prey to exploiters of all kinds who recruit them to achieve their narrow ends, usually engaging them in anti-social and criminal activities. The human potential of these youth is not fully realised. Dalit youth seeking employment is another story of sorrow and disappointment.

The real problem of the Dalits is not just economic, but social. The attitudes of many Dalit people have remained the same for generations. They still believe in what has been instilled in them for centuries; that their present shameful existence is because of their *Karma*, sins of their previous birth and that their oppressors have been blessed to enjoy life.

They resign themselves to a defeatist situation and accept injustice without complaint. Centuries of this suffering based on religious and social indoctrination has stunted the minds of the Dalit people, resulting in a lack of self-respect and human dignity. Lacking in spiritual and psychological growth their problems of their inner-self remains tormented.

Today social discrimination has been mostly replaced by social prejudice in urban areas. Insecurity abounds both individually and socially among Dalit population. This insecurity continues to breed even greater psychological problems like fear, inferiority feelings, guilt, shame, etc. A number of communal divisions based on occupations for generations exist among the Dalits, leading to disunity. They are unable to perform collectively and are politically exploited. Their powerlessness and lack of control over their destiny makes them react to life's encounters with resignation and suppressed anger. They spend their meager wages on alcohol and ignore their families. The existence of liquor shops near Dalit communities perpetuates poverty. The family ends up fending for itself. Women and children are most affected by this dehumanizing situation. Women are forced to go out to work and children drop out of school because they too must work. Illiteracy, ignorance and poverty have condemned them to a culture of silence, apathy and self-resignation. Searching for a new identity, the Scheduled Caste people resort to conversions to other religions. But they face prejudice and discrimination even in other religions, and their situation is not significantly altered.

As an initial step to remedy the above situation, we selected the unemployed Dalit Youth to infuse in them a feeling of self-awareness and a belief in themselves so that they might realize their potential. Our Trust provides counselling to enable youth to tackle the problems of life and society, to seek advice and ideas for local action and to share local and personal problems. The goal is to instill confidence in the Dalit young men and women and to change the real circumstances of their lives. The psychological wounds inflicted on Dalits by fear goes deep into their souls and makes them subservient to others. This situation denies the dignity of self. Dalit people are denied of Human Rights. The healing of the wounded psyche is done through an empowering educational programme in the youth camps of discovering their true humanity and dignity. In the process of expressing love and respect for each human being, an opportunity is provided to create a new social order. It is important that one is liberated from his own fears, doubts, victim acts and feelings to be authentic to lay the foundation for a new society which can be formed with new thinking and new self one discovers. In the youth camps I organized, a space is created for each participant to realise the possibility of creating a new society with equity and justice.

The Dalit Youth Camp fulfils the deepest needs of our youth: the repairing of their wounded psyche and the restoration of a sense of dignity, self-worth and personal initiative. The healing of the mind, the emergence of the human self, or what Dr Ambedkar calls "the reclamation of human personality," of Dalit youth is accomplished by natural, educational activities, and by providing space for human fellowship and communication.

The word *education* is derived from the Greek word *educara* which means to bring forth, to draw out the inner potential of a student. Real education should bring out the inner talents of a human being. In this sense, education should empower young people to bring out their inner human resource to the betterment of society. This is what we do in our Dalit Youth Camps. We bring out the hidden human potential of the youth participant and in the process enable them to work for a new social order based on Human Rights.

Our objects are that the youth from untouchable communities: (1) become self-reliant. (2) take self-oriented, independent initiatives. (3) take a group support. (4) form local action and service groups. (5) express their commitment for service. (6) organise co-operative societies, seeking self-employment with higher goals and alternative goals in job seeking, to succeed in employment seeking efforts, interviews, etc. The emphasis of the Dalit Youth Leadership Camp is to integrate the following activities:-

1. To impart information regarding economic realities through lectures and games;
2. Ideas of inter-personal communication are introduced to the youth and they participate in various group communication exercises;
3. A social awakening is attempted through dramatizations utilizing puppet shows, street plays and
4. Music-group singing;
5. Lectures, are not mere monologues, but influence participation from the youth through demonstration;
6. And seminar–type–participatory discussion;
7. Cultural events are organized to make the youth come out of their shells and gain inner confidence in themselves;
8. The youth are guided on how to prepare and present themselves when seeking employment. Trial interviews are conducted and each participant's performance is analyzed by a panel and helpful suggestions offered;
9. In an attempt to create awareness of how to function as effective participants in the society, the youth are divided into

several groups to take care of various camp activities. The groups also engage themselves in discussions of contemporary problems;

10. Games are arranged in which participants shed their inhibition;
11. The 'lighting a lamp' festival is symbolic of the liberation experienced by the Dalit youth. This lighting programme has the theme: You light yourself, light your neighbour and you light up the world. Each participant lights a lamp, experiences a sense of liberation and an expression of their social commitment to liberate their people through education. The atmosphere is filled with joyous celebration.

The Camp is usually held for five days. A camp participant said: "The Camp has ended, but we realize our mission starts only now". The results were beyond our expectation as a definite shift in attitudes discovering a newself has been experienced by participants–indeed a very inspiring experiences as each Camp took us to new level of quality of service and we found a freshness of life and fellowship–as they spoke of: 'I am born free-free from fears, to live and experience life'. 'I have strength and courage within me to fight injustice'; I am born anew, etc. Our object is a process of transformation, that the participants become aware of self and of society-instead of suffering from wounds of injustice and discrimination–to recover their true source of power–their real self and experiencing completeness and wholeness. Our work raised the level of consciousness through awareness education. The youth camps not only concentrated on youth fellowship, but created self-worth and brought human dignity to deprived youth. In the process of our service to the downtrodden youth we realize the experience of oneness of humanity as we live among the very oppressed young people with whom we share our life.

Methodology of the Camp

Dalit youth are informed of this camp and its benefits through spoken word and through seminars organized by the local community organizers. First, they register their names by paying Rs.10/-as an expression of their commitment to participate in the youth camp. The participants pay their own travel to and fro to the Camp site, wherever it is located. The DLET bears the expenses of food, accommodation, course fees etc., which is given as scholarship by raising funds from donor agencies. On arrival at the camp, we asked the participants to write about their life, problems, and painful experiences and expectations from the Camp. Some methods adopted are given below:-

1. The camp organizer explains how the camp works and some of the ground rules by which the camp works. Every participant is given an option either to stay and fully participate in Camp activities till the end or may opt out at the introduction stage if they have other important engagements. They are encouraged to freely communicate their need and problems with counsellors available in the Camp;
2. The following methods of communication are used: 15 to 30 minutes lecture followed by questions and answers followed by a discussion. Enabling the participants to ask questions. Questions and answer sessions are scheduled to encourage two way communication;
3. Demonstration by role models;
4. Exercises in communication on how to communicate in groups is provided;
5. Participants are encouraged to act and participate in cultural activities by copying village people character roles, play music, sing and dance, creating awareness among the communities and social problems;
6. Physical Exercises in the morning and games in the evening are provided to experience sound body which can house a sound mind;
7. A slide show on human body including how the brain works is scheduled as part of Know Yourself realization;
8. Instead of talks, experience oriented practicals are given.

Achievements of the Youth Camps: Some of the benefits commonly reported are overcoming fear, gaining confidence to face people and to communicate freely, developing social skills, and organizing abilities. Unemployed youth find it easy to fare well in job interviews. Volunteering to become Community Organizers the youth are able to stand by the victims of injustice and to fight for social justice in local areas. The youth who became motivated become agents of social change in the villages. As community organizers, they organize many community events and become responsible for the blossoming of the people's movements in their areas. Some of them played an active role in forming Dalit Youth for Human Rights from 1987 to 1990 and organised processions and events like "Run for Human Rights", on World Human Rights Day. From 1990 this youth movement in turn contributed to the formation of the Human Rights Education Movement of India to prevent violence through education and forming village level network.

Thus, in 19 years about 4000 young people in 70 youth camps were trained and many more thousands were reached by service and mass media. In addition to the youth camps, we encouraged Dalit youth to start voluntary service societies wherever the caste atrocities and violence against Dalit women had occurred. We facilitated their organising into a functional entity in the community to take up local issues. Their groups are doing good work within their limitations, without any financial commitment by us. Many of them learnt the skills to obtain funds from government schemes and donor agencies. For those who would like to be associated with our Trust, the parent body, we have developed a programme of networking. There are many groups working in rural districts with the leadership of youth trained in our youth camps. This experience opened up the possibility of organizing the people for their liberation. The Dalit Liberation Education Trust founded several rural education centres. Women in several centres have taken the initiative to form rural women's associations and to hold regular meetings to discuss their problems and to take organized action.

For the first time I made it possible for my Dalit people from the dehumanized conditions of life to experience, realize their human dignity, self-worth and to develop their human potential for nation building activities. In this pioneering effort by bringing the dimension of human rights to the Dalit discrimination, which is usually called local caste issues, highlighted a dignity for the human struggle of equality and social justice.

The Positive Impact of the Project

The camp participants became community organizers, facilitators, educators and formed voluntary service organizations in their villages to champion the cause of Dalits, to become leaders in their respective communities as councillors in village councils. By giving human rights education inputs it was possible to prevent violence and violation of human rights. There has been widespread appreciation from the community for the young people becoming agents for social change. Sixty women who have been trained as health ambassadors in a 15-day capsule course became effective community organizers in the villages. Some degrading traditions disappeared as a silent revolution took place, when people refused to be sexually abused stopping violation of their human dignity. A simple declaration and assertion of their human rights and human dignity through educational seminars brought self-esteem to the people that their violators stopped harassing them. The project demonstrates, it is possible to effect social change through educational process in a non-violent manner.

Since the methods of education is used and human nature is universal, it can be easily introduced in any country to overcome discrimination as all ideas of prejudices and discriminations are based on social inputs of conditioning the mind, it is possible to educate people to decondition the human mind to experience human dignity. International visitors and educators have expressed their appreciation.

Empowerment of Women

Our Community organizers enrolled Dalit women in large numbers to become members of the Human Rights Education Movement. They play an active role in movement building, organising village sangams and taking up local cases of rape, dowry, wife beating and desertion. Most of the women members have developed political awareness and have participated in the electoral politics effectively; in one block above 31 Dalit Councillors were elected in October 2001 Panchayat Elections.

Dalit women suffer triple discrimination—from (1) men and family, (2) the usual social-caste-based discrimination or social customs and (3) by religious or political systems. So, the focus of our work is increased participation of women in the community and strengthening their social awareness and income-generating economic programmes. The project has organised women to take care of practical needs of the villages. Women are recognised as important agents of social change in improving the status of Dalits in general. Decision making in the process of selection of members for availing loans and small saving schemes is completely handled by women leaders in the sangam.

The practical gender needs of women such as water, electricity, ration shop, health problems, legal education, caste-based violence, transport, and alcohol issues have been taken up by women leaders and our Trust facilitated in their empowerment programmes.

Here I would like to share the success of social transformation women achieved in a remote village in a southern district of Tamil Nadu. Due to the delicate nature of the dignity of women involved and the assurance given to them that I will not use this success story for publicity, I am not giving names and other details. In this particular village there was a tradition that any Dalit woman, either married or not, can be picked up by caste men in the night to be abused, as most of them depend on the wages they earn by working in the fields of these caste men. The women felt that they were abused because they were not treated as human beings and they did not have human rights. Organizing them by a human rights education woman co-ordinator, they held meetings and decided that they will declare themselves to be members of the Human rights Education Movement of India and made a declaration that they will not allow themselves to be abused nor will they be available for further abuse. The abusing tradition has to stop. A mere declaration of human rights and the assertion of their human right made by women in this village transformed the village and the women, who gained the right to live in human dignity. The abusing tradition has stopped. This is the kind of profound transformation which human rights education can achieve for oppressed people who have been exploited in the name of social traditions.

Human Rights Education and Movement Building

In the broadest sense Human Rights is the right of every citizen in this country to be treated with dignity-regardless of caste, community, gender-and thereby realise his or her own capabilities and capacities. Since 1990 Human Rights Education has been the focus of our Trust. Special thrust and emphasis given to the Dalit issue being viewed as a human rights issue made us promote literacy as a way of educating people about their civil and political rights, as well as social, economic and cultural rights. By promoting awareness on the safeguards that are available for the protection of these rights through the media, seminars, campaigns, education is being imparted at the grassroots level through empowerment programmes for women and youth. Education is also a tool to encourage the Dalit community to face struggles and develop skills to solve their day-to-day problems. The Dalits are being motivated and encouraged by our staff to view and demand right to free education, agricultural land, employment, fair wages without gender bias, water, food, health and housing as basic rights to a life of dignity and self respect. We have produced audiotapes and developed cultural teams to reach out to Dalit people in rural areas. Through cultural plays, a human rights message is communicated. Songs, dance, drama, posters and publications are useful tools to disseminate information. The Movement grew with 4640 active members in 127 villages from the rural areas of seven districts in 1999. The essential object of the movement is to realise human rights and dignity through solidarity. It is also a forum to raise the voice of Dalits and to fight against human rights violations. At the village level this is being linked to social, economic and cultural rights of Dalits. The right to education is being achieved through organising night schools, adult education and social awareness programmes. The right to fair wages without gender discrimination and also to the right to agricultural land is being fought through mass protests and rallies. The road to Dalit Liberation through Human Rights Education has not been an easy one, as there are thorny bushes along the way. The words of Dr. B. R. Ambedkar, has been a source of inspiration to us: "Noble is your aim and sublime and glorious is your mission."

Blessed are those who are awakened to their duty to those among whom they are born. Glory to those who devote their time, talents and their all to the amelioration of slavery. Glory to those who would keep their struggle for the liberation of the enslaved in spite of heavy odds, carping humiliations, storms and dangers till the downtrodden secure their Human Rights". [33]

Criticism of Human Rights Movement

Several years ago a group of Sudanese Students met me and invited me to a meeting to discuss their Human Rights Problem. I was happy to attend the meeting. After my initial introductory remarks I was asked several questions and severely criticised by these students from Sudan, most of whom are of the Islamic faith. Some of the criticisms are now widely discussed:

1. Human Rights are a product of capitalist countries to promote globalization, multinationalism etc.
2. It is a Western idea not applicable to the Africans, Asians, particularly Hindus and Muslims. In this sense, it is implied that Human Rights Movement is a Christian concept, used largely for conversions as was stated by BJP Government sponsored NGO's in Durban.
3. When you speak of universalism, it ignores cultural diversity and neglects the rights of pluralistic societies and their ethos. For instance, Nagas, Mizos and Sikhs who assert their political and cultural rights want ethnic pluralism and cultural diversity of their indigenous groups. Universalism contradicts or negates the rights of ethnic minorities, leading to tensions and conflicts. As a result, the NGOs are not liked by militants.

Some of you may remember that a few years ago, an NGO Activist, Sanjay Ghose, was kidnapped and eventually killed by ULFA terrorists in upper Assam. It is in this kind of predicament that we have to examine in promoting of Human Rights. I am convinced that these criticisms are motivated for several local reasons. Let me answer these criticisms:

Just because Human Rights Declaration was proclaimed in the United States where the UN Head Quarters is situated, it doesn't become an American Capitalist product. The Universal Declaration of Human Rights was the product of great humanists and intellectuals, who protected the dignity of human beings. Discoveries in Medical Science, innovations, transplants surgeries, are hailed as indicators of human progress. Science is a science where ever it is proved with experiments and reason. The medicine taught in the United States works very well in India. For example, the Prime Minister of India had knee surgery at Mumbai performed by a doctor from America. There is always a commonality to certain things which benefit humanity. The dignity of human beings is a common good, whose universalism is applicable to all people. In this, there should be no discrimination on any grounds.

The Universality Issue has been well stated by Yale University Professor Charles Norchi, Executive Director of the International League Human Rights during World Conference on Human Rights at Vienna, "The world community must understand which such expressions are commensurate with those Human Rights standards which are the obligations of states under customary and codified international law. And it must be underscored that the Universal Declaration has now been crystallized as customary international law."

"Indeed, the question is not "are Human Rights relative?" but "within the context of the 'universal' standards of the world community, how is human dignity demanded across cultures" and "How can those demands be given effect?" It is the values of the distinct cultures of our planet that contribute to the strengthening of the universality of the Human Rights system. For, although practises may vary across cultures, all human beings demand, fundamentally, the same values. This is why we must never accept the 'cultural relativism' justification by a state for the denial of human dignity to its people."

Truth, Goodness and Beauty are Universal ideals and belongs both to the World and to Human Nature. The Moral Law is binding on all people in all countries on the basis of which Judicial System, Governmental and Social Developments have taken place. The German philosopher Immanuel Kant spoke of Ethics to be Universal, "The moral imperative is unconditional; that is, its imperative force is not tempered by the conditional. Kant advocated that reason dictates a categorical imperative for moral action. He gives at least three formulations of the Categorical Imperative.

1. "Act only according to that maxim by which you can at the same time will that it should become a universal law."
2. "Act as though the maxim of your action were by your will to become a universal law of nature."
3. "Act so that you treat humanity, whether in your own person or in that of another, always as an end and never as a means only."

If we remove all subjectivity and particularity from motivation we are only left with will to universality. The question "what rule determines what I ought to do in this situation?" – becomes "what rule ought to universally guide action?" What we must do in any situation of moral

(*Metaphysics*, Internet Encyclopedia of Philosophy Immanuel Kant–Author Dr. Matt McCormick 'California State University, Sacramento.)

choice is act according to a maxim that we would will everyone to act according to.

The Universal Nature of Moral Law has been prevalent among the Asian Cultures. 'Tao' is the Chinese concept of the path and the way, a law conceived by the Chinese people, who respect the divine principle in the Universe, which also exists in Human Beings. Eastern Religion and philosophies had an intuition of modern physics as explained by Prof. Fritjof Capra in his book Tao of Physics. The Chinese idea of "Wu lei" integrates Natural Law and Moral Law. "Wu Li" ("The Way") governs the physical world about which the Esalen Institute (USA) has done research. * The Dancing Wu Li Masters: An Overview of the New Physics by Gary Zukav, Bantam Books.

Buddhism speaks of the moral universe of "Dhamma". The Law of righteousness has been the guiding principle for human conduct. The "Hindus" spoke of "Dharma", Moral Law Force that is prevailing in the Universe. According to Bansi Pandit, Author of Hindu Mind & Hindu Dharma, "The original name of Hindu Dharma is Sanãtana Dharma, or "universal religion." A religion is universal if its appeal is not restricted to any particular segment of humanity, religious group, nation, race, class, country or age. All religions have some universal aspects."

"A true spiritual experience is always rooted in the universal vision of mankind.

The mystics of all religions have invariably held that beyond the apparent diversity of the physical phenomena, there is a perfect unity."

"Thousands of years ago, Hindu sages declared that *dharma* (righteousness), *ahimsã* (non-violence), *dayã* (compassion), *abhaya* (fearlessness) and recognition of the unity of existence are the supreme virtues for mankind. Today these ideals form the fundamental charter of the United Nations organization.

In personal life *dharma* is expressed as virtues and duties. In the political life *dharma* is expressed as the just and equitable laws which restrain evil and promote virtuous life. In the Hindu polity, politicians are required to inspire virtue and loyalty to the laws of the state by their own examples. In Hindu legal literature the word *dharma* conveys the same meaning as the words *ethical, reasonable,* and *equitable* in Western legal literature."

Dharma (morality or righteousness) is the cornerstone of a just and equitable state. *Dharma* preserves the individuals and the society. The oft-quoted axiom is: "Hunger, sleep, fear, and sex are common to all

---

* Chapter 12: *Why is Hindu Dharma a Universal Religion?* BASIN PANDIT Hindu Dharma, A New Comprehensive Guide to Hindu Way of Life, ISBN: 0-9634798-3-0, soft cover, 120 pp.

animals, human and sub-human. It is the additional attribute of *dharma* that differentiates man from the beast." Thus, the political philosophy (*danda-nîti*) of the state must be grounded in *dharma*.

The Native Dravidian poet-sage "Thiruvalluvar" and "Thirumoolar" propounded "Aram" or "Virtue" the Moral Law as a governing force. Hence Human Rights which respect Human dignity and Human Rights only be Universal and cannot be related to any particular culture. Human Rights is not a Christian concept, because in every religion the respect for all human beings is preached. In every religion there are streams of spirituality, which are liberal, open, universal. In every religion there is a liberative stream, which embraces people all over the world, of all cultures and religions. In every religion there is an oppressive force, an oppressive streak, which simply drags people into a web of traditions and superstitions that make people to lose humanity, become dehumanized and lost! There are two tracks in every religion, one that leads toward human rights, justice and peace and the other which leads to customs, rituals and ideas, which are oppressive. The basis for Human Rights is inter-religious, multi-cultural. It depends on who interprets and for what advantage it is being interpreted. The Hindu Bhakti movements embraced all people, overcoming the barriers of the day, as forerunners of Human Rights. Dr R. M. Pal writing on the Indian Heritage of Human Rights states, "One of the most significant contributions of Buddhism was the introduction and spread of secular education—education for all. Organised universities came to be established under the direct influence of Buddhism."[34] Dr. Pal further argues, "There were other aspects–non-vedic-like the *Nath, Yoga Siddharcara* who too, like the Buddhists, found the key to all religious mysteries in the human body itself. The position of the *nath-panthi siddhas* and *jogis* in Hindu society needs to be understood. Most of the *nath-panthi siddhas* and *jogies* belonged to the low castes, opposed caste-based inequalities, denounced the religion of works favoured by the *Brahmins*, and did not favour image worship".[35] Women played an important part in these sects, particularly in the Tantra".

"Bhakti, the path of devotion, implies belief in the Supreme Person, not a Supreme Abstraction. It is, therefore, a very straight forward and unsophisticated belief. This movement has non-Aryan roots; in fact, according to some scholars, it originated in the Dravidian country. It was opposed by the *Brahmins* for a long time because of its utter disregard for caste divisions, religious rituals and ceremonies, in which people of different social and economic categories, women and children are treated equally."[36]

While Universal Declaration protects the rights of individuals and the rights of indigenous people and ethnic minorities, we have to examine whether our loyalty to our culture, language, tribe, etc. makes us liberated, open to have compassion for others and respect the rights of other groups, that is loving our neighbour as ourselves. Often cultural fundamentalist mentality is to protect our little groups and nothing to do with others who differ from us in ideas, faith, church, colour, race, etc. Tribal cultural heritage and ethnic diversity can be an enriching factor rather than a barrier for our outreach. If one's culture, or faith, or religion, or language helps one to be free from oppressive ideas, it will be a great way for transformation in the world. If a religion, belief, occupation helps a person to communicate freely, then that tradition and culture is worth having. Usually what happens to people is to hold on to oppressive ideas and traditions for the sake of survival, and use these outmoded ideas for power and political purpose and popularity. Out of fear people hold on to these victimizing ideas. Fascism, Nazism, and Stalinism are monuments to social oppression of the individual in the name of security and in the process introduced dehumanization. For example, in India, the right wing fundamentalists of Hindu religion used the word *Hindutva* for political gain of achieving Hindu unity and Hindu religious rule, or to uphold the Hindu Dharma. Hindu Dharma, when universally applicable to all people and to the universe becomes Sanathana Dharma which embraces all humanity, aptly described as *Vasudeva Kudumbam*. The same word Dharma can be used in a restricted sense to mean *Varna*shrma Dharma which advocated the four fold caste structure, which has become discriminatory and oppressive in actual practise socially enslaving Dalits for centuries. This led our late great leader Babasaheb Dr. B. R. Ambedkar to lead a revolt against Hinduism and to embrace Buddhism with half a million people at Nagpur in 1956.

Ancient indigenous people all over the world had a view of life and the world. In India, the ancient *Sidhars* in Tamil Nadu require mention here. Many modern psychological and self-development programmes are similar to the teachings of the ancient sages of Tamil Nadu–the Siddhars mastered life and nature. Their mysticism of Nature leading to self-realisation instead of institutionalisation of religion is quite distinctive. They come from the marginalised communities in Tamil Nadu. They were able to see humanity as one whole in a positive perspective and condemned discrimination perpetuated by the Brahminical religion on the basis of caste, race, sex, etc. They spoke of one God. They propagated the slogan: One race, One God – "Onre Kulam, Oruvane Thevan". The spirituality of the marginalised people must be recognised as distinct from the dominant Hindu Religious beliefs and

Theology. The Siddhars used herbs and metals for medicine and read the pulse of a person. Their view of world was based on natural elements which created the world and people. They dealt with consciousness of human beings, which encompasses all tribes, races, cultures and is pretty universal. They respected the spirit of human beings and sanctified human dignity and empowered people. They were known as prophets of counter-culture as they condemned oppressive systems, superstition and encouraged self-analysis, rational thinking and mastery of self, mastery of human nature, to attain super natural powers.

Educational material should be non-religious and available and relevant to all, irrespective of religion, race, caste, class, culture, ethnicity and gender. We should realize that the study of the human body made medical science applicable to all people, whether Africans or Americans or Asians. Human consciousness is universal, as are values of compassion, service, health care, nursing, etc. Human values like dignity of human life should be acceptable to all nationalities all over the world.

The next problem is that the Western countries emphasise the worth of an individual, and individual rights and do not speak of community and societal rights. Western thought is associated with Reason, Rationality, the Cartesian philosophy which stresses the importance of man. The antithesis to individual rights is the collective rights of Marx. The rise of reason and the rights of man made 19th century scholars comment that God is dead. The climax of industry and machines, the ascendancy of science and technology made people in the 20th century to comment that Man is dead, whereas in the 21st Century it is possible for both the Divine and the human to become alive in the frame work of Human Rights.

So far, no single idea has provided the solution to the many problems which we in India have countered in the last fifty years. The concepts of economic development has not tackled the problems related to poverty, disease and ignorance. Man-made disasters are continuously rattling the globe. Democracy has been weakened by political groups capturing power to loot the wealth of the state and plunder it for personal benefits. Lamenting on the governing situation Professor Meghnad Desai says, "With social and economic interest running contrary to politics, there was a clash of ideas", "Literacy figuring low on the priority list not for lack of resources but because it threatened certain social powers", "This when making people literate is much cheaper than building a nuclear bomb." "Calling for a certain degree of respect for fellow–citizens, India's problems–which had been rendered more grave by caste and political influences over the years–could be solved through politics. What is needed today is 'active citizenship' in which people voluntarily came forward to stem the rot which had set into the democratic character of the nation."

Advocating the need for a more active role by NGOs Prof. Desai said, people were needed to provide information to ordinary citizens on "where to shop for better politics."[43]

The civil society in India is fragmented and views of the NGOs are not seriously taken by Government. It is observed that some NGOs work with cross-purposes. Some are depending on government grants which imposes certain conditions on them for their survival, restricting their free voice. Some NGOs depend on foreign donors who are dictated by their major funding institutions like Religion, Church, Government, or Western ideologies which are also restricting the freedom of the NGOs, and to this extent their strength and courage to be independent is affected. The fragmentation of Dalit civil society is still worse plagued by divisions created by discrimination based on occupational sub-castes by descent.

While we debate and worry over these worldly matters, during a recent visit to a village I see agricultural landless labourers in rural south India working in the fields, living in a different world of survival. A female farm worker with three children working on sporadic daily wage of Rs. 20 a day seems to be totally ignorant of what goes on in the rest of the world, as she ekes out her living in her world of being ignorant, poor, socially and economically deprived. Yet her life shines with human dignity which transcends her difficulties and problems of survival. Here I see an element or a basis of transformation. The world has some hope of new life, as people toil to make life worth living. There is beauty and rhythm of human life in work, making things work, and making the world work for everyone. The simple people who earn their living in daily wages, working in the field, close to nature, enjoy their work and in that process make life possible despite the difficulties they encounter. This natural experience of rural people is missed among urban educated elitists and socialites. Many life styles of urban Indians seem to be artificial and uncomfortable, often based on money or business profits, contacts and conversations are devoid of real human encounters. It is a good experience to meet rural poor people whose life moves with some dynamism that energises the world. If you see from this perspective of humanity, some great people, mystics, poets, philosophers, spiritual leaders are able to see humanity in its entirety and able to bring transformation. It is sad that often very educated scholars and religious people use their intelligence to oppress the growth of human spirit and to control human initiatives for betterment and progress instead of contributing to the liberation and the enrichment of the human spirit. A solace from these intelligent creatures, are the poets and mystics whose intuitional genius nourishes human spirit. Here is a poetic view of the Universe, "To see a World in a Grain of sand, and a Heaven in a Wild Flower, Hold Infinity in the palm of your hand, And Eternity in an hour."[37]

An American Indian Tribal Chief, Seattle, in *Writing to the US President (1855)* said: "We do not own the freshness of the air, or the sparkle of the water. You cannot buy them from us.... One thing we know, which the White Man may one day discover: Our God is the same God.... compassion is equal for the Red Man and the White. To harm the earth is to heap contempt on its Creator." [38]

All people belong to one human family. Often good Christians insist that one should be a member of church of a particular denomination and should adhere that denominational faith as a good Anglican, Baptist, Methodist, Adventist, etc. Thereby it is easy to get the idea that is confined to the four walls of the Church, and in that mindset, *one may miss the view that God is for all people.* The great religious leaders have said *love your enemies; receive the stranger to home; and be compassionate to the poor.* Similarly, if I'm a good Hindu, my first preference is to my caste and I'm least bothered about other caste people. Likewise, it is not right to kill my tribe / caste, but it is different for others because you don't consider other caste people as humans with the same human values. Actually, this kind of process is a primeval evolution characteristic of early societies, which existed on the survival of closed communities and tribes, where an alien is unacceptable. In today's world, in which humanity is capable of moving faster to a higher purpose, outmoded ideas and belief systems will reverse the process of growth to primitive and sub-human levels. In order to transform society and change attitudes, we have to move on from the ideas of 'my tribe', my caste to the humanity at large and to 'the world'. I belong to humanity. My vision is people of the world. We cannot function in isolation. We have to express our humanity and be part of the humanity. The great Sufi saint-poet of Konya, *Jalaluddin Rumi* (1207-1273) beautifully speaks of a world which transcends barriers:

"Not Christian or Jew or Muslim,
not Hindu, Buddhist, Sufi or Zen.
Not any religion or cultural system.
I am not from the East or the West."

The great mystics and poets had a vision of a world view of life, like the Tamil saying "one humankind and one God", the world is my home all are my kinsman. Here we find the Universal message of love developing. The Judeo-Christian heritage had the ethos and seeds of human rights. The Old Testament books show the transition from a tribal religion and tribal ethics of "an eye for an eye and a tooth for a tooth" to justice for all-especially for the oppressed, propounded by the Prophets. Jewish Prophet Isaiah, shows a spirituality which goes beyond Judaism. He leads us to Universal Religion saying: "The kind of fasting I want is this: Remove the chains of oppression and the yoke of injustice, and let the oppressed go free.

"Share your food with the hungry and open your homes to the homeless poor. Give clothes to those who have nothing to wear, and do not refuse to help your own relatives.

"Then my favour will shine on you like the morning sun, and your wounds will be quickly healed. I will always be with you to save you; my presence will protect you on every side.

"When you pray, I will answer you. When you call to me, I will respond. If you put an end to oppression, to every gesture of contempt, and to every evil word.

"If you give food to the hungry and satisfy those who are in need, then the darkness around you will turn to the brightness of noon.

"And I will always guide you and satisfy you with good things. I will keep you strong and well. You will be like a garden that has plenty of water, like a spring of water that never runs dry.

"Your people will rebuild what has long been in ruins, building again on the old foundations. You will be known as the people who rebuilt the walls, who restored the ruined houses." (Ch.5 lambs will eat together; lions will eat straw, as cattle do, and snakes will no longer be dangerous. On Zion, my sacred hill, there will be nothing harmful or evil."

Amidst chaos, destruction, sorrow, poverty, disease, to create new tools and categories of understanding which are required to cope up with the problems of the increasing complexities of the world, we should accelerate the increasing understanding of human nature. As you are looking for a new paradigm for 21st Century, it looks to me a paradigm of Human Rights, is a possibility for a future. Its accessibility and availability is easy; its teaching is fairly simple, though neglected, we got lost in big theories and ideas. A simple truth like respecting human dignity in human life is indispensable for all humans.

It is said that the present condition of human beings is that we are becoming global citizens with the mind-set of a closed community, of a closed nation. That is, people who seek world unity are struggling to overcome their own personal prejudices and limitations. The Late Dag Hammarskjold, Secretary General of the United Nations in 1958, recalling his vast experience of working with the international community mentioned, "The conflict between different approaches to the liberty of man and mind or between different view of human dignity and the right of the individual is continuous. The dividing line goes within ourselves, within our own people and also within other nations. It does not coincide with any political or geographical boundaries. The ultimate fight is one between the human and the subhuman. We are on dangerous ground if we believe that any individual, any nation or any ideology has a monopoly on rightness, liberty and human dignity. When we fully recognize this and translate our insight into words and action, we may also be able to re-establish full human contact and communications across geographical and political boundaries". We have to move on in the human evolution with a vision for humankind.

It is obvious that we are groping for a new paradigm. After analysing the dynamics underlying the great problems we face, the famous physicist–author Fritj Capra offers a holistic paradigm of science and spirit. It is in the spirituality of ancient people and the culture of the indigenous people, we find a world view of life, a common ground for ecology and human rights, development and environment, synthesis of individual rights with community well being and living in harmony with the world. It is the mystics and spiritual leaders who have an insight into this nature of world and human consciousness contribute to individual transformation as well as to social transformation. It is a mystic who awakens the mystic in everyone. It is a great master who draws the humanity in every person. Affirming life or life affirmation is found among ancient and indigenous people. Affirmation of life is very essential for Human Rights.

Dietrich Bonhoeffer, the theologian who was imprisoned and suffered under Nazi rule in Germany spoke of 'rights' and the living human body as the repository of the rights, related to natural life. "Other worldliness is the temptation of those who cannot bear the earth as it is." He prayed that "Thy Kingdom Come: The Prayer of the Church for God's Kingdom on Earth." The kingdom of God on earth will assure all human rights for all, for justice and peace. St John mentions that Christ said, "The kingdom of God is within you." (John 14:15). It is for us to claim and realize the kingdom of human rights.

"But, whether we go bail for small measures or great, a decision is imperative. Mankind lies groaning, half crushed beneath the weight of its own progress. Men do not sufficiently realize that their future is in their own hands. Theirs is the task of determining first of all whether they want to go on living or not. Theirs the responsibility, then, for deciding if they want merely to live, or intend to make just the extra effort required for fulfilling, even on their refractory planet, the essential function of the universe, which is a machine for the making of gods."[39]

"The challenge is to build a culture of human rights awareness and commitment in all countries. The World community needs to return to the audacious vision of those who drafted the Universal Declaration of Human Rights."[40]

Dr. Jonas Salk once said, "There are few indeed who can make choices of direction that would lead to the avoidance of catastrophe and the solution of problems that have arisen in the course of evolution. But such individuals do exist. It matters little that they are few in number. Only a few are needed to visualize and initiate a process that would become self-organizing, self-propelling, and self-propagating, as is characteristic of evolutionary process.

Our first need is to counter the anti-evolutionary influences and to move consciously into the next stage of human evolution. There is a qualitative difference in all aspects of this new reality. It is a new beginning. It should be seen both in terms of the opportunities that exist as well as in terms of the dangers. Both opportunity and danger exist in every crisis. The present is no exception. The best way to resolve any crisis is by choosing the path of opportunity–the evolutionary advantageous path–and avoiding the path of danger.[41]

As one serving the cause of downtrodden Dalits during the last twenty years and going through different phases of struggles, having participated in the United Nations Working Group on Minorities and other human rights commission meetings for few years here in Geneva, let me share my vision for humanity.

The end of cold war and the disintegration of erstwhile USSR triggered off violence in Europe based on ethnic cultural and linguistic identities. The violent conflict resulted in great suffering to people as a result children, women, and family life suffered much adding to new set of problems to conflict areas around the world increasing the distress to the already afflicted and ailing humanity.

The word *terrorism* causes complex conflicts which cannot be solved easily or causes prolonged delay in finding solutions. It is ideal to avoid negative reactions towards our idealistic goals and to encourage positive contribution of minorities, and the educated and intelligent citizens of the world by gaining confidence of the State and other people sympathetic to our cause. This can be achieved only by educating people at grass roots communities and mobilizing people to bring the desired results.

Sharing Indian Experiences

India is a multi-cultural and multi-lingual country where in one state a linguistic majority becomes a minority in the neighbouring state. This initiate necessitates providing adequate protection for minorities. When intolerance and political exploitation of a conflict arises it burst into violence, using machinery of oppression and denial of justice. Sharing of river waters is a recent feature which resulted in such conflicts where people become angry with linguistic minorities and inflict violence.

The Christian population in India is only about 3%. It is an insignificant minority considering India's population of one billion people! However it has become a significant minority which contributed to the growth of education and healing people by establishing the best schools and hospitals. Similarly it should be possible for all minorities to develop education and medical facilities without mixing indoctrination of religious belief or conversions.

While the right to self determination is respected as a principle of human right, as people belonging to the human race, every one has an obligation to the people of the world for peaceful co-existence and to enjoy life in peace, so that our children can grow as future citizens of emerging new world. I have a vision of our minority community people around the world instead of being victims and marginalized become a powerful persons of social change, engaged in teaching, educating people to make a better world.

In order to ensure continuity, sustainability and credibility to the work of leaders of minority communities, it is my proposal placed before this august body of international delegates that we set up a peace corps of volunteers who can serve in areas of conflict. It should be non-aligned, truly neutral to conflict and like Red Cross serve suffering humanity. The present world climate is conducive to promote a positive contribution of minorities like setting up a Peace Corps. This Peace Corps may operate under the umbrella of international Red Cross and the UN system to encourage educated volunteers to serve the twin purposes of (1) caring the victims of conflict and violence, and (2) to create confidence among people to remove discrimination and prejudice through multi-culture education. Hereby the minorities will get an opportunity to transcend their feelings of isolation to an opportunity of integrating with the rest of humanity through humanitarian services, to build a new humanity based on values of equal opportunity and human dignity. This Peace Corps may easily find both financial and moral support from several inter-governmental agencies like European Union, Middle Eastern countries and International development organizations.

This Peace Corps of committed educated volunteers will sow the seeds for non-violent conflict resolution within the context of international Justice. The establishment of the Peace Corps will avoid danger of young people being branded and exploited as terrorists and will encourage young people to be drawn into an area of human rights and will positively contribute to a peaceful society, in which opportunities for growth will flourish, establishing continuity, credibility, and sustainability.

"Today, like every other day, we wake up empty
And frightened. Don't open the door to the study
and begin reading. Take down a musical instrument.
Let the beauty we love be what we do.
There are hundreds of ways to kneel and kiss the ground
Out beyond ideas of wrong doing and right doing,
there is a field. I'll meet you there."

—Sufi saint-poet, Jalaluddin Rumi

Let us all create a new world where our own Human Rights Peace Corps volunteers will become torch bearers of emerging new humanity. All of us present here are uniquely privileged to witness the dawn of new millennium, . We had a glimpse of what 21st Century would look like. I do believe that you and I are called to create a world of justice, peace and progress for all. We are called to be co-creators of a new earth with a new social order ensuring human dignity and human rights for all. We are called to be partners in creating a new culture of peace, a new civilization, which will further evolve into a humane world - a new heaven on earth.

References

1. Mumford, *The Conduct of Life*, New York, 1951, pp.14-16.
2. From the speech delivered by Mrs.Mary Robinson at New Delhi in November 2001.
3. Ibid.
4. Ibid.
5. Ibid.
6. The Voice of the Voiceless, The NGO Forum at LDC III.
7. Ibid.
8. World Bank Report 1995, Vol. V & IX.
9. William F.Felice, 'Taking Suffering Seriously-Collective
10. Human Rights' in A World Society.
11. Human Development Report, 2000, p.8.
12. Human Development Report, 1994.
13. Former Food Minister of India, Late Mr.C.Subramaniam.
14. UN Report.
15. *The Hindu*, Madras, 11.08.1997.
16. Ibid.
17. Marukkalampatti is the Dalit Village where recently the Dalits are deprived of their fundamental rights in a caste based clash. They are not allowed to wear chapels, decent dressing and they are provided tea in a separate tumbler used exclusively for them as they are identified as untouchables. Opposing all these violations, a Dalits woman was beaten to death and number of Dalits were chased away from the village.
18. Dr.B.R.Ambedkar's Speeches & Writings, Vol.III, Bombay 1989.

19. *United Nations Research Institute for Social Development Bulletin,* Summer 2000, Number 22, Switzerland, Aug. 8, 2000, p.2.
20. Ibid., p.2.
21. *Women : Challenges to the Year 2000,* a UN Report.
22. *Human Development Report, 1994,* op.cit.
23. *Universal Declaration of Human Rights* (Abbreviated).
24. National Organization of Women Report, 1992.
25. William F.Felice, op.cit.
26. HDR, 2000, op.cit.
27. *The Hindu,* New Delhi, July 7, 1988; *Vilakku,* DLET, 1988, p.13.
28. Speech by Dr.Kofi Annan, UN Secretary-General.
29. Ibid.
30. Dr.Kofi Annan, UN Secretary-General, UNIC Press Release, Durban, South Africa, August 30, 2001.
31. Ibid.
32. *1991 Census Report–Population.*
33. Speech delivered at All-India Radio by Dr.B.R.Ambedkar.
34. R.M.Pal, 'Human Rights Education, India's Heritage', in Henry Thiagaraj (Ed.), *Human Rights from the Dalit Perspective,* Chennai, 1996, p.145.
35. Ibid., p.145.
36. Ibid., p.145.
37. William Blake, The Sane Society.
38. Seattle, *Writing to the US President,* New York, 1855.
39. Bergson.
40. Diana Ayton-Shenker, 'The Challenge of Human Rights and Cultural Diversity', *Human Rights,* a Newsletter by United Nations Department of Public Information, New York, March 1995.
41. Jonas Salk, *Anatomy of Reality,* 1983; Benjamin B.Ferencz & Ken Keyes, *Planethood,* Jr.Love line books, 1991.

Annexures

Annexure - I

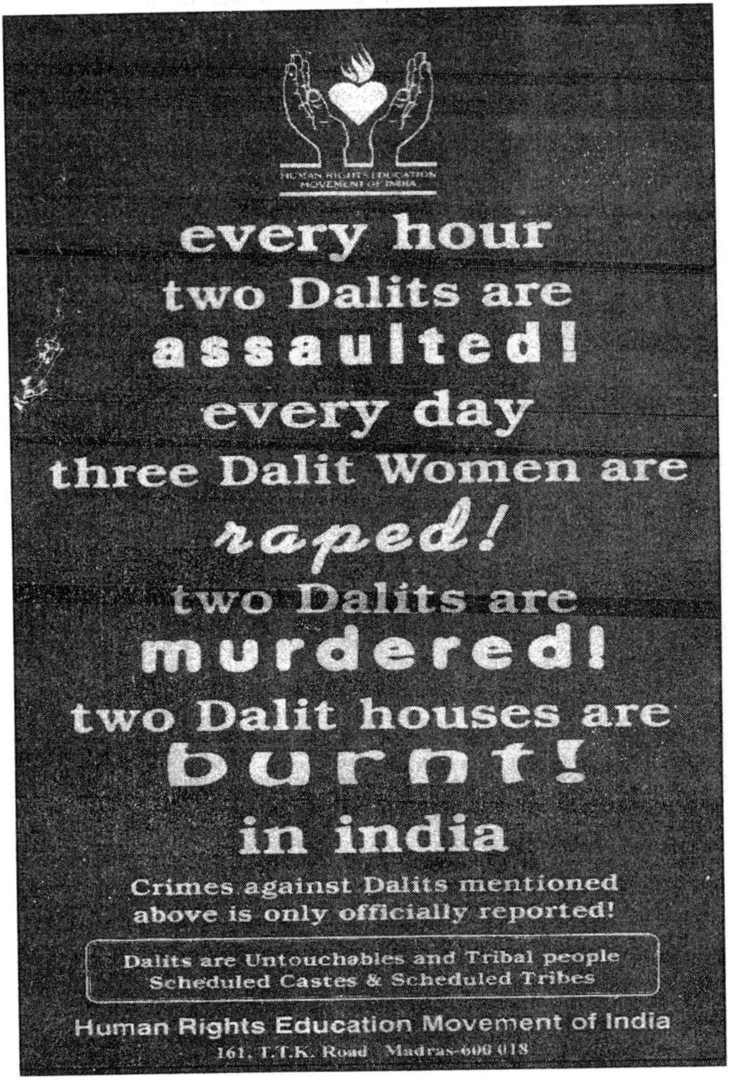

This land mark Poster designed by Dr. Henry Thiagaraj in June 1963 for United Conference in Human Rights held in Vienna, Austria sensitised the UN Community and NGO's in Europe the struggle of Dalits. The text of the poster is widely used by NGO's.

Annexure - II

Number of Cases of Crimes against Dalits (Scheduled Castes and Scheduled Tribes) in India

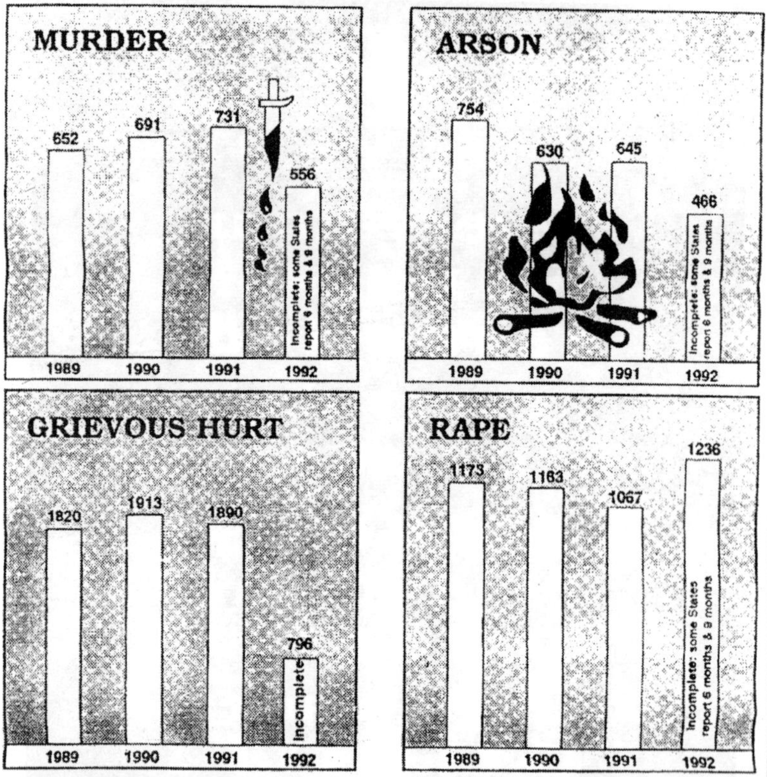

Other Crimes against Dalits under the Indian Penal Code of India

Year	Total Number of Cases Registered
1989	15023
1990	16880
1991	17029
1992 Incomplete: Some States reported for 6 months and some 9 months only	12797

Total Number of Cases of Crimes againts Dalits - Scheduled Castes and Scheduled Tribes in India

Year	Total Number of Cases Registered
1989	19422
1990	21307
1991	21362
1992 Incomplete: Some States reported for 6 months and some 9 months only	13,393

Chart first published in the booklet Dalits of India—The wounded society published by Mr. HENRY THIAGRAJ for distribution at World Conference on Human Rights in 1993.

Annexure - III

People of India

The people of India are derived from six main ethnic groups: 1. Negrito, 2. Proto-Australoids or Austrics, 3. Mongoloids, 4. Mediterranean or Dravidian, 5. Western Brachycephals and 6. Nordic Aryans anthropological

Very little people research has been done regarding the ethnic origins of the Indian population. The Indian population is polygenetic and is a confusing mixture of various racial strains. Few, if any, can claim to belong to any particular stock. Nevertheless, many Indians pride themselves on their Aryan descent. The Aryans must have come into India between 2000 and 1500 B.C. Negroids from Africa were the oldest people to have come to India. These people are now found only in patches among the hiss tribes of South India (Irulas, Kodars, Paniyans and Kurumbas) on the main land.

The Dravidians comprise all the three sub-types: Paleo-Mediterranean, the true Mediterranean and Oriental Mediterranean. The Dravidians must have spread to the whole of India, supplanting Austrics and Negritos alike. Dravidians who had big towns with fortifications and brick structures and many of the amenities of a quite high city civilization. The Indus people were essentially the city dwellers while the Aryans were the pastoral race.

Castes: The caste system is fundamental to Hindu religious beliefs. It is part of the Hindu law-Dharma-*Varna*shma–Dharma. There are four castes: The *Brahmins*–Priests, The Warrior-*Kshatriyas,* The Merchant–Vaisyas and the farming labourers-Sudras. They live outside the caste village. Within each caste, there are hereditary sub-castescalled Jatis. The les perform those tasks that the other castes will not do obeying the Hindu law. There is the fear of damaging their chances of advancing up the chain of re-incarnation–that is by disobedience to Hindu law.

Segregated Housing of Dalits

Every Indian village portrays a reality of age-long discrimination in housing 1. The Caste village, where Hindu upper caste people live around or near a Hindu Temple and 2. Dalit "Colonies" or "Cheries", adjoining a caste village where the oppressed-untouchables live at least half a kilometer away. In Tamil Nadu, of which Madras is the capital, the Dalits are usually known as "Adi-Dravidars"-"the earliest" or "the oldest" of the Dravidian race living in South India.

Social Realities and Caste Taboos

Article 17 of the Indian Constitution has expressly abolished untouchability and made it a legal offence, an offence punishable under law to practise it in any form. Though provisions to this effect exist in the law (Protection of Civil Rights Act 1955), untouchability is still practised in many ways in Tamil Nadu especially in rural areas. The system of landlordism in many parts of the State reinforce such feudal and social practises with cultural manifestations.

Dalit settlements (Cheries) separated from other communities by a long distance is the general phenomenon in almost all the villages in the State. In addition to this physical separation, untouchability is practised in several other ways like:

a. Prohibition to draw water from village common well.
b. Prohibition to enter into a village temple.
c. Separation in Dinning Halls-Restaurants.
d. In some areas keeping separate vessels for serving the Dalits in the hotels are still practised.
e. Burning of the houses and launching of violent attacks on the Dalit people who question the social system are common practise. For example, on April 14, 1992-the Birthday of Dr. Ambedkar 20 houses of Dalits were burnt at Kadalur village 80 kms away from Madras. Social tension prevailed there for three months.

In addition to loss of property, they were assaulted and arrested.

Dalits Worship Nature and Spirit

One visible evidence of the oldest Dravidian people is nature worship of the Dalits, despite 2000 years of Hindu indoctrination. For example: the spirit of nature–the Divine Force is worshipped as represented by a green tree-symbol of fertility and "Mother Earth"-represented by a stone–these are found in open areas of Dalit settlements and not covered by temples. Sometimes a mini-house for the "Sprit-Divine"–is built underneath the tree. Usual name for this "Mother

Nature" is "Amma" or "Amman"-and "Mart". "Mart"-"Amman" represents water or Mother Rain. A "Spirit"-which is like a wind is on the tree referred to as "Muni" a belief in Spiritism-is prevalent among the people.

Dalit means the oppressed, broken people-people

The Dalits are given local names according to the region in which they live. For example, in Maharashtra they are called *Mahars* and *Mongs*. In Andhra Pradesh *Malas* and *Madhikas*. In Tamil Nadu some local names of large groups are: *Adi Dravidars, Pallars, parayars,* and *Chakiliyars* in Punjab areas *Chamars* and *Balmikis*.

The Dalits are contrasted with the Hindu Aryan race and religion of India, as pointed out by Dr. B.R. Ambedkar, a great Dalit leader and intellectural (14.04.1891-06.10.1956) whose birth centenary was celebrated during the year 1991-92. Dr. Ambedkar was the leader of Dalits of India as contrasted to Gandhi' who was considered as a leader of the Hindus in India, (like Jinnah for Muslims-Father of Pakistan). All these three leaders were contemporaries.

NAMES FOR THE UNTOUCHABLES IN INDIA

1. UNTOUCHABLES Hindu Orthodoxy
2. OUTCASTES
3. CHANDALAS
4. PANCHAMAS
5. SCHEDULED CASTES-British classification used in Indian constitution and Indian Govt.
6. HARIJANS-Used by Mahatma Gandhi
7. DEPRESSED CLASSES-Political Parties
8. OPPRESSED COMMUNITIES-Political Parties
9. DALIT-Used by Dr. Ambedkar, Constitution maker of India.

Who is a Sudra?

A *Sudra* is born within the Hindu caste society, but belongs to the lowest status. They are at the bottom. The *Avarnas*, Out-caste are literally and physically outside the caste system and the forefold Varnsrama Dharma. Sudras are the fourth category people whereas the untouchables are the fifth category of people also called as *Panchamas*. A *sudra* can enter the Hindu temple whereas the *Panchamas* are not allowed to enter the Hindu temple historically to draw water even from the Shudhra areas.

Manu dharmashastra, Chapter 8. Sloka 415 says that Sudras are of seven kinds. One becomes a *Sudra* under any one of these circumstances:-

- One who ran away as a coward, from war.
- One who was captured as a prisoner of war.
- One who serves *Brahmins* with devotion.
- Son of an adulteress.
- Persons bought for money.
- One who belongs to a line of persons serving others for several generations.

The socio-legal study made turns round the above definition of a Sudra, by Manu in his *Dharmasastra;* and this definition is accepted by the Law of the Land. The Hindu Law, even today, recognizes only two castes: the twice-born or the *Brahmins,* and all the rest of the Hindus, who are not twice-born, the *Shudras* and the outcastes.

Who are the Untouchables?

The *Dharmasastras* declare the *Chandalas* to be the progeny of unions between a Brahmin female and a Sudra male. The age of the *Dharmasastras* is difficult to be determined. But from the available evidence it may be held that the 6th and 5th century B.C. formed the period of the *Dharmasastras.* Thus, ideas about the *Chandala* and the ceremonial purity might have appeared before 500 B.C.

References to Pratiloma castes appear in the *Arthasatra* as well as in Patanjali's Mahabhashya of about 500-150 B.C. Manu develops the idea of the degradation of the *Chandalas.* He states that the *Chandalas* were to reside only outside the villages and were subject to various inhibitions. they were not allowed to use gold or silver ornaments or wear cotton, much less silk clothing. The use of skins of corpses alone was permitted for them. The duty assigned to the *Chandalas* was to serve as hangmen and as undertakers for unclaimed corpses"

Chandalas are included in the Depressed Classes. They are also called '*Avarnas*' 'Untouchables' or 'External Castes', or later called "Harijans" and Dalits. The following social taboos are enforced on them by the upper caste people:

1. *Brahmins* should not server themfor disregarding the prohibitions.
2. Barbers, water carriers, tailors and such other who serve the caste Hindus. Should not serve the *Chandalas.*
3. The out-castes pollute a high-caste Hindu by contact or by proximity.
4. A caste Hindu cannot take water from the out-caste.
5. They are debarred from public conveniences such as roads, ferries, wells or schools.
6. They are debarred from the use of Hindu temples.

7. An educated man of the caste cannot be treated as an equal by the educated out-caste HIndu.
8. It is depressed only on account of the occupation followed.
9. The upper caste doesnot become merely depressed on account of its own ignorance, illiteracy or poverty; and but for that, would be subject to no social disability.[1]

In December 1930 the "Kallar" caste in Ramanathapuram propounded eight prohibitions, the disregard of which led to the violence by the Kallars who furiously set fire to the huts and destroyed the properties of the depressed classes (Adi-Dravidas) These eight prohibitions were:

1. That the Adi-Dravidas shall not wear any ornament of gold or silver.
2. That the males should not be allowed to wear their clothes below their knees or above the hips.
3. Males not to wear coats, shirts or vests.
4. Nor were they to have their hair cropped.
5. Only earthen vessels were to be used.
6. Women were not to cover the upper portion of their bodies with jckets and an upper cloth.
7. Nor were they allowed to used flowers or saffron paste.
8. The people obviously the males, were not to used umbrellas or sandals.

In 1931, the Kallars, not satisfied with the above eight restrictions, drew up a list of eleven prohibitions. These included that: (1) The Adi-Dravidas should not read or get educated (2) should be asked to tend the cattle of the Mirasdars or landowners and plough their land and (3) must work as coolies only and not to own lands. It is commonly thought that the *Brahmins* are responsible for the abuses of the Cate system; but it is not so. True, they have laid the foundation of the caste complex and paved the way for castism. But in later times the caste Hindu non-*Brahmins* were the people who extended them to the extreme limit.

References

1. Dr. K.K. Pillay, "Studies in the History of India with Special References to Tamil Nadu", Madras, 1979.
2. Manorma Year Book, 1992.

Annexure - IV

Oppression of Women in Indian Society

It was Manu the law giver, who created the caste system and discriminated the class of untouchables by segregating housing and other atrocious taboos. He made women subordinate to man and a slave to him. Family life deteriorated, giving rise to polygamy and prostitution including temple prostitution.

Many enjoyed a special status as the bread winner and administrator of the family matters, while the woman's freedom was generally restricted to bringing up the children, attending to her husband's needs slavishly, performing house hold chores of cooking and maintaining the house. Motherhood was glorified at least in principal and was used as a tool of exploitation. Wives, however, had little initiative. It was considered a wife's duty to wait on her husband, fetching and carrying for him, rubbing his feet when he was weary, rising before him, eating and sleeping after him (according to the law of Manu). The following gives an idea what was expected of a wife:-

"She should do nothing independently even in her own house. In childhood subject to her father, in youth to her husband, and when her husband is dead to her sons."

"She should always be cheerful, and skillful in her domestic duties, with her household vessels well cleansed and her hand tight on the purse-strings..."

"In season and out of season her lord, who wed her with sacred rites, ever gives happiness to his wife, both here and in the other world".

"Though he be uncouth and prone to pleasure, though he have no good points at all, the virtuous wife should ever worship her lord as a God"..*

*Manu as quoted by A.L. Basham-The Wonder that was India-
Used as a source book for this paper.

Passages of this type are frequent in literature of a religious and semi-religious type and stories of obedient and faithful wives are numerous. The great models of Indian womanhood are Sita who faithfully followed her husband Rama into exile and endured great hardships and temptations for his sake and Savitri who followed hfer husband Sathyavant when he was being carried away by the death-God Yama, and so impressed the God with her loyalty that he released her lord.

According to Arthasastra 3rd Century B.C., a woman was allowed some personal property like jewellery and clothing, but the husband alone had rights over his wife's property that he might sell it in dire emergency or restrain his wife from giving it away wantonly.

The true function of woman is marriage and the care of men folk and children. A study of ancient India shows that kings and chiefs were invariably polygamous, as were many Brahmins and wealthier members of lower status. In Arthasastra, polygamous marriages were frequently mentioned that one may assume that they were fairly common in all sections of community who can afford them. Women kept in royal harem (anthapura) which were closely guarded and were not allowed to leave their harems. The women were not allowed to help her parents, as they became members of their husband's families. Rajput (warriors and kings) familiesdestroyed their infant girls. Some communities still practice this atrocious custom, as often reported in the Press.

Complied by Mrs. Philomena Thiagaraj

Annexure - V

The Bhopal Declaration

Adopted Unanimously By

The Bhopal Conference: 27th February 2002

Charting A New Course For Dalits For The 21st Century

Held at Bhopal, Madhya Pradesh, India, 12-13 January 2002

We— intellectuals and activists assembled at the Bhopal Conference, 12-13 January 2002, to deliberate the issues concerning the welfare of and justice to the 250 million —are:

Declaring our belief in Babasaheb Dr. B. R. Ambedkar's ideal of Social Democracy and his prophecy that, "A democratic form of Government presupposes a democratic form of society. The formal framework of democracy is of no value and would indeed be a misfit if there was no social democracy",

Endorsing the ideals of civil society enshrined in the Constitution of India, particularly its Preamble that declares the Indian State's commitment to Justice, Liberty, Equality and Fraternity,

Recognising that the tenets established by the Universal Declaration of Human Rights and various other charters of the United Nations which our nation has acceded to also emphasise the same principles,

Recognising also the tribals' legitimate and historical rights over forest and forest-produce,

Acknowledging the role of tribal communities, particularly tribal women, to the protection and conservation of the country's rich biodiversity and natural resources as well as its culture and civilisation

Acknowledging also the need to ensure that SCs and STs are given due representation in all bodies of decision making,

Recalling the struggles that Babasaheb had waged for the emancipation of his people and the historic rights he had won for them,

Mindful of the fact that even after 54 years of Independence, the Dalit community is denied of its basic human rights and is also at the receiving end of the most brutal and oppressive forms of discrimination and exclusion,

Reaffirming that concerted action by society as a whole – especially coordination among the political leadership, officials and grassroots activists – is necessary for the over-all development of the most oppressed of India,

Bearing in mind the responsibility to take forward our struggle at this critical juncture in spite of the fact that most political formations are reluctant to pursue any policy favourable to the Dalits,

Recognising that the social consensus over the Dalit cause – reluctantly agreed upon at the time of Independence – has by and large broken down,

Convinced that informed and democratic discourse at all levels is essential to re-negotiate a new consensus over redeeming the pledges of the founding fathers of the Republic to do justice to Dalits,

Convinced also that the national psyche and public discourse in the country accepts uncritically the rigid hierarchy and discrimination caused by caste and thereby denies that caste is a major source of prejudice and brutal violence,

Emphasizing that Babasaheb's stress on struggle through democratic and constitutional means is relevant today,

Regretting that the post-Ambedkar Dalit intelligentsia has failed both in carrying forward his emancipatory movement as well as making a dent in the country's intellectual life,

Recognizing the need for Dalits to make common cause with other liberation and human rights movements in and outside the country,

Conscious of the hurdles that caste-Hindu society – and its tentacles in government, media, voluntary sector, etc., – is likely to hurl at any serious movement that challenges the entrenched system of discrimination and exclusion,

Noting that women - especially Dalit women - represent the most oppressed sections of our society, and that they face multiple forms of discrimination, including caste-based, religious and patriarchal ideology and practices,

Welcoming the winds of change the world over that are conducive to Inclusion, Equal Opportunity, Diversity, Democratisation and Civil Society, and against discrimination, stereotype, stigma, exclusion and caste society,

Hoping that this country will no longer remain an exception to the global norm of Progress, Equality, Justice, Peace and Social Harmony, and

We hereby **Solemnly proclaim** that while we rededicate ourselves to work in unison to achieve basic rights of Dalits, we are convinced that unless the following issues are resolved no amount of activism on our part and pro-active measures from the State can liberate the community from the scourges of untouchability and exploitation.

We therefore demand....

21-POINT ACTION AGENDA FOR THE 21ST CENTURY

1. Ensure that each Dalit family will own enough cultivable land for socio-economic well-being. The government should pursue all possible measures including the distribution of surplus land, government revenue lands and temple lands within a specific timeframe. If the need be, the government should purchase cultivate land and distribute it among Dalits.
2. Enact legislation and enforce it stringently to enable Dalits have an equitable share in the appropriation and use of the rural and urban common property resources. The law must be amended to ensure that lengthy litigation with the ulterior motive of denying Dalits of legal redressal, is not resorted to.
3. Enact legislation and enforce the right of Dalit agricultural labourers to living wages, to gender parity in wages, to job security, to better working conditions and welfare measures, and ensure punitive measures against offenders.
4. Appoint Statutory Committees at the national and state level to identify within specified time-frame all the Depressed Class lands occupied by non-Dalits, to assess the quantum of compensation to be paid by non-Dalits for their illegal utilization of lands, to identify the original owners and their nearest kith and kin for restoring these lands back to them, to expedite legal proceedings in courts specially appointed for this purpose against the illegal occupants and to ensure punitive measures against them.
5. Ensure the restoration of the alienated lands to the tribals, restore their rights over forest and forest-produce, provide them with compensation and rehabilitation measures, extend resources and

capacity building measures for gainful utilization of their lands and forests and make those Dalits displaced due to construction of dams/developmental projects as shareholders of such enterprises.

6. Democratise the capital so as to ensure proportionate share for SCs and STs. Make budgetary allocation for SCs and STs to enable them enter the market economy with adequate investment resources, and develop their capacities and skills for such market enterprises.
7. Enforce with stringent measures the Bonded Labour System (Abolition) Act, 1976 and abolish forthwith child labour to ensure freedom with dignity for all the Dalits, and accordingly make suitable amendments in the appropriate legislations.
8. Amend Art. 21 of the Constitution of India: Fundamental Rights so as to include the following rights for all citizens, but with special emphasis for SCs and STs, and on the basis of two criteria, namely low economic income and without religious discrimination: the rights to a standard of living adequate for the health and well-being of women and men equally, including food, safe drinking water, clothing, housing, public health and medical care, social security and social services; the right to living wage and the right to own 5 acres of cultivable land or to gainf! ul employment.
9. Implement compulsory, free and high quality education for all Dalits immediately, make allocation of funds proportionate to the number and level of the illiterates, ensure compensation to those families which forfeit their income from child-labour, increase the number and amount of scholarships, and provide better infrastructural facilities in SC and ST schools and offer market-oriented vocational and technical education.
10. Make the reservation quota applicable in all the public and private educational institutions from primary to technical and professional levels. Every SC/ST child with low income-base must be given quality free-education at State's expense. And every English medium school must implement Diversity in Admissions.
11. Recognize SC and ST women as a distinct category among women, and accordingly make segregated data on Dalit women available in census reports, action taken reports and progress reports, evolve national and state level perspective plan for mainstreaming SC and ST women in developmental programmes, market enterprises, financial allocation, reservation facilities in education, employment and health facilities, and mandate the National and State

Commissions for SC and ST and for Women to study and report specifically the status of SC and ST women in their annual reports.

12. Implement effectively in letter and spirit the SC and ST (Prevention of Atrocities) Act, 1989 & Rules1995, especially with regard to atrocities against Dalit women, and accordingly prosecute the dominant caste leaders and their minions who stoke the fire of caste clashes and the police officials acting in connivance with them. In cases of atrocities against SC/STs, a system of collective punishment has to be evolved as oppressors enjoy community support and protection and escape the law.
13. Ensure diversity or SC/STs' due representation in all public institutions of India, whether universities or academic or autonomous or registered bodies. Those institutions, which do not abide by the principle of Affirmative Action, must lose recognition and state funding. All private industry/ corporate houses must accept and implement Diversity in workforce immediately.
14. Ensure that in all state and national budgets allocations are made as per the proportion of SC and ST population and penal action taken against unutilisation or diversion of funds meant for these sections.
15. Every government and private organization must implement Supplier Diversity from socially disadvantaged businesses and Dealership Diversity in all goods and services.
16. The State must assume sole responsibility in protecting the SCs and STs. The State must identify those atrocity prone areas and deploy forces. In addition, provide arms licences to the SCs & STs as stipulated in the Atrocities Act for self-defence purposes, make the setting up of Dalit self-defence groups from village onwards mandatory, and specially train Dalit women to handle weapons in self-defence against the perpetrators of crimes and atrocities.
17. Eliminate the humiliating practice of manual scavenging on an urgent footing through effective rehabilitation, alternative and sustainable employment measures and developmental programmes, and prosecute violators of the Employment of Manual Scavengers and Construction of Dry Latrines (Prohibition) Act, 1993, especially the gross violators Railways, Defence and Urban Local bodies.
18. Make it statutory for Parliament and State Assemblies to debate on the Annual Reports of the National and State level Commissions for SC/ST and Safai Karamcharis within the following year, and

ensure that these annual reports and the action-taken reports of the government are made public.

19. Make reservation mandatory in the private and corporate sector in the same proportion as in the public sector and government institutions and develop the capacities and skills of Dalits to help them cope up with the demands of these different sectors.
20. Implement policy of reservation to SCs and STs at all levels of judiciary and defence forces. And make transparent appointment processes in Judiciary by doing away with the nomination system.
21. Bring out a Truth Paper in two years on the status of reservation during the past 25 years and place it before Parliament and State Assemblies for debate, and on a war footing fill immediately all the backlog posts meant for Dalits and that, too, only with Dalit candidates.

Source : India Together, January 2002

Annexure - VI

Comments on Bhopal Declaration

SARDAR BUTA SINGH
Member of Parliament

1. We Commend all those who had spent their time energy and money, in organizing an exclusive Conference at Bhopal on Dalit Issues, reportedly to Chart a '**New Course for Dalits for the 21st Century'** and in preparing and publishing the Bhopal **Declaration and Document.**
2. While We Congratulate them for this, we will be failing in our Duty and Commitment to the SC & ST Dalits and Dalit Cause, if we do not speak honestly about the failures and gaps, in the otherwise beautifully printed Bhopal Declaration and Document, their shortcomings and limitations.
3. It is sad that the Conference had remained exclusive, to a select few or many co-opted elements, looking for some awards or special placements, excluding many real SC & ST Dalit Representatives. Particularly left out, perhaps deliberately were, senior SC & ST Parliamentarians, Dalit Intellectuals and Scholars, Ambedkar Chair Professors and all those associated with the Ambedkar Foundation New Delhi, recognized grassroots workers, selflessly working silent Dalit Activists, and the few committed officials.
4. We must Confess that the 21st Point Action Agenda for the 21st Century, released at the Bhopal Conference, sure makes an interesting reading. But it appears to be slip-shod, repetitive, confused and verbose, with each point covering multiple issues.
5. Though we must concede that many Dalit Issues and Problems have been covered by the Action Agenda, we see a lot of

confusion and hurry in drafting and finalizing the Agenda. And, not all the Dalit Issues have been touched upon.

6. We find that those in the Conference at Bhopal had exhibited a clear lack of understanding of the Constitutional Mandate of Reservation, as evolved in this country. The participants had failed to keep in their mind or remember that Reservations for SC & ST Dalits today, is the direct result of the endless Struggles of the Dalits, particularly under the great leadership of Baba Saheb Dr. BR Ambedkar. The reservation here, which is distinctly different from the Affirmative Action of America for the Blacks, is a Fundamental Right, enshrined in the Constitution. On the other hand, the AA in USA was adopted there purely for Political Reasons, that too in the face of Internal Pressures and International Criticisms. It is a Political Right there, but neither is it a Fundamental Right, nor has it any Constitutional Mandate.
7. Be that ignorant others or the shallow dalit writers, let none belittle the Great Concept of Reservation as agreed by Baba Saheb Dr. B.R. Ambedkar, and signed as the Poona Pact 1932. Baba Saheb inked it then at Yerawadha in Pune, after a massive long struggle. That, all must remember, in the face of great threats to his person, life and safety. That was and still is, a solemn Agreement that remains alive. It has not ever been abrogated by any one. So it remains, as it was on of the most crucial basic Agreements of Nation Making, and constitutional Process in this Country. That was and is an Agreement between all the Dalits who number more than 260 million in the country today, and the few dominant caste hindus. That was signed by Baba Saheb on behalf of all the Dalits of this Country, after a tenuous but tense long and protracted negotiations–frustrating most of the times; with Gandhi standing for the DCHs Yerawadha Jail, many of his followers and Congress. And hence, it was built into the Constitution of Free India, by Baba Saheb right in the Chapter on Fundamental Rights of the People of this Nation.
8. Equating or loosely using AA, while talking about or referring to Reservation for SCs & STs in this Country, betrays the shallow understanding and hollowness of Bhopal Conference. That is the major Weakness of those who had organized the Conferenc, all those who attended and participated in the discussions; drafted, finalized, accepted and brought out the 21 point action agenda, and the other Declarations of the Bhopal Conference.

9. The documents had also been prepared so callously and haphazardly that, there is neither any sequence and order, nor any priority in the way the Agenda Points have been ordered. These, thus appear to be only a shortsighted Wish list, to be taken around by the Dalits before various Authorities and Govts as one more New Petition.
10. Those behind the Declarations, had apparently not done their home-works. They had confortably neglected the designated role and failures in the lives and developments of SC & ST Dalits, of National Institutions like NSFDC, TRIFED, Ambedkar Foundation, Ambedkar Chairs in various Universities; and the Ambedkar Fellows who had been to various Western Universities of repute; and the way they are being controlled and sabotaged by others and vested interests of different shades. They also appear to have been interested in avoiding the Parliamentary Forum of SCs & STs, and the Parliamentary Committees on SCs & STs.
11. The Major Failure of the Conference and its Declarations is that, it had for reasons not stated skirted all the Sensitive Issues and Burning Problems in the Country, that have serious impacts on the life survival and future of SC & ST.

Annexure - VII

Statement made by Mr. Henry Thiagraj Managing Trustee of the Dalit Liberation Education Trust on the Situation of Untouchable People (Dalits) in South Asia Region, at the World Conference on Human Rights of the United Nations on 24th June 93 at Astoria Centre, Vienna during the 11th meeting of the Main Committee.

Madam Chairperson:

The World Conference on Human Rights is an epoch making event in which everyone participating has a unique privilege to shape the future of humanity as a whole. This historical event in Vienna reflects the anguish of humanity today-the growing pains caused by violence and violation of human rights around the world, as seen by the varity of exhibits, documents and personal testimoniespresented by more than 1, 000 NGOs around the world-at the lower levels of the Austria Centre. At the same time, this great Global Conference offers great hope to people seeking solutions to the painful problems and violations. Several distinguished speakers representing many countries expressed support to the opening theme of this Conference to make "human rights as the common language of all humanity". We are heartened to hear that "Human Rights permeates all activities "of the United Nations to evaluate all activities of development and government.

It is in achieving the supreme goal of "all human rights for all" we bring to the attention of this august body the plight of the 250 million untouchable people in the South Asia Region. The sheer magnitude of the number of people suffering discrimination alone is sufficient to attract the attention of this World Body. The NGO Forum meeting in Vienna had set up a separate workshop to deal with Casteism and the conclusions of this workshop have been given in Document A/Conf. 157/7 14 June 1993, page 23 for the consideration of this World Conference.

When our group arrived in Vienna, a friend took us to visit Mauthausen, near Linz, to see the site of a concentration camp of the Nazis–which now has memorials of the people who suffered inhuman torture and death. This reminded us of the experience of our own Dalit people's suffering, violence and pain. It is very clear to us that "casteism" and its untouchability doctrine is a manifestation of Nazism still practiced in modern times in South Asia. It has all the dangerous ingredients of racism which manifests in ugly forms.

As untouchable people, we have chosen a name for ourselves–Dalits, the broken people—to overcome the stigma of being born in an untouchable community. Untouchability is worse than apartheid, as it is not colour but the community and the place in which one is born that stigmatizes and causes one to suffer discrimination. Discrimination of one's very existence, one's being–starts from birth and continues to haunt all through life and goes beyond death by separate burial / cremation grounds. This anachronistic belief system sanctioned by the Hindu religion, has been absorbed by other religious through social practices and taboos. This pernicious doctrine is insidious, showing up in discrimination of occupation, marriage, and segregated housing. Casteism is a man-made myth, which was designed to keep a class of people under servitude. Historically it originated from the powerful invaders who created segregated communities to oppress the native indigenous people and to enslave the conquered communities by imposing discriminatory to boos: denial of ownership of land, denial of education, denial of worship and spirituality, denial of growth of human personality, denial of drinking water, and access to public roads.

Dalits were condemned to engage in degrading occupations like carrying dead corpses, leather workers, cobblers, scavengers, street sweepers, and agricultural coolies. All kinds of dirty, difficult and dangerous work are assigned to the Dalits who in many places are still treated like slaves–as their masters are born by birth to lord over them and enjoy the fruits of their labour. This practice of "casteism", dehumanizing people for over 2, 500 years, enforced deplorable living conditions. This reality is easily seen even today in rural areas–where feudalistic social structures and attitudes, supported by a colonial bureaucracy, keep people in oppressed conditions: as landless labourers and bonded labourers. Women are induced or forced to enter prostitution (the Devadasi system) and nude worship, in the name of religion. Dalits are subjected to all kinds of humiliation and violence. Dalit Villages have been set afire, sometimes with people still inside. Other examples of murder and criminal assaults have been well documented.

As per a published official document, in the year 1991 total number of criminal cases against Dalits and officially registered by the Government was 21362. In the same year 1067 Dalit women were raped, 731 Dalits murdered, 645 incidents of arson took place, and 1890 dalits were grievously hurt. Another 17029 cases of offenses against Dalits were registered. In other words it amounts to: ***Every hour two Dalits are assaulted, every day three Dalit women are raped, two Dalits are murdered, two Dalit houses are burnt***. Under these circumstances child labour abounds.

The national press has pointed out how tormentors go free while victims await for justice with pain from wounds inflicted on their body and soul. Justice delayed is justice denied, and our people suffer with anguish. Despite clear laws abolishing untouchability, the crimes committed against Dalits reveal the deep-rooted prejudices which cannot be changed by legislation alone. Efficient law enforcing machinery and the will of people in power to implement the laws are urgently required. In this area the United Nations Human Rights Commission can play a vital role.

When Dalits want to escape from the oppressive social system by seeking faith and comfort in other religions, they are denied of the benefits of the Government. In other words they are denied the freedom of belief, though they continue to suffer the same socio-economic disadvantages. This is clear violation of article 18 of U.N. Human Rights. Several protests and petitions against this discrimination on the basis of religion have not produced any remedial measures.

This World Conference highlighted the inter-relationship of human rights with democracy and development. This new paradigm heralds a new revolution in the world based on justice. The removal of poverty and social development and enjoyment of human rights by the Dalit people. Dalits remain untouched by development. Literacy, disease and poverty remain concentrated among the Dalit people, as does exploitation by age-old barbaric customs. It is in this context of socio-economic realities we would like to urge the United Nations Human Rights Commission to establish a commission to end the racist manifestation of untouchability which is a crime against humanity.

We would like to emphasise a preventive education of human rights as a must to remove deep-rooted prejudices to end atrocities and discrimination of Dalit people. We also whole heartedly welcome and support the Secretary General's project, as he outlined in his opening speech: "to help States change attitudes, convince them to undertake structural reforms educate their citizens and set up regulatory mechanisms that respect democracy and concern for human rights" This "global workshop" project will bring together the NGOs working at grassroots level of the people and the governments–bridging the existing gap, and will remove suspicions and conflict.

As a grassroot people's organization, we are engaged in non-violenct educational methods and communication to promote Human Rights education as a people's movement. As we affirm our conviction on the Universal Declaration of Human rights, we recall the words of a great champion of human rights for Dalits, Dr. B.R. Ambedkar: "The world owes a duty to the untouchables, as it does to all oppressed people to break their shackles and to set them free". We plead that the United Nations which is the conscience of the world's humanity to accord high priority to appoint a Special Commissioner to study the situation of untouchable people and to initiate measures to end violations of human rights against Dalits and other vulnerable groups. Human Rights is an "idea whose time has come" (Victor Hugo)–to bring real humanity to the deprived millions of Dalit people in the Asian region, through justice and progress.

Thank you, Madam Chairperson.

Sunday, April 11, 2004 – 12:08:20 AM

Annexure - VIII

United Nations Sub-Commission on Prevention of Discrimination and Protection of Minorities

50th Session 3-28 August 1998
Agenda Item 4: The realization of Economic, Social, and Cultural Rights
Item 6: Contemporary Forms of Slavery

Mr. Chairman:

The World Council of Churches expresses its warm appreciation on the pioneering work done by this Sub-Commission on the subject of the realization of economic, social and cultural rights. During this 50th Session very scholarly papers have been presented by experts on vital issues of development like the right of access of everyone to drinking water and the right to food, which give human dignity to the poor of the world. The link between poverty, income distribution, and globalization and the importance of holistic and integrated approach to human rights education has been highlighted in the deliberations of this Sub-Commission. We thank the scholars who have taken the efforts to give these new dimensions and insight into the realization of human rights.

Mr. Chairman, if there is one single issue that requires this Sub-Commission's kind attention, it is the discrimination based on untouchability and caste violence inflicted on millions of people in the South Asian Region, as a result of which the right to development of 300 million people have been severely curtailed. Despite its magnitude, and the anguish suffered by these people, this has escaped the attention of this august body. The one issue which stands out in all the items of the agenda and discussions, is insidious caste discrimination and violence which portrays the pathetic plight of the untouchable people, the Dalits, who are subject to the contemporary forms of slavery rooted in an ancient social system, which condemned people to "dehumanized" conditions for over two thousand years, as pointed out by Dr. B. R. Ambedkar, the champion of human rights in India. The Dalit Liberation Education Trust has participated in the Working Group on Minorities in the last two years and made statements on the plights of the Dalits (this subject) earlier.

It is mentioned that two million children are working in hazardous industries. Most of these children are Dalits who are socially oppressed and economically poor. Whether it is child labor, bonded labor, sex exploitation and rape victims,-most of the people affected are Dalits.

Discrimination against Dalits in India is the major human rights issue.Unlike apartheid the basis for discrimination against the Dalit is the community in which the person is born. The Dalit people are denied their legitimate development; they live even today in segregated colonies, denied access to drinking water, accessible roads, and made to live without development opportunities. The prestigious journal, The Economic and Political Weekly, has pointed out the sad neglect of Dalits in the development process of India and the urgent need to uplift the people living in discriminatory and degrading conditions. The 20th October 1997 issue of the TIME magazine brought out a special cover picture article on the violence suffered by Dalits.

Mr. Chairman, the Government has provided laws against untouchability, yet they are not implemented. Mr. H.Hanumanthappa, Member of Parliament and the Chairman of National Commission for Scheduled Castes and Scheduled Tribes, describes the conditions of Dalits as follows:

"The Dalits are in different stages of socio-economic development and are engaged in divergent forms of work for their living. The practice of such traditional unclean occupations as scavenging, carrying night-soil, removing dead animals, leather work, beating of drums, etc. gave them a low position in the traditional caste hierarchy and they are viewed as occupying the lowest rung of the social ladder. The vast majority of Dalits are landless and work as agricultural laborers and wage earners to eke out their livelihood. Dependence on upper-caste landowners for agricultural labor and perpetual subjugation forces many of them to live as bonded laborers. On the educational front the Scheduled Castes lag far behind the general population of India. The general literacy rate in 1991 was 52.19% while the literacy among the Scheduled castes was only 37.41%. The condition of the Dalit women is particularly deplorable. They are doubly under-privileged being women belonging to the Scheduled Castes. They constitute the major work force doing hard manual labor and engaged in agricultural operations and their exposure to outdoor work and interaction with the cunning employers make them vulnerable to sexual exploitation. Abject poverty forces Dalit women to become victims of Devadasi, the institutionalized prostitution system prevalent...."

"The Dalits constitute the weakest of the weaker sections of the society. Landlessness, a low level of literacy, and social discrimination arising out of the practice of untouchability not only account for their miseries but are also factors contributing to perpetration of atrocities against them. They are victims ofatrocities, which include heinous crimes like murder, grievous hurt, rape, arson, etc. During 1995, the number of reported cases of atrocities committed on the Scheduled Castes in the country was 35, 262 which included 688 cases of murder, 2156 grievous hurt, 1143 rape, and 729 arson cases." Because of discrimination and their segregated living, the violence against Dalits is increasing. This rise of violence against Dalits is graphically stated by the leading newspaper, The Hindu (11.08.97) in an article by a well known journalist, Prem Shankar Jha: "More than 300 Dalits were already killed in inter-caste violence in the first half of 1997 against a similar number in the whole of 1995 and around 490 in 1996."

In addition to the above, the National Human Rights Commission (NHRC) in its recently released Annual Report made the following observations:

"The Commission considers it deeply offensive to human dignity that the degrading practice requiring the manual handling of night soil is still allowed to continue in our country, fifty years after independence (5.25). "Despite the launching of nation-wide scheme in March 1992 to free those engaged in such work, and to rehabilitate them in other occupations, the implementation has remained dismal. "For all practical purposes, little follow-up action have been taken.(5.27). Further the NHRC stated: That despite the existence of the Protection of Civil Rights Act 1976, the violation of human rights of Dalits had increased. The implementation of the Act left much to be desired; investigations into atrocities against Dalits were often inadequate or biased." The Report points out the need for greater sensitization of all the agencies of government, the judiciary and law enforcement machinery in particular, to the special problems posed in protecting the rights of Dalits.

The Special Rapporteur on Religious Intolerance has published a report on his visit to India vide Document Ref. No: E/CN.4/1997/91/ Add.1 dated 14.02.97, which in para 61 refers to the assurance of the Secretary of the Ministry of Law, of the Government of India, who has accepted the loss of privileges of Dalit Christians, that the proposal to remove discrimination against Dalit Christians would be placed in the Parliament. Mr. Chairman, the Government of India has not yet introduced the proposed law to remove discrimination on the Dalit Christians in the Parliament. In view of their long standing struggle for equal treatment before the law, it should be impressed on the Government to remove the discrimination against Dalit Christians in view of Article 27 of the International Covenant of Civil and Political Rights which makes it obligatory on the States that have ratified the Covenant to ensure that all individuals under their jurisdiction enjoy the equal rights; this may require specific action to correct inequalities to which minorities are subject. Therefore the legitimate demand of the Dalit Christians to remove discrimination against them should be accorded priority.

It is very significant that UNDP during this 50th Anniversary of Declaration of Human Rights published a policy statement entitled:"Integrating Human Rights with Sustainable Human Development." Millions of Dalits have been denied development opportunities by discriminatory social and religious customs for centuries. We plead with UNDP and other specialised Agencies like UNESCO, UNICEF, ILO, WHO, etc. in India to reorient their projects and policies to protect the Human Rights of the Dalits, to improve their socio-economic conditions in the light of latest UNDP policy guidelines and to uplift the Dalit people from their down-trodden life.

India has the third largest scientific and technical and manpower in the world. India uses its scientific knowledge and progress for nuclear test explosions. The Indian Government should be persuaded to use the same scientific knowledge to solve the problems of the people, to remove poverty and discrimination and to respect the right to development of the millions of Dalits. The question of Discrimination of Dalits in the Indian sub-continent must receive the attention of this world body, which stands for protecting the Universal Human Rights of the people. The Sub-Commission should undertake a study on discrimination and discriminatory practices based on untouchability and the caste system and its manifestations in contemporary forms of slavery in the South Asian Region.

Thank you, Mr. Chairman.

The above oral statement was made by Mr Henry Thiagaraj, Managing Trustee, Dalit Liberation Education Trust, on 14.8.98 at Geneva on behalf of the World Council of Churches.

Annexure - IX

Memorandum Presented to Ms. Mary Robinson,

High Commissioner For Human Rights of The United Nations, at the United Nations Information Centre, New Delhi on 17 February 1999

Respected Madam,

We are extremely pleased that you are visiting India at an appropriate time. During this month we are witnessing many human rights violations which you would have noticed through the press reports. Our Trust had the privilege of bringing these violations particularly the atrocities inflicted on untouchable people of India, Dalits, before different forums of UN Human Rights Commission. If there is one single issue that requires the attention of the UN in the field of Human Rights, it is the discrimination based on untouchability and caste violence inflicted on millions of people in the South Asian Region. As a result, the right to development of 300 million people has been curtailed. Despite its magnitude and the anguish suffered by our people this has escaped the attention of the United Nations. The one issue which stands out in all items of the agenda of Human Rights Commission like contemporary forms of slavery, the right to development, etc., is the insidious caste discrimination and violence depicted by the pathetic living conditions of the untouchable people. As per the Indian Government reports of 1993 we have worked out that every hour two Dalits are assaulted, every day three Dalit women are raped, two Dalits are murdered and two Dalit houses are burnt.

The caste violence is on the increase. A leading newspaper, The Hindu, dated 11.8.1997 in an article mentioned "More than 300 Dalits were already killed in inter caste violence of 1997 against a similar number in the whole of 1995 and around 490 in 1996. The National Human Rights Commission recently released its Annual Report has deplored the pathetic life of the Dalit people. On February 12, 1999, The New Indian Express of Chennai has reported that in Bihar 12 Dalits were massacred within 15 days of earlier massacre of 22 Dalits including violence on women. It is also reported that police oppression on Dalit women and youth are severe in the state of Tamil Nadu. Many other states like Orissa, Madhya Pradesh, Maharashtra and Rajasthan have records of atrocities committed on Dalits, some of whom belong to the minority religions.

With great anguish, we once again appeal to you to use your good offices to enable the United Nations to wake up to see the sufferings of our people and to take urgent action to appoint a Special Rapporteur to study the caste violence and human rights violations based on discrimination of untouchability in South Asia Region and to launch human rights education to prevent caste violence.

Yours sincerely
HENRY THIAGARAJ
Managing Trustee–Dalit Liberation Education Trust Co-Convener–National Campaign on Dalit Human Rights Convener–Human Rights Education Movement of India.

> *"As we see all around us, racism and racial discrimination continue unabated. Although we refer to our world as a global village, it is a world sadly lacking in the sense of closeness towards neighbour and community which the world village implies. In each region, and within all countries, there are problems stemming from either a lack of respect for, or lack of acceptance of, the inherent dignity and equality of all human beings. Our world is witness to serious ethnic conflicts; to discrimination against minorities, indigenous peoples and migrants workers; the accusation of institutionalized racism in police forces; harsh immigration and asylum policies; hate sites on the Internet and youth groups promoting intolerance and xenophobia."*
>
> **-Ms.Mary Robinson**
> United Nations High Commissioner for Human Rights
> 24 March 1999

Annexure - X

Human Rights Day – 10 December 2005

On December 10th, the international community celebrates and observes Human Rights Day. It is in observance of the ratification of the Universal Declaration of Human Rights in 1948 by the United Nations General Assembly.

THE SECRETARY-GENERAL'S MESSAGE ON HUMAN RIGHTS DAY

10 December 2005

Fifty-seven years after the Universal Declaration of Human Rights prohibited all forms of torture and cruel, inhuman or degrading treatment or punishment, torture remains unacceptably common. Recent times have witnessed an especially disturbing trend of countries claiming exceptions to the prohibition on torture based on their own national security perceptions.

Let us be clear: torture can never be an instrument to fight terror, for torture is an instrument of terror.

The prohibition on torture is well established under international law. It is also unambiguous and absolute. It is binding on all States in all territories under their jurisdiction or effective control. It applies in all circumstances, in times of war as in times of peace. Nor is torture permissible when it is called something else: cruel and inhuman treatment is unacceptable and illegal, irrespective of the name we give it.

States must honour this prohibition and vigorously combat the impunity of perpetrators of torture. Those who conceive of or authorize any form of torture and other cruel, inhuman or degrading treatment, and those who commit such acts, should not go unpunished. Nor may any State condone torture by a third party. This means that individuals must never be rendered to another State if there is any danger that doing so may subject them to torture.

The international community must speak forcefully, and with one voice, against torture in all its forms. Today, I call on all States who have not done so to ratify the Convention against Torture and Other Cruel, Inhuman or Degrading Treatment or Punishment, as well as the Optional

Protocol to the Torture Convention. And I urge all States to allow the United Nations' Special Rapporteur on Torture independent access to detainees within their control. Unimpeded access is an essential protection for these individuals, whose isolation makes them especially vulnerable to abuse. Together, we must give voice, and redress, to abused detainees as well as to all victims and survivors of torture.

Humanity faces grave challenges today. The threat of terror is real and immediate. Yet fear of terrorists can never justify adopting their methods. Nor can we be complacent about the broader prevalence of cruel and inhuman punishment, which in so many of our societies disproportionately affects the most vulnerable people: the imprisoned, the politically powerless and the economically deprived. Instead, we must respond to this evil wherever we find it by reaffirming humanity's most basic values. Today, on Human Rights Day, let us recommit ourselves to the principles of the Universal Declaration of Human Rights, and let us rededicate ourselves to wiping the scourge of torture from the face of the earth.

Annexure - XI

Human Rights Day 10 December 2006

On 10 December 1948, the United Nations General Assembly adopted the Universal Declaration of Human Rights, which has become a universal standard for defending and promoting human rights. Every year on 10 December, Human Rights Day marks the adoption of the Universal Declaration. On Human Rights Day it is celebrated around the globe that "All human beings are born with equal and inalienable rights and fundamental freedoms".

This year Human Rights Day focuses on **fighting poverty** as a matter of obligation, not of charity. Poverty is a cause and a product of human rights violations. It is this double edge that makes poverty probably the gravest human rights challenge in the world. The links between human rights and poverty should be obvious: People whose rights are denied – victims of discrimination or persecution, for example – are more likely to be poor. Generally they find it harder or impossible to participate in the labour market and have little or no access to basic services and resources. Meanwhile, the poor in many societies cannot enjoy their rights to education, health and housing simply because they cannot afford them. And poverty affects all human rights: for example, low income can prevent people from accessing education – an "economic and social" right – which in turn inhibits their participation in public life – a "civil and political" right – and their ability to influence policies affecting them.

Governments and those in a position of authority can, indeed are obliged to, do something about poverty. They have committed to it by overwhelmingly accepting a number of human rights treaties and by signing on to the international consensus to make poverty history, through the Millennium Declaration and the Millennium Development Goals, as well as most recently the 2005 World Summit Outcome. The realization of human rights - including the fight against poverty – is a duty, not a mere aspiration.

Today, poverty prevails as the gravest human rights challenge in the world. Combating poverty, deprivation and exclusion is not a matter of charity, and it does not depend on how rich a country is.

By tackling poverty as a matter of human rights obligation, the world will have a better chance of abolishing this scourge in our lifetime...Poverty eradication is an achievable goal.

Louise Arbour

UN High Commissioner for Human Rights

POVERTY AND HUMAN RIGHTS

Poverty is a cause and a product of human rights violations. It is this double edge that makes poverty probably the gravest human rights challenge in the world. The links between human rights and poverty should be obvious : People whose rights are denied – victims of discrimination or persecution, for example – are more likely to be poor. Generally they find it harder or impossible to participate in the labour market and have little or no access to basic services and resources. Meanwhile, the poor in many societies cannot enjoy their rights to education, health and housing simply because they cannot afford them. And poverty affects all human rights: for example, low income can prevent people from accessing education – an "economic and social" right – which in turn inhibits their participation in public life – a "civil and political" right – and their ability to influence policies affecting them.

Yet, poverty is still rarely seen thought the lens of human rights. Rather it is often perceived as tragic but inevitable, and even as the responsibility of those who suffer it. At best those living in poverty – countries and individuals – are portrayed as unfortunate, at worst as lazy and undeserving.

The reality is different. Many ingredients go into making poverty, but factors like discrimination, unequal access to resources, and social and cultural stigmatization have always characterized it. These "factors" have another name: the denial of human rights and human dignity. What's more, these are factors governments and those in a position of authority can, indeed are obliged to, do something about. They have committed to it by overwhelmingly accepting a number of human rights treaties and by signing on to the international consensus to make poverty history, through the Millennium Declaration and the Millennium Development Goals, as well as most recently the 2005 World Summit Outcome. The realization of human rights - including the fight against poverty – is a duty, not a mere aspiration.

More information on the link between poverty eradication and human rights is available in the Secretary-General's Report [A/61/308] (5 September 2006)

Source: Office of the UN High Commissioner for Human Rights

Annexure - XII

Dalits Break Through UN Wall of Silence on Caste Discrimination

Geneva, April 20 2005: The UN Commission on Human Rights today adopted by consensus a decision to appoint two Special Rapporteurs to tackle the entrenched problem of caste-based discrimination. The Commission was endorsing an earlier decision taken by its Sub-Commission on the Promotion and Protection of Human Rights to conduct a comprehensive analysis of the problem and find solutions for its eradication. This is the first time a political body of the UN has referred directly to the problem, and the decision is seen as a crucial step in the campaign for justice for South Asia's Dalits (formerly known as 'untouchables') and communities suffering from similar forms of discrimination around the world. The seven-month long wait from 12th August 2004 to 19th April 2005 and hard work of international NGO's achieved a historical breakthrough in the passing of a resolution appointing Mr. Yolo Yokota and Ms Chin-Sung Chung as Special Rapporteurs to study caste-based discrimination. This has opened an avenue to voice Dalit concerns in the UN. Dalit activists congratulate International Dalit Solidarity Network (ISDN) and its team of dedicated activists for this achievement.

The Sub-Commission will now undertake a 3-year study, led by two experts given the title of 'Special Rapporteurs', and will draft a set of Principles and Guidelines to eliminate this form of discrimination.

The relevant UN documents and the Katmandu Dalit Declaration are available at www.idsn.org

Source: bahujan@yahoogroups.com

The above achievement is possible because of the pioneering and foundation work done by Dr. Henry Thiagaraj, Managing Trustee of the Dalit Liberation Education Trust during 1987-98 details of which can be found in the book: "Human Rights from Dalit Perspective" published in 1996 and reprinted in 1998 and this edition.

Annexure - XIII

United Nations Human Rights Sub-Commission

Resolution E/CN.4/Sub.2/2004/L.8

The Sub Commission on the Promotion and Protection of Human Rights,

Reaffirming its resolution 2000/4 of 11 August 2000, in which it declared that discrimination based on work and descent is a form of discrimination prohibited by international human rights law,

Acknowledging the constitutional, legislative and administrative measures taken by some States to abolish practices of discrimination based on work and descent, as outlined in the expanded working paper on this topic submitted by Mr. Asbjørn Eide and Mr. Yozo Yokota (E/CN.4/Sub.2/2004/31),

Concerned that discrimination based on work and descent affects communities in many regions of the world,

Noting the need for further study on this topic, and for the formulation of principles and guidelines for the elimination of discrimination based on work and descent,

1. *Urges* concerned States to ensure that all necessary constitutional, legislative and administrative measures, including appropriate forms of affirmative action and public education programmes, are in place to prevent and redress discrimination based on work and descent, and that such measures are respected and implemented by all State authorities at all levels;
2. *Welcomes* the expanded working paper on discrimination based on work and descent submitted by Mr. Asbjørn Eide

and Mr. Yozo Yokota (E/CN.4/Sub.2/2004/31) and endorses the conclusions and recommendations contained therein, including with regard to the importance of undertaking a study on the issue of discrimination based on work and descent and the preparation of a draft set of principles and guidelines for the elimination of discrimination based on work and descent,

3. *Decides* to appoint Mr. Yozo Yokota and Ms Chin-Sung Chung as Special Rapporteurs with the task of preparing a comprehensive study on discrimination based on work and descent on the basis of the three working papers submitted on this issue (E/CN.4/Sub.2/2001/16, E/CN.4/Sub.2/2003/24 and E/CN.4/Sub.2/2004/31) as well as the comments made and discussions that took place during the sessions of the Sub Commission to which those working papers were submitted, and requests the Special Rapporteurs to submit a preliminary report to the Sub Commission at its fifty-seventh session, a progress report at its fifty-eighth session and a final report at its fifty-ninth session;

4. *Requests* the Special Rapporteurs to focus on the finalization of a draft set of principles and guidelines for the effective elimination of discrimination based on work and descent, addressing all relevant actors including Governments, local authorities, private sector entities, schools, religious institutions and the media, based on existing applicable standards and best practices and taking into account the framework proposed in the third working paper and the contents of General Recommendation XXIX (2002) of the Committee on the Elimination of Racial Discrimination.

5. *Also requests* the Special Rapporteurs, for the purpose of identifying best practices, to obtain more comprehensive information on constitutional, legislative, judicial, administrative and educational measures taken to address discrimination based on work and descent, including through the elaboration and submission of a questionnaire to Governments, national human rights institutions, relevant organs and agencies of the United Nations system and non-governmental organizations.

6. *Encourages* the Special Rapporteurs to undertake this study in cooperation and collaboration with relevant treaty bodies and United Nations organs, agencies and mandates, including the Committee on the Elimination of Racial Discrimination, the Special Rapporteur on contemporary forms of racism, the International Labour Organization and the United Nations Educational, Scientific and Cultural Organization, and in consultation with representatives of affected communities.
7. *Requests* the Secretary-General and the United Nations High Commissioner for Human Rights to provide the Special Rapporteurs with all the assistance necessary to enable them to accomplish this task;
8. *Recommends* the following draft decision to the Commission on Human Rights for adoption:

   "The Commission on Human Rights, taking note of resolution 2004/... of ... August 2004 of the Sub-Commission on the Promotion and Protection of Human Rights, approves the decision of the Sub-Commission to appoint Mr. Yozo Yokota and Ms. Chin-Sung Chung as Special Rapporteurs with the task of preparing a comprehensive study on discrimination based on work and descent, on the basis of the three working papers submitted to the Sub-Commission on this topic (E/CN.4/Sub.2/2001/16, E/CN.4/Sub.2/2003/24 and E/CN.4/Sub.2/2004/31), the comments made during the sessions of the Sub Commission at which these working papers were submitted and the provisions of the above-mentioned resolution, and of responses from Governments, national human rights institution, relevant organs and agencies of the United Nations system and non-governmental organizations to a questionnaires to be elaborated and circulated by the Special Rapporteurs. The Commission also approves the request to the Special Rapporteurs to submit a preliminary report to the Sub Commission at its fifty-seventh session, a progress report at its fifty-eighth session, and a final report at its fifty-ninth session, and the request to the Secretary-General and the United Nations High Commissioner for Human Rights to provide the Special Rapporteurs with all the assistance necessary to enable them to accomplish this task."
9. *Decides* to continue consideration of this question at its fifty-seventh session under the same agenda item.

Annexure - XIV

United Nations and the Elimination of Racism and Racial Discrimination

UN is Concerned about Racism and Racial Discrimination

In 1945 the nations tried to make a new start. After suffering two world wars, they turned from the old world of colonial empires and from ideas of racial superiority and ideologies which had caused the elimination of millions of people due to their race or religion. The nations founded the United Nations and pledged themselves to develop a just and peaceful world community in which all people would be treated with respect and have equal opportunities to lead decent lives.

Many parts of the UN system worked on different aspects of the human rights and fundamental freedoms called for in the UN Charter. Some gave attention to political rights, others to the right to education, health care, fair employment and the like.

It was soon recognized that this work would be difficult and slow. Although the nations had committed themselves to basic human rights, some people had been brought up to feel that certain groups were superior to others because of the colours of their skins, their religions, their race, sex, ethnic or political backgrounds. In some places, certain groups were not allowed to own land or rent homes; in others some children were given inferior or no education; some jobs were closed to various groups and so on. In the most extreme case, apartheid, the government itself (South Africa) denied to the black majority in the country the enjoyment of basic human rights agreed upon by the United Nations Member States.

It was difficult to put the ideals of the United Nations Charter into practice, and peace and development were impeded when people suffered such injustices. But what was to be done? How could the world community insist that these nations abide by basic human rights?

How could people's feelings and behavior change? As time went on, the United Nations devised many ways to deal with this problem.

What the United Nations is doing about racism and racial discrimination

A. Setting standards

In the United Nations Charter Member States decided that everyone had equal dignity and worth without distinction of any kind, such as race, colour, sex, language, religion, political or other opinion, national or social origin, property, birth or other status. Soon after, in the Universal Declaration of Human Rights, nations said they believed that each person had certain basic rights and fundamental freedoms. The United Nations Covenants on Civil and Political Rights and on Economic, Social and Cultural Rights put these ideas into legal from; nations who ratified these pledged to carry out their provisions.

A special declaration and convention on racism and racial discrimination followed. In these nations agreed that none of the human rights guaranteed in the Charter and Human Rights Conventions could be denied to people because of their race, colour, descent or national or ethnic origin. The United Nations Declaration on the Elimination of All Forms of Racial Discrimination includes the following considerations:

* that any doctrine which holds that one race is superior to another is "scientifically false, morally condemnable, socially unjust and dangerous, and that there is no justification for racial discrimination either in theory or in practice;

* that racial discrimination harms not only those who are its objects but also those who practice it. "The Declaration calls on all States to put its principles into law. It also asks that they take measures to combat prejudices which lead to discrimination and to promote, through education and information, understanding, tolerance and friendship among racial groups.

International Convention on the Elimination of All **Forms of Racial Discrimination**

The principles set out in the United Nations Declaration on the Elimination of All Forms of Racial Discrimination are reaffirmed in the International Convention on the Elimination of All Forms of Racial Discrimination, adopted by the General Assembly in 1965 and ratified or acceded to by 118 states.

Under the Convention, each State Party undertakes to prohibit and to eliminate racial discrimination in all its forms and to guarantee the right to everyone, without distinction as to race, colour or ethnic origin, equality before the law in the enjoyment of a long list of human rights and fundamental freedoms. The list contains several rights not mentioned specifically in the Universal Declaration of Human Rights, such as the right to inherit and the right to access to any place or service intended for use by the general public, including transport, hotels, restaurants, cafes, theatres and parks. The Convention lists specifically, among the rights in regard to which discrimination is prohibited, the right to work, the right to join trade unions, and the right to housing.

B. Implementing the Standards

The Committee on the Elimination of Racial Discrimination

The committee on the Elimination of Racial Discrimination, which consists of 18 independent experts, reviews reports submitted by States Parties on the actions they have taken to eliminate racial discrimination and makes proposals and general recommendations. The Committee may also receive and consider communications from individuals or groups of individuals to that effect, and prepare proposals and recommendations in regard to such communications. The Committee also co-operates with the United Nations bodies concerned with dependent Territories in dealing with petitions from the inhabitants of such Territories, which contain allegations of racial discrimination.

From time to time the Committee comments upon particular situations involving racial discrimination or draws them to the attention of the General Assembly. It also indicates matters on which it would like to receive detailed information from States Parties to the Convention.

The Committee holds two sessions a year at which it examines reports by the States Parties to the Convention and by United Nations organs concerned with dependent Territories. Representatives of States Parties are invited to be present at, and take part in, the discussions when their reports are under consideration. At the two sessions when their reports are under consideration. At the two sessions in 1982, for example, the reports of 40 countries were examined. They dealt with measures taken by States Parties in fields such as the following: The advancement and promotion of gypsies, States relations with South Africa, the rights of minorities to use their own languages, the rights of migrant workers, etc.

Role of the United Nations: moral force

At times of violence or chaos students need to appreciate the power of moral standards. The primary incentives for nations to live up to the ideals of the United Nations Charter are the approval of other Member States and the chance to participate in the world community. Nations are deterred from antisocial behaviour by disapproval and the threat of exclusion as well as by economic sanctions. The sense that there are standards and that nations for the most part abide by them will help young people to feel more secure. At the same time they will understand better the real strength of the United Nations.

To deal with these matters, students can study the United Nations Covenants on Civil and Political Rights and on Economic, social and Cultural Rights and the Convention on the Elimination of All Forms of Racial Discrimination. Then they can see how these matters are dealt with in their own constitutions. They can also analyze stories or simulations showing how people learn to respect the rights of others and to abide by the good of the community. The theme of decolonization can also be used as an example of the United Nations moral force.

Studies and Seminars

As part of its on-going work relating to racial discrimination, UNESCO has sponsored research which has shown there is absolutely no scientific foundations for considering one race superior to another. They firmly rejected the idea that there are fundamental difference in the human species and unequivocally condemned theories based on the superiority of one or more races. They pointed out that differences in cultural achievements are to be explained by the cultural history of a people rather than differences in intelligence or innate ability, and that other differences might be more closely linked to the social and economic opportunities the society permitted.

Other studies done within the UN have included: "Apartheid as a collective form of slavery". "The problem of discrimination against indigenous populations" and "Equality in the administration of justice".

Numerous seminars have been held in all parts of the world on topics relating to racial discrimination in such areas as recourse procedures for victims of discrimination and the dangers of a return to racist ideologies.

3. Mobilizing World Action

In order to give added urgency to the fight against racism and racial discrimination, the United Nations has held conferences and designed a year, a decade and an international day and week to be devoted to this subject.

1971: International Year for Action to Combat Racism and Racial Discrimination

1973-

1983: Decade for Action to Combat Racism and Racial Discrimination

In launching the Decade, the General assembly declared that racial discrimination in all its forms and manifestations is a total negation of the purposes and principles of the United Nations Charter, and that it militates against human progress, peace and justice. The programme of Action for the Decade calls for a continuing effort by all peoples, Governments and institutions to eradicate racial discrimination and to promote respect for human rights and fundamental freedoms for all.

1978: First World Conference to Combat Racism and Racial Discrimination

1983: Second World Conference to Combat Racism and Racial Discrimination

This reviewed and assessed the activities undertaken during the Decade and also formulated measures to ensure full and universal implementation of United Nations decisions on racism, racial discrimination and apartheid.

In addition to Human Rights Day (10 December), there is the International Day for the Elimination of racial Discrimination (21 March) and the Week of Solidarity with the peoples Struggling against Racism and Racial Discrimination (the week beginning 21 March). These may be celebrated with assemblies, films, exhibits, demonstrations and other activities in communities, schools and universities.

Role of individual People: Student involvement

Racial discrimination is a useful theme for international education because it is not far-off and abstract but sometimes present even in the home societies. Much may have been accomplished, particularly in recent years, but there are still societies, which have not wiped out every vestige of discrimination. Laws may have been passed and redress be possible but de facto discrimination and attitudes of superiority of one group towards another probably remain. (Students themselves can affect what happens).

Students can become aware of the situation of people in their home communities through local media, surveys and other investigations and field trips. For example, students of one school sketched scenes of discrimination in different daily situations. They should also become aware of their own attitudes and behaviour and learn that when they fail to actively repudiate discrimination, they are actually contributing to it. They can also study the local laws relating to discrimination in various fields and ways that people can obtain redress when the laws are violated. In conclusion, many schools undertake action projects to eliminate instances of discrimination in school or in the community. They can learn that in doing so they are contributing to the elimination of racial discrimination everywhere. Celebrating Human Rights Day and Racial Discrimination Days can give them the sense that they are part of this worldwide effort.

Realistic expectations: the pace of change

Although technology can bring swift changes, human relations evolve only very slowly. Students need to accept the idea that signs of improvement will not become immediately visible. This, however, should not deter them from the work.

Regional and national action

Different regions monitor how the States carry out human rights. The Council of Europe and the Organization of American States (OAS) have each a Commission and a Court on Human Rights. At the national level States Parties have passed laws and made efforts to enforce them. They are also trying through education and information to help people to be aware of discrimination and to combat it wherever it exists.

III. What remains to be done

The United Nations and the Governments

The fight against racism and racial discrimination is not over. In spite of the standards set, the laws and their implementation, much remains to be done. There are some nations that have not yet become parties to the Convention and these are urged to do so. Some who are Party to the Convention still have to intensify their efforts. Changes are still needed in the ways people treat one another.

To change attitudes and behaviour, education is important. This is what the United Nations and the States Parties consider especially urgent. Through schools and the media people can learn about the worth, dignity and quality of all people.

What Can YOU Do to Help?

A great deal of what happens now depends on individuals like yourselves. Attitudes and behaviour which people absorb unconsciously are slow and difficult to change. You can help them, however, to become aware of discrimination. You yourself can help people to understand

"He who shames him, does not he know he shames himself"

Annexure - XV

Human Rights Education

"Education shall be directed to the full development of the human personality and to the strengthening of respect for human rights and fundamental freedoms. It shall promote understanding, tolerance and friendship among all nations, racial or religious groups, and shall further the activities of the United Nations for the maintenance of peace"

Universal Declaration of Human Rights, Article 26.2

Human Rights Day 2004 is dedicated to human rights education. On 10 December, the United Nations General Assembly is devoting a special plenary session to mark the end of the United Nations Decade for Human Rights Education (1995-2004). At the meeting, the General Assembly is expected to proclaim a World Programme for Human Rights Education. The first phase of the Programme, to run from 2005 to 2007, is to be devoted to human rights education in the primary and secondary school systems.

Announcing the theme, Mrs. Louise Arbour, the UN High Commissioner for Human Rights, stated in Geneva on 16 November 2004: "Every year, Human Rights Day reminds us of persisting human rights problems in our communities and in the world, and of the huge effort still needed, on the part of each and everyone of us, to make human rights a reality for all".

UNESCO Director-General Koïchiro Matsuura stated that "Human rights education is indispensable for every individual to fully enjoy and claim a life of security and dignity. It is indispensable for public officials to give effect to human rights commitments by the State. Finally, it is indispensable for the entire society to develop and nurture a human rights culture as a prerequisite of harmonious and peaceful development".

The High Commissioner and the Director-General have called on everyone to take the opportunity provided by Human Rights Day to organize educational activities, disseminate good practices and launch future initiatives in this area, "in a spirit of cooperation and mutual respect among all those involved. Human Rights Day should provide us with an opportunity to pay tribute to human rights educators – indeed, human rights defenders - who, in formal and informal settings, in small or large communities, and often encountering difficulties and hazards, contribute to building a universal culture of human rights".

The Office of the High Commissioner for Human Rights is the coordinator of the United Nations Decade for Human Rights Education (1995-2004). It has been carrying out many activities related to the Decade in cooperation with UNESCO.

Background

The importance of human rights education has long been recognized by the international community. The prominence accorded to it at the Vienna World Conference on Human Rights in 1993, and the fact that the United Nations decided to establish the Decade for Human Rights Education, are evidence of this.

In the words of the General Assembly resolution establishing the Decade, human rights education is intended to be "a life-long process by which people at all levels of development and in all strata of society learn respect for the dignity of others and the means of ensuring that respect in all societies". In this sense, human rights education significantly contributes to promoting equality and sustainable development, preventing conflict and human rights violations and enhancing participation and democratic processes, with a view to developing societies in which all human rights of all are valued and respected.

During the Decade, Governments, international organizations, national institutions, non-governmental organizations, professional associations, all sectors of civil society and individuals were asked to establish partnerships and to concentrate their efforts on promoting a universal culture of human rights through human rights education, training and public information. The international Plan of Action for the Decade set out detailed objectives for the international community: the assessment of needs and formulation of effective strategies; the building and strengthening of programmes and capacities for human rights education at the international, regional, national and local levels; the coordinated development of effective materials; the strengthening of the role and capacity of the mass media; and the global dissemination of the Universal Declaration of Human Rights.

In February 2004, the High Commissioner for Human Rights submitted to the United Nations Commission on Human Rights, at its request, a report on the achievements and shortcomings of the Decade and on future United Nations activities in this area, based on consultations with Member States (document E/CN.4/2004/93). In that report, most responding Governments reported on their increased human rights education activities, within or outside the Decade's framework. Most Governments mentioned that human rights education will still remain a priority in their countries, since specific groups or issues have not been dealt with and appropriate coordination mechanisms for human rights education are not yet in place.

In April 2004, the Commission on Human Rights adopted resolution 2004/71, in which it took note of the need to continue a global framework for human rights education beyond the Decade. Accordingly, the Commission recommended the proclamation of a world programme for human rights education, to begin on 1 January 2005, structured in consecutive phases, in order to maintain and develop the implementation of human rights education programmes in all sectors. The Commission also requested the Office of the High Commissioner to prepare, in cooperation with UNESCO and other relevant governmental and non-governmental actors, and submit for consideration and adoption to the General Assembly at its 2004 session, a plan of action for the first phase (2005-2007) of the proposed world programme, focusing on the primary and secondary school systems, which is available as document A/59/525.

Conclusion

Fifty-six years ago, the United Nations General Assembly recognized the equal and inalienable rights accorded to every human being by adopting the Universal Declaration of Human Rights. The Declaration calls upon every individual and every institution of society to strive, by teaching and education, to promote respect for human rights and to secure their universal and effective recognition and implementation.

The proclamation of the United Nations Decade for Human Rights Education represented not the beginning but the maturation of the global effort for human rights education. Consistent with the provisions of Article One of the Charter, United Nations activities in the field of human rights have, for more than fifty years, been devoted to promoting and encouraging respect for human rights and for fundamental freedoms. Specific human rights education obligations have been embodied in the main United Nations human rights instruments, ensuring the sound legal basis of the right to human rights education. Thus, States have undertaken legal obligations, within the framework of international treaties, to provide not only education in general, but education in and for human rights in particular.

Still, more efforts are needed to realize everybody's right to human rights education. The proposed World Programme for Human Rights Education, if adopted by the General Assembly, will ensure a priority focus on human rights education within the international agenda, provide a common collective framework for action for all relevant actors, support existing programmes and provide an incentive for the development of new ones, as well as enhance partnership and cooperation at all levels.

Human Rights Day

Message of the UN Secretary-General Kofi Annan

Every year, International Human Rights Day reminds us of persisting human rights problems in our communities and in the world, and of the enormous efforts still required to make human rights a reality for all.

Human rights education is a vital part of such efforts, designed to equip new generations with the knowledge of their inalienable rights, and the means to exercise and defend them. These rights include rights to health, to education, to food, to housing, to marry and found a family, to participate in public life, to be free from torture, arbitrary arrest and detention — in short, the rights needed to be free from want and fear.

Today, the General Assembly marks the conclusion of the United Nations Decade for Human Rights Education (1995-2004) with a plenary session, in which the recommendation to proclaim a World Programme for Human Rights Education will be considered. The first three years of such a Programme, from 2005 to 2007, would focus on primary and secondary education, through integrating human rights issues into curricula, changing educational processes and teaching methods and, most importantly, improving the environment in which education takes place.

Human rights education is much more than a lesson in schools or a theme for a day; it is a process to equip people with the tools they need to live lives of security and dignity. On this International Human Rights Day, let us continue to work together to develop and nurture in future generations a culture of human rights, to promote freedom, security and peace in all nations.

Annexure - XVI

The Declaration af a Global Ethic

"There will be peace on earth when there is peace among the world religions."

"No world peace without peace among religions;
no peace among religions without dialog between religions."

From "Global Responsibility," a book by Hans Küng, Theologian

Preamble

"...Time and again we see leaders and members of religions incite aggression, fanaticism, hate and xenophobia - even inspire and legitimize violent and bloody conflicts. Religion is often misused for purely power-political goals, including war. We are filled with disgust...."

II. A fundamental demand: every human being must be treated humanely

"...Of course, religions are credible only when they eliminate those conflicts which spring from the religions themselves, dismantling mutual arrogance, mistrust, prejudice, and even hostile images, and thus demonstrating respect for the traditions, holy places, feasts and rituals of people who believed differently..."

III. Irrevocable directives: Commitment to a culture of non-violence and respect for life

"...Every people, every race, every religion must show tolerance and respect - indeed high appreciation - for every other. Minorities need protection and support, whether they be racial, ethnic or religious."

III. Irrevocable directives: Commitment to a culture of tolerance and a life of truthfulness

"...All over the world, we find endless lies and deceit, swindling and hypocrisy, ideology and demagoguery... Representatives of religions who dismiss other religions as of little value and who preach fanaticism and intolerance instead of respect and understanding..No woman or man, no institution, no state or church or religious community has the right to speak lies to other humans...This is especially true...for representatives of religion - when they stir up prejudice, hatred and enmity towards those of different belief, or even incite or legitimize religious wars, they deserve the condemnation of humankind and the loss of their adherents."

III. Irrevocable directives: Commitment to a culture of equal rights and partnership between men and women

"...We have the duty to resist whenever the domination of one sex over the other is preached - even in the name of religious conviction..."

The following declaration was prepared by about 200 scholars who represented many world religions after a two year consultation. It was presented at the 1993 Parliament of the World's Religions, held in Chicago, IL on 1993-SEP-4. The declaration, with The Principles of a Global Ethic appended, was signed by 143 respected leaders from all of the world's major faiths, including Baha'i World Faith, Brahmanism, Brahma Kumaris, Buddhism, Christianity, Hinduism, Indigenous, Interfaith, Islam, Jainism, Judaism, Native American, Neo-Pagan, Sikhism, Taoism, Theosophist, Unitarian Universalist and Zoroastrian. The Council for a Parliament of the World's Religions offers it to the world as an initial statement of a group of rules for living on which all of the world's religions can agree.

Towards a Global Ethic (An Initial Declaration)

The world is in agony. The agony is so pervasive and urgent that we are compelled to name its manifestations so that the depth of this pain may be made clear.

Peace eludes us...the planet is being destroyed...neighbors live in fear...women and men are estranged from each other...children die!

This is abhorrent!

We condemn the abuses of Earth's ecosystems.

We condemn the poverty that stifles life's potential; the hunger that weakens the human body; the economic disparities that threaten so many families with ruin.

We condemn the social disarray of the nations; the disregard for justice which pushes citizens to the margin; the anarchy overtaking our communities; and the insane death of children from violence. In particular we condemn aggression and hatred in the name of religion.

But this agony need not be.

It need not be because the basis for an ethic already exists. This ethic offers the possibility of a better individual and global order, and leads individuals away from despair and societies away from chaos.

We are women and men who have embraced the precepts and practices of the world's religions:

We affirm that there is an irrevocable, unconditional norm for all areas of life, for families and communities, for races, nations, and religions. There already exist ancient guidelines for human behavior which are found in the teachings of the religions of the world and which are the condition for a sustainable world order.

We Declare:

We are interdependent. Each of us depends on the well-being of the whole, and so we have respect for the community of living beings, for people, animals, and plants, and for the preservation of Earth, the air, water and soil.

We take individual responsibility for all we do. All our decisions, actions, and failures to act have consequences.

We must treat others as we wish others to treat us. We make a commitment to respect life and dignity, individuality and diversity, so that every person is treated humanely, without exception. We must have patience and acceptance. We must be able to forgive, learning form the past but never allowing ourselves to be enslaved by memories of hate. Opening our hearts to one another, we must sink our narrow differences for the cause of world community, practicing a culture of solidarity and relatedness.

We consider humankind a family. We must strive to be kind and generous. We must not live for ourselves alone, but should also serve others, never forgetting the children, the aged, the poor, the suffering, the disabled, the refugees and the lonely. No person should ever be considered or treated as a second-class citizen, or be exploited in any way whatsoever. There should be equal partnership between men and women We must not commit any kind of sexual immorality. We must put behind us all forms of domination or abuse.

We commit ourselves to a culture of non-violence, respect, justice, and peace. We shall not oppress, injure, torture, or kill other human beings, forsaking violence as a means of settling differences.

We must strive for a just social and economic order, in which everyone has an equal chance to reach full potential as a human being. We must speak and act truthfully and with compassion, dealing fairly with all, and avoiding prejudice and hatred. We must not steal. We must move beyond the dominance of greed for power, prestige, money, and consumption to make a just and peaceful world.

Earth cannot be changed for the better unless the consciousness of individuals is changed first. We pledge to increase our awareness by disciplining our minds, by meditation, by prayer, or by positive thinking. Without risk and a readiness to sacrifice there can be no fundamental change in our situation. Therefore we commit ourselves to this global ethic, to understanding one another, and to socially beneficial, peace-fostering, and nature-friendly ways of life.

We invite all people, whether religious or not, to do the same.

Annexure - XVII

Poster designed by Dr. Henry Thiagaraj for display and distribution at 16 UN-World Conference Against Racism, Durban, South Africa, Sept. 2001.

Annexure - XVII

Activists allege police harassment

They took part in the November 10 protest against killing of Dalits in Khairlanji

I was molested, faeces-mixed water thrown at me: Dalit woma

Muthumari narrating her tale of woe at a press conference in Madurai on Monday. — Photo: S. James

They were skinning a dead cow to sell hide; local VHP, Sena spread rumour of cow slaughter

Five Dalits lynched, entire administration watches

Seven Dalits burnt to death

Fallout of caste clash in Karnataka

Dalit beaten to death

Caste clash claims 8 lives in Kolar village

KARNATAKA / MOB VIOLENCE

Dalit beaten, loses limbs

Upper caste Jats attack farmworker for speaking out

SPOTLIGHT

Brutality: Bant Singh of Jhabbar village in Punjab, who was beaten up by members of the upper caste Jat community in January. A Deccan Chronicle photograph

Two Dalits made to eat human faeces

PM regrets continuing atrocities against Dalits

Caste atrocities in Karnataka

Boycott of Dalits in Kadkol was only the latest in the long list of atrocities against Scheduled Castes and Scheduled Tribes.

Right to worship denied to Dalits in Ramnad village

Dalits embrace Buddhism, Christianity

A system against Dalits

Bibipur is a metaphor. Locally it is a symbol of unrelieved Dalit suffering in Haryana. Nationally it is about the staggering insensitivity of the state machinery to a community grievously wronged by history.

Dalit residents of Bibipur Brahmnan. — PHOTO: S. SUBRAMANIUM

Acquittal of Kolar massacre accused a setback to Dalits

Forum wants the Government to move High Cou

- Seven Dalits were burnt alive in their house at Kambalpalli
- Murder of an upper caste waterman was the immediate provocation

More panchayat chiefs admit caste discrimination: study

Dalit houses looted

Unruly mob goes on the rampage at Mela Orappanur

Chennai Monday 20 November 2006

Dalit chief 'auctioned' for Rs 2.16 lakh

SPECIAL

Index

D

G

H

I

J

S

T